Certified Rehabilitation Counselor Examination Preparation

Fong Chan, PhD, CRC, is a professor and department chair, and Norman L. and Barbara M. Berven Professor of Rehabilitation Psychology, Department of Rehabilitation Psychology and Special Education, University of Wisconsin–Madison. Dr. Chan is also the codirector of the Rehabilitation Research and Training Center on Evidence-Based Practice in Vocational Rehabilitation.

Malachy Bishop, PhD, CRC, is a professor of rehabilitation counseling and director of the rehabilitation counseling doctoral program, Department of Early Childhood, Special Education, and Rehabilitation Counseling, University of Kentucky.

Julie Chronister, PhD, CRC, is a professor in the Department of Counseling, San Francisco State University.

Eun-Jeong Lee, PhD, CRC, is an associate professor and director of the counseling and rehabilitation science division, Department of Psychology, Illinois Institute of Technology.

Chungyi Chiu, PhD, CRC, is an assistant professor, Department of Kinesiology and Community Health, University of Illinois at Urbana–Champaign.

Certified Rehabilitation Counselor Examination Preparation

Second Edition

Fong Chan, PhD, CRC
Malachy Bishop, PhD, CRC
Julie Chronister, PhD, CRC
Eun-Jeong Lee, PhD, CRC
Chungyi Chiu, PhD, CRC

SPRINGER PUBLISHING COMPANY

Copyright © 2018 Springer Publishing Company, LLC

Springer Publishing Company, LLC
11 West 42nd Street
New York, NY 10036
www.springerpub.com

Acquisitions Editor: Sheri W. Sussman
Compositor: diacriTech

ISBN: 978-0-8261-3314-4
Ebook ISBN: 978-0-8261-3315-1

17 18 19 20 21 / 5 4 3 2 1

Library of Congress Cataloging-in-Publication Data
Names: Chan, Fong, | Bishop, Malachy, | Chronister, Julie A., | Lee, Eun-Jeong, | Chiu, Chungyi
Title: Certified rehabilitation counselor examination preparation /Fong Chan, Malachy Bishop, Julie Chronister, Eun-Jeong Lee, Chungyi Chiu.
Other titles: CRC® examination preparation.
Description: Second edition. | New York, NY : Springer Publishing Company, LLC, [2018] | Preceded by CRC® examination preparation / Fong Chan ... [et al.], editors. c2012. | Includes bibliographical references and index.
Identifiers: LCCN 2017021484 | ISBN 9780826133144 | ISBN 9780826133151 (e-book)
Subjects: | MESH: Rehabilitation—methods | Counseling—ethics | Disabled Persons—rehabilitation | Examination Questions
Classification: LCC RC466 | NLM WB 18.2 | DDC 362.2/04256076—dc23
  LC record available at https://lccn.loc.gov/2017021484

Printed in the United States of America by Bradford & Bigelow.

Contents

Contributors

Christina Espinosa Bard, MRC, CRC, is community education director, Human Development Institute, University of Kentucky, Lexington, Kentucky.

Malachy Bishop, PhD, CRC, is a professor of rehabilitation counseling and director of the rehabilitation counseling doctoral program, Department of Early Childhood, Special Education, and Rehabilitation Counseling, University of Kentucky.

Jessica M. Brooks, PhD, CRC, is a research fellow at the Department of Psychiatry, Geisel School of Medicine at Dartmouth College. Dr. Brooks is also an assistant professor, Department of Rehabilitation and Health Services, University of North Texas, Denton, Texas.

Fong Chan, PhD, CRC, is a professor and department chair, and Norman L. and Barbara M. Berven Professor of Rehabilitation Psychology, Department of Rehabilitation Psychology and Special Education, University of Wisconsin–Madison. Dr. Chan is also the codirector of the Rehabilitation Research and Training Center on Evidence-Based Practice in Vocational Rehabilitation.

Chungyi Chiu, PhD, CRC, is an assistant professor, Department of Kinesiology and Community Health, University of Illinois at Urbana–Champaign, Champaign, Illinois.

Julie Chronister, PhD, CRC, is a professor in the Department of Counseling, San Francisco State University, San Francisco, California.

Nicole Ditchman, PhD, CRC, LCPC, is an associate professor, Department of Psychology, Illinois Institute of Technology, Chicago, Illinois.

Sandra Fitzgerald, PhD, CRC, is an assistant professor in the Department of Counseling, San Francisco State University, San Francisco, California.

Kanako Iwanaga, MS, CRC, is a doctoral student, Department of Rehabilitation Psychology and Special Education, University of Wisconsin–Madison, Madison, Wisconsin.

Kristin Kosyluk, PhD, CRC, is an assistant professor in the rehabilitation counseling program, University of Texas at El Paso, El Paso, Texas.

Eun-Jeong Lee, PhD, CRC, is an associate professor and director of the counseling and rehabilitation science division, Department of Psychology, Illinois Institute of Technology.

Bradley McDaniels, MS, CRC, is a doctoral student in the rehabilitation counselor education program, Department of Special Education and Rehabilitation Counseling, University of Kentucky, Lexington, Kentucky.

Veronica Muller, PhD, CRC, is an assistant professor, Department of Educational Foundation and Counseling Programs, Hunter College, City University of New York, New York, New York.

Jinhee Park, PhD, CRC, is an assistant professor, Department of Special Education, Rehabilitation, and Counseling, Auburn University, Auburn, Alabama.

Phillip Rumrill, PhD, CRC, is a professor and coordinator of rehabilitation counseling and director of the Center for Disability Studies at Kent State University, Kent, Ohio.

David Strand, PhD, CRC, is a rehabilitation counselor at the Neurology Vocational Services Unit at Harborview Medical Center, University of Washington, Seattle, Washington. Dr. Strand is also an adjunct instructor in the rehabilitation counseling program at Western Washington University.

Connie Sung, PhD, CRC, LLPC, is an assistant professor, Office of Rehabilitation and Disability Studies, Department of Counseling, Educational Psychology, and Special Education, Michigan State University, East Lansing, Michigan.

Veronica I. Umeasiegbu, PhD, CRC, is an assistant professor, School of Rehabilitation Services and Counseling, University of Texas Rio Grande Valley, Edinburg, Texas.

Emre Umucu, MS, CRC, is an assistant professor of rehabilitation counseling, University of Texas at El Paso.

Preface

Rehabilitation counseling is a systematic process that assists persons with physical, mental, developmental, cognitive, and emotional disabilities to achieve their personal, career, and independent living goals in the most integrated settings possible through the application of the counseling process. The counseling process involves communication, goal setting, and beneficial growth or change through self-advocacy, psychological, vocational, social, and behavioral interventions (Commission on Rehabilitation Counselor Certification [CRCC], 2017). With the passage of the Workforce Innovation and Opportunity Act (WIOA) and the Rehabilitation Act amendments in 2014, innovative approaches for improving the training and employment of people with disabilities are occurring. Rehabilitation counselors in state vocational rehabilitation agencies are required to be competent in local labor market analysis, employer relations, customized training, secondary transition, and postsecondary education. At the same time, the rehabilitation counseling profession is becoming a specialization within the broader counseling profession requiring a broad and diverse spectrum of general counseling and rehabilitation counseling competencies. Rehabilitation counseling consumers are culturally diverse and our services and settings are continually evolving (Leahy, Chan, Sung, & Kim, 2013) to meet the above-average growth trajectory for rehabilitation and health professions in the United States (Bureau of Labor Statistics, 2017). Rehabilitation counselor education programs are charged with ensuring rehabilitation counselors are trained to meet the accreditation and licensure standards of counselors, while at the same time preserving vocational rehabilitation training and the profession's identity.

In the first edition, we indicated that ". . . the purpose of the book is to provide a concise yet comprehensive preparation guide for the CRCC's Certified Rehabilitation Counselor (CRC®) examination." The purpose of this edition is to provide a complete and up-to-date detailed review of the CRC examination contents in a well-organized and user-friendly manner that reflects the expanding professional landscape of rehabilitation counseling. The content of this book is based on the most recent empirically derived rehabilitation counselor roles and functions studies (Leahy et al., 2013) that inform the test specifications for the CRC examination. In addition, this book corresponds to accreditation standards for master's degree programs in rehabilitation counseling. These standards are addressed in this book's chapters: Professional Identity and Ethical Behavior; Psychosocial Aspects of Health, Mental Health, and Disability; Human Growth and Development; Employment and Career Development; Counseling Theories, Skills, and Principles of Practice; Group Work and Family Dynamics; Assessment and Evaluation; Research Methods and Evidence-Based Practice; Biopsychosocial Aspects of Chronic Illness and Disability; and Rehabilitation Services, Case Management, and Related Services. Each chapter provides a concise overview of the key concepts, summary tables of the key concepts, practice questions (with annotated answers), and links to web-based materials for further study and review. This edition is highly valuable to rehabilitation counseling graduate students, working rehabilitation counselors seeking to obtain the CRC credential, and those in allied rehabilitation professions seeking to become a CRC through additional coursework. In addition, rehabilitation counselor educators who use the CRC examination as an alternative to a comprehensive examination for graduation may find this book useful to offer and/or require of students. We encourage rehabilitation counselor educators to build a CRC-preparation strategy into master's level rehabilitation programs—preparation that begins early in the program and positions students to take the CRC examination prior to graduation.

In summary, there have been significant changes in the delivery of rehabilitation counseling services related to legislative mandates (e.g., the Workforce Innovation and Opportunity Act), health care reform, increasing service provision to multicultural, younger, and older populations, evidence-based practices, changes in accreditation bodies, and shifts in the economic and business environment. Nearly every rehabilitation counseling practice setting (e.g., public, private-for-profit, and community-based rehabilitation organizations) has undergone significant changes in the services delivered to persons with disabilities, requiring new knowledge and skills for rehabilitation practitioners (Leahy et al., 2013). In light of these changes, we have updated this book to provide a contemporary, user-friendly, and expert-written preparation guide for counselors and students preparing for the CRC examination.

References

Bureau of Labor Statistics, U.S. Department of Labor. (2017). *Occupational outlook handbook, 2016–17 edition.* Rehabilitation Counselors. Retrieved from https://www.bls.gov/ooh/community-and-social-service/rehabilitation-counselors.htm

Commission on Rehabilitation Counselor Certification. (2017). Rehabilitation counseling scope of practice. Retrieved from https://www.crccertification.com/scope-of-practice

Leahy, M., Chan, F., Sung, C., & Kim, M. (2013). Empirically derived test specifications for the certified rehabilitation counselor examination. *Rehabilitation Counseling Bulletin, 56*, 199–214.

Certified Rehabilitation Counselor Examination Preparation

1

Professional Identity and Ethical Behavior

CONNIE SUNG, VERONICA MULLER, FONG CHAN, JESSICA M. BROOKS, DAVID STRAND, AND EMRE UMUCU

Rehabilitation counselors have long played an instrumental role in helping persons with disabilities achieve independent living and employment goals (Maki & Tarvydas, 2011; Martin, West-Evans, & Connelly, 2010). Although rehabilitation counseling (RC) evolved from the state–federal vocational rehabilitation (VR) program, the professional practice of RC is no longer restricted to state VR agencies. Today, rehabilitation counselors work in diverse settings and are required to meet the varied and often complex needs of a range of disability groups (Leahy, Chan, & Saunders, 2003; Leahy, Chan, Sung, & Kim, 2013). This chapter reviews the history and background regarding rehabilitation and related legislation, professional identity of RC, and professional ethics for rehabilitation counselors.

Learning Objectives

By the end of this unit you should be able to:

1. Understand rehabilitation and the impact of related legislation on RC practices and the inclusion and participation of people with disabilities.
2. Understand the evolution of RC and professional issues related to the profession.
3. Understand the basic principles of ethics and ethical behavior related to the professional practice of RC.

Key Concepts

I. Rehabilitation and Related Legislation

The state-federal VR program is the oldest and most successful public program supporting the employment and independence of individuals with disabilities (Martin et al., 2010). It is also one of the major practice settings for VR counselors. The Smith-Fess Act of 1920, also known as the Civilian Vocational Rehabilitation Act, is considered the starting point of public rehabilitation for people with physical disabilities. State VR services were expanded in 1943 to include people with mental disabilities. To be qualified for state VR services, people with disabilities must meet two eligibility criteria. Specifically, the individual must demonstrate (a) the presence of a physical or mental impairment that constitutes or results in a substantial impediment to employment and (b) the potential to benefit from employment secured through the assistance of VR services.

With the passage of the Rehabilitation Act of 1973 emphasizing services to people with severe disabilities, the philosophy of rehabilitation has evolved from an "economic-return" philosophy to a "disability-rights" philosophy (Rubin & Roessler, 2008). The goals of VR have been identified as (a) inclusion, (b) opportunity, (c) independence, (d) empowerment, (e) rehabilitation, and (f) quality of life. Table 1.1 provides a description of the purpose and implications of key rehabilitation legislation. Figure 1.1 depicts the evolution of major rehabilitation and related legislation.

TABLE 1.1 Rehabilitation Legislation

Rehabilitation Legislation	Purpose
The Smith-Hughes Act of 1917	Provided Federal funding to states on a matching basis for vocational education programs.
The Solder's Rehabilitation Act of 1918	Authorized VR services for World War I veterans.
The Smith-Fess Act of 1920	Expanded rehabilitation services to civilians.
The Social Security Act of 1935	Made the state–federal VR program permanent.
The Randolph-Sheppard Act of 1936	Authorized people with blindness to operate vending stands in federal buildings.
The Wagner-O'Day Act of 1938	Required the federal government to purchase designated products produced in workshops by persons with blindness.
The Barden-LaFollette Act of 1943	Expanded services to include people with mental disabilities. It also established the state–federal program for individuals with blindness.
The Vocational Rehabilitation Act Amendments of 1954	Provided funding to universities to train master's level rehabilitation counselors and resulted in the professionalization of the RC profession.
The Vocational Rehabilitation Act Amendment of 1965	Added extended evaluation to the VR process.
The Rehabilitation Act of 1973	Mandated services for people with the most severe disabilities; established the IWRP to ensure consumer involvement in the rehabilitation process; implemented CAPs to provide assistance with application and advocacy services; established demonstration projects in rehabilitation and/or independent living services; increased funding for rehabilitation and disability research and established the National Institute of Handicapped Research; mandated program evaluation; and guaranteed employment rights of people with disabilities through Title V which included sections covering: • Section 501 (affirmative action in federal hiring) • Section 502 (enforcement of accessibility standards for federal buildings) • Section 503 (affirmative action by federal contract recipient) • Section 504 (equal opportunities)
The Rehabilitation Act Amendments of 1978	Mandated the provision of independent living services.
The Rehabilitation Act Amendments of 1984	Mandated the establishment of CAPs.
The Rehabilitation Act Amendments of 1986	Added the provision of rehabilitation engineering services and established supported employment as an acceptable goal for rehabilitation services.

(continued)

TABLE 1.1 Rehabilitation Legislation (*continued*)

The ADA of 1990	Provided the most comprehensive civil rights protections for people with disabilities to date. It was the most sweeping disability-rights legislation in history. See Section II for more details.
Individuals with Disabilities Education Act (IDEA) of 1990	Included categories of eligibility for special education services. Stated that children with disabilities (3–21 years of age) are entitled to a free appropriate public education to meet their unique needs and prepare them for further education, employment, and independent living. Each child's education will be planned and monitored with an individualized education program or an individualized family service plan with aims to promote the involvement of the family and to offer a wide range of services and specialists to support the child in a least restrictive environment.
The Rehabilitation Act Amendments of 1992	Advanced the concepts of empowerment, self-determination, and informed choice at both individual and agency levels; required state VR agencies to establish "qualified personnel" standards for rehabilitation counselors as mandated by the development of the CSPD within state VR agencies; established, via the CSPD, qualified personnel standards to ensure the quality of state–federal VR; lead to an emphasis on master's level degree and counselor certification in the delivery of VR services. Other highlights include: • Presumption of (employ)ability • Career-based job placement • Improved services to minority groups • Increased client involvement in the IWRP • Establishment of Rehabilitation Advisory Councils • Determination of eligibility within 60 days of application • Order of selection • Use of existing data • Increased federal share of the state–federal funding match to 78.7% • Rehabilitation engineering • Training of rehabilitation counselors from minority backgrounds
The STWOA of 1994	Provided federal venture capital grants to state and local agencies to help restructure educational systems and to establish school-to-work systems; provided specific funding for technical assistance, capacity building, outreach, and research and evaluation.
Individuals with Disabilities Education Act Amendments of 1997	Shifted the focus of IDEA to improve teaching and learning through emphasizing the individual educational plan as a primary tool for educational planning, increasing the role of parents in educational decision-making and promoting meaningful access to the general curriculum.
The WIA of 1998	Linked the state–federal VR program to the state's workforce investment system; consolidated several employment and training programs into a unified statewide workforce investment system in which customers can easily access employment information and services through a one-stop center. VR became a mandated partner.
The Rehabilitation Act Amendments of 1998	Replaced the IWRP with the IPE to emphasize the employment focus and to support the exercise of informed choice of the individual with a significant disability in the selection of employment outcomes, specific services, service providers, and methods to procure the services; established automatic eligibility for people already receiving SSI or SSDI benefits to streamline VR administrative procedures; introduced a new category of service, i.e., provision of technical assistance and consultation to individuals to pursue self-employment, telecommuting, or a small business operation; emphasized outreach to minorities and encouraged school-to-work transition service provision to students with disabilities, including employment; required the establishment of mediation policies and procedures to improve due process provisions.

(*continued*)

TABLE 1.1   Rehabilitation Legislation (*continued*)

Rehabilitation Legislation	Purpose
The TWWIIA of 1999	Expanded Medicare and Medicaid coverage for individuals with disabilities; offered those with disabilities a "ticket" with which they could obtain VR and support services from an employment network of their choice.
The ADA Amendments Act of 2008	Revised definition of *disability* and broadened the scope of coverage for those who have a disability.
The WIOA of 2014	Introduced significant changes to Title I of the Rehabilitation Act of 1973, affecting the state–federal VR program, including replacing the WIA and amending the Rehabilitation Act of 1973; establishing an Advisory Committee on Increasing Competitive Integrated Employment for Individuals with Disabilities; mandating state VR agencies to allocate at least 15% of their federal funding to provide preemployment transition services to improve transition outcomes of students with disabilities; emphasizing local labor market analysis, employer engagement, and customized work-based learning experiences (e.g., apprenticeships and internships); identifying primary performance indicators to measure employment outcomes across programs. Introduced significant changes to Title IV of the Rehabilitation Act, governing the supported employment-program, including allotment of significant funds (not less than 10%) to support youth with the most significant disabilities to obtain competitive integrated employment; transferred a number of programs from the DOE to the DHHS.

ADA, Americans with Disabilities Act; CAPs, Client Assistance Programs; CSPD, Comprehensive System of Personnel Development; DHHS, Department of Health and Human Services; DOE, Department of Education; IPE, Individualized Plan for Employment; IWRP, Individualized Written Rehabilitation Program; RC, rehabilitation counseling; TWWIIA, Ticket to Work and Work Incentives Improvement Act; SSDI, Social Security Disability Insurance; SSI, Supplemental Security Income; STWOA, School-to-Work Opportunities Act; WIA, Workforce Investment Act; WIOA, Workforce Innovation and Opportunity Act; VR, vocational rehabilitation.

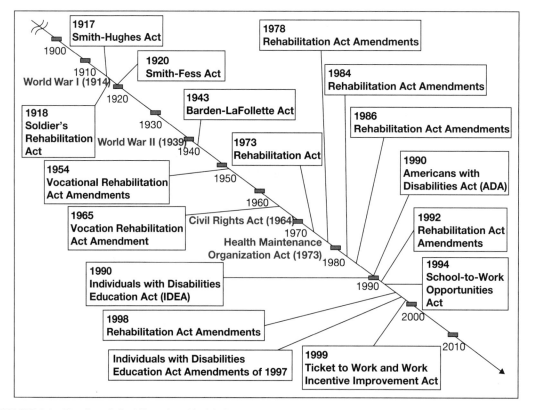

FIGURE 1.1   Timeline of disability-related legislation.

II. The Americans with Disabilities Act

The Americans with Disabilities Act (ADA) of 1990 is a federal *civil rights* law designed to prevent discrimination and enable individuals with disabilities to participate fully in all aspects of society. The ADA guarantees equal opportunity for individuals with disabilities in employment (Title I), public services (Title II), public accommodations (Title III), telecommunications (Title IV), and other miscellaneous provisions (Title V). The employment provisions of Title I of the ADA are particularly relevant to rehabilitation counselors because the goal of VR is employment. An individual with a disability under the ADA is a person with a physical or mental impairment that substantially limits a major life activity (e.g., caring for oneself, performing manual tasks, seeing, hearing, eating, sleeping, walking, standing, lifting, bending, speaking, breathing, learning, reading, concentrating, thinking, communicating, and working). The impairment must be severe, not temporary, and must have a permanent or long-term impact on the individual. The ADA may also protect a person who has a record of impairment or who is regarded by others as a person with impairment. The *regarded as* standard applies to a person who is excluded from any basic life activity, including employment, or is otherwise discriminated against because of a covered entity's (e.g., an employer's) negative attitudes toward the person regarded as having an impairment.

The ADA Amendments Act (ADAAA) of 2008 overturns the controversial Supreme Court decisions in *Sutton v. United Airlines, Inc.* (1999) and *Toyota Motor Manufacturing, Kentucky, Inc. v. Williams* (2002). The Supreme Court stated that courts should interpret the definition of "disability" strictly in order to create a demanding standard for qualifying as having a disability, denying individuals with epilepsy, diabetes, cancer, HIV, or mental illness protection from disability discrimination—the very people whom Congress intended to protect. The ADAAA of 2008 asserts that the definition of *disability* is intended to be a less demanding standard than that applied by the court. Specifically, the ADAAA clarifies and expands the meaning and application of the definition of *disability* in the following ways:

- It provides that the definition of *disability* shall be construed in favor of *broad coverage* of individuals under this act, to the maximum extent permitted by the terms of the act.

- It prohibits consideration of *mitigating* measures such as medication, assistive technology, accommodations, or modifications when determining whether an impairment substantially limits a major life activity.

- It removes from the "regarded as" clause of the disability definition.

Although the ADAAA is important, it addresses mostly Title I (employment provisions) of the act, which suggests that the remaining four titles (mostly public-access provisions) are working rather well (McMahon, 2010). Table 1.2 provides a description of key ADA concepts.

TABLE 1.2   Key ADA Concepts

Key ADA Concepts	Definition
Major life activities	An impairment must substantially limit one or more major life activities in order to be a disability covered by the ADA. These are activities that an average person can perform with little or no difficulty. Examples are walking, speaking, breathing, performing manual tasks, seeing, hearing, learning, caring for oneself, and working. These are only examples. Other activities such as sitting, standing, lifting, or reading are also major life activities.

(continued)

TABLE 1.2   Key ADA Concepts (*continued*)

Key ADA Concepts	Definition
Substantially limiting	An impairment is a "disability" under the ADA only if it substantially limits one or more major life activities. An individual must be unable to perform, or be significantly limited in the ability to perform, an activity compared with an average person in the general population. The regulations provide three factors to consider in determining whether a person's impairment substantially limits a major life activity: • Nature and severity • Expected duration • Expected impact
Qualified individual with a disability	A person with a disability who satisfies the requisite skill, experience, education, and other job-related requirements of the desired or held employment position and who, with or without reasonable accommodation, can perform the essential functions of such a position.
Essential function	1. The position exists to perform the function. 2. There are a limited number of other employees available to perform the function or among whom the function can be distributed. 3. A function is highly specialized, and the person in the position is hired for special expertise or ability to perform it.
Reasonable accommodation	Reasonable accommodation is a modification or adjustment to a job, the work environment, or routine that enables a qualified individual with a disability to benefit from an equal employment opportunity. The ADA requires reasonable accommodation in three aspects of employment: (a) to ensure equal opportunity in the application process, (b) to enable a qualified individual with a disability to perform the essential functions of a job, and (c) to enable an employee with a disability to enjoy equal benefits and privileges of employment.
Undue hardship	An *undue hardship* is an action that requires "significant difficulty or expense" in relation to the size of the employer, the resources available, and the nature of the operation. The concept of undue hardship includes any action (a) that is unduly costly, (b) that is extensive, (c) that is substantial, (d) that is disruptive, or (e) that would fundamentally alter the nature or operation of the business.

ADA, Americans with Disabilities Act.

III. The Workforce Innovation and Opportunity Act

The Workforce Innovation and Opportunity Act (WIOA), which replaces the Workforce Investment Act of 1998 (WIA), was passed on July 22, 2014, and amends the Rehabilitation Act of 1973 (U.S. Department of Labor, 2016). The purpose of the WIOA is to increase employment opportunities of individuals who face barriers to employment, including people with disabilities, and to strengthen the connection between education and career preparation (U.S. Department of Education, 2016). The WIOA imposes significant changes to Title I and Title VI of the Rehabilitation Act of 1973 that affect state–federal VR and supported employment programs (U.S. Department of Education, 2016). Specifically, the WIOA amendments include transition-related definitions regarding the scope and provision of both group and individual preemployment transition services, requirements and considerations related to formal interagency agreements between state educational agencies and VR agencies, and limitations on the use of subminimum wage. The passage of the WIOA has several implications for the state–federal VR program, and these implications are discussed next.

A. Promote Competitive Integrated Employment Outcomes

The WIOA established an Advisory Committee on Increasing Competitive Integrated Employment for Individuals with Disabilities under Section 609 of the Rehabilitation Act of 1973. Its goal is to develop strategies for improving training and career opportunities for individuals with disabilities, especially those with the most significant disabilities, through customized employment, supported employment, and other individualized services (U.S. Department of Labor, 2015).

B. Underscore Transition Services

The WIOA mandates state VR agencies to allocate at least 15% of their federal funding to providing preemployment transition services for youth with disabilities and to prioritize assistance in the area of transition from secondary to postsecondary education programs and/or competitive integrated employment with the ultimate goal of facilitating career development, upward mobility, and improved transition outcomes. Furthermore, the act calls for increased collaboration among schools, VR, and community agencies in the delivery of services and allows state VR agencies to support advanced training in the fields of science, technology, engineering, mathematics (STEM) and other technical professions (Association of University Centers on Disabilities, 2014; White House, 2014; U.S. Department of Education, 2016; U.S. Department of Labor, 2016).

C. Emphasize Demand-Side Employment

The WIOA emphasizes local labor market analysis, employer engagement, and customized training; it requires state VR agencies to describe in their state plans how they will work with employers to increase competitive integrated employment opportunities and assist employers in providing work-based learning experiences, including apprenticeships and internships, for individuals with disabilities.

D. Promote Collaboration, Efficiency, and Accountability

The WIOA emphasizes service coordination between federal programs that provide employment support/VR services, workforce development, and adult education (Association of University Centers on Disabilities, 2014; U.S. Department of Education, 2016). Through the establishment of common employment-outcome measures across core programs, the act enhances accountability of federal programs and places stronger emphasis on outcome measures. Consequently, primary performance indicators were established for both adult and youth clients.

E. Expand Support Employment Services

The WIOA dedicates a significant amount of the funds for the federal supported employment program to help youth with the most significant disabilities to obtain competitive integrated employment (Association of University Centers on Disabilities, 2014). It also extends the time for the provision of supported employment from 18 to 24 months and requires not less than a 10% match for the amount of funds reserved to serve youth with the most significant disabilities (U.S. Department of Education, 2016).

F. Transfer Programs

The WIOA transferred certain programs from the U.S. Department of Education (DOE) to the Department of Health and Human Services (DHHS). The State Independent Living Services program, Centers for Independent Living program, National Institute on Disability and Rehabilitation Research (NIDRR), and programs under the Assistive Technology Act of 1998 have been transferred from the DOE to the DHHS. Specifically, the name of NIDRR has officially changed to the National Institute on Disability, Independent Living, and Rehabilitation Research (NIDILRR). The WIOA also repealed several programs such as the State Vocational Rehabilitation Unit In-Service Training program, the Projects with Industry program, the Migrants and Seasonal Farmworkers program, and the Recreation Programs for Individuals with Disabilities program.

IV. Informed Choice and Consumer Empowerment

Empowerment, self-determination, and informed choice promulgated by the Rehabilitation Act Amendments of 1992 are central to the philosophy of contemporary rehabilitation practices. It is generally agreed that the goals of rehabilitation can be better achieved when there is maximal consumer involvement in the development, implementation, and use of VR services. West and Parent (1992) defined *empowerment* as the transfer of power and control over decisions, choices, and values from external entities to the consumers of disability services. *Informed choice* in RC refers to the process by which consumers make insightful decisions about personal goals and necessary services. *Self-determination* refers to directing one's own course of action, which requires active personal agency in implementing informed choices. Kosciulek and Wheaton (2003) indicated that informed choice and self-determination, along with an effective counselor–consumer working alliance, are the necessary components of increased consumer empowerment.

The Rehabilitation Counseling Profession

Rehabilitation counselors play a central role in the VR process. RC has been described as a process in which the counselor works collaboratively with the client to understand existing problems, barriers, and potentials to facilitate the client's effective use of personal and environmental resources for career, personal, social, and community adjustment following disability. In carrying out this multifaceted process, rehabilitation counselors must be prepared to assist individuals in adapting to the environment, assist environments in accommodating the needs of the individuals, and work toward the full participation of individuals in all aspects of society, with particular focus on independent living and work (Parker & Szymanski, 1998).

The professionalization of RC has been shaped significantly by graduate training programs that provide students with the knowledge and skills necessary for working with persons with physical and mental disabilities within the state–federal VR program. The professional practice of RC, however, is no longer restricted to the state VR agency setting. Today, rehabilitation counselors work in various settings, including private practice, private nonprofit rehabilitation facilities/organizations, private-for-profit rehabilitation firms, insurance companies, medical centers or general hospitals, and businesses/corporations. Across these settings, rehabilitation counselors are required to meet the diverse needs of a wider and more complex spectrum of disability groups with various degrees of severity.

I. Commission on Rehabilitation Counselor Certification and Council on Rehabilitation Education

To ensure that VR services will be provided in a manner that meets the national standards of quality and protect the best interest of the client, the Commission on Rehabilitation Counselor Certification (CRCC) was officially incorporated in 1974 to conduct certification activities on a nationwide basis for rehabilitation counselors. The typical pathway to certification is a master's degree in RC from an RC program accredited by the Council on Rehabilitation Education (CORE). CORE was incorporated in 1972 to support the effective delivery of rehabilitation services to individuals with disabilities by promoting and fostering continuing review and improvement of RC programs. In July 2017, CORE became a corporate affiliate of the Council for Accreditation of Counseling and Related Educational Programs (CACREP), which began carrying out the mission of both CORE and CACREP (Council for Accreditation of Counseling and Related Educational Programs, 2015). As part of the merger agreement, CACREP and CORE have agreed to develop a joint process that will allow RC programs to become dually accredited as both a Clinical Rehabilitation Counseling (ClRC) program and a Clinical Mental Health Counseling (CMHC) program.

II. Roles and Functions

In their seminal roles and functions study, Muthard and Salamone (1969) found that state VR counselors divide their time equally among three areas: (a) counseling and guidance; (b) clerical work, planning, recording, and placement; and (c) professional growth, public relations, reporting, resource development, travel, and supervisory administrative duties. In addition, Leahy et al. (2013) identified eight major job functions that are essential to the professional practice of RC in today's practice environment; these include (a) job placement, (b) vocational assessment and career counseling, (c) occupational information analysis, (d) counseling, (e) psychosocial interventions, (f) case management and advocacy, (g) demand-side employment, and (h) workers' compensation and forensic services. Leahy et al. (2013) further identified ten knowledge and skill domains reported by certified rehabilitation counselors as important for contemporary practice, including (a) assessment, appraisal, and vocational evaluation; (b) job development, job placement, and career and lifestyle development; (c) vocational consultation and services for employers; (d) case management, professional roles and practices, and use of community resources; (e) foundations of counseling, professional orientation and ethical practice, theories, social and cultural issues, and human growth and development; (f) group and family counseling; (g) mental health counseling; (h) medical, functional, and psychosocial aspects of disability; (i) disability management; and (j) research, program evaluation, and evidence-based practice.

III. Current Issues

Determining the roles and functions of rehabilitation counselors has been subjected to considerable debate. C. H. Patterson (1968) proposed that the practice of RC is primarily a subspecialty within the broader field of counseling and involves two fundamental roles. Specifically, Patterson posited that state VR agencies should employ graduate-level–trained rehabilitation counselors to function as either psychological counselors or rehabilitation coordinators; the former role would involve working with clients who need personal adjustment counseling, and the latter role would involve providing case management and vocational adjustment counseling. Whereas Patterson (1968) advocated a "two hats theory," Whitehouse (1975) advocated the "big hat theory," proposing that RC involves a number of roles and functions that justify a separate and distinct practice area that should not be subsumed under the greater rubric of counseling. Specifically, Whitehouse (1975) suggested that rehabilitation counselors should be trained to work with the whole person and should have skills that encompass many roles, including those of a therapist, guidance counselor, case manager, case coordinator, psychometrician, vocational evaluator, educator, community and consumer advocate, and placement counselor. This "big-hat" definition of RC has become the primary model used in the development of rehabilitation education and training curricula and certification since the 1970s. Although this approach facilitated the development of a separate professional status for RC, it also weakened the relationship of RC to the broader field of counseling.

Today, the external pressure of the counselor licensure movement has reignited the debate about the wisdom of maintaining a separate professional status for RC or aligning RC firmly as a specialty of counseling. Leahy (2002) is a major proponent for the adoption of the 60-hour credit requirement as the educational standard for a master's level RC program. He views generic licensure as a threat to the survival of RC. With the American Counseling Association and the American Association of State Counselor Licensure Boards working closely to develop portability standards, Leahy (2002) contends that it will ultimately drive the standardization of educational requirements and give even more momentum to the 60-hour requirement. The current 48-credit educational requirement for rehabilitation counselors may place the RC profession in a vulnerable position and, in fact, threatens its professional viability. Conversely, J. Patterson and Parker (2003) expressed concern about aligning CORE standards with state licensure requirements, suggesting that this alignment weakens the identity of RC and will be detrimental to the preparation of students for employment in state VR agencies and community-based rehabilitation programs. Havranek and Brodwin (1994) proposed a model that suggests streamlining current core rehabilitation and counseling specialty courses and providing students the opportunity to take 12 addition elective credits to develop informal specializations such as clinical counseling, community-based rehabilitation, assistive technology, or disability management. This option allows students to pursue jobs in an array of settings, such as mental health agencies, nonprofit rehabilitation agencies, or private rehabilitation, and allows them to pursue licensure. With the CORE/CACREP merger, however, the 48-credit versus 60-credit debate appears to be no longer relevant, whereas the debate concerning the wisdom of de-emphasizing VR knowledge and skills underscored by the WIOA in favor of mental health counseling knowledge and skills will be important in crystallizing the professional identity of the RC profession.

Professional Ethics

Ethics and ethical behavior encompassing legal, value, and moral issues are inherently complex (J. Patterson, 1998). Rehabilitation counselors must be able to use their rehabilitation knowledge and skills in an ethical manner, recognize ethical dilemmas fundamental to the profession, and apply ethical decision-making skills to solve ethical dilemmas. *Ethics* is defined as a set of moral principles or values that govern the conduct of an individual or group. Ethical behavior is therefore essential to the professional practice of RC. To recognize ethical dilemmas, a rehabilitation counselor must first have a working knowledge of the codes of ethics. The most recent Code of Professional Ethics for Rehabilitation Counselors (CRCC, 2017) was effective as of January 1, 2017. The new code clearly delineates that the primary obligation of rehabilitation counselors is to their clients. The basic objectives of the code are to (a) promote public welfare by specifying the ethical behavior expected of rehabilitation counselors, (b) establish the principles that define ethical behavior and the best practices of rehabilitation counselors, (c) serve as an ethical guide designed to assist rehabilitation counselors in constructing a professional course of action that best serves those using RC services, and (d) serve as the basis for the processing of alleged code violations by certified rehabilitation counselors (CRCC, 2017). The code explicitly states that rehabilitation counselors are committed to facilitating the personal, social, and economic independence of individuals with disabilities. In fulfilling this commitment, rehabilitation counselors recognize *diversity* and embrace a cultural approach in support of the worth, dignity, potential, and uniqueness of individuals with disabilities within their social and cultural context. The CRCC Code of Professional Ethics for Rehabilitation Counselors includes the following 12 enforceable standards:

1. The counseling relationship
2. Confidentiality, privileged communication, and privacy
3. Advocacy and accessibility
4. Professional responsibility
5. Relationships with other professionals and employers
6. Forensic services
7. Assessment and evaluation
8. Supervision, training, and teaching
9. Research and publication
10. Technology, social media, and distance counseling
11. Business practices
12. Resolving ethical issues

I. Ethical Principles

The fundamental spirit of caring and respect with which the code is written is based on six principles of ethical behaviors (adapted from CRCC, 2017):

- *Autonomy:* refers to the right of clients to make their own decision, and to the counselor's respect for the client's individual freedom and self-determination
- *Beneficence:* refers to promoting the welfare and well-being of the client; ensuring that the work of the counselor is for the benefit of the client
- *Fidelity:* means to be faithful, to keep promises, and to behave in ways that are consistent with truth and trustworthiness
- *Justice:* this principle refers to the requirement that counselors treat clients and others fairly, justly, and equally
- *Nonmaleficence:* means, literally, to do no harm; to ensure that the counselor's work does not cause or promote harm to clients and others
- *Veracity:* refers to truth, honesty, and respecting the trust that clients place in counselors

These ethical principles can be tremendously helpful in ethical decision-making, yet may also conflict with one another. For example, rehabilitation counselors may be faced with an ethical dilemma when they encourage consumer autonomy in career choice but the consumer selects occupational preferences beyond their abilities, possibly resulting in disappointment and poor employment outcomes (nonmaleficence). J. Patterson (1998) suggested that when principles are in conflict, rehabilitation counselors should use ethical theory for guidance. There are three types of ethical theories: (a) normative ethical theories, (b) metaethical theories, and (c) good-reasons theories.

When ethical principles are in conflict, rehabilitation counselors should use the good-reasons approach and ask themselves the following two questions: (a) would they want this for themselves or their loved ones in the same situation, and (b) would this action produce the least amount of avoidable harm? However, rehabilitation counselors' ethical behaviors are governed primarily by normative ethical theories, which focus on establishing general principles for determining right or wrong. The CRCC determines the seriousness of unethical behavior based on the potential harm (teleological principles) and the extent to which the behavior is deliberate and persistent. Unethical behavior can be influenced by multiple factors, including developmental ethical reasoning ability, which can be described along the following continuum:

1. **Punishment orientation:** following unbendingly social standards related to punishment
2. **Institutional orientation:** focusing on the expectations of an institution or other higher authorities
3. **Societal orientation:** maintaining societal standards, getting approval of others, and avoiding difficulties
4. **Individual orientation:** promoting individual welfare without undermining the laws and welfare of society
5. **Principle or conscience orientation:** demonstrating concern for the client based on internal standards without regard for legal and social consequences

II. Client Rights

A. Professional Disclosure Statement

According to the CRCC Code of Professional Ethics, rehabilitation counselors have an obligation to review with clients orally, in writing, and in a manner that best accommodates any of the limitations of clients, the rights of clients, and the responsibilities of both rehabilitation counselors and clients. Disclosure at the outset of the counseling relationship should minimally include (a) the qualifications, credentials, and relevant experience of the rehabilitation counselor; (b) purposes, goals, techniques, limitations, and the nature of the potential risks and benefits of services; (c) the frequency and length of services; (d) confidentiality and the limitations regarding confidentiality (including how a supervisor and/or treatment team professional is involved); (e) contingencies for continuation of services on the incapacitation or death of the rehabilitation counselor; (f) fees and billing arrangements; (g) record preservation and release policies; (h) risks associated with electronic communication; and, (i) legal issues affecting services.

B. Informed Consent

Rehabilitation counselors must recognize that clients have the freedom to choose whether to enter into or remain in an RC relationship. Rehabilitation counselors should respect the rights of clients to participate in ongoing RC planning and to make decisions to refuse any services or modality changes while also ensuring that clients are advised of the consequences of such refusal.

C. Cultural Sensitivity

Rehabilitation counselors must communicate information in ways that are both developmentally and culturally appropriate. Rehabilitation counselors should provide accommodation services (e.g., qualified interpreter or translator) when necessary to ensure comprehension by clients.

III. Ethical Issues in RC

The CRCC Code of Professional Ethics identifies several ethical issues germane to RC practices. According to the code, rehabilitation counselors must respect the privacy rights of clients and should not solicit private information that is not beneficial to the counseling process. The concepts of privacy, confidentiality, and privileged communication are defined as follows:

- *Privacy*: the right of the individuals to choose for themselves the time and the circumstances under which, and the extent to which, personal beliefs, behaviors, and opinions are to be shared or withheld from others (The right to privacy belongs to clients and protects clients [not counselors], and only clients can waive that right.)

- *Confidentiality*: the ethical responsibility of the rehabilitation counselor to safeguard clients from unauthorized disclosures of information given in the therapeutic relationship

- *Privileged communication*: the legal right that exists by statute and that protects the client from having confidences revealed publicly and without her or his permission on the witness stand during legal proceedings

IV. Limits of Confidentiality

According to the CRCC Code of Professional Ethics, rehabilitation counselors must inform their clients of the limitations of confidentiality, including the qualification that they will share confidential information with client consent or without consent when sound legal or ethical justification is given. For example, in the workers' compensation system, clients are presumed to have given up a large measure of their right to privacy by accepting the benefits offered. Client records are routinely exchanged among claim adjustors, rehabilitation professionals, and attorneys. The code requires that clients be informed of such limits of confidentiality at the onset of the counseling relationship. As another example, suspicion of child abuse and neglect abrogates nearly all privileges that might otherwise exist. *Tarasoff v. Regents of University of California* established that the counselor has a duty to protect or a duty to warn. The duty is a mandate for the counselor to take some actions to prevent foreseeable harm to a third party (an "identifiable victim") by the client. Thus, it may require the counselor to warn the intended victim, to notify the police, or to take whatever steps are reasonably necessary under the circumstances. Similarly, when clients disclose that they have a disease commonly known to be both communicable and life-threatening (e.g., HIV/AIDS), rehabilitation counselors may be justified in disclosing information to identifiable third parties, if they are known to be at demonstrable and high risk of contracting the disease.

V. Dual Relationships

The CRCC Code of Professional Ethics explicitly prohibits sexual or romantic rehabilitation counselor–client interactions or relationships with current clients, their romantic partners, or their immediate family members. Rehabilitation counselors cannot have sexual or romantic relationships with former clients for a period of five years following the last professional contact. Rehabilitation counselors cannot engage in sexual or romantic relationships with clients with significant cognitive impairments regardless of the length of time elapsed since termination of the client relationships.

VI. Recent Movement in Ethics—Applied Participatory Ethics

Traditionally, ethical decision-making models were designed to assist professionals in systematically resolving ethical dilemmas (Tarvydas, Vazquez-Ramos, & Estrada-Hernandez, 2015). Prilleltensky and Gonick (1996) significantly added to the literature by suggesting that counselors seek to involve clients as stakeholders in the ethical decision-making process. Extrapolating from this participatory framework, Tarvydas et al. (2015) developed a set of applied participatory ethics, which is composed of four interactive elements that facilitate client participation in the process of ethical decision-making: ethical knowledge and practices, the therapeutic alliance or relationship, client involvement, and client empowerment. A pilot study was conducted by Tarvydas, Estrada-Hernandez, Vazquez-Ramos, and Saunders (2017) to validate this applied participatory ethical decision-making model. This study empirically supports the development and initial validation of the Participatory Ethics Scale (PES), which is designed to assess self-reported ethical orientation in relation to client participation in the solution of ethical dilemmas. Using Delphi methodology, ethical knowledge and practice domains related to participatory ethics were identified to capture the predisposition of rehabilitation counselors to using a participatory ethical orientation. The results of the study further support the usefulness of the instrument in measuring ethical knowledge and practice, therapeutic alliance, consumer involvement, and consumer empowerment as significant factors in maximizing full consumer participation during the rehabilitation process.

Internet Resources

Commission on Rehabilitation Counselor Certification Code of Professional Ethics for Rehabilitation Counselors website:
>   www.crccertification.com/code-of-ethics-3

2017 Code of Professional Ethics for Rehabilitation Counselors:
>   www.crccertification.com/filebin/pdf/Final_CRCC_Code_Eff_20170101.pdf

Kenneth Pope's Therapy, Ethics, Malpractice, Forensics, Critical Thinking website:
>   http://kspope.com/index.php

Multiple-Choice Questions

1. Which of the following is considered the starting point of public rehabilitation for people with disabilities?

    A. The Rehabilitation Act of 1973

    B. The Smith-Fess Act of 1920

    C. The Smith-Hughes Act of 1917

    D. The Vocational Rehabilitation Act Amendments of 1954

2. Although the rehabilitation counseling profession evolved from the state–federal vocational rehabilitation (VR) program, professional practice is not restricted only to state VR agencies. Where can rehabilitation counselors work?

    A. Private practice

    B. Private nonprofit rehabilitation organizations

   C. Hospitals

   D. Insurance companies

   E. All of the above

3. The professionals who have the primary responsibility for providing vocational rehabilitation services to assist people with disabilities to meet their needs for equal employment opportunities and quality of life satisfaction are:

   A. Job-placement specialists

   B. Employee assistance counselors

   C. Rehabilitation counselors

   D. Rehabilitation psychologists

4. The first piece of rehabilitation legislation enacted supporting of the practice of vocational rehabilitation was:

   A. The Soldiers Rehabilitation Act of 1918

   B. The Smith-Fess Act of 1920

   C. The Social Security Act of 1935

   D. The States Rights Rehabilitation Act of 1902

5. Which of the following made the state–federal VR program permanent?

   A. The Social Security Act of 1935

   B. The Randolph-Sheppard Act of 1936

   C. The Wagner-O'Day Act of 1938

   D. The Barden-LaFollette Act of 1943

6. Which of the following resulted in the professionalization of the rehabilitation counseling profession?

   A. The Social Security Act of 1935

   B. The Randolph-Sheppard Act of 1936

   C. The Barden-LaFollette Act of 1943

   D. The Vocational Rehabilitation Act Amendments of 1954

7. The Rehabilitation Act of 1973 mandated which of the following as a high-priority state-federal program rehabilitation service?

   A. Persons with behavioral disorders

   B. All industrially injured workers

   C. Socially disadvantaged persons

   D. Persons with severe disabilities

8. The Rehabilitation Act Amendments of 1984:

   A. Mandated that all public transit buses be equipped with lifts

   B. Extended services to children 12 years of age and older

    C. Required each state rehabilitation agency to have an Individualized Plan for Employment

    D. Required each state rehabilitation agency to have a Client Assistance Program

9. What is true about Client Assistance Programs?

    A. They became the required programs for every state in 1984

    B. They were established with the passage of the Rehabilitation Act of 1973

    C. They ensured that clients could receive assistance with application and advocacy services

    D. All of the above

10. The Americans with Disabilities Act of 1990 is a:

    A. Federal civil rights law

    B. Federal education act

    C. Veterans protection act

    D. None of the above

11. An individual with a disability under the Americans with Disabilities Act of 1990 is a person with a physical or mental impairment that substantially limits a major life activity. Which of the following is *NOT* considered a major life activity?

    A. Breathing

    B. Walking

    C. Caring for oneself

    D. Weight-lifting

    E. Working

12. An impairment is only a "disability" under the Americans with Disabilities Act of 1990 if it substantially limits one or more major life activities. The concept of *substantially limiting* is based on:

    A. Severity

    B. Duration

    C. Impact

    D. All of the above

13. An undue hardship is an action that requires "significant difficulty or expense" in relation to:

    A. The size of the employer

    B. The resources available

    C. The nature of the operation

    D. All of the above

14. Which of the following is *NOT* one of the main purposes of the Workforce Innovation and Opportunities Act?

    A. Increasing employment opportunities of individuals who face barriers to employment, including people with disabilities

B. Providing preemployment transition services

C. Conducting transition-related research in educational settings

D. Strengthening connections between education and career preparation

15. There are several major concepts in the Americans with Disabilities Act of 1990. Which of the following is *NOT* one of them?

A. Major life events

B. Substantial limitation

C. Qualified individual with a disability

D. Mandated accommodation

E. Undue hardship

16. The Americans with Disabilities Act of 1990 requires reasonable accommodation in three aspects of employment. Which of the following is NOT one of them?

A. To ensure equal opportunity in the application process

B. To ensure that an individual with a disability has the required educational background before getting a particular job

C. To enable a qualified individual with a disability to perform the essential functions of a job

D. To enable an employee with a disability to enjoy equal benefits and privileges of employment.

17. Which of the following is *INCORRECT* regarding *essential function* in the Americans with Disabilities Act of 1990?

A. The building has to be accessible

B. The position exists to perform the function

C. There are a limited number of other employees available to perform the function or among whom the function can be distributed

D. A function is highly specialized, and the person in the position is hired for special expertise or the ability to perform the function

18. The Workforce Innovation and Opportunity Act mandated state VR agencies allocate at least ____% of their federal funding to provide preemployment transition services for youth with disabilities and to prioritize assistance in the area of transition from secondary to post-secondary education programs and/or competitive integrated employment.

A. 5

B. 10

C. 15

D. 20

E. 25

19. Which of the following is *NOT* true about ethics?

A. Ethicists impose punishments or penalties when people fail to follow ethical guidelines

B. *Ethics* is defined as a set of moral principles

C. Ethical behavior is essential to the professional practices of rehabilitation counseling

D. Rehabilitation counselors' ethical behaviors are governed primarily by normative ethical theories

20. What strategy should rehabilitation counselors use when they want to solve ethical dilemmas?

A. Rehabilitation knowledge and skills

B. Awareness of ethical dilemmas fundamental to the profession

C. Application of ethical decision-making models

D. All of the above

21. Rehabilitation counselors must have _____ to effectively recognize ethical dilemmas?

A. A great supervisor

B. A doctoral degree

C. A working knowledge of the codes of ethics

D. Membership in a professional organization

22. Which of the following is *TRUE* concerning dual relationships?

A. The Commission on Rehabilitation Counselor Certification (CRCC) Code of Professional Ethics prohibits sexual or romantic rehabilitation counselor–client interactions or relationships with current clients

B. Rehabilitation counselors cannot have sexual or romantic relationships with former clients for a period of three years following the last professional contact

C. As long as a rehabilitation counselor–client relationship is reported to the CRCC board, it is allowed to continue under ongoing monitoring

D. The CRCC code allows rehabilitation counselors to have sexual or romantic relationships with their current clients' immediate family

23. The Commission on Rehabilitation Counselor Certification Code of Professional Ethics is *NOT* based on which of the following?

A. Nonmaleficence (i.e., inflict no harm)

B. Autonomy

C. Justice (i.e., fairness)

D. Dignity

24. All of the following are acceptable disclosures of confidentiality by rehabilitation counselors *EXCEPT*:

A. Disclosing to prevent foreseeable harm to a third party (an "identifiable victim") by the client

B. Reporting child abuse or neglect to authorities

C. Reporting to the authorities when a client with a communicable and life-threatening disease is putting others at risk

D. Sharing the counseling record with a client's spouse to fix the marriage

E. Disclosing the appropriate case record when an attorney sends a subpoena

25. Council on Rehabilitation Education is:

A. The certification body that ensures the quality of rehabilitation counseling services and the protection of clients

B. The accreditation body of rehabilitation counseling education programs

C. A division of the American Psychological Association

D. A governing body that oversees all counseling specialties

Answer Key

1B, 2E, 3C, 4A, 5A, 6D, 7D, 8D, 9D, 10A, 11D, 12D, 13D, 14C, 15D, 16B, 17A, 18C, 19A, 20D, 21C, 22A, 23D, 24D, 25B

Advanced Multiple-Choice Questions

1. The Randolph-Sheppard Act of 1936:

A. Made it mandatory for the federal government to purchase designated products from workshops for individuals with cognitive impairments

B. Created federal employment opportunities for individuals with deafness

C. Enabled individuals with blindness to operate vending stands in federal property

D. None of the above

2. Which of the following expanded services to people with mental disabilities?

A. The Smith-Fess Act of 1920

B. The Randolph-Sheppard Act of 1936

C. The Barden-LaFollette Act of 1943

D. The Rehabilitation Act of 1973

E. The Americans with Disabilities Act of 1990

3. The professionalization of rehabilitation counseling has been shaped significantly by graduate training programs. Which of the following provided funding to universities to train master's level rehabilitation counselors?

A. The Vocational Rehabilitation Act Amendments of 1954

B. The Rehabilitation Act of 1973

C. The Americans with Disabilities Act of 1990

D. The School-to-Work Opportunities Act of 1994

E. The Workforce Investment Act of 1998

4. The following are all true regarding the Rehabilitation Act of 1973, *EXCEPT*:

   A. Increased funding for rehabilitation and disability research and established the National Institute of Handicapped Research

   B. Mandated that states serve individuals with the most severe disabilities before serving persons with less severe disabilities

   C. Established the Individualized Written Rehabilitation Program to ensure consumer involvement in the rehabilitation process

   D. Implemented Client Assistance Programs to provide assistance with application and advocacy services

5. The Rehabilitation Act of 1973 also mandated:

   A. Program evaluation for state–federal rehabilitation agencies

   B. A reduction in the federal–state funding split from 80-20 to 70-30

   C. Rehabilitation services for the culturally deprived

   D. More emphasis on behavioral disorders (e.g., alcoholics, drug abusers)

6. What is true regarding the philosophy of rehabilitation after the passage of the Rehabilitation Act of 1973?

   A. The philosophy of rehabilitation has evolved from a "pathological" to a "functionality" point of view

   B. The philosophy of rehabilitation has evolved from a "medical" to an "ability" point of view

   C. The philosophy of rehabilitation has evolved from a "pathological" to a "disability-rights" point of view

   D. The philosophy of rehabilitation has evolved from an "economic-return" to a "disability-rights" point of view

   E. The philosophy of rehabilitation has evolved from a "pathological" to a "disability-rights" point of view

7. To be qualified for state vocational rehabilitation services, people with disabilities must meet the following criteria *EXCEPT*:

   A. The presence of a family history of receiving Social Security and Supplemental Security Income

   B. The presence of a physical or mental impairment that constitutes or results in a substantial impediment to employment

   C. The individual with disability benefiting in terms of an employment outcome from vocational rehabilitation services

   D. The presence of a history of using recreational drugs

   E. A and D

8. Which of the following is considered a goal of vocational rehabilitation?

   A. Empowerment

   B. Independence

   C. Quality of life

D. Inclusion

E. All of the above

9. Under the Rehabilitation Act Amendments of 1992, rehabilitation counselors must determine whether an individual is eligible for VR services within a reasonable period, not to exceed _____ days:

A. 120

B. 90

C. 60

D. 30

10. The Americans with Disabilities Act of 1990 guarantees equal opportunity for people with disabilities in five aspects (Titles). Which of the following is *NOT* one of the five Titles in this legislation?

A. Employment

B. Public services

C. Independent contractors

D. Telecommunications

E. Other miscellaneous provisions

11. Which of the following statement is *NOT* true about *substantially limiting*?

A. An individual must be unable to perform, or be significantly limited in the ability to perform, an activity compared with an average person in the general population

B. An impairment is a "disability" under the ADA only if it substantially limits three or more major life activities

C. The impairment's nature and severity must be considered when determining the impairment

D. How long the impairment will last or is expected to last is also a factor to consider

12. Which of the following is not promulgated by the Rehabilitation Act Amendments of 1992 or central to the philosophy of contemporary rehabilitation practices?

A. Independent living

B. Empowerment

C. Self-determination

D. Informed choices

13. In which legislation was the Individual Written Rehabilitation Plan replaced by the Individualized Plan for Employment?

A. The Rehabilitation Act of 1973

B. The Americans with Disabilities Act of 1990

C. The Rehabilitation Act Amendments of 1998

D. The Ticket to Work and Work Incentives Improvement Act of 1999

E. The Workforce Innovation and Opportunity Act of 2014

14. What is *NOT* a primary function of counselors in the rehabilitation counseling process?

    A. Assist individuals with disabilities in adapting to the environment

    B. Assist environments in accommodating the needs of individuals with disabilities

    C. Work toward the full participation of individuals in all aspects of society

    D. Maximize the cash benefits an individual can receive with the minimum work hours

15. The following are all basic objectives of the Code of Professional Ethics for Rehabilitation Counselors *EXCEPT*:

    A. Promote public welfare by specifying ethical behavior expected of rehabilitation counselors

    B. Establish laws and regulations that punish rehabilitation counselors who do not follow best practices

    C. Serve as an ethical guide designed to assist rehabilitation counselors in constructing a professional course of action that best serves those using rehabilitation counseling services

    D. Serve as the basis for the processing of alleged code violations by certified rehabilitation counselors

16. Certain client rights are protected under the Commission on Rehabilitation Counselor Certification (CRCC) Code of Professional Ethics. Which of the following is *NOT* one of the client rights listed in this code?

    A. Professional disclosure statement should be provided

    B. Informed consent should be included in the intake session

    C. Official transcripts of the counselor should be provided to ensure the quality of the counseling services

    D. Counselors should possess cultural sensitivity

17. Six ethical principles are fundamental to the Commission on Rehabilitation Counselor Certification Code of Professional Ethics. Which of the following is the definition of *beneficence*?

    A. To do good to others

    B. To do no harm to others

    C. To respect the rights of clients to be self-governing within their social and cultural framework

    D. To be fair in the treatment of all clients

    E. To be honest

    F. To be faithful

18. What is the definition of *privileged communication*?

    A. The right of the individuals to choose for themselves the time and the circumstances under which, and the extent to which, personal beliefs, behaviors, and opinions can be shared or withheld from others

    B. The legal right that exists by statute and that protects the client from having confidences revealed publicly from the witness stand during legal proceedings without her or his permission

C. The ethical responsibility of the rehabilitation counselor to safeguard clients from unauthorized disclosures of information given in the therapeutic relationship

D. To be faithful; to keep promises and honor the trust placed in rehabilitation counselors

E. To respect the rights of clients to be self-governing within their social and cultural framework

19. A new participatory ethical decision-making model is proposed to better involve clients in the decision-making process. This model consists of four interactive elements that facilitate client participation. Which of the following is *NOT* one of the four elements?

A. Ethical knowledge and practices

B. Therapeutic alliance or relationship

C. Client involvement

D. Client empowerment

E. Consultation with third-party organizations

20. Rehabilitation counselors must provide several disclosures to clients before they engage in the rehabilitation counseling process. Which of the following is *NOT* one of them?

A. Limitation of confidentiality

B. Educational background and credentials

C. Fees and billing arrangement

D. Record preservation and release policies

E. Identities of other clients

21. Which of the following is true about the stance of J. Patterson and Parker (2003) on licensure?

A. Concerned about alignment CORE standards with state licensure requirements

B. Suggested that alignment with state licensure requirements will weaken the identity of rehabilitation counseling

C. Afraid that aligning with state licensure requirements will be detrimental to the preparation of students for employment in state vocational rehabilitation agencies and community-based rehabilitation programs

D. All of the above

E. None of the above

22. All of the following are true about the stance of Havranek and Brodwin (1994) on licensure, EXCEPT:

A. Described a qualified provider as one who is certified and licensed

B. Suggested students take 12 addition elective credits to develop informal specialization

C. Suggested that students could have the ability to work in various settings with the additional credits

D. Suggested that specializations include, but not be limited to, clinical counseling, assistive technology, and disability management

23. The "two-hats theory" and "big-hat theory" debate regarding the roles and functions of rehabilitation counselors have been reignited in the form of the 48- versus 60-credit debate. The most important concern about the "two-hats theory" and the 60-credit approach is:

    A. It will weaken the identity of rehabilitation counseling

    B. It will weaken the relationship of rehabilitation counseling to the broader field of counseling

    C. It will be detrimental to the preparation of students for employment in state VR agencies and community-based rehabilitation programs

    D. A & C

    E. None of the above

24. Which of the following is *TRUE* regarding *empowerment*?

    A. It is defined as the transfer of power and control over decisions, choices, and values from external entities to the consumers of disability services

    B. It is defined as the process by which consumers make insightful decisions about personal goals and necessary services

    C. It is defined as directing one's own course of action, which requires active personal agency in implementing informed choices

    D. It is a process in which the counselor works collaboratively with the client

25. Leahy et al. (2013) identified eight major job functions that are essential to the professional practice of rehabilitation counseling in today's practice environment. Which of the following is *NOT* one of them?

    A. Job placement

    B. Personality assessment

    C. Case management

    D. Forensic services

    E. Counseling

Answer Key and Explanation of Answers

1C: The Randolph-Sheppard Act of 1936 is an example of specific legislation for individuals with blindness.

2C: The Smith-Fess Act of 1920 is the starting point of public rehabilitation for people with physical disabilities; the Randolph-Sheppard Act of 1936 is specific legislation for individuals with blindness; the Barden-LaFollette Act of 1943 expanded services to include people with mental disabilities; the Rehabilitation Act of 1973 mandated services for people with the most severe disabilities; and the Americans with Disabilities Act of 1990 provided the most comprehensive civil rights protections for people with disabilities.

3A: The Vocational Rehabilitation Act Amendments of 1954 provided funding to universities to train master's level rehabilitation counselors and resulted in the professionalization of rehabilitation counseling.

4A: The Rehabilitation Act of 1973 increased funding for rehabilitation and disability research and established the National Institute of Handicapped Research.

5A: The Rehabilitation Act of 1973 mandated program evaluation and services for people with the most severe disabilities, established the Individualized Written Rehabilitation Program and demonstration projects in rehabilitation and/or independent living services, and increased funding for rehabilitation and disability research.

6D: With the passage of the Rehabilitation Act of 1973, which emphasized services to people with severe disabilities, the philosophy of rehabilitation evolved from an "economic-return" philosophy to a "disability-rights" philosophy.

7E: To be qualified for state vocational rehabilitation services, people with disabilities must meet two eligibility criteria: (a) the presence of a physical or mental impairment that for such individual constitutes or results in a substantial impediment to employment and (b) the individual with disability benefiting in terms of an employment outcome from vocational rehabilitation services.

8E: The goals of vocational rehabilitation have been identified as (a) inclusion, (b) opportunity, (c) independence, (d) empowerment, (e) rehabilitation, and (f) quality life.

9C: Under the Rehabilitation Act Amendments of 1992, rehabilitation counselors must determine eligibility within 60 days and clients must stay on a job for 90 days to be considered as successful closure.

10C: The Americans with Disabilities Act of 1990 guarantees equal opportunity for individuals with disabilities in employment (Title I), public services (Title II), public accommodations (Title III), telecommunications (Title IV), and other miscellaneous provisions (Title V). Private contractors are not protected by this legislation.

11B: An impairment is only a "disability" under the Americans with Disabilities Act of 1990 if it substantially limits one or more major life activities.

12A: All the statements except "independent living" are promulgated by the Rehabilitation Act Amendments of 1992 and are central to the philosophy of contemporary rehabilitation practices. It is generally agreed that the goals of rehabilitation can be better achieved when there is maximal consumer involvement in the development, implementation, and use of vocational rehabilitation services.

13C: The Individualized Written Rehabilitation Program was established during the Rehabilitation Act of 1973 and was replaced by the Individualized Plan for Employment with the passage of the Rehabilitation Act Amendments of 1998.

14D: In carrying out the multifaceted process of rehabilitation counseling, rehabilitation counselors must be prepared to assist individuals in adapting to the environment, assist environments in accommodating the needs of individuals with disabilities, and work toward the full participation of individuals in all aspects of society, with a particular focus on independent living and work.

15B: The basic objectives of the Code of Professional Ethics for Rehabilitation Counselors are to (a) promote public welfare by specifying the ethical behavior expected of rehabilitation counselors, (b) establish principles that define the ethical behavior and best practices of rehabilitation counselors, (c) serve as an ethical guide designed to assist rehabilitation counselors in constructing a professional course of action that best serves those using rehabilitation counseling services, and (d) serve as the basis for the processing of alleged violations by certified rehabilitation counselors (CRCC, 2017).

16C: Counselors' qualifications, credentials, and relevant experience in rehabilitation counseling should be included in the professional disclosure, but the official transcript is not necessary.

17A: The rest of the definitions are for *nonmaleficence, autonomy, justice, veracity, and fidelity,* respectively.

18B: Answer A is the definition of *privacy;* Answer C is the definition of *confidentiality;* Answer D is the definition of *fidelity;* Answer E is the definition of *autonomy.*

19E: This model, introduced by Tarvydas et al. (2015), is composed of four interactive elements that facilitate client participation in the process of ethical decision-making: ethical knowledge and practices, the therapeutic alliance or relationship, client involvement, and client empowerment.

20E: According to the Commission on Rehabilitation Counselor Certification Code of Professional Ethics, disclosure at the onset of the counseling relationship should minimally include (a) qualifications, credentials, and relevant experience of the rehabilitation counselor; (b) purposes, goals, techniques, limitations, and nature of potential risks and benefits of services; (c) frequency and length of services; (d) confidentiality and limitations regarding confidentiality (including how a supervisor and/or treatment team professional is involved); (e) contingencies for continuating services on the incapacitation or death of the rehabilitation counselor; (f) fees and billing arrangements; (g) record preservation and release policies; (h) risks associated with electronic communication; and (i) legal issues affecting services.

21D: J. Patterson and Parker (2003) expressed concern about aligning Council on Rehabilitation Education standards with state licensure requirements, suggesting that this alignment weakens the identity of rehabilitation counseling and could be detrimental to the preparation of students for employment in state vocational rehabilitation agencies and community-based rehabilitation programs.

22A: Leahy (2004), instead of Havranek and Brodwin (1994), describes a qualified provider as one who is certified and licensed.

23D: The most important concern about the "two-hats theory" and the 60-credit approach is that it will weaken the identity of rehabilitation counseling and be detrimental to the preparation of students for employment in state vocational rehabilitation agencies and community-based rehabilitation programs.

24A: Answer B is the definition of *informed choice;* Answer C is the definition of *self-determination;* and Answer D is a general description of rehabilitation counseling. In addition, Kosciulek and Wheaton (2003) indicated that informed choice and self-determination, along with an effective counselor–consumer working alliance, are the necessary components of increased consumer empowerment.

25B: Rehabilitation counselors can administer vocational, but not personality, assessment for the purpose of career counseling.

References

Association of University Centers on Disabilities. (2014). WIOA changes to Rehab Act. Retrieved from https://www.aucd.org/docs/wioa-changes-to-rehab-act%20(1).pdf

Commission on Rehabilitation Counselor Certification. (2017). *Code of professional ethics for rehabilitation counselors.* Retrieved from https://www.crccertification.com/filebin/pdf/CRCC_Code_Eff_20170101.pdf

Council for Accreditation of Counseling and Related Educational Programs. (2015). Plan of merger agreement between the Council on Rehabilitation Education (CORE) and the Council for Accreditation of Counseling and Related Educational Programs (CACREP) [Press release]. Retrieved from http://www.cacrep.org/wp-content/uploads/2017/05/Press-Release-on-Merger-7-20-15.pdf

Havranek, J. E., & Brodwin, M. G. (1994). Rehabilitation counselor curricula: Time for a change. *Rehabilitation Education, 8,* 369–379.

Kosciulek, J. F., & Wheaton, J. E. (2003). Rehabilitation counseling with individuals with disabilities: An empowerment framework. *Rehabilitation Education, 17,* 207–214.

Leahy, M. J. (2002). Professionalism in rehabilitation counseling: A retrospective review. *Journal of Rehabilitation Administration, 26,* 99–109.

Leahy, M. J. (2004). Qualified providers. In T. F. Riggar & D. R. Maki (Eds.), *Handbook of rehabilitation counseling* (pp. 142–158). New York, NY: Springer Publishing.

Leahy, M. J., Chan, F., & Saunders, J. L. (2003). Job functions and knowledge requirements of certified rehabilitation counselors in the 21st century. *Rehabilitation Counseling Bulletin, 46,* 66–81.

Leahy, M. J., Chan, F., Sung, C., & Kim, M. (2013). Empirically derived test specifications for the certified rehabilitation counselor examination. *Rehabilitation Counseling Bulletin, 56,* 199–214.

Maki, D., & Tarvydas, V. (2011). *Professional practice of rehabilitation counseling.* New York, NY: Springer Publishing.

Martin, R., West-Evans, K., & Connelly, J. (2010). Vocational rehabilitation: Celebrating 90 years of careers and independence. *American Rehabilitation,* Special Edition/Summer, 15–18.

McMahon, B. T. (2010). The ADA Amendments Act of 2008: Pocket guide for rehabilitation professionals. *The Rehabilitation Counseling Professional, 18,* 11–18.

Muthard, J. E., & Salamone, P. R. (1969). The roles and functions of the rehabilitation counselor. *Rehabilitation Counseling Bulletin, 13,* 81–168.

Parker, R. M., & Szymanski, E. M. (1998). *Rehabilitation counseling: Basics and beyond* (3rd ed.). Austin, TX: Pro-Ed.

Patterson, C. H. (1968). Rehabilitation counseling: A profession or a trade? *Personnel and Guidance Journal, 46,* 567–571.

Patterson, J. (1998). Ethics and ethical decision making in rehabilitation counseling. In R. Parker & E. Szymanski (Eds.), *Rehabilitation counseling: Basics and beyond* (pp. 181–207). Austin, TX: Pro-Ed.

Patterson, J., & Parker, R. M. (2003). Rehabilitation counselor education at the crossroads: Private practice or human service? *Rehabilitation Education, 17,* 9–18.

Prilleltensky, I., & Gonick, L. (1996). Polities change, oppression remains: On the psychology and politics of oppression. *Political Psychology, 17*(1), 127–148.

Rubin, S. E., & Roessler, R. T. (2008). *Foundations of the vocational rehabilitation process* (6th ed.). Austin, TX: Pro-Ed.

Sutton v. United Air Lines, Inc. 527 U.S. 471 (1999).

Tarasoff v. Regents of University of California, 17 Cal. 3d 425 (Cal. 1976).

Tarvydas, V. M., Estrada-Hernandez, N., Vazquez-Ramos, R. A., & Saunders, J. L. (2017). Development and initial psychometric properties of the Participatory Ethics Scale. *Rehabilitation Counseling Bulletin, 60*(4), 195–202.

Tarvydas, V. M., Vazquez-Ramos, R. A., & Estrada-Hernandez, N. (2015). Applied participatory ethics: Bridging the social justice chasm between counselor and client. *Counseling and Values, 60*(2), 218–233.

Toyota Motor Manufacturing, Kentucky, Inc. v. Williams, 534 U.S. 184 (2002).

U.S. Department of Education. (2016). RSA: Workforce Innovation and Opportunity Act. Retrieved from http://www2.ed.gov/about/offices/list/osers/rsa/wioa-reauthorization.html#overview

U.S. Department of Education. (2016). State vocational rehabilitation services program; state supported employment services program; limitations on use of subminimum wage. Retrieved from https://www.federalregister.gov/articles/2016/08/19/2016-15980/state-vocational-rehabilitation-services-program-state-supported-employment-services-program

U.S. Department of Labor. (2015). Advisory committee on increasing competitive integrated employment for individuals with disabilities. Retrieved from https://www.dol.gov/odep/pdf/20150808.pdf

U.S. Department of Labor. (2016). Workforce Innovation and Opportunity Act; joint rule for unified and combined state plans, performance accountability, and the one-stop system joint provisions; final rule. Retrieved from https://www.doleta.gov/wioa/Final_Rules_Resources.cfm

West, M., & Parent, W. (1992). Consumer choice and empowerment in supported employment services: Issues and strategies. *Journal of the Association for Persons with Severe Handicaps, 17*, 47–52.

White House. (2014). Ready to work: Job-driven training and American opportunity. Retrieved from https://obamawhitehouse.archives.gov/sites/default/files/docs/skills_report.pdf

Whitehouse, F. A. (1975). Rehabilitation clinician. *Journal of Rehabilitation, 41*, 24–26.

2

Psychosocial Aspects of Health, Mental Health, and Disability

JULIE CHRONISTER AND SANDRA FITZGERALD

Living with a disabling health or mental health condition is an idiosyncratic experience that reflects the intersection of a diverse number of personal and contextual factors. Particularly, the level of disability for one individual with a health condition varies from that of another individual living with the same condition with health conditions varying significantly across and within specific conditions. To help the student understand the psychosocial experience of persons with disabling health conditions, this chapter reviews the literature related to (a) models of disability, health, and mental health; (b) society and disability; (c) development, aging, sexuality, and disability; (d) culture and disability; (e) psychological response to disability theories; and (f) contemporary psychosocial issues in rehabilitation and mental health counseling.

Key Concepts

Learning Objectives

By the end of this unit you should be able to:

1. Understand the medical, social, functional, and biopsychosocial models of disability.
2. Understand the World Health Organization's International Classification of Functioning, Disability and Health.
3. Understand the Mental Health Recovery Model.
4. Understand the types and functions of social support.

I. Models of Disability, Health, and Mental Health

The **medical model** conceptualizes disability as a medically diagnosed health or mental health condition that causes deficient functioning and requires medical intervention (Bingham, Clarke, Michielsens, & Van de Meer, 2013). The medical model seeks to increase access and equality for people with disabilities by eliminating the cause of, or "fixing" the medical condition (Bingham et al., 2013). In the United States, the medical model is used to determine eligibility for educational, vocational, financial, legal, and government entitlement programs (e.g., Social Security Disability Insurance [SSDI], Supplemental Security Income [SSI]; Chan, Leahy, & Saunders, 2005; Tarvydas, Peterson, & Michaelson, 2005). Specifically, medical professionals perform *disability determinations* based on their clinical impression of the severity of the condition and its impact on the person's ability to learn, communicate, work, and perform daily activities (e.g., bathing, dressing, cooking). Medical professionals are trained to diagnose, treat, and cure health conditions, but their process of disability determination ignores societal and environmental factors that influence the disability experience and perpetuate the societal attitude that people with disabilities are "abnormal" or "defective" (Humpage, 2007). Nonetheless, the model has advanced science to better understand illness and disease etiology, process, and survival rates (Peterson, 2009).

The medical model is the foundation for the **functional model**, which posits that disability is based on *functional limitations* (e.g., mobility, communication, social, or psychological limitations) that influence an individual's ability to perform daily activities and participation in work, school, and social life. The functional model determines disability based on the severity of functional limitations caused by the medical diagnosis. For example, an individual with chronic back pain or post-polio syndrome may experience fatigue, weakness and pain, resulting in functional limitations associated with standing, walking, and endurance, which increases their level of disability within their home, work, and social contexts. Although the functional model originates from the medical model, the difference lies in the functional model's focus on determining what aspect of an individual's school, work, and social life is impacted (e.g., a professional athlete would be much more affected by mobility impairments than a software designer) and what environmental **accommodations, modifications**, and **assistive technology devices** can be used as remedies to increase access and equality for people with disabilities (vs. medical intervention only). **Accommodations** include any alteration or change in the individual's environment, such as a ramp, reduced work schedule, extra time on exam, standing desk, chair, or service animal, that is designed to reduce the impact of functional limitations and increase access and equality. **Modifications** are alterations to existing work or school tasks that alter formats or schedules/duties to allow persons with disabilities fair access to perform tasks or assignments. **Assistive technology devices** are commonly used to decrease the level of disability within a particular context (e.g., memory devices, computer software, audiology devices, and talking devices/software). Smartphones, tablets, software, and accessible computer technology have increased the availability and universality of assistive technology for all persons.

The **social model** posits that health or mental health conditions are not inherently disabling; it is societal exclusion and inaccessible environments (e.g., a missing curb cut, lack of an entrance ramp, a poorly placed elevator, lack of Braille signage) designed for the able-bodied that are disabling. As such, society is responsible for eliminating disabilities through social change and political action that promotes universal access and policies and laws that prevent discrimination and injustices toward people living with health or mental health conditions (Bingham et al., 2013; Peterson, 2009). The *Americans with Disabilities Act Amendments Act* (ADAAA, 2008) is an example of a law to protect persons with disabilities from discrimination, injustice, and inaccessibility. Similarly, the *Individuals with Disabilities Educational Act* of 1990 and *Section 504 of the Rehabilitation Act of 1973* were designed to reduce barriers to school, work, and the community for persons with disabilities. The social model considers health and mental health conditions as components of cultural diversity versus a biological deficiency.

The **minority group model** and the **independent living model** are iterations of the social model, also proposing that disability is not a personal attribute but is caused by, and should thus be remedied by, society (Smart, 2009). While popular today, the social model is not universally accepted (Barney, 2012). Some argue that separating health conditions from an environmentally imposed disability prevents a full understanding of the individual's experience (Palmer & Harley, 2012). In addition, critics argue that the social model does not account for the various differences among those living with health and mental health conditions, ignoring that people experience conditions differently. In addition, this model does not take into account the various intersecting cultural identities (e.g., age, race, ethnicity, sexual orientation, gender identity, religion, geographical location) among people with disabilities; these identities contribute to many forms and layers of prejudice and discrimination such as ageism, racism, sexism, homonegativism, and transphobia (Flintoff, Fitzgerald, & Scraton, 2008).

The social model is grounded in the disability rights movement, and thus **self-advocacy** is a critical component of the social model of disability. Self-advocacy is based on Americans with disabilities engaging in social and political collective action to shape their social role and legal treatment (Scotch, 2009). In contrast to the potential consequences of the medical model (e.g., dependency, marginality, and social exclusion), self-advocacy is taking control of one's life, speaking up for oneself, being in control of one's resources, and having the right to make life decisions without undue influence or control from others. Self-advocacy organizations have been instrumental in advocating for the rights of persons with disabilities by promoting independence, access, justice, and disability as diversity and by fighting to eliminate disability as a stigmatized status (Scotch, 2009). Self-advocacy is rooted in the American ideals of autonomy and **self-determination**, and self-determination is rooted in theories of human agency. *Human agency* refers to the capacity of human beings to make choices and to impose those choices on the world. According to Bandura (2001), to be an agent "is to intentionally make things happen by one's actions" (p. 2). Thus, self-determination is about people being active contributors to, or "authors" of their own behavior (Walker et al., 2011). Self-determination reflects a change from "shoulds" to "decisions and behaviors" (Corrigan et al., 2012). Application of self-determination principles may foster greater client participation in treatment, leading to better outcomes (Fitzgerald et al., 2015). According to the Developmental Disabilities Assistance and Bill of Rights Act of 2000, self-determination skills include (a) communicating and making personal decisions; (b) communicating choices and exercising control over supports and services received; (c) controlling resources needed to access services, supports, and other assistance; (d) using opportunities to participate and contribute to communities; and (e) supporting for and training in self-advocating to develop leadership skills, participate in coalitions, and educate policymakers (Table 2.1).

TABLE 2.1 Comparison Between Medical and Social Models of Disability Discourse

Topic	Medical Model	Social Model
Definition of *disability*	An individual or medical phenomenon that results from impairments in body functions or structures; a deficiency or abnormality	A social construct that is imposed on top of impairments by society; a difference
Access to treatment or services	Referral by diagnosis	Self-referral, experience driven
Targets of interventions	"Fixing" the disability to the greatest extent possible; "normalizing"	Social or political change in an effort to decrease environmental barriers and increase levels of understanding

(*continued*)

TABLE 2.1 Comparison Between Medical and Social Models of Disability Discourse (*continued*)

Topic	Medical Model	Social Model
Outcome of interventions	Normalized function; functioning member of existing society	Self-advocacy, changes in environment and understanding, social inclusion
The agent of remedy	The professional	Potentially, the individual, an advocate or anyone who positively affects the arrangements between the individual and society
Effects on individuals who are typically functioning	Society remains the same	Society evolves to be more inclusive
Perceptions toward individuals with disabilities	The individual is faulty	The individual is unique
Cognitive authority	Scientists and physician	Academics and advocates with disabilities
Perception of disability	Being disabled is negative	Being disabled, in itself, is neither positive nor negative

Source: Haegele and Hodge (2016).

The **biopsychosocial (BPS) model** was developed in the 1970s by Engel (1977), who argued for a BPS model of medicine. This model expanded the understanding and treatment of illness and disease to include not only the biological component (e.g., decreased dopamine production in Parkinson's disease), but also the psychological (e.g., emotional response to disease/illness) and social (e.g., social support, impact on family, societal response) components. The World Health Organization (WHO) **International Classification of Functioning, Disability and Health** (ICF; WHO, 2001) is the world's leading BPS approach to conceptualizing and measuring level of disability (Peterson, 2005). Simply put, disability cannot be defined in isolation; it is understood as an outcome of interacting **functional** (body function/structure, activity, participation) and **contextual** (personal and environmental) variables (Chan, Gelman, Ditchman, Kim, & Chiu, 2009). As shown in Figure 2.1, "disability" is not included as a factor in the model but is an outcome of the intersecting variables. See Figure 2.2 for examples of application of ICF with individuals.

The components of the ICF model include the functional (body function/structure, activities, participation) and the contextual (environmental and personal) components (Table 2.2). See Table 2.3 for description of function components including body function and structure, activity and participation and the context components including personal and environmental factors which reflect the unique factors that intersect with functioning, to determine level of disability. **Environmental** factors include phenomena such as societal attitudes, architectural barriers/access, available and accessible institutional support (e.g., medical services, educational programs and technological supports, political and religious groups), living conditions, availability of job opportunities, accessibility of worksites, legal and social structures and policies, transportation systems, social and community support, climate, and terrain. **Social support** is a particularly important environmental factor for those living with health and mental

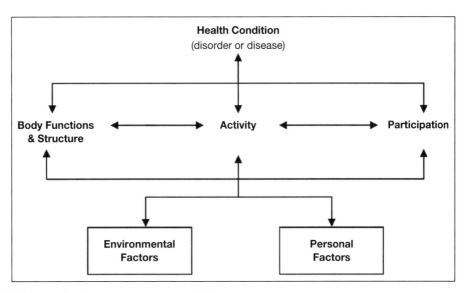

FIGURE 2.1 Interaction between components of ICF.

ICF, International Classification of Functioning, Disability and Health.

Source: World Health Organization (2001). Reprinted with permission.

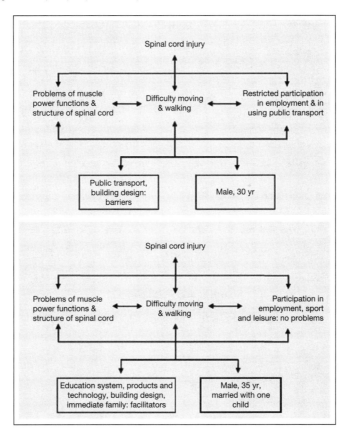

FIGURE 2.2 Examples of ICF use with individuals.

ICF, International Classification of Functioning, Disability and Health.

Source: World Health Organization (2001). Reprinted with permission.

TABLE 2.2 Definitions of ICF Components

Body functions are physiological functions of body systems (including psychological functions).

Body structures are anatomical parts of the body such as organs, limbs, and their components.

Impairments are problems in body function or structure such as a significant deviation or loss.

Activity is the execution of a task or action by an individual.

Participation is involvement in a life situation.

Activity limitations are difficulties an individual may have in executing activities.

Participation restrictions are problems an individual may experience in involvement in life situations.

Environmental factors make up the physical, social, and attiudinal environments in which people live and conduct their lives.

ICF, International Classification of Functioning, Disability and Health.

Source: World Health Organization (2001). Reprinted with permission.

TABLE 2.3 Components of the ICF Model

Body	
Function	**Structure**
Mental functions	Structure of the nervous system
Sensory functions and pain	The eye, ear, and related structures
Voice and speech functions	Structures involved in voice and speech
Functions of the cardiovascular, hematological, immunological, and respiratory systems	Structures of the cardiovascular, immunological, and respiratory systems
Functions of the digestive, metabolic, and endocrine systems	Structures related to the digestive, metabolic, and endocrine systems
Genitourinary and reproductive functions	Structures related to genitourinary and reproductive systems
Neuromusculoskeletal and movement-related functions	Structures related to movement
Functions of the skin and related structures	Skin and related structures

Activities and Participation
Learning and applying knowledge
General tasks and demands
Communication
Mobility
Self-care
Domestic life
Interpersonal interactions and relationships

(continued)

TABLE 2.3 Components of the ICF Model (*continued*)

Activities and Participation
Major life areas
Community, social, and civic life
Environmental Factors
Products and technology
Natural environment and human-made changes to environment
Support and relationships
Attitudes
Services, systems, and policies

ICF, International Classification of Functioning, Disability and Health.
Source: World Health Organization (2001). Reprinted with permission.

health conditions. Decades of research shows that social support is linked to better physical and mental health, reduced mortality and morbidity rates, longevity, and recovery from trauma (Cohen & Janicki-Deverts, 2009; Ertel, Glymour, & Berkman, 2009; Uchino, 2004; Umberson & Montez, 2010). In addition, social support has been linked to numerous rehabilitation outcomes (Chronister, Chou, Frain, & da Silva Cardoso, 2008; Chou & Chronister, 2012; Chronister, Chou, & Liao, 2013; Chronister, Chou, Fitzgerald, & Liao, 2016), including (a) increased well-being, happiness, and higher occupational functioning among individuals with spinal cord injuries (Devereux, Bullock, Bargmann-Losche, & Kyriakou, 2005; Hampton, 2004); (b) reduced emotional distress and better vocational outcomes among those living with brain injuries (Kaplan, 1990); (c) reduced mental health conditions among those with intellectual disabilities (Scott & Havercamp, 2014); and (d) reduced sick leave from work, fewer career barriers, more career choices, successful job seeking, job retention, and improved job performance among persons with disabilities (Antonson, Danermark, & Lundström, 2006; E. C. Dunn, Wewiorski, & Rogers, 2010; Fabian, Beveridge, & Ethridge, 2009). In addition, many contemporary theoretical models of health and functioning include social support as a key environmental variable; examples include Kumpfer's Transactional Framework of Resilience (1999), Lewinsohn, Hoberman, Teri, and Hautzinger's Integrative Model of Depression (1985), and as described previously, the ICF Model (WHO, 2001). Indeed, decades of research suggest that high levels of social support have the potential to reduce the level of disability.

Given that persons with disabilities have smaller social support systems than the general population (Chronister, 2009), report fewer opportunities to access support, and often experience negative social ties that perpetuate dependency and exclusion, rehabilitation counselors must assess client's social support systems and provide strategies to strengthen their support network. Social support assessment includes an analysis of the *structure* of an individual's support system (size, frequency of interactions) as well as the *functional* aspect (e.g., type and quality) of their support providers (peers, friends, family, service providers). Typically defined as the social resources or provisions that a person perceives to be available or that have actually been provided by a support provider (Cohen, Mermelstein, Kamarck, & Hoberman, 1985; Thoits, 2011), functional support is conceptualized to include two overarching types of support, **emotional support**—which involves the provision of caring, empathy, love, and trust (House, 1981;

Krause, 1986) that leads to feelings of being cared for and loved, feelings of being esteemed and valued, and belongingness (Cobb, 1976), and **instrumental support**—which is the provision of tangible goods, aid, services, or concrete assistance that is intended to solve a problem or accomplish a task (Barrera, 1986; Cutrona & Russell, 1990). Theoretically, social support works through a direct salutary effect on health or by buffering the negative impact of stress on health (Cohen & Wills, 1985; House, 1981; Uchino, 2004; Umberson & Montez, 2010).

Most research shows that functional support is a better predictor of health and well-being than the structural dimension of social support (Southwick, Vythilingam, & Charney 2005). In fact, functional support is one of the most well-documented psychosocial factors influencing physical health outcomes (Berkman, Glass, Brissette, & Seeman, 2000). Compelling evidence from a meta-analytic study showed that functional support was significantly related to lower risk for all-cause mortality (Holt-Lunstad, Smith, & Layton, 2010). In addition, high levels of support appear to buffer or protect against the negative impact of mental and physical illness, whereas low levels are associated with mood disorders and comorbid depression accompanying conditions such as multiple sclerosis, cancer, and rheumatoid arthritis (Hassan et al., 2006; Hershey, Morton, Davis, Reichgott, 1980; Jung, 1990).

Numerous social support measures have been designed to assess structural and functional support. Population-specific measures of support are particularly useful for those living with health or mental health conditions (e.g., diabetes, psychiatric disabilities, cancer). (See Chronister, 2009; Chronister, Johnson, & Berven, 2006; Cohen, Underwood, & Gottlieb, 2000 for in-depth reviews of social support assessment.) In addition, informal support assessments can be easily accomplished through intake interviews and on-going clinical inquiry by collaboratively drawing on the client's social network to determine sources of positive and negative ties, to determine the types of supports provided by these ties, and to explore ways to capitalize on existing social supports and facilitate an increase in the quantity and quality of supports.

Personal factors include demographic and cultural characteristics (e.g., age, gender, sexual orientation, religion, geographical location, heritage, immigration status, socioeconomic status) and other personal characteristics (e.g., health care, work, social, education histories; health, mental health, substance abuse, and trauma histories; coping styles; and other psychological presentations related to self-determination, self-advocacy, and health literacy) that influence how disability is experienced by the individual. In addition, personal experiences related to the health condition's time of onset (congenital, acquired), type of onset (insidious vs. acute), course (direction, pace of movement, degree of predictability) and frequency and duration of hospitalizations are also relevant personal factors (Smart, 2009).

II. Mental Health Recovery Model

According to Anthony (1993), mental health—or more contemporarily referred to as *behavioral health*—recovery is,

> a deeply personal, unique process of changing one's attitude, values feelings, and goals and/or roles. It is a way of living a satisfying, hopeful, and contributing life even with the limitations caused by illness. Recovery involves the development of new meaning and purpose in one's life (p. 15).

According to the Substance Abuse and Mental Health Services Administration (SAMHSA; 2012), mental health recovery is "a process of change through which individuals improve their health and wellness, live a self-directed life, and strive to reach their full potential." The four areas of recovery include (a) health (overcoming or managing one's disease or symptoms); (b) home (a stable place to live); (c) purpose (meaningful daily activities, such as a job, school, volunteer-ism, caretaking, or creative endeavors, as well as the independence, incomes, and resources to participate in society); and (d) community (relationships or social networks that provide support, friendship, love, and hope). The 10 guiding principles underlying this model include *hope; respect; person-driven; holistic; multiple pathways to recovery; addresses trauma; culturally informed services; support of peers and allies; relationship and social network support; and individual, family, and community strengths and responsibility* (SAMHSA, 2012).

Traditional service-delivery models guide client treatment by telling clients what to do or by having tasks done with minimal to no client input. Services based on recovery principles emphasize client strengths and empowerment and propose that clients who have greater control and choice in their treatment have increased control and initiative in their lives. Client recovery relies heavily on social and community supports and can occur without professional intervention. In fact, providers do not make decisions for clients but provide information and support regarding possible outcomes associated with client decisions. Recovery is not a linear process that aims for being symptom free; recovery includes symptom reoccurrence and symptom management.

Key Concepts

Learning Objectives

By the end of this unit you should be able to:

1. Understand the social, economic, and other environmental factors affecting individuals with disabilities and presenting barriers to rehabilitation.

2. Understand attitude formation and strategies to reduce attitudinal barriers affecting people with disabilities.

I. Society and Disability

Minority stress theory, originally conceptualized to explain the experiences of gender, racial, and ethnic marginalized communities, can also be understood within the context of disability communities. Although not all persons with disabilities consider themselves to be part of a marginalized community, as a group, people with disabilities have endured a long history of minority-type stressors similar to those from historically marginalized communities. Minority stress theory posits that nondominant group members, including persons with disabilities, experience chronic stress related to **negative societal attitudes, stigma, ableism, discrimination, prejudice, and microaggressions**; this stress leads to health disparities and work, school, social, and housing inequities and injustices (Meyer, 2003; Sue et al., 2007)

Attitudes are defined as the observable consequences of customs, practices, ideologies, values, norms, factual beliefs, and religious beliefs (Chan, Livneh, Pruett, Wang, & Zheng, 2009). Specifically, an attitude is "an evaluative statement (favorable or unfavorable) related to a person, object or event" (Chan, Livneh, et al., 2009, p. 335). Attitudes are typically composed of **affect** (feelings), **cognitions** (beliefs), and **behaviors** that predispose individuals to behave, interpret, and evaluate in particular ways based on attitudinal influence (Chan, Livneh, et al., 2009; Eagly, Mladinic, & Otto, 1994). Attitudes also reduce discomfort in negotiating the environment (Marini, Glover-Graf, & Millington, 2011). Numerous studies suggest that societal attitudes toward people with disabilities are negative (Chan, Livneh, et al., 2009; Chubon, 1994; Donaldson, 1980; Livneh, 1988; Olkin, 1999; Wright, 1988). Common negative attitudes toward people with disabilities include that they are "perpetual children," objects of pity, menaces to society, sick and incompetent, and psychological and economic burdens to society—a sentiment aligned with those held by the Nazis and eugenicists, which ultimately led to confinement, sterilization, and extermination (Marini et al., 2011). Yuker (1988) and Wright (1988) also identified physical attractiveness, competence and social skills as areas that have long be known to influence societal attitudes toward all people, including those with disabilities. Wright (1983) articulated how **spread** occurs when society assumes, for example, that a wheelchair user is cognitively impaired, spreading the health condition to encompass all aspects of the individual.

Antonak and Livneh (1991) and other scholars (e.g., Plotnik, 1996; Smart, 2009; Szymanski, Ryan, Merz, Trevino, & Johnston-Rodriguez, 1996; Wright, 1960, 1983) identified 15 origins of attitudes toward people with disabilities, including (a) **attributional origins** (causes of events, other people, and own behavior); (b) **blaming of the victim** (psychological safety net that minimizes the fear that the event could happen to someone); (c) **disability as a punishment for sin**; (d) **anxiety-provoking situations** (unstructured or ambiguous social situation resulting in avoidance of a person with a disability); (e) **childhood influences** (negative messages, experiences, or influences related to disability); (f) **sociocultural conditioning** (societal norms of beauty, physique, agility); (g) **psychodynamic factors** (unconscious expectation of mourning/ sadness, just world belief); (h) **existential angst** (fearing becoming disabled if near a person with a disability); (i) **aesthetic aversion** (aesthetic-sexual aversion related to nonnormative physical differences); (j) **minority status** (intersecting marginalized identities); (k) **prejudice-inviting behavior** (acting in a way that strengthens societal stereotypes); (l) **disability-related factors** (hierarchy of stigma toward different types of disabilities; (m) **media portrayals of disability** (usually negative); (n) **demographic variables** related to nondisabled persons (age, gender, education, income, personality, self-concept, body-image of able-bodied individuals influences attitudes); and (o) **perceptions of burden** (assumption of burden related to caring for person with disability). Notably, while society does assign positive characteristics (e.g., inspirational, admirable, saintly) to persons with disabilities who obtain notable achievements (Olympic runner, actor, president), the underlying message conveys that persons with disabilities who do not achieve these rare achievements lack the motivation and desire to succeed. Individuals who do experience these rare achievements or fame, are often referred to by persons with disabilities as "super crips" (Smart, 2009) because they represent a small, yet tokenized group of persons with disabilities that set an unreachable standard for the majority of those living with a disabling condition.

II. Negative Attitudes Toward Disability

Additional concepts related to society attitudes include **stereotype, prejudice, discrimination, ableism, microaggressions,** and **stigma.** Allport (1968) defined **stereotype** as "an exaggerated belief associated with a category" (p. 191). Examples of stereotypes follow: Asians are good at math, people with Down syndrome are always happy, and African Americans are good at sports. Stereotypic views are sources of prejudice and discrimination that lead to **invisible attitudinal barriers** in the environment (Chan, Livneh, et al., 2009). Stereotypic views of persons with disabilities stem from (a) the **safety threat** in which persons with disabilities are perceived to be a threat to the physical safety of persons without disabilities; (b) the **ambiguity of disability**, which results in the tendency to ascribe negative aspects or greater limitations to the disability;

(c) the **salience of the disability** which considers the disability to be the most important or the only aspect of the individual; (d) **spread or overgeneralization**, which involves discounting and underrating all of the abilities of persons with disabilities and focusing on the disability as the sole aspect of their identity; (e) **moral accountability for the cause and management of the disability**, which involves placing blame on persons with disabilities for the cause of and the way that they deal with their condition; (f) **inferred emotional consequences of the disability**, which assumes that all persons with disabilities experience negative emotions because of their condition; and (g) the **fear of acquiring a disability**, which involves an unfounded fear by others that if they interact with persons with disabilities they will "catch" the disability. These stereotypic views have a negative impact on rehabilitation outcomes (Chan, Livneh, et al., 2009). Patterson, McFarlane, & Sax (2005) assert that rehabilitation counselors should evaluate their own attitudes (i.e., awareness, feelings, actions) and stereotypes through self-exploration questions such as, "Am I afraid of persons with psychiatric conditions?" or "Do I think someone with an intellectual disability can attend school?"

Prejudice is a negative generalization toward a group of people and the assumption that an individual belonging to that group has the characteristics based on the generalization. Examples include the following: All persons with disabilities are intellectually inferior, and persons with psychiatric conditions are violent (Chan, Livneh, et al., 2009). **Discrimination** is the *action* carried out based on prejudice. For example, an employer does not hire a person with a disability because of the belief that the person with the disability is "unsafe," or individuals with a psychiatric condition are not provided silverware or sharp pencils because of the fear that they will be violent. **Ableism** is the unique form of discrimination experienced by person with disabilities based on their disabilities. Ableism favors abled-bodied individuals, maintaining disability as a negative state and experience. "Implicit within ableism is an able-centric worldview, which endorses the belief that there is a 'normal' manner in which to perceive and/or manipulate stimuli and a 'normal' manner of accomplishing tasks of daily living" (Keller & Galgay, 2010, p. 242). Ableism perpetuates the belief that disability is a deviation from societal norms.

Microaggressions are defined as "everyday verbal, nonverbal, and environmental slights, snubs, or insults, whether intentional or unintentional, that communicate hostile, derogatory, or negative messages to target persons based solely upon their marginalized group membership" (Sue, 2010, p. 3). Microaggressions are more distinct from traditional and overt forms of discrimination in that otherwise well-intentioned individuals can deliver them unconsciously, unaware of their potential harmful effects (Gonzales, Davidoff, Nadal, & Yanos, 2015). Sue et al. (2007) identified three major categories: (a) microassaults, which involve explicit attacks and are parallel to traditional forms of racism or ableism; (b) microinsults, which are insensitive and demeaning remarks; and (c) microinvalidations, which negate an individual's experience of reality. According to Sue et al. (2007), microaggressions are the most insidious and harmful forms of prejudices. Studies show that microaggressions contribute to minority stress among a variety of nondominant groups (Nadal, 2013), including persons with disabilities. For example, microaggressions toward marginalized racial and sexual communities are associated with stress, depression, and alcohol abuse (Blume, Lovato, Thyken, & Denny, 2012; Nadal, 2013; Torres, Driscoll, & Burrow, 2010). Keller and Galgay (2010) identified eight types of microaggressions targeting people with disabilities including (a) denial of identity, (b) denial of privacy, (c) helplessness, (d) secondary gain, (e) spread effect, (f) patronization, (g) second-class citizen, and (h) desexualization.

Stigma is a term that encompasses the problems associated with stereotyping, prejudice, discrimination, ableism, and microaggressions—the chain of events resulting from negative attitudes and beliefs. Persons with disabilities who are stigmatized often cannot access work, housing, and other community resources because of stigmatizing attitudes that have led to discriminatory behavior (Chan, Livneh, et al., 2009). According to Hatzenbuehler, Phelan, and Link (2013), stigma is a fundamental cause of health, work, school and social disparities, as well as inequalities for people with disabilities, because it contributes to the unequal distribution of power and resources through multiple routes. Societal stigma is a pervasive phenomenon that is positively linked to **internalized stigma**, which is the psychological internalization of the negative stereotypes, biases, and assumptions about one's stigmatized group and the application these negative messages to oneself (Corrigan & Watson, 2002; Link, Cullen, Struening, Shrout, & Dohrenwend, 1989). Internalized stigma has been associated with lower levels of hope, self-esteem, empowerment, treatment adherence, and recovery and higher levels of psychiatric symptoms (Boyd, Adler, Otilingam, & Peters, 2014; Drapalski et al., 2013; Livingston & Boyd, 2010). Stigma impacts disability communities in different ways, often depending on the type of disability. For example, some health and mental health conditions experience more societal stigma than others. Often conceptualized as the **hierarchy of stigma** (Livneh, 1982), persons with psychiatric, substance abuse, HIV/AIDS, and other sexually transmitted conditions experience more stigmatizing attitudes because society often attribute the cause of these conditions to the individual, whereas those with physical disabilities such as cerebral palsy, muscular dystrophy, and multiple sclerosis, experience more favorable attitudes (D. Cook, 1998). Differing levels of stigma occur, depending on how others perceive the individual's control or lack of control over the cause of the condition and the ambiguity of a condition. For example, health conditions such as cancer and cardiovascular conditions may be less ambiguous than chronic pain syndromes or fibromyalgia.

III. Attitude-Change Strategies

Stigma-reduction and attitude-change interventions aim to change stigmatizers' beliefs and attitudes, refute stereotypes and causal attributions, and diminish feelings of difference (J. E. Cook, Purdie-Vaughns, Meyer, & Busch, 2014; Corrigan & Kosyluk, 2013; Paluck & Green, 2009). Attitudes toward persons with disabilities are considered complex, stable, and impervious to change (D. Cook, 1998). Popular interventions include (a) contact or personal experience, (b) information and education, (c) social influence and persuasion, (d) disability simulation, (e) protest, (f) affirmative action or legislative and political efforts, and (g) impression management (Chan, Livneh, et al., 2009; Donaldson, 1980; Smart, 2001). **Contact** refers to face-to-face interactions between persons with a disability and the public (Shaver, Curtis, Jesunathadas, & Strong, 1987). A meta-analysis confirmed that contact with persons with severe mental illness was linked to improved attitudes (Kolodziej & Johnson, 1996). Contact has been identified as the most effective strategy for reducing negative attitudes when combined with information provision (Corrigan & Penn, 1999).

Information and education includes factual information regarding the etiology, characteristics, treatment, and problems experienced by individuals with disabilities (Yuker, 1988). Information and education have been shown to positively influence attitude change by appealing to an individual's desire for being informed about the correct action or position, which motivates attitude change (e.g., hiring people with disabilities; Gottlieb & Hall, 1980). **Persuasive communication** focuses on attitude change through an individual's ego defense system, whereby a valued integrated ego is supported. **Disability simulations** modify attitudes toward people with disabilities by placing able-bodied individuals in situations that simulate a person with a disability's experience, with the goal to facilitate understanding and empathy (Flower, Burns, & Bottsford-Miller, 2007). Empirical support for simulation exercises is mixed; Shaver et al. (1987) conducted a meta-analysis and found a medium effect for simulation on negative attitudes, whereas Flower et al. (2007) found a small to negligible effect, indicating that disability simulations may be an ineffective strategy for modifying negative attitudes.

Protest strategies are actions taken to fight against moral injustices of stigma, publicly criticizing social injustices (Corrigan, 2006). Although anecdotal evidence suggests that protests change some behaviors (Wahl, 1995), such as media behavior, research suggests that protesting has no effect (Corrigan, Edwards, Green, Diwan, & Penn, 2001). **Affirmative action** is a legal approach designed to address disparities based on historical data to improve basic rights and access to education and employment opportunities for people with disabilities (Corrigan & Lam, 2007). Affirmative action can provide a legal avenue for challenging structural and institutional discrimination toward people with disabilities (Corrigan & Lam, 2007). The Americans with Disabilities Act Amendments Act (ADAAA, 2008) is one example of affirmative action. However, the success of the Americans with Disabilities Act of 1990 in altering attitudes toward people with disabilities has yet to be shown (Chan et al., 2005; McMahon, Hurley, Chan, Rumrill, & Roessler, 2008). **Impression management** includes skills used by people with disabilities to cope with and/or control the impressions that others form of people with disabilities (e.g., self-presentation or self-impression management skills). These skills are used to influence the attitude of other people about the image of a person, an object, or an event by managing the information in the interaction.

Key Concepts

Learning Objectives

By the end of this unit you should be able to:

1. Understand the meaning and influence of culture and cultural intersectionality, social roles, and contextual factors on the lives of persons with disabilities.

2. Understand sexual orientations, gender identities, and nonbinary gender orientations within the context of living with a disability.

3. Understand societal attitudes, including heteronormativity, toward marginalized lesbian, gay, bisexual, transgender, and queer individuals (LGBTQ) communities within the context of living with a disability.

4. Understand the influence of Western values on the rehabilitation process and those from non-Western cultures.

5. Understand developmental stages, aging and end-of-life care, and sexuality within the context of living with a disability.

I. Culture and Disability

Culture involves the sharing of values, beliefs, practices and behavioral norms within a specific group of people, giving them a common identity (Lefley, 2002). **Cultural groups** may be characterized by (but not limited to) age, gender identity, race, ethnicity, sexual orientation, socioeconomic class, religion and spirituality, disability status, heritage, and geographic location. Arredondo and Toporek (2004) also identified language, physicality, relationship status, work experience, hobbies, and recreational interests as important cultural factors to consider in client conceptualization. **Intersectionality theory** posits that systems of oppression work together to produce inequality (Cole, 2009; Schulz & Mullings, 2006). As such, individuals from multiple marginalized groups, including persons with disabilities, must be understood within the context of intersecting social roles and identities (e.g., age, gender, race, ethnicity, class, religion, ability, geographic location). Intersectionality is rooted in the writings of U.S. Black feminists, who challenged the notion of a universal gendered experience and argued that Black women's experiences were also shaped by race and class (Collins, 1990). Intersectionality is not an additive approach whereby gender, race, disability and class "add up" to explain life experiences; this approach states that social roles and identities, including privilege and marginalization, interact fluidly and flexibly to influence the human experience (Dhamoon & Hankivsky, 2011). Intersectionality challenges the binary approach to understanding individuals, stating that categories such as man/woman, Black/White, able-bodied/disabled are limiting and do not reflect the full experience of people.

Indeed, the level of disability experienced by an individual with a health or mental health condition cannot be understood without knowledge of that person and that person's context. **Cultural factors** (e.g., age, race, ethnicity, gender identity, sexual orientation, ability status, religion, geographic location), **social roles** (e.g., child, parent, sibling, employee, student, activist, caregiver, care recipient, relative), health-related factors, socioeconomic status, educational experience, work history, and co-occurring conditions intersect. Similarly, intersecting **contextual factors** also influence an individual's lived experience; these include family, social, and community support; access to health care; education and employment; societal, physical, and attitudinal barriers and facilitators (e.g., transportation, building access, accommodations, assistive technology, stigma, discrimination, microaggressions); and living environments.

The intersectionality of disability, sexual orientation, and gender identity (e.g., **LGBTQ**) is common. See Table 2.4 for definitions. According to Fredriksen-Goldsen, Kim, and Barkan (2012), the prevalence of disability is higher among **lesbian, gay, and bisexual (LGB)** adults compared with their **cisgendered** counterparts. In addition, LBG adults with disabilities are significantly younger than cisgendered adults with disabilities. According to Disabled World (2017), 30% of men and 36% of women have a disability among LGB adults. Lesbians and bisexual women are also more likely than cisgendered women to have a disability, with approximately 25% of cisgendered women, 36% of bisexual women, and 36% of lesbians experiencing disability. In addition, the probability of having a disability is higher for gay and bisexual men than for cisgendered men, even after considering their age, with approximately 22% of cisgendered men, 40% of bisexual men, and 26% of gay men experiencing disability. Members of the LGBTQ communities compose various cultures and subcultures. Language, lifestyle and the stigma, microaggressions, and discrimination associated with **heteronormativity** (the belief that heterosexuality is the only sexual orientation and sexual and marital relations are fitting only between people of opposite sexes) must be acknowledged and broached in the counseling relationship. Rehabilitation counselors must follow the same cultural competency strategies and practices for LGBTQ persons with disabilities as those outlined for working with persons with disabilities from diverse age, racial, ethnic, religious, and geographical backgrounds.

Sexuality and gender knowledge is also important to practicing culturally competent rehabilitation counseling. *Sex* refers to the biological and physiological characteristics that define men and women, and *gender* refers to the socially constructed roles, behaviors, activities, and attributes that a given society considers appropriate for men and women. Simply put, male and female are sex categories, whereas masculine and feminine are gender categories. Sex does not vary substantially between different societies, whereas aspects of gender may vary greatly and can change over time. Many terms are used to explain gender diversity. For example,

TABLE 2.4 Gender and Sexual Orientation Definitions

Bisexual	Refers to a male or female person who is sexually attracted to both males and females.
Cisgender	When a person's gender identity and expression is in line with their sex assigned at birth, non-trans person.
Gay	Refers to a male person whose primary sexual attraction is toward males.
Gender identity	The gender one identifies with, such as man, woman or an alternative gender.
Gender expression	The way one expresses gender by use of certain clothes, hairstyles, accessories, make-up and other attributes.
Gender queer, gender nonbinary, intergender	A person, regardless of sex assigned at birth, identifying outside of the gender binary, not being male or female, perhaps being in between genders or a whole other gender. Queer may also refer to a person who is in the questioning process of arriving at a clearer sense of their sexual orientation.
Intersex	When a person is born with reproductive or sexual anatomy that appears as male or female on the outside but have the opposite sexual anatomy on the inside; or, when a person is born with genitals that seem to be in-between the usual male and female types.
LGB	Lesbian, gay, bisexual.
LGBT	Lesbian, gay, bisexual, transgender.
LGBTQ	Lesbian, gay, bisexual, transgender, queer.
LGBTTQ	Lesbian, gay, bisexual, transgender, transsexual, queer.
LGBTTQQI	Lesbian, gay, bisexual, transgender, transsexual, queer, questioning, intersex.
Transgender/trans	Refers to a person whose gender identity is neither exclusively masculine nor feminine.
Transsexual	Refers to a person whose gender identity is the opposite of their biological sex.
Trans feminine	A person who was assigned male at birth, identifying or presenting as female or feminine.
Trans masculine	A person who was assigned female at birth, identifying or presenting as male or masculine.
Transvestite/ crossdresser	A person who expresses their gender differently from their sex assigned at birth, as a way of expressing their identity.

Source: Zeluf et al. (2016).

transgender individuals are a heterogeneous group of people whose gender identity and/or expression differ from the sex assigned to them at birth (Beek et al., 2016). In this context, *sex* refers to bodily characteristics believed to determine whether a body is male or female, whereas gender identity refers to the person's internal feeling of masculinity and femininity or an alternative gender (Tate, Ledbetter, & Youssef, 2013). *Cisgender* refers to when a person's gender identity and expression aligns with the assigned sex at birth—a non-trans person. *Queer* refers to a person who, regardless of assigned sex at birth, identifies outside of the gender binary—not being masculine or feminine—or perhaps identifies as in between genders or a whole other gender. *Queer* may also refer to a person who is in the **questioning** process of determining sexual orientation. Finally, persons who identify as queer, gender nonbinary, intergender, or transgender may prefer nonbinary pronouns (e.g., they) versus binary pronouns (e.g., he or she) (Zeluf et al., 2016).

Gender roles and norms, influence susceptibility to different health conditions, health and well-being, access to health care, and health outcomes. When individuals or groups do not "fit" established gender norms, they often face stigma, discrimination, and social exclusion. As such, it is important for rehabilitation counselors to be sensitive to clients with gender identities that do not fit into the traditional binary masculine or feminine categories.

Despite the changing nature of gender roles and norms and the move toward a less binary approach to gender, rehabilitation counselors working with women with disabling health or mental health conditions should be conscientious of the following potential psychosocial issues: (a) women may consider themselves incapable of succeeding in male-dominated occupations; (b) women may question their ability to successfully balance family, home, and career; (c) women may experience double discrimination (being a woman and seen as fragile with a disability may heighten stereotypes); (d) women may experience loss as an assault to the self that leads to greater loss of identity; (e) women may experience higher rates of depression and grief, which further compound the negative impact of the disability; and (f) women usually have more favorable attitudes toward persons with disabilities than their counterparts (Chan, Livneh, et al., 2009). Rehabilitation counselors need to explore women's vocational aspirations by understanding their knowledge of occupations, work values, and career goals. Restrictions often result from (a) the nature and type of disability, (b) socialization that may restrict the range of a career to traditional jobs held by women, and (c) limited opportunities of mentors or role models (Patterson et al., 2005).

Rehabilitation counselors working with men with disabling health or mental health conditions should be conscientious of the following potential psychosocial issues: (a) society rewards able-bodies, so the loss of physical functioning may be difficult for men; (b) men often define themselves through their work identity, so those who can no longer participate in their chosen career may experience a loss of identity; (c) men equate their masculinity with the ability to have intercourse, so men who experience physical limitations associated with sexual performance may feel emasculated; (d) men often cope with sadness and grief through distractions such as sports, physical fitness activity, or other activities, so when limitations prevent participation in these activities, they may be at greater risk for depression; and (e) in some cultures, men are the sole providers, so those whose disability impacts or alters their work or career may perceive themselves as disappointments to their family (Patterson et al., 2005).

Patterson et al. (2005) suggest that men and women respond differently to various disabilities. For example, in the area of spinal cord injury, men experience greater difficulties around sexual functioning than woman, resulting in feelings of loss of "manhood" or "masculinity." In regard to HIV/AIDS, women are more socially isolated than men because of the cultural backgrounds commonly associated with females with HIV/AIDS and because transmission rates are lower and transmission methods differ for women. Women with HIV/AIDS also experience reproductive issues related to the transmission from mother to child. With respect to myocardial infarction, men return to work sooner than woman and typically participate in physical activity to cope with the stressors related to the condition. This type of coping style, which may be advantageous for men, is not beneficial for woman (Patterson et al., 2005).

Rehabilitation counseling, as indicated by the Section 21 of the U.S. Rehabilitation Act Amendments of 1992 requires rehabilitation counselors to work with persons with disabilities who are also members of other historically marginalized communities (e.g., racial, ethnic, religious, LGBTQ). Studies show a disproportionate number of persons with disabilities from historically marginalized communities in the United States (Cartwright, 2001), and these individuals likely experience multiple negative experiences or "double" discrimination and stigmatization (Brodwin, 1995), which arguably influences their response to disability (Chronister & Johnson, 2009). For example, an African American gay man with bipolar disorder is likely to experience multiple forms of discrimination, whereas a White man with a physical disability is likely to experience fewer barriers and acts of discrimination. In fact, studies show that persons with disabilities from historically marginalized communities are accepted less often, have fewer case closures, and receive less training and less case expenditures in the public vocational rehabilitation system than those from the majority culture (Atkins & Wright, 1980; Wilson, Harley, & Alston, 2001).

Rehabilitation counseling is shaped by Western cultural values such as independence, work, achievement, medicine, science, and self-sufficiency (Sotnik & Jezewski, 2005), and these values may conflict with the values held by those from non-Western cultures. For example, in contrast to Western culture's medical and scientific values, some non-Western cultures approach health and disability from a metaphysical-spiritual realm, where disability is predetermined by fate and should therefore not be altered through medicine, science, or technology (Sotnik & Jezewski, 2005). In addition, some non-Western cultures believe family should care for the family member with a health or behavioral health condition, and thus independent living and employment may not be acceptable. Finally, culture informs how communities view help-seeking, accessing services and Western medicine.

II. Development, Sexuality, and Aging

Developmental stages such as those identified by Erikson (1968) may be influenced by a health or behavioral health condition in childhood or during adulthood depending on whether the disability is **congenital** (occurred at birth) or **acquired** (occurred later in life). For example, an **infant's** primary task is to establish trust through a relationship with primary caregiver. Factors that may disrupt the establishment of trust include long periods of hospitalizations, disruptive or rotating care by various health providers, and emotional difficulties experienced by parents who are coping with a child with a congenital health condition (Smart, 2009). For a **preschool child**, the developmental tasks of mastering their environment, gaining independence from their primary caregiver, and learning to communicate may be influenced by a health or behavioral health condition. For example, children with cognitive or intellectual disabilities may have delayed speech, expressive and receptive language difficulties, delayed social skill development, and increased dependence on primary caregivers for eating, sleeping, and getting dressed. Overprotection by family members may also limit the child's independence (Smart, 2009).

For **elementary school–aged children**, the developmental milestones of achieving industry such as doing homework and negotiating peer relationships may be negatively influenced by a disabling health or behavioral health condition. For example, health-related complications may interrupt school attendance and learning, disrupt participation in playdates and other peer activities, and slow overall social skill practice and development. Negative psychosocial experiences may slow the development of an industrious and competent self-concept, increase frustration, and contribute to low self-esteem and emotional difficulties. Elementary school–aged children may also begin to experience negative feedback from peers, ridicule, and exclusion. In addition, physical and psychological changes associated with puberty may interact with the health-related condition during the preteen or "tween" years (ages 9 through 12).

Adolescence is marked by the teenage years, between 13 and 19, and is often considered the transitional stage from childhood to adulthood. Adolescence is characterized by identity development, independence, social life, romantic interests, sexual orientation, gender identity, and pressures and decisions related to substance use, alcohol, appearance, and sexuality. Adolescents with disabilities accessing vocational rehabilitation services are often referred to **transition-age youth (TAY)**. For adolescents with disabling conditions, this can be a challenging period due to the heavy focus on others' evaluation and feedback—which may be clouded by exclusion, ableism, and stigma. In addition, adolescents with disabilities may be excluded from socially prized benchmarks such as driving or participating in sports or other normative teenage activities. Social and intimate relationships may also be influenced by societal and peer attitudes related to disability and sexual functioning (Smart, 2009).

During **early adulthood**, establishing a work identity and a career path, developing longer-term relationships, and/or starting a family are common developmental tasks. For persons with disabling conditions, fewer opportunities for career development may occur because of limited exposure, low expectations from others, and other negative attitudinal and physical barriers to employment. Establishing a family may also be hindered due to negative societal attitudes that persons with disabilities are asexual, should not have children, and are not capable of caring for a family. Sexuality and establishing relationships are especially important during this stage, and for many people with disabilities, their perception of themselves as a sexual being is severely compromised (Smart, 2009). **Middle adulthood** is typically a time of individual and career achievement. Personal satisfaction and feelings of mastery are at their greatest during this stage, and preparation for retirement may begin. Individuals who experience a disabling health condition during this stage may experience a loss of identity, status, and economic security (Smart, 2009). Work and/or family life may be disrupted and future plans altered. Individuals accessing rehabilitation services may experience difficulty identifying new and meaningful work options that are commensurate with their current abilities and limitations. The use of additional supports, accommodations, and/or caregiving services may be a new, yet difficult transition.

According to the U.S. Census Bureau (2016), one in five Americans will be an **older adult** (65 or older) by 2050. In the United States., 78 million "baby boomers" turned 70 in 2016; of these individuals, approximately 66% have at least one health or behavioral health condition, and 20% have five or more conditions. **Aging** involves multiple life transitions, including retirement or sudden loss of work and changes in health, social roles, social support, transportation, monetary and economic position, and purpose. In addition, aging is often associated with an increased loss of loved ones, role strain (e.g., caregiving for spouse, partner, or family member), and transition to assistive living settings or moving living with family. Older adults may face **ageism**, which is a form of prejudice and discrimination based on Western values of youthfulness, agility, productivity, independence, achievement, and competition (Smart, 2009; Zola, 1988). Older adults may be stereotyped as senile, sick, frail, and asexual, as well as a burden on their families and society due to entitlements (e.g. Social Security, Medicare).

The impact of disabling health conditions on older adults' independence and functioning varies significantly due to genetics, personal and environmental factors, and prior health conditions. Nonetheless, the "graying of the American workforce," coupled with the large proportion of older adults living with disabling health conditions, has resulted in rehabilitation counselors providing services for this population—particularly given the increased cost of living and lack of adequate health insurance. Common functional limitations experienced by older adults with disabling health conditions include decreased mobility, cognitive changes, depression, visual and hearing loss, inability to drive, restricted activities of daily living, and limited work and social participation. Limited technological skills may also be a disadvantage for obtaining work. Older adults with disabling health conditions may experience multiple, intersecting forms of oppression and discrimination, requiring advocacy and culturally competent rehabilitation counseling.

Rehabilitation counselors working with terminally ill clients should provide supportive **end-of-life** care in collaboration with those trained in palliative and/or hospice care. According to the Code of Professional Ethics for Rehabilitation Counselors (Commission on Rehabilitation Counselor Certification, 2010), rehabilitation counselors should obtain high-quality end-of-life care for clients' physical, emotional, social, and spiritual needs; facilitate **self-determination** and **informed decision-making**; and facilitate **competency assessment** as needed. Rehabilitation counselors must seek consultation and/or supervision from trained end-of-life care professionals, particularly when there are competency and end-of-life medical decisions to be made. Rehabilitation counselors working with terminally ill individuals must also be competent in discussing death and dying within the counseling relationship.

Sexuality is a complex concept that must be understood and addressed within the context of rehabilitation counseling. Sexuality involves multiple elements, all of which influence how individuals behave and perceive themselves in relation to their gender (Marini et al., 2011). According to the WHO (2010), sexuality "includes gender roles and sexual orientation and is influenced by the interaction of biological, psychological, cognitive, social, political, cultural, ethical, legal, historical, religious, and spiritual factors" (p. 4). Dailey (1979) identified five aspects of sexuality: identity, intimacy, sensuality, sexualization, and reproductive aspects. *Identity* is the dynamic process of an individual is in relation to sexuality; *intimacy* is the emotional connectedness with others; *sensuality* is experiencing one's body through the five senses; *sexualization* is when the body is used for control, influence, and manipulation; and *reproductive aspects* are the functions associated with conceiving and parenting (Dailey, 1979). These components interact with societal and cultural norms that govern what is acceptable and tolerated, including sexual behaviors, partners, and the factors that constitute legal marriage (Marini et al., 2011).

Persons with disabilities have a long history of sexual stigmatization beginning with societal sanctions to eliminate a "defective gene pool" (Marini et al., 2011). Although society has progressed in its' treatment and acceptance of people with disabilities (Vash & Crewe, 2004), sexual myths about people with disabilities are pervasive, negatively impacting their self-esteem, body image and motivation to engage in relationships (Marini et al., 2011). Sexual myths about persons with disabilities include lack of sex drive, asexuality, inability to sexually perform or experience orgasm, unable to make decisions about their sexuality, sexual inappropriateness, and inability to conceive, give birth, or parent (Magnan, Reynolds, & Galvin, 2006; Olkin, 1999). Societal values of beauty and physique further the sexual stigmatization of persons with disabilities, contributing to barriers to developing friendships and intimate relationships (Howland & Rintala, 2001; Marini et al., 2011). Research supports the negative impact of sexual stigmatization on people with disabilities. For example, studies show that people with disabilities are less likely to have partners or marry than those without disabilities (Taleporos & McCabe, 2003). In addition, the more severe the disability, the less likely a person without a disability desires a relationship. Specifically, people without disabilities are more willing to be friends with persons with physical disabilities and less willing to be friends or marry a person with intellectual and psychiatric disabilities (Gordon, Tantillo, Feldman, & Perrone, 2004).

Key Concepts

Learning Objectives

By the end of this unit you should be able to:

1. Understand psychological theories and models of response to disability, including somatopsychology, acceptance, stage, disability centrality, and coping models.

2. Understand contemporary psychosocial issues impacting the lives of persons with disabilities, including health disparities, population health, health promotion, self-management, and health literacy.

3. Understand the role of trauma in the lives of persons with disabilities.

I. Psychological Response to Disability

Adaptation, adjustment, and **acceptance** of disability are concepts traditionally used to describe the process and outcome associated with psychological response to disability (Lindemann, 1981; Linkowski & Dunn, 1974; Livneh, 1986). *Adaptation* is defined as the dynamic process a person with a disability experiences to achieve the final state of optimal person–environment congruence known as *adjustment* (Smedema, Bakken-Gillen, & Dalton, 2009). Coined by Wright (1960, 1983), disability **acceptance** occurs when disability is incorporated as part of the individual's self-concept and is accepted as non-devaluing (Smedema et al., 2009). Today, *response* to disability is considered a more accurate way of describing the psychological process because it is a neutral term communicating that the experience is not necessarily negative, but a subjective and dynamic process, not a one-time event (Smart, 2009; Wortman & Silver, 1989).

   Somatopsychology has roots in Lewin's (1935, 1936) field theory. Lewin posited that environmental factors influence the lives of people with disabilities significantly more than personal factors, including personality or other dispositional variables (Nisbet, 1980; Nisbett & Ross, 1991). Lewin believed that people with disabilities' perception of their social and physical environments or "situation" profoundly impacts their actions and subjective experiences. He emphasized understanding the total situation, whereby the person's behavior (B) is a function of the person (P) and the environment (E), or $B = f(P, E)$. Aligned with this theory, **somatopsychology** focuses on the interaction between the person and his or her situational sociopsychological factors, explaining how society and the self perceive and react to physical disability. The Person × Situation interaction is the focus of somatopsychology and emphasizes that the personal meaning of the others in a person's life is important in understanding response to disability. Whereas psychosomatic relationships focus on the influence of the psychological functioning on physical and physiological functioning, somatopsychology focuses on the opposite relationship—the influence of physical and physiological processes on the psychological functioning of the individual (Smedema et al., 2009).

   Disability acceptance. Based on the principles of somatopsychology, Wright (1960, 1983) developed the **disability acceptance model,** which is a cognitive restructuring framework also known as the "coping versus succumbing" model. In this model, **succumbing** involves focusing on the negative effects of physical disability and neglects challenges for change and meaningful adaptation. Conversely, **coping** focuses on individual assets and is oriented toward what an individual can do (Smedema et al., 2009). Wright (1983) proposed four major value changes, or cognitions, that reflect acceptance: (a) **enlargement of the scope of values**, which entails subscribing to values not in conflict with the disability; (b) **subordination of the physique**, which occurs when the individual focuses on other nonphysical assets, such as personality, intelligence, or creativity, versus viewing their body as the only symbol of worth, desirability, or competency; (c) **containment of disability effects**, which occurs when the individual does not deny the disability but contains or limits the effects, realizing there are other activities that they can do; and (d) **transformation from comparative status to asset values**, which occurs when the individual does not compare oneself to others and focuses on their assets (Smart, 2009). **Disability acceptance** therefore occurs when an individual's values and cognitions are consistent with those described and are incorporated as part of the individual's self-concept, at which point disability is accepted as nondevaluing (Smedema et al., 2009).

   Stage model. The stage model characterizes the disability process as a linear series of psychological stages through which one progresses, with the final stage conceptualized as adjustment. Many stage models have been proposed to describe phases of adjustment (e.g., M. E. Dunn, 1975; Fink, 1967; Roessler & Bolton, 1978; Shontz, 1965). The most common stages include shock, denial, anger, depression, and adaptation. Livneh (1986) described five broad stages: (a) initial impact, which includes shock and anxiety; (b) defense mobilization, which includes bargaining and denial; (c) initial realization, which includes mourning, depression, and internalized anger; (d) retaliation, which includes externalized anger or aggression; and (e) reintegration or reorganization, which includes acknowledgement, acceptance, and final adjustment. Stage models provide a structure for understanding and predicting the course and outcome of an individual's response to disability process (Smart, 2009). For example, rehabilitation counselors may draw on this model to better understand and respond to verbal attacks, low motivation, or withdrawal—understanding that these responses may reflect a process being used to move toward positive coping and integration. Nonetheless, the applicability of the stage theory has been criticized for the following reasons: (a) "stages" are not universally experienced, (b) a state of final adjustment (e.g., resolution, acceptance, assimilation) is not always achieved, and (c) psychological response to disability does not follow a linear stage-like sequence (Livneh, 1986). Finally, the existence of a universal, progressive, phase-like, orderly sequence of predetermined psychosocial reactions to disability has not been adequately supported by empirical research (Livneh & Antonak, 1997).

Disability centrality model. Developed by Bishop (2005), this model posits that a person's response to disability is related to the quality-of-life satisfaction and perceived control over medical and environmental circumstances. Specifically, Bishop proposed that the onset of a health or behavioral health condition results in an initial reduction in **central** satisfying activities (e.g., sports, writing, hiking), personal control, and overall quality of life. The degree to which an individual's quality of life is reduced depends on how many central satisfying activities are affected by the health condition and the degree to which the individual establishes new central satisfying activities commensurate with their abilities. According to Bishop (2005), people strive to close the gaps by changing their values and interests to be aligned with their abilities and use strategies to increase perceived control over health and environment. Alternatively, those that do not strive to close the gap between prior central satisfying activities and activities consistent with abilities experience poor quality of life and distress (Bishop & Feist-Price, 2002; Devins et al., 1983).

Coping. *Coping* refers to strategies people use to manage stress (Chronister & Chan, 2007) According to Lazarus and Folkman (1984), people appraise or evaluate the significance of a stressor and then manage the demands of the stressor using coping strategies. Coping has been conceptualized in various ways, with the most popular taxonomic structure including three types of coping approaches: (a) **emotion-focused** (reducing distress by changing or managing emotions), (b) **problem-focused** (reducing stress by problem-solving), and (c) **appraisal-focused** (reducing stress by altering one's appraisal, assumptions, or perception of the stressor) (Chronister & Chan, 2007). Coping approaches include various cognitive, behavioral, and affective coping responses. **Cognitive** coping refers to how an individual chooses to think or view the stressor. For example, "Even if I've lost functioning in my leg, I can still have intimate relationships" (appraisal-focused approach). **Behavioral** coping refers to actions taken to manage the stress (e.g., treatment compliance, seeking out of social support, return to work, self-advocacy, use of substances, exercise, avoidance of friends, and impression management). For example, an individual who seeks social support for assistance getting to an appointment for needed assistive device or who goes to a movie to reduce social isolation is using problem-focused behavioral coping to reduce the stress by solving the problem with action. **Emotional** or **affective** coping refers to how the individual manages the emotions associated with the stressor (Smart, 2009). An individual who shares with a friend the frustration and anger associated with health care or lack of accessible bathrooms at the office is using emotion-focused coping by venting emotions with a friend to reduce negative feelings. An individual who feels less depressed about a stigmatizing experience after talking to a friend is using emotion-focused coping by reducing negative feelings associated with the stress of being stigmatized. Coping can be adaptive or maladaptive; for example, an adaptive coping strategy within the context of disability may include having a realistic view of the disability and an awareness of limitations but not an exaggeration of the limitations (Yoshida, 1993). Conversely, a maladaptive coping strategy may involve using substances or blaming oneself or others for the disability. Positive, adaptive coping strategies such as seeking out social support or redefining life goals may improve body image and quality of life and decrease social isolation and feelings of helplessness.

II. Contemporary Psychosocial Issues

According to Healthy People 2020, a primary goal for people with disabling health and behavioral health conditions is to maximize health, prevent chronic disease, and improve **health disparities**. Health disparity occurs when health outcomes vary by groups or populations. Factors influencing health disparities include economic stability, education, health and health care, neighborhood and built environment, and social and community context (U.S. Department of Health and Human Services, 2000). **Population health** is a research and health care practice approach that focuses on identification and intervention related to health outcomes and the distribution of health among populations (e.g., race or ethnic groups, gender, persons with disabilities, LGBTQ communities, geographical populations, tribal nations or communities, prisoners, employees, college students). Population health is an integrative, BPS approach that considers the multiplicity and patterns of **determinants** (e.g., genetics, individual behavior, medical care, public health interventions, income, education, employment, culture, urban design, clean air, toxic environments) that influence the health of particular populations. Health outcomes, distribution, and determinants are all used to develop strategies for change and improve health care delivery for particular populations, such as those living with disabilities. For example, to address the high rates of obesity in the United States, a population health approach examines not only health outcomes and the distribution of these outcomes among persons identified as obese, but also seeks to understand the determinants of these outcomes and develop strategies to improve the health and well-being of this population (Kindig & Stoddart, 2003).

Understanding health disparities and the population health model is important to rehabilitation counseling. Specifically, people with disabilities are one of the largest underserved communities in health care, experiencing differences in health care access, quality and outcomes (Drum, Brownson, Denmark, & Smith, 2009). Studies suggest that incidence, prevalence, mortality, and burden of disease outcomes vary significantly between people with and without disabilities. In addition, persons with disabilities are more likely to have secondary conditions, less likely to receive preventive health care, and have less access to fitness facilities and health information technology compared with able-bodied individuals. People with disabilities are at greater risk for heart disease, type 2 diabetes, stroke, hypertension, osteoarthritis, colon cancer, depression, and obesity due to physical inactivity and sedentary lifestyles (U. S. Preventive Services Task Force, 2003). Health disparities among people with disabilities are linked to multiple determinant factors, including low SES, transportation barriers, lack of social supports and prevention services, inaccessible fitness devices, and attitudinal barriers.

Barriers to health care vary by type of disability. For example, people with sensory limitations (e.g., poor vision or hearing) generally experience positive health outcomes (Harrison, Mackert, & Watkins, 2010; Muñoz-Baell, Ruiz-Cantero, Álvarez-Dardet, Ferreiro-Lago, & Aroca-Fernández,

2011; Pereira & Fortes, 2010), whereas people with mobility limitations have poorer health outcomes related to lack of physical activity/exercise accommodations, pain, secondary conditions, and obesity (Hollar, 2013; Iezzoni, Park, & Kilbridge, 2011; WHO, 2011). In addition, people with behavioral health, intellectual, and development disabilities experience significant attitudinal barriers to health care and **health promotion**. Health promotion is any combination of educational, organizational, economic, and environmental supports for healthy behavior (Green & Johnson, 1983). A BPS approach to health promotion emphasizes (a) biological factors (person's health contributes to whether microorganisms cause disease); (b) psychological factors (feelings, thoughts, and behaviors related to engaging in health care, such as belief systems, trust, and health behaviors [e.g., scheduling, attending appointments, medication adherence]) and (c) socioenvironmental factors (attitudes, ableism, accessible health care) (Ray, 2004). **Health-promotion programs** for persons with disabilities are typically designed to address the health-promotion needs of persons with particular types of functional limitations. For example, *Living Well with a Disability* is a client-directed, lifestyle change-oriented health promotion program for people with mobility limitations (Ravesloot et al., 1998); *Project Shake-It-Up* promotes health and empowerment through case coordination, physical activity, and recreation and independent living skills for persons with spinal cord injuries and other neurological conditions (Block, Skeels, Keys, & Rimmer, 2005). Health-promotion programs have also been designed for those with Down syndrome (Heller, Hsieh, & Rimmer, 2004), serious behavioral health conditions (Pelletier, Nguyen, Bradley, Johnson, & McKay, 2005), chronic back pain (Friedrich, Gittler, Arendasy, & Friedrich, 2005), and aging adults (Teri, McCurry, & Logsdon, 1997). Full health promotion for persons with disabilities and aging adults, however, requires accessible and inclusive health education material and fitness programs. Negative attitudes, ableism, stigma, and inaccessible fitness machines significantly impact motivation and desire to participate (Lynch & Chui, 2009).

Self-management is an important component to health promotion. *Self-management* refers to the daily activities that individuals undertake to keep a health condition under control, minimize its impact on health status and functioning, and cope with its psychosocial sequelae (Clark et al., 1991). Although these activities are typically undertaken in cooperation with a health care provider, self-management is more than just strict adherence to a prescribed behavioral regimen. It involves a high level of control on the part of the individual, some autonomy with respect to adjusting the regimen as necessary, and deliberate decision making and problem solving (Gallant, 2003). Successful self-management requires mastery of three sets of tasks: making informed decisions about care, performing activities aimed at management of the condition and applying the skills necessary for maintaining adequate psychosocial functioning (Clark et al., 1991). Although self-management tasks are illness specific (e.g., measuring blood glucose for diabetes), there is a common core of self-management tasks that cuts across specific health conditions. These include, but are not limited to, recognizing and responding to symptoms, using medications, managing acute episodes, maintaining diet and physical activity, quitting smoking, managing relations with significant others, and managing the psychological responses to illness (Clark et al., 1991).

Health literacy is "the degree to which individuals have the capacity to obtain, process, and understand basic health information and services needed to make appropriate health decisions" (Hernandez, 2009, p. 1). The impact of health literacy extends beyond understanding and making health care decisions to include empowering people to handle the structural barriers to health care (Egbert & Nanna, 2009) Health literacy is important to accessible health care, health promotion, and improvement of health outcomes. Health literacy is important to people with disabilities, given the significant health disparities between persons with and without disabilities. Studies show that persons with disabilities have low levels of health literacy and report inadequate health information and autonomy in health decisions (National Council on Disability, 2009), which in turn, increases health risk behaviors that influence health outcomes, employment, and social participation (Brucker & Houtenville, 2015; Hollar & Moore, 2004; Rimmer, Rowland, & Yamaki, 2007). Persons with psychiatric, cognitive, intellectual, and developmental disabilities are at risk for poor health literacy, requiring health information to be communicated in an accessible format (Chew, Iacono, & Tracy, 2009). Facilitating health literacy among people with disabilities requires accommodations and modifications to health education material and programs and valid and accessible health literacy assessment tools (Field & Jette, 2007; D. W. Hollar, 2005; Hollar, McAweeney, & Moore, 2008; Hollar & Moore, 2004).

Trauma is an event or enduring condition/situation that is an actual threat or perceived threat to the life and integrity of an individual (Keesler, 2014). The nature of the event is so overwhelming and deleterious to the individual that there is an inability to effectively integrate an emotional response to the event with prior cognitions and experiences (Saakvitne, Gamble, Pearlman, & Lev, 2000). The impact of trauma is typically enduring, resulting in various BPS consequences such as unpredictable emotions, flashbacks, strained relationships, and physical symptoms (Keesler, 2014). Although these types of responses are appropriate given the nature of trauma experiences, the sequelae often become a persistent influence on a person's current presentation and perspective (Brown, Baker, & Wilcox, 2012; Harris & Fallot, 2001), making it difficult to move forward in life.

Notably, numerous studies show that adverse, traumatic events can also lead to positive outcomes such as **posttraumatic growth** (Lahav, Solomon, & Levin, 2016). Posttraumatic growth is characterized by an increased positive self-perception, improved interpersonal relationships, and a more optimistic view of the world. It is considered a genuine transformation in core beliefs about the self and the world as a result of the difficulties associated with the traumatic experience (Calhoun & Tedeschi, 2014; Schaefer & Moos, 1998; Tedeschi & Calhoun, 2004). Posttraumatic growth has been shown among survivors of various traumatic events, including disasters, war, sexual assault, and illness (Calhoun & Tedeschi, 2014; Linley & Joseph, 2004), as well as among mothers of children with acquired disabilities (Konrad, 2006), husbands of breast cancer survivors (Weiss, 2004), spouses of myocardial infarction patients (Senol-Durak & Ayvasik, 2010), and wives of war veterans (McCormack, Hagger, & Joseph, 2011).

Experiencing physical, sexual, and emotional abuse toward oneself and/or witnessing abuse are the most commonly reported adverse, traumatic events (Keesler, 2014). In addition, experiences related to health conditions, injury, accidents, hospitalizations, loss of employment, and bereavement are also potentially traumatic situations (Hastings, Hatton, Taylor, & Maddison, 2004). **Disability** has been linked to trauma and posttraumatic stress disorder (PTSD) in various ways. First and foremost, persons with disabilities are at higher risk for experiencing traumatic life events, with studies showing specific disability populations exposed to more trauma events than the general population (Hatton & Emerson, 2004). Indeed, chronic societal injustices, exclusionary practices, stigma, discrimination and microaggressions are enduring adverse events that contribute to trauma-related symptoms for persons with disabilities. A traumatic experience for a person with a disability may be "the subjective meaning one makes of being starved of the means to take on the basic challenges and pleasures of life while surrounded by fellow citizens granted full access" (Watermeyer & Swartz, 2016, p. 270). For example, the wheelchair user living in an inaccessible environment continually observes those around them access public transportation, restaurants, beaches, travel, shops, homes of friends, and other public amenities (Mutua, 2001). Another example is a deaf person who lives in a community where no one else has been taught sign language, yet education for other locally prevalent languages is a priority (Watermeyer & Swartz, 2016). Trauma can also lead to disability and trigger trauma symptoms by being a persistent reminder of the traumatic experience

(Asmundson, Coons, Taylor, & Katz, 2002; Jurišić & Marušič, 2009). In addition, individuals with PTSD are more likely to develop a physical disability (O'Donnell et al., 2013; Ramchand, Marshall, Schell, & Jaycox, 2008) due to stress-related changes in neurobiology and immune functioning, poor health behaviors, avoidance of health care, and increased health-risk behaviors (Schnurr & Green, 2004). Conversely, persons with disabilities are more likely to develop PTSD because of reduced access to needed socioeconomic resources after an adverse event compared with those without disabilities (Peek & Stough, 2010; Shih, Schell, Hambarsoomian, Marshall, & Belzberg, 2010).

With respect to particular disability populations, persons with intellectual and developmental disabilities experience more trauma experiences than the general population, given institutionalized living and dependency on caregivers (Hastings et al., 2004; Hatton & Emerson 2004; Wigham, Hatton, & Taylor, 2011). Parental death may be devastating for a person with an intellectual or developmental disability because it may also result in the loss of primary caregivers and a home (Hollins & Esterhuyzen 1997; Levitas & Gilson, 2001). Veterans, who often have multiple service-connected disabilities, are also at risk for PTSD. Approximately 23% of Iraq/Afghanistan veterans develop clinically significant levels of PTSD (Fulton et al., 2015), and there is extensive literature reporting a strong link between PTSD and functional impairment across multiple domains among veterans (Rodriguez, Holowka, & Marx, 2012). For example, research shows that veterans with PTSD are 19% less likely to be employed at discharge than those without PTSD (Resnick & Rosenheck, 2008). Indeed, PTSD is considered one of the "signature" injuries—with traumatic brain injury (TBI) being the other—of veterans serving in the Iraq war (Burke, Degeneffe, & Olney, 2009). The combination of TBI and PTSD has been identified as a new disability classification for the rehabilitation counseling profession (Burke et al., 2009). Rehabilitation counseling professionals serving veterans with both PTSD and TBI need to consider applying for an extended period of evaluation and to offer counseling, assistive technology, other individualized services, and therapeutic interventions (Burke et al., 2009). For example, the Army offers a teaching program to educate soldiers and family members about the signs and symptoms of behavioral and mental health issues, including TBI and PTSD (Burke et al., 2009). Additional trauma-related interventions useful for soldiers and veterans experiencing PTSD include cognitive behavioral therapy and exposure-type interventions, including virtual reality techniques (Burke et al., 2009).

Individuals with trauma-related backgrounds and symptoms often access multiple rehabilitation and other health care-related services within a fragmented service delivery system. These access points can often be retraumatizing, and thus, accessing care comes with a high personal and social cost (Fallot & Harris, 2009). One strategy for decreasing the service delivery fragmentation and discontinuation of service use is to provide increased social support surrounding access to and continuation of health and rehabilitation-related service use (Ben-David, Cole, Spencer, Jaccard, & Munson, 2017). For example, rehabilitation and mental health counselors can provide emotional support related to encouragement and support for seeking help when needed; they can also provide instrumental support related to health and mental health literacy information that includes types and locations of services and information about knowledge, skills, and strategies needed to access services (Ben-David et al., 2017). In related fields, health messages have been found to be associated with seeking treatment and continued engagement, among other outcomes (Kreuter et al., 2007). In addition, **trauma-informed care**, discussed in more detail in Chapter 5, is a service-delivery framework that acknowledges the pervasiveness of trauma in the lives of all persons (Keesler, 2014). Trauma-informed care is woven into the fabric of the organization; considers clients, families, and service providers; and uses a common language and approach that reduces the likelihood of retraumatization (Bath, 2008; Brown et al., 2012; Jennings, 2004).

Multiple-Choice Questions

1. This model of disability defines *disability* as a deficiency within the individual.

    A. Social model

    B. Functional model

    C. Medical model

    D. Minority model

2. Individuals who experience disability at this developmental stage may experience loss of identity, loss of status, and loss of economic security.

    A. Early adulthood

    B. Adolescence

    C. Preschool age

    D. Middle adulthood

3. The World Health Organization's International Classification of Functioning, Disability and Health conceptualizes level of disability based on the following major domains *EXCEPT*:

    A. Body function and structure

    B. Activities and participation

    C. Person and environment

    D. Psychosocial adjustment to disability

4. This is an evaluative statement (favorable or unfavorable) related to a person, object, or event.

    A. Stigma

    B. Prejudice

    C. Discrimination

    D. Attitude

5. This model considers medical diagnosis in disability determination but determines what aspect of an individual's school, work, and social life is impacted and uses environmental accommodations, modifications, and assistive technology devices as remedies to increase access and equality for people with disabilities.

    A. Independent living model

    B. Minority model

    C. Functional model

    D. Environmental model

    E. Sociopolitical model

6. This occurs when persons with psychiatric disorders, substance abuse, and HIV/AIDS and other sexually transmitted conditions experience more stigmatizing attitudes than those with physical disabilities such as cerebral palsy, muscular dystrophy, and multiple sclerosis.

    A. Attributional errors

    B. Top-down approach

    C. Hierarchy of stigma

    D. Levels of stigma

7. When individuals make personal decisions, communicate choices, exercise control over the supports and services received, and participate and contribute to their communities, they are said to be exercising _____skills.

    A. Self-advocacy

    B. Social

    C. Self-management

    D. Self-determination

8. Health, home, purpose, and community are four major areas of this model of mental health care.

    A. Assertive community treatment model

    B. Independent living model

    C. Recovery model

    D. Continuum of care model

9. This model conceptualizes disability as an outcome of interacting functional and contextual factors.

    A. Somatopsychology model

    B. Biopsychosocial model

    C. International Classification of Functioning, Disability and Health model

    D. Functional model

    E. Socioenvironmental model

10. This model posits that a person's response to disability is related to quality of life satisfaction and perceived control over medical and environmental circumstances.

    A. Personal control model

    B. Disability centrality model

    C. Field theory

    D. Acceptance theory

Answer Key

1C, 2D, 3D, 4D, 5C, 6C, 7D, 8C, 9C, 10B

Advanced Multiple-Choice Questions

1. When disability is perceived to be the sole aspect of an individual's identity and all other aspects of the person are discounted or underrated, this is called:

   A. Ambiguity of disability

   B. Spread

   C. Safety threat

   D. Invisible barrier

2. This form of discrimination favors abled-bodied individuals, maintains disability as a negative state and experience, and perpetuates the belief that disability is a deviation from societal norms.

   A. Homonegativism

   B. Racism

   C. Ableism

   D. Microaggression

3. This strategy to change societal attitudes refers to face-to-face interactions between persons with a disability and the public.

   A. Contact

   B. Protest

   C. Simulations

   D. Information and education

4. Rehabilitation counselors are practicing _____ counseling when they exhibit an awareness of their assumptions about human behavior, values, preconceived notions, limitations and biases; an understanding of the worldview of clients who are culturally different without imposing negative judgments; and an ability to develop and practice appropriately with culturally different clients.

   A. Multicultural

   B. Ethical

   C. Lawful

   D. Culturally competent

5. This theory states that social roles and identities, including privilege and marginalization, interact fluidly and flexibly to influence the human experience and explain life experiences.

   A. Minority stress theory

   B. Intersectionality theory

   C. Racial identity theory

   D. Cross-cultural counseling theory

6. These are everyday verbal, nonverbal, and environmental slights, snubs, or insults, whether intentional or unintentional, that communicate hostile, derogatory, or negative messages to target persons based solely on their marginalized group membership.

    A. Discrimination

    B. Assaults

    C. Exclusion

    D. Microaggressions

7. These individuals are a heterogeneous group of people whose gender identity and/or expression differ from the sex assigned to them at birth.

    A. Cisgender

    B. Homosexual

    C. Transvestite

    D. Transgender

8. Sexual myths about persons with disabilities include which of the following?

    A. Persons with disabilities are sexual beings.

    B. Persons with disabilities' sex drive depends on their biological makeup.

    C. Persons with disabilities cannot give birth or be a parent.

    D. Persons with disabilities can decide their sexual orientation and sexual interests.

    E. Persons with disabilities cannot experience an orgasm.

    F. None of the above

    G. C and E

9. This refers to any combination of educational, organizational, economic, and environmental supports for healthy behavior.

    A. Population health

    B. Health promotion

    C. Health education

    D. Health literacy

10. This type of service delivery framework acknowledges the pervasiveness of trauma in the lives of all persons irrespective of whether clients enter services with a trauma-related diagnosis or a record of such.

    A. Integrated care

    B. Continuum of care

    C. Trauma-informed care

    D. Clinically sensitive care

Answer Key and Explanation of Answers

1B: According to Wright (1983), **spread** occurs when society assumes, for example, that a wheelchair user is cognitively impaired, spreading the health condition to encompass all aspects of the individual.

2C: Ableism is the unique form of discrimination experienced by persons with disabilities based on their disabilities. Ableism favors abled-bodied individuals, maintaining disability as a negative state and experience. "Implicit within ableism is an able-centric worldview, which endorses the belief that there is a 'normal' manner in which to perceive and/or manipulate stimuli and a 'normal' manner of accomplishing tasks of daily living" (Keller & Galgay, 2010, p. 242). Ableism perpetuates the belief that disability is a deviation from societal norms.

3A: Contact refers to face-to-face interactions between persons with a disability and the public (Shaver et al., 1987). A meta-analysis confirmed that contact with persons with severe mental illness was linked to improved attitudes (Kolodziej & Johnson, 1996). Contact has been identified as the most effective strategy for reducing negative attitudes when combined with information provision (Corrigan & Penn, 1999).

4C: Self-management refers to the daily activities that individuals undertake to keep their health condition under control, minimize its impact on health status and functioning, and cope with the psychosocial sequelae of the health condition (Clark et al., 1991). Successful self-management requires mastery of three sets of tasks: making informed decisions about care, performing activities aimed at management of the condition, and applying the skills necessary for maintaining adequate psychosocial functioning (Clark et al., 1991). The common core of self-management tasks include, but are not limited to, recognizing and responding to symptoms, using medications, managing acute episodes, maintaining diet and physical activity, quitting smoking, managing relations with significant others, and managing psychological responses to illness (Clark et al., 1991).

5B: Intersectionality theory posits that systems of oppression work together to produce inequality (Cole, 2009; Schulz & Mullings, 2006). Intersectionality is not an additive approach whereby gender, race, disability, and class "add up" to explain life experiences; this approach states that social roles and identities, including privilege and marginalization, interact fluidly and flexibly to influence the human experience (Dhamoon & Hankivsky, 2011). Intersectionality challenges the binary approach to understanding individuals, stating that categories such as men/woman, Black/White, and able-bodied/disabled are limiting and do not reflect the full experience of people.

6D: Microaggressions are "everyday verbal, nonverbal, and environmental slights, snubs, or insults, whether intentional or unintentional, that communicate hostile, derogatory, or negative messages to target persons based solely upon their marginalized group membership" (Sue, 2010, p. 3). Microaggressions are more distinct from traditional and overt forms of discrimination in that otherwise well-intentioned individuals can deliver them unconsciously, unaware of their potential harmful effects (Gonzales et al., 2015). According to Sue et al. (2007), microaggressions are the most insidious and harmful forms of prejudices. Keller and Galgay (2010) identified eight types of microaggressions targeting people with disabilities, including: denial of identity, denial of privacy, helplessness, secondary gain, spread effect, patronization, second-class citizen, and desexualization.

7D: Transgender individuals are a heterogeneous group of people whose gender identity and/or expression differ from the sex assigned to them at birth (Beek et al., 2016). In this context, *sex* refers to bodily characteristics believed to determine whether a body is male or female, whereas *gender identity* refers to the person's internal feeling of masculinity and femininity or an alternative gender (Tate et al., 2013).

8G: Sexual myths about people with disabilities are pervasive, negatively impacting their self-esteem, body image, and motivation to engage in relationships (Marini et al., 2011). Sexual myths about persons with disabilities include lack of sex drive, asexuality, **inability to sexually perform or experience orgasm**, inability to make decisions about their sexuality, sexual inappropriateness, and **inability to conceive, give birth**, or parent (Magnan et al., 2006; Olkin, 1999).

9B: Health promotion is any combination of educational, organizational, economic, and environmental supports for healthy behavior (Green & Johnson, 1983). A biopsychosocial approach to health promotion emphasizes (a) biological factors (person's health contributes to whether microorganisms cause disease); (b) psychological factors (feelings, thoughts, and behaviors related to engaging in health care such as belief systems, trust, health behaviors [e.g., as scheduling, attending appointments, medication adherence]); and (c) socioenvironmental factors (attitudes, ableism, accessible health care) (Ray, 2004).

10C: Trauma-informed care is a service-delivery framework that acknowledges the pervasiveness of trauma in the lives of all persons (Keesler, 2014). Trauma-informed care is woven into the fabric of the organization; considers clients, families and service providers; and uses a common language and approach that reduces the likelihood of retraumatization (Bath, 2008; Brown et al., 2012; Jennings, 2004).

References

Allport, G. W. (1968). *The person in psychology: Selected essays*. Boston, MA: Beacon Press.

Americans with Disabilities Act Amendments Act of 2008, Pub. L. No. 110–325, S 3406 (2008).

Anthony, W. A. (1993). Recovery from mental illness: The guiding vision of the mental health service system in the 1990s. *Psychosocial Rehabilitation Journal, 16*(4), 11.

Antonak, R. F., & Livneh, H. (1991). A hierarchy of reactions to disability. *International Journal of Rehabilitation Research, 14*(1), 13–24.

Antonson, S., Danermark, B., & Lundström, I. (2006). Importance of social support for hard-of-hearing students in pursuing their "educational careers." *Scandinavian Journal of Disability Research, 8*(4), 298–316.

Arredondo, P., & Toporek, R. (2004). Multicultural counseling competencies = ethical practice. *Journal of Mental Health Counseling, 26*(1), 44–55.

Asmundson, G. J., Coons, M. J., Taylor, S., & Katz, J. (2002). PTSD and the experience of pain: Research and clinical implications of shared vulnerability and mutual maintenance models. *The Canadian Journal of Psychiatry, 47*(10), 930–937.

Atkins, B. J., & Wright, G. N. (1980). Vocational rehabilitation of Blacks. The statement. *Journal of Rehabilitation, 46*(2), 40–49.

Bandura, A. (2001). Social cognitive theory: An agentic perspective. *Annual Review of Psychology, 52*(1), 1–26.

Barney, K. W. (2012). Disability simulations: Using the social model of disability to update an experiential educational practice. *SCHOLE: A Journal of Leisure Studies and Recreation Education, 27*(1). Retrieved from http://www.nrpa.org/globalassets/journals/schole/2012/schole-volume-27-number-1-pp-1-11.pdf

Barrera, M. (1986). Distinctions between social support concepts, measures, and models. *American Journal of Community Psychology, 14*(4), 413–445.

Bath, H. (2008). The three pillars of trauma-informed care. *Reclaiming Children and Youth, 17*(3), 17–21.

Beek, T. F., Cohen-Kettenis, P. T., Bouman, W. P., de Vries, A. L., Steensma, T. D., Witcomb, G. L., . . . Kreukels, B. P. (2016). Gender incongruence of adolescence and adulthood: Acceptability and clinical utility of the World Health Organization's proposed ICD-11 criteria. *PLOS ONE, 11*(10), e0160066.

Ben-David, S., Cole, A., Spencer, R., Jaccard, J., & Munson, M. R. (2017). Social context in mental health service use among young adults. *Journal of Social Service Research, 43*(1), 85–99.

Berkman, L. F., Glass, T., Brissette, I., & Seeman, T. E. (2000). From social integration to health: Durkheim in the new millennium. *Social Science & Medicine, 51*(6), 843–857.

Bingham, C., Clarke, L., Michielsens, E., & Van de Meer, M. (2013). Towards a social model approach? British and Dutch disability policies in the health sector compared. *Personnel Review, 42*(5), 613–637.

Bishop, M. (2005). Quality of life and psychosocial adaptation to chronic illness and disability preliminary analysis of a conceptual and theoretical synthesis. *Rehabilitation Counseling Bulletin, 48*(4), 219–231.

Bishop, M., & Feist-Price, S. (2002). Quality of life assessment in the rehabilitation counseling relationship: Strategies and measures. *Journal of Applied Rehabilitation Counseling, 33*(1), 35.

Block, P., Skeels, S. E., Keys, C. B., & Rimmer, J. H. (2005). Shake-It-Up: health promotion and capacity building for people with spinal cord injuries and related neurological disabilities. *Disability and Rehabilitation, 27*(4), 185–190.

Blume, A. W., Lovato, L. V., Thyken, B. N., & Denny, N. (2012). The relationship of microaggressions with alcohol use and anxiety among ethnic minority college students in a historically White institution. *Cultural Diversity and Ethnic Minority Psychology, 18*(1), 45–54.

Boyd, J. E., Adler, E. P., Otilingam, P. G., & Peters, T. (2014). Internalized Stigma of Mental Illness (ISMI) scale: A multinational review. *Comprehensive Psychiatry, 55*(1), 221–231.

Brodwin, M. G. (1995). Barriers to multicultural understanding: Improving university rehabilitation counselor education programs. In S. Walker, K. A. Turner, M. Haile-Michael, A. Vincent, & M. D. Miles (Eds.), *Disability and diversity: New leadership for a new era* (pp. 39–44). Washington, DC: Howard University Research and Training Center.

Brown, S. M., Baker, C. N., & Wilcox, P. (2012). Risking connection trauma training: A pathway toward trauma-informed care in child congregate care settings. *Psychological Trauma: Theory, Research, Practice, and Policy, 4*(5), 507–515.

Brucker, D. L., & Houtenville, A. J. (2015). People with disabilities in the United States. *Archives of Physical Medicine and Rehabilitation, 96*(5), 771–774.

Burke, H. S., Degeneffe, C. E., & Olney, M. F. (2009). A new disability for rehabilitation counselors: Iraq war veterans with traumatic brain injury and post-traumatic stress disorder. *Journal of Rehabilitation, 75*(3), 5.

Calhoun, L. G., & Tedeschi, R. G. (2014). *Handbook of posttraumatic growth: Research and practice.* New York, NY: Psychology Press.

Cartwright, B. Y. (2001). Multicultural counseling training: A survey of CORE-accredited programs. *Rehabilitation Education, 15*(3), 233–242.

Chan, F., Gelman, J. S., Ditchman, N., Kim, J. H., & Chiu, C. Y. (2009). The World Health Organization ICF model as a conceptual framework of disability. In F. Chan, E. Da Silva Cardoso, & J. A. Chronister (Eds.), *Psychosocial interventions for people with chronic illness and disability: A handbook for evidence-based rehabilitation health professionals* (pp. 23–74). New York, NY: Springer Publishing.

Chan, F., Leahy, M. J., & Saunders, J. L. (Eds.). (2005). *Case management for rehabilitation health professionals.* Linn Creek, MO: Aspen Professional Services.

Chan, F., Livneh, H., Pruett, S., Wang, C. C., & Zheng, L. X. (2009). Societal attitudes toward disability: Concepts, measurements, and interventions. In F. Chan, E. Da Silva Cardoso, & J. A. Chronister (Eds.), *Understanding psychosocial adjustment to chronic illness and disability* (pp. 333–370). New York, NY: Springer Publishing.

Chew, K. L., Iacono, T., & Tracy, J. (2009). Overcoming communication barriers: Working with patients with intellectual disabilities. *Australian Family Physician, 38*(1/2), 10–14.

Chou, C. C., & Chronister, J. A. (2012). Social tie characteristics and psychiatric rehabilitation outcomes among adults with serious mental illness. *Rehabilitation Counseling Bulletin, 55*(2), 92–102.

Chronister, J. (2009). Social support and rehabilitation: Theory, research and measurement. In F. Chan, E. Da Silva Cardoso, & J. A. Chronister (Eds.), *Understanding psychosocial adjustment to chronic illness and disability: A handbook for evidence-based practitioners in rehabilitation* (pp. 149–183). New York, NY: Springer Publishing.

Chronister, J. A., & Chan, F. (2007). Hierarchical coping: A conceptual framework for understanding coping within the context of chronic illness and disability. In E. Martz & H. Livneh (Eds.), *Coping with chronic illness and disability* (pp. 49–71). New York, NY: Springer.

Chronister, J. A., Chou, C. C., & Liao, H. Y. (2013). The role of stigma coping and social support in mediating the effect of societal stigma on internalized stigma, mental health recovery, and quality of life among people with serious mental illness. *Journal of Community Psychology, 41*(5), 582–600.

Chronister, J. A., Chou, C. C., Fitzgerald, S., & Liao, H. Y. (2016). Social support and persons with psychiatric disabilities: A cluster analysis. *Journal of Applied Rehabilitation Counseling, 47*(3), 29–40.

Chronister, J. A., Chou, C. C., Frain, M., & da Silva Cardoso, E. (2008). The relationship between social support and rehabilitation related outcomes: A meta-analysis. *Journal of Rehabilitation, 74*(2), 16–32.

Chronister, J. A., & Johnson, E. K. (2009). Multiculturalism and adjustment to disability. In F. Chan, E. Da Silva Cardoso, & J. A. Chronister (Eds.), *Understanding psychosocial adjustment to chronic illness and disability* (pp. 479–518). New York, NY: Springer Publishing.

Chronister, J. A., Johnson, E. K., & Berven, N. L. (2006). Measuring social support in rehabilitation. *Disability and Rehabilitation, 28*(2), 75–84.

Chubon, R. A. (1994). *Social and psychological foundations of rehabilitation.* Springfield, IL: Charles C Thomas.

Clark, N. M., Becker, M. H., Janz, N. K., Lorig, K., Rakowski, W., & Anderson, L. (1991). Self-management of chronic disease by older adults: A review and questions for research. *Journal of Aging and Health, 3*(1), 3–27.

Cobb, S. (1976). Social support as a moderator of life stress. *Psychosomatic Medicine, 38*(5), 300–314.

Cohen, S., & Janicki-Deverts, D. (2009). Can we improve our physical health by altering our social networks? *Perspectives on Psychological Science, 4*(4), 375–378.

Cohen, S., Mermelstein, R., Kamarck, T., & Hoberman, H. M. (1985). Measuring the functional components of social support. In I. G. Sarason & B. R. Sarason (Eds.), *Social support: Theory, research and applications* (Vol. 24, pp. 73–94). Dordrecht, The Netherlands: Springer.

Cohen, S., Underwood, L. G., & Gottlieb, B. H. (Eds.). (2000). *Social support measurement and intervention: A guide for health and social scientists.* New York, NY: Oxford University Press.

Cohen, S., & Wills, T. A. (1985). Stress, social support, and the buffering hypothesis. *Psychological Bulletin, 98*(2), 310–357.

Cole, E. R. (2009). Intersectionality and research in psychology. *American Psychologist, 64*(3), 170–180.

Collins, P. H. (1990). *Black feminist thought: Knowledge, consciousness and the politics.* Chicago, IL: University of Chicago Press.

Commission on Rehabilitation Counselor Certification (2010). *Code of professional ethics for rehabilitation counselors.* Schaumburg, IL: Author.

Cook, D. (1998). Psychosocial impact of disability. In R. M. Parker & E. M. Szymanski (Eds.), *Rehabilitation counseling: Basics and beyond* (pp. 303–326). Austin, TX: Pro-Ed.

Cook, J. E., Purdie-Vaughns, V., Meyer, I. H., & Busch, J. T. (2014). Intervening within and across levels: A multilevel approach to stigma and public health. *Social Science & Medicine, 103*, 101–109.

Corrigan, P. W. (2006). Impact of consumer-operated services on empowerment and recovery of people with psychiatric disabilities. *Psychiatric Services, 57*(10), 1493–1496.

Corrigan, P. W., Angell, B., Davidson, L., Marcus, S. C., Salzer, M. S., Kottsieper, P., … Stanhope, V. (2012). From adherence to self-determination: Evolution of a treatment paradigm for people with serious mental illnesses. *Psychiatric Services, 63*(2), 169–173.

Corrigan, P. W., Edwards, A. B., Green, A., Diwan, S. L., & Penn, D. L. (2001). Prejudice, social distance, and familiarity with mental illness. *Schizophrenia Bulletin, 27*(2), 219–225.

Corrigan, P. W., & Kosyluk, K. A. (2013). Erasing the stigma: Where science meets advocacy. *Basic and Applied Social Psychology, 35*(1), 131–140.

Corrigan, P. W., & Lam, C. (2007). Challenging the structural discrimination of psychiatric disabilities: Lessons learned from the American disability community. *Rehabilitation Education, 21*(1), 53–58.

Corrigan, P. W., & Penn, D. L. (1999). Lessons from social psychology on discrediting psychiatric stigma. *American Psychologist, 54*(9), 765–776.

Corrigan, P. W., & Watson, A. C. (2002). The paradox of self-stigma and mental illness. *Clinical Psychology: Science and Practice, 9*(1), 35–53.

Cutrona, C. E., & Russell, D. W. (1990). Type of social support and specific stress: Toward a theory of optimal matching. In B. R. Sarason, I. G. Sarason, & G. R. Pierce (Eds.), *Social support: An interactional view* (pp. 319–366). New York, NY: Wiley.

Dailey, D. M. (1979). Adjustment of heterosexual and homosexual couples in pairing relationships: An exploratory study. *Journal of Sex Research, 15*(2), 143–157.

Devereux, P. G., Bullock, C. C., Bargmann-Losche, J., & Kyriakou, M. (2005). Maintaining support in people with paralysis: What works? *Qualitative Health Research, 15*(10), 1360–1376.

Devins, G. M., Blinik, Y. M., Hutchinson, T. A., Hollomby, D. J., Barre, P. E., & Guttmann, R. D. (1983). The emotional impact of end-stage renal disease: Importance of patients' perceptions of intrusiveness and control. *International Journal of Psychiatry in Medicine, 13*(4), 327–343.

Dhamoon, R. K., & Hankivsky, O. (2011). Why the theory and practice of intersectionality matter to health research and policy. In O. Hankivsky (Ed.), *Health inequities in Canada: Intersectional frameworks and practices* (pp. 16–50). Vancouver, BC, Canada: UBC Press.

Disabled World. (2017). LGBT health: People with disabilities. Retrieved from https://www.disabledworld.com/disability/sexuality/lgbt-health.php

Donaldson, J. (1980). Changing attitudes toward handicapped persons: A review and analysis of research. *Exceptional Children, 46*(7), 504–514.

Drapalski, A. L., Lucksted, A., Perrin, P. B., Aakre, J. M., Brown, C. H., DeForge, B. R., & Boyd, J. E. (2013). A model of internalized stigma and its effects on people with mental illness. *Psychiatric Services, 64*(3), 264–269.

Drum, D. J, Brownson, C, Denmark, A. B, Smith, S. E. (2009). New data on the nature of suicidal crises in college students: Shifting the paradigm. *Professional Psychology: Research and Practice, 40*(3), 213–222. doi:10.1037/a0014465

Dunn, E. C., Wewiorski, N. J., & Rogers, E. S. (2010). A qualitative investigation of individual and contextual factors associated with vocational recovery among people with serious mental illness. *American Journal of Orthopsychiatry, 80*(2), 185–194.

Dunn, M. E. (1975). Psychological intervention in a spinal cord injury center. *Rehabilitation Psychology, 22*(4), 165–178.

Eagly, A. H., Mladinic, A., & Otto, S. (1994). Cognitive and affective bases of attitudes toward social groups and social policies. *Journal of Experimental Social Psychology, 30*(2), 113–137.

Egbert, N., & Nanna, K. M. (2009). Health literacy: Challenges and strategies. *The Online Journal of Issues in Nursing, 14*(3), Manuscript 1. doi:10.3912/OJIN.Vol14No03Man01

Engel, G. L. (1977). The care of the patient: Art or science? *The Johns Hopkins Medical Journal, 140*(5), 222–232.

Erikson, E. H. (1968). *Identity: Youth and crisis.* New York, NY: W. W. Norton.

Ertel, K. A., Glymour, M. M., & Berkman, L. F. (2009). Social networks and health: A life course perspective integrating observational and experimental evidence. *Journal of Social and Personal Relationships, 26*(1), 73–92.

Fabian, E. S., Beveridge, S., & Ethridge, G. (2009). Differences in perceptions of career barriers and supports for people with disabilities by demographic, background and case status factors. *Journal of Rehabilitation, 75*(1), 41–49.

Fallot, R., & Harris, M. (2009). Creating Cultures of Trauma-Informed Care (CCTIC): A self-assessment and planning protocol. *Community Connections, 2*(2), 1–18.

Field, M. J., & Jette, A. M. (Eds.). (2007). *The future of disability in America. Committee on Disability in America.* Washington, DC: National Academies Press.

Fink, S. L. (1967). Crisis and motivation: A theoretical model. *Archives of Physical Medicine and Rehabilitation, 48*(11), 592–597.

Fitzgerald, S., Umucu, E., Arora, S., Huck, G., Benton, S. F., & Chan, F. (2015). Psychometric validation of the Clubhouse climate questionnaire as an autonomy support measure for people with severe mental illness. *Journal of Mental Health, 24*(1), 38–42.

Flintoff, A., Fitzgerald, H., & Scraton, S. (2008). The challenges of intersectionality: Researching difference in physical education 1. *International Studies in Sociology of Education, 18*(2), 73–85.

Flower, A., Burns, M. K., & Bottsford-Miller, N. A. (2007). Meta-analysis of disability simulation research. *Remedial and Special Education, 28*(2), 72–79.

Fredriksen-Goldsen, K. I., Kim, H. J., & Barkan, S. E. (2012). Disability among lesbian, gay, and bisexual adults: Disparities in prevalence and risk. *American Journal of Public Health, 102*(1), e16–e21.

Friedrich, M., Gittler, G., Arendasy, M., & Friedrich, K. M. (2005). Long-term effect of a combined exercise and motivational program on the level of disability of patients with chronic low back pain. *Spine, 30*(9), 995–1000.

Fulton, J. J., Calhoun, P. S., Wagner, H. R., Schry, A. R., Hair, L. P., Feeling, N., … Beckham, J. C. (2015). The prevalence of posttraumatic stress disorder in Operation Enduring Freedom/Operation Iraqi Freedom (OEF/OIF) Veterans: A meta-analysis. *Journal of Anxiety Disorders, 31,* 98–107.

Gallant, M. P. (2003). The influence of social support on chronic illness self-management: A review and directions for research. *Health Education & Behavior, 30*(2), 170–195.

Gonzales, L., Davidoff, K. C., Nadal, K. L., & Yanos, P. T. (2015). Microaggressions experienced by persons with mental illnesses: An exploratory study. *Psychiatric Rehabilitation Journal, 38*(3), 234–241.

Gordon, P. A., Tantillo, J. C., Feldman, D., & Perrone, K. (2004). Attitudes regarding interpersonal relationships with persons with mental illness and mental retardation. *Journal of Rehabilitation, 70*(1), 50–56.

Gottlieb, B. H., & Hall, A. (1980). *Prevention and mental health.* Beverly Hills, CA: Sage.

Green, L. W., & Johnson, K. W. (1983). Health education and health promotion. In D. Mechanic (Ed.), *Handbook of health, health care, and the health professions* (pp. 744–765). New York, NY: Wiley.

Haegele, J. A., & Hodge, S. (2016). Disability discourse: Overview and critiques of the medical and social models. *Quest, 68*(2), 193–206.

Hampton, N. Z. (2004). Subjective well-being among people with spinal cord injuries: The role of self-efficacy, perceived social support, and perceived health. *Rehabilitation Counseling Bulletin, 48*(1), 31–37.

Harris, M. E., & Fallot, R. D. (2001). *Using trauma theory to design service systems.* San Francisco, CA: Jossey-Bass.

Harrison, T. C., Mackert, M., & Watkins, C. (2010). Health literacy issues among women with visual impairments. *Research in Gerontological Nursing, 3*(1), 49–60.

Hassan, N. B., Hasanah, C. I., Foong, K., Naing, L., Awang, R., Ismail, S. B., … Shaharom, M. H. (2006). Identification of psychosocial factors of noncompliance in hypertensive patients. *Journal of Human Hypertension, 20*(1), 23–29.

Hastings, R. P., Hatton, C., Taylor, J. L., & Maddison, C. (2004). Life events and psychiatric symptoms in adults with intellectual disabilities. *Journal of Intellectual Disability Research, 48*(1), 42–46.

Hatton, C., & Emerson, E. (2004). The relationship between life events and psychopathology amongst children with intellectual disabilities. *Journal of Applied Research in Intellectual Disabilities, 17*(2), 109–117.

Hatzenbuehler, M. L., Phelan, J. C., & Link, B. G. (2013). Stigma as a fundamental cause of population health inequalities. *American Journal of Public Health, 103*(5), 813–821.

Heller, T., Hsieh, K., & Rimmer, J. H. (2004). Attitudinal and psychosocial outcomes of a fitness and health education program on adults with Down syndrome. *American Journal on Mental Retardation, 109*(2), 175–185.

Hernandez, L. M. (Ed.). (2009). *Health literacy, eHealth, and communication: Putting the consumer first: Workshop summary.* Washington, DC: National Academies Press.

Hershey, J. C., Morton, B. G., Davis, J. B., & Reichgott, M. J. (1980). Patient compliance with antihypertensive medication. *American Journal of Public Health, 70*(10), 1081–1089.

Hollar, D. W. (2005). Risk behaviors for varying categories of disability in NELS:88. *Journal of School Health, 75*(9), 350–358.

Hollar, D. W. (2013). Cross-sectional patterns of allostatic load among persons with varying disabilities, NHANES: 2001–2010. *Disability and Health Journal, 6,* 177–187.

Hollar, D. W., McAweeney, M., & Moore, D. (2008). The relationship between substance use disorders and unsuccessful case closures in vocational rehabilitation agencies. *Journal of Applied Rehabilitation Counseling, 39*(2), 25–29.

Hollar, D. W., & Moore, D. (2004). Relationship of substance use by students with disabilities to long-term educational and social outcomes. *Substance Use & Misuse, 39*(6), 929–960.

Hollins, S., & Esterhuyzen, A. (1997). Bereavement and grief in adults with learning disabilities. *The British Journal of Psychiatry, 170*(6), 497–501.

Holt-Lunstad, J., Smith, T. B., & Layton, J. B. (2010). Social relationships and mortality risk: A meta-analytic review. *PLOS Medicine, 7*(7), e1000316. doi:10.1371/journal.pmed.1000316

House, J. S. (1981). *Work stress and social support.* Reading, MA: Addison-Wesley.

Howland, C. A., & Rintala, D. H. (2001). Dating behaviors of women with physical disabilities. *Sexuality and Disability, 19*(1), 41–70.

Humpage, L. (2007). Models of disability, work and welfare in Australia. *Social Policy & Administration, 41*(3), 215–231.

Iezzoni, L. I., Park, E. R., & Kilbridge, K. L. (2011). Implications of mobility impairment on the diagnosis and treatment of breast cancer. *Journal of Women's Health, 20*(1), 45–52.

Jennings, A. (2004). *Models for developing trauma-informed behavioral health systems and trauma-specific services.* Alexandria, VA: National Association of State Mental Health Program Directors, National Technical Assistance Center for State Mental Health Planning.

Jung, J. (1990). The role of reciprocity in social support. *Basic and Applied Social Psychology, 11*(3), 243–253.

Jurišić, B., & Marušič, A. (2009). Suicidal ideation and behavior and some psychological correlates in physically disabled motor-vehicle accident survivors. *Crisis, 30*(1), 34–38.

Kaplan, S. P. (1990). Social support, emotional distress, and vocational outcomes among persons with brain injuries. *Rehabilitation Counseling Bulletin, 34*(1), 16–23.

Keesler, J. M. (2014). A call for the integration of trauma-informed care among intellectual and developmental disability organizations. *Journal of Policy and Practice in Intellectual Disabilities, 11*(1), 34–42.

Keller, R. M., & Galgay, C. E. (2010). Microaggressive experiences of people with disabilities. In D. W. Sue (Ed.), *Microaggressions and marginality: Manifestation, dynamics, and impact* (pp. 241–268). Hoboken, NJ: Wiley.

Kindig, D., & Stoddart, G. (2003). What is population health? *American Journal of Public Health, 93*(3), 380–383.

Kolodziej, M. E., & Johnson, B. T. (1996). Interpersonal contact and acceptance of persons with psychiatric disorders: A research synthesis. *Journal of Consulting and Clinical Psychology, 64*(6), 1387–1396.

Konrad, S. C. (2006). Posttraumatic growth in mothers of children with acquired disabilities. *Journal of Loss and Trauma, 11*(1), 101–113.

Krause, N. (1986). Social support, stress, and well-being among older adults. *Journal of Gerontology, 41*(4), 512–519.

Kreuter, M. W., Green, M. C., Cappella, J. N., Slater, M. D., Wise, M. E., Storey, D., … Hinyard, L. J. (2007). Narrative communication in cancer prevention and control: A framework to guide research and application. *Annals of Behavioral Medicine, 33*(3), 221–235.

Kumpfer, K. L. (1999). *Strengthening America's families: Exemplary parenting and family strategies for delinquency prevention.* Salt Lake City: University of Utah.

Lahav, Y., Solomon, Z., & Levin, Y. (2016). Posttraumatic growth and perceived health: The role of posttraumatic stress symptoms. *American Journal of Orthopsychiatry, 86*(6), 693–703.

Lazarus, R. S., & Folkman, S. (1984). Coping and adaptation. In W. D. Gentry (Ed.), *The handbook of behavioral medicine* (pp. 282–325). New York, NY: Guilford Press.

Lefley, H. P. (2002). Ethical issues in mental health services for culturally diverse communities. In P. Backlar & D. L. Cutler (Eds.), *Ethics in community mental health care* (pp. 3–22). New York, NY: Kluwer Academic Press.

Levitas, A., & Gilson, S. F. (2001). Predictable crises in the lives of people with mental retardation. *Mental Health Aspects of Developmental Disabilities, 4*, 89–100.

Lewin, K. (1935). *A dynamic theory of personality: Selected papers* (D. K. Adams & K. E. Zener, Trans.). New York, NY: McGraw-Hill.

Lewin, K. (1936). Some social-psychological differences between the United States and Germany. *Journal of Personality, 4*(4), 265–293.

Lewinsohn, P. M., Hoberman, H., Teri, L., & Hautzinger, M. (1985). An integrative theory of depression. In S. Reiss & R. R. Bootzin (Eds.), *Theoretical issues in behavior therapy* (pp. 331–359). San Diego, CA: Academic Press.

Lindemann, J. E. (1981). General considerations for evaluating and counseling the physically handicapped. In J. E. Lindemann (Ed.), *Psychological and behavioral aspects of physical disability* (pp. 1–19). New York, NY: Plenum Press.

Link, B. G., Cullen, F. T., Struening, E., Shrout, P. E., & Dohrenwend, B. P. (1989). A modified labeling theory approach to mental disorders: An empirical assessment. *American Sociological Review, 54,* 400–423.

Linkowski, D. C., & Dunn, M. A. (1974). Self-concept and acceptance of disability. *Rehabilitation Counseling Bulletin, 18,* 28–32.

Linley, P. A., & Joseph, S. (2004). Positive change following trauma and adversity: A review. *Journal of Traumatic Stress, 17*(1), 11–21.

Livingston, J. D., & Boyd, J. E. (2010). Correlates and consequences of internalized stigma for people living with mental illness: A systematic review and meta-analysis. *Social Science & Medicine, 71*(12), 2150–2161.

Livneh, H. (1982). On the origins of negative attitudes towards people with disabilities. *Rehabilitation Literature, 43,* 338–347.

Livneh, H. (1986). A unified approach to existing models of adaptation to disability: I. A model adaptation. *Journal of Applied Rehabilitation Counseling, 17,* 5–16.

Livneh, H. (1988). A dimensional perspective on the origin of negative attitudes toward persons with disabilities. In H. E. Yuker (Ed.), *Attitudes toward persons with disabilities* (pp. 35–46). New York, NY: Springer Publishing.

Livneh, H., & Antonak, R. F. (1997). *Psychosocial adaptation to chronic illness and disability.* Osage Beach, MO: Aspen Professional Services.

Lynch, R. T., & Chiu, C. Y. (2009). Health promotion interventions for people with chronic illness and disability. In F. Chan, E. Da Silva Cardoso, & J. A. Chronister (Eds.), *Psychosocial interventions for people with chronic illness and disability: A handbook for evidence-based rehabilitation health professionals* (pp. 277–305). New York, NY: Springer Publishing.

Magnan, M. A., Reynolds, K. E., & Galvin, E. A. (2006). Barriers to addressing patient sexuality in nursing practice. *Dermatology Nursing, 18*(5), 448.

Marini, I., Glover-Graf, N. M., & Millington, M. J. (2011). *Psychosocial aspects of disability: Insider perspectives and strategies for counselors.* New York, NY: Springer Publishing.

McCormack, L., Hagger, M., & Joseph, S. (2011). Vicarious growth in wives of Vietnam veterans: A phenomenological investigation into decades of 'lived' experience. *The Journal of Humanistic Psychology, 51,* 273–290.

McMahon, B. T., Hurley, J. E., Chan, F., Rumrill, P. D., & Roessler, R. (2008). Drivers of hiring discrimination for individuals with disabilities. *Journal of Occupational Rehabilitation, 18*(2), 133–139.

Meyer, I. H. (2003). Prejudice, social stress, and mental health in lesbian, gay, and bisexual populations: Conceptual issues and research evidence. *Psychological Bulletin, 129*(5), 674–697.

Muñoz-Baell, I. M., Ruiz-Cantero, M. T., Álvarez-Dardet, C., Ferreiro-Lago, E., & Aroca-Fernández, E. (2011). Comunidades sordas: ¿pacientes o ciudadanas? *Gaceta Sanitaria, 25*(1), 72–78.

Mutua, M. W. (2001). Savages, victims, and saviors: The metaphor of human rights. *Harvard International Law Journal, 42,* 201–245.

Nadal, K. L. (2013). *That's so gay! Microaggressions and the lesbian, gay, bisexual, and transgender community.* Washington, DC: American Psychological Association.

National Council on Disability. (2009). The current state of healthcare for people with disabilities. Retrieved from http://www.ncd.gov/publications/2009/Sept302009

Nisbet, R. A. (1980). *History of the idea of progress.* New Brunswick, NJ: Transaction Publishers.

Nisbett, R., & Ross, L. (1991). *The person and the situation.* New York, NY: McGraw-Hill.

O'Donnell, M. L., Varker, T., Holmes, A. C., Ellen, S., Wade, D., Creamer, M., … Forbes, D. (2013). Original research disability after injury: The cumulative burden of physical and mental health. *Journal of Clinical Psychiatry, 74*(2), e137–e143.

Olkin, R. (1999). The personal, professional and political when clients have disabilities. *Women & Therapy, 22*(2), 87–103.

Palmer, M., & Harley, D. (2012). Models and measurement in disability: An international review. *Health Policy and Planning, 27*(5), 357–364.

Paluck, E. L., & Green, D. P. (2009). Prejudice reduction: What works? A review and assessment of research and practice. *Annual Review of Psychology, 60*, 339–367.

Patterson, J. B., McFarlane, F. R., & Sax, C. (2005). Challenges to a legacy: Retaining CORE accreditation of rehabilitation counselor education programs. *Rehabilitation Education, 19*(4), 203–214.

Peek, L., & Stough, L. M. (2010). Children with disabilities in the context of disaster: A social vulnerability perspective. *Child Development, 81*(4), 1260–1270.

Pelletier, J. R., Nguyen, M., Bradley, K., Johnsen, M., & McKay, C. (2005). A study of a structured exercise program with members of an ICCD Certified Clubhouse: Program design, benefits, and implications for feasibility. *Psychiatric Rehabilitation Journal, 29*, 89–96.

Pereira, P. C., & Fortes, P. A. (2010). Communication and information barriers to health assistance for deaf patients. *American Annals of the Deaf, 155*(1), 31–37.

Peterson, D. B. (2005). International classification of functioning, disability and health: An introduction for rehabilitation psychologists. *Rehabilitation Psychology, 50*(2), 105–112.

Peterson, D. B. (2009). The International Classification of Functioning, Disability & Health: Application to professional counseling. In I. Marini & M. A. Stebnicki (Eds.), *The professional counselor's desk reference* (pp. 529–542). New York, NY: Springer Publishing.

Plotnik, R. (1996). *Introduction to psychology* (4th ed.). Pacific Grove, CA: Brooks/Cole.

Ramchand, R., Marshall, G. N., Schell, T. L., & Jaycox, L. H. (2008). Posttraumatic distress and physical functioning: A longitudinal study of injured survivors of community violence. *Journal of Consulting and Clinical Psychology, 76*(4), 668–676.

Ravesloot, C., Young, Q. R., Norris, K., Szalda-Petree, A., Seekins, T., White, G., … Lopez, C. (1998). *Living well with a disability: A workbook for promoting health and wellness.* Missoula: The University of Montana Rural Institute.

Ray, O. (2004). How the mind hurts and heals the body. *American Psychologist, 59*(1), 29.

Resnick, S. G., & Rosenheck, R. A. (2008). Integrating peer-provided services: A quasi-experimental study of recovery orientation, confidence, and empowerment. *Psychiatric Services, 59*(11), 1307–1314.

Rimmer, J. H., Rowland, J. L., & Yamaki, K. (2007). Obesity and secondary conditions in adolescents with disabilities: Addressing the needs of an underserved population. *Journal of Adolescent Health, 41*, 224–229.

Rodriguez, P., Holowka, D. W., & Marx, B. P. (2012). Assessment of posttraumatic stress disorder-related functional impairment: A review. *Journal of Rehabilitation Research and Development, 49*(5), 649–666.

Roessler, R., & Bolton, B. (1978). *Psychosocial adjustment to disability.* Baltimore, MD: University Park Press.

Saakvitne, K. W., Gamble, S. J., Pearlman, L. A., & Lev, B. T. (2000). *Risking connection: A training curriculum for work with survivors of childhood abuse.* Baltimore, MD: Sidran Institute Press.

Schaefer, J. A., & Moos, R. H. (1998). The context for posttraumatic growth: Life crises, individual and social resources, and coping. In R. G. Tedeschi, C. L. Park, L. G. Calhoun (Eds.), *Posttraumatic growth: Positive changes in the aftermath of crisis* (pp. 99–125). Mahwah, NJ: Erlbaum.

Schnurr, P. P., & Green, B. L. (2004). *Trauma and health: Physical health consequences of exposure to extreme stress.* Washington, DC: American Psychological Association.

Schulz, A. J., & Mullings, L. (Eds.). (2006). *Gender, race, class, and health: Intersectional approaches* (p. 146). New York, NY: Wiley.

Scotch, R. (2009). *From good will to civil rights: Transforming federal disability policy.* Philadelphia, PA: Temple University Press.

Scott, H. M., & Havercamp, S. M. (2014). Race and health disparities in adults with intellectual and developmental disabilities living in the United States. *Intellectual and Developmental Disabilities, 52*(6), 409–418.

Senol-Durak, E., & Ayvasik, H. B. (2010). Factors associated with posttraumatic growth among myocardial infarction patients: Perceived social support, perception of the event and coping. *Journal of Clinical Psychology in Medical Settings, 17*(2), 150–158.

Shaver, J. P., Curtis, C. K., Jesunathadas, J., & Strong, C. J. (1987). *The modification of attitudes toward persons with handicaps: A comprehensive integrative review of research* (Project No. 023CH50160). Logan: Utah State University, Bureau of Research Services.

Shih, R. A., Schell, T. L., Hambarsoomian, K., Marshall, G. N., & Belzberg, H. (2010). Prevalence of PTSD and major depression following trauma-center hospitalization. *The Journal of Trauma, 69*(6), 1560–1566.

Shontz, F. C. (1965). Reactions to crisis. *Volta Review, 67*(5), 364–370.

Smart, J. F. (2001). *Disability, society, and the individual.* Austin, TX: Pro-Ed.

Smart, J. F. (2009). The power of models of disability. *Journal of Rehabilitation, 75*(2), 3–11.

Smedema, S. M., Bakken-Gillen, S. K., & Dalton, J. (2009). Psychosocial adaptation to chronic illness and disability: Models and measurement. In F. Chan, E. D. Cardoso, & J. A. Chronister (Eds.), *Understanding psychosocial adjustment to chronic illness and disability: A handbook for evidence-based practitioners in rehabilitation* (pp. 51–73). New York, NY: Springer Publishing.

Sotnik, P., & Jezewski, M. (2005). Cultural and disability services. In J. H. Stone (Ed.), *Culture and disability; Providing culturally competent services* (pp. 15–36). Thousand Oaks, CA: Sage.

Southwick, S. M., Vythilingam, M., & Charney, D. S. (2005). The psychobiology of depression and resilience to stress: Implications for prevention and treatment. *Annual Review of Clinical Psychology, 1*, 255–291.

Substance Abuse and Mental Health Services Administration. (2016). Recovery and recovery support. Retrieved from https://www.samhsa.gov/recovery

Sue, D. W. (2010). Microaggressions in everyday life: Race, gender, and sexual orientation. New York, NY: Wiley.

Sue, D. W., Capodilupo, C. M., Torino, G. C., Bucceri, J. M., Holder, A., Nadal, K. L., & Esquilin, M. (2007). Racial microaggressions in everyday life: Implications for clinical practice. *American Psychologist, 62*(4), 271–286.

Szymanski, E. M., Ryan, C., Merz, M. A., Trevino, B., & Johnston-Rodriguez, S. (1996). Psychosocial and economic aspects of work: Implications for people with disabilities. In E. M. Szymanski & R. M. Parker (Eds.), *Work and disability: Issues and strategies in career development and job placement* (pp. 9–38). Austin, TX: Pro-Ed.

Taleporos, G., & McCabe, M. P. (2003). Relationships, sexuality and adjustment among people with physical disability. *Sexual and Relationship Therapy, 18*(1), 25–43.

Tarvydas, V. M., Peterson, D. B., & Michaelson, S. D. (2005). Ethical issues in case management. In F. Chan, M. Leahy, & J. L. Saunders (Eds.), *Case management for rehabilitation health professionals* (pp. 144–175). Osage Beach, MO: Aspen Professional Services.

Tate, C. C., Ledbetter, J. N., & Youssef, C. P. (2013). A two-question method for assessing gender categories in the social and medical sciences. *Journal of Sex Research, 50*(8), 767–776.

Tedeschi, R. G., & Calhoun, L. G. (2004). Posttraumatic growth: Conceptual foundations and empirical evidence. *Psychological Inquiry, 15*(1), 1–18.

Teri, L., McCurry, S. M., & Logsdon, R. G. (1997). Memory, thinking, and aging: What we know about what we know. *Western Journal of Medicine, 167*(4), 269–275.

Thoits, P. A. (2011). Mechanisms linking social ties and support to physical and mental health. *Journal of Health and Social Behavior, 52*(2), 145–161.

Torres, L., Driscoll, M. W., & Burrow, A. L. (2010). Racial microaggressions and psychological functioning among highly achieving African-Americans: A mixed-methods approach. *Journal of Social and Clinical Psychology, 29*(10), 1074–1099.

Uchino, B. N. (2004). *Social support and physical health: Understanding the health consequences of relationships.* New Haven, CT: Yale University Press.

Umberson, D., & Montez, J. K. (2010). Social relationships and health a flashpoint for health policy. *Journal of Health and Social Behavior, 51*(1 Suppl.), S54–S66.

U.S. Census Bureau. (2016). Minority population tops 100 million. Retrieved from http://www.census.gov/Press-Release/www/releases/archives/population/010048.html

U.S. Department of Health and Human Services, Office of Disease Prevention and Health Promotion. (2000). Healthy people 2020. Retrieved from https://www.healthypeople.gov

U.S. Preventive Services Task Force. (2003). *Guide to clinical preventive services: Methods* (Vol. 1). Washington, DC: U.S. Department of Health and Human Services, Office of Disease Prevention and Health Promotion, U.S. Preventive Services Task Force.

Vash, C. L., & Crewe, N. M. (2004). *Psychology of disability* (2nd ed.). New York, NY: Springer Publishing.

Wahl, O. (1995). *Media madness: Public images of mental illness.* New Brunswick, NJ: Rutgers University Press.

Walker, H. M., Calkins, C., Wehmeyer, M. L., Walker, L., Bacon, A., Palmer, S. B., ... Abery, B. H. (2011). A social-ecological approach to promote self-determination. *Exceptionality, 19*(1), 6–18.

Watermeyer, B., & Swartz, L. (2016) Disablism, identity and self: Discrimination as a traumatic assault on subjectivity. *Journal of Community & Applied Social Psychology, 26,* 268–276. doi:10.1002/casp.2266

Weiss, T. (2004). Correlates of posttraumatic growth in married breast cancer survivors. *Journal of Social and Clinical Psychology, 23*(5), 733–746.

Wigham, S., Hatton, C., & Taylor, J. L. (2011). The effects of traumatizing life events on people with intellectual disabilities: A systematic review. *Journal of Mental Health Research in Intellectual Disabilities, 4*(1), 19–39.

Wilson, K. B., Harley, D. A., & Alston, R. J. (2001). Race as a correlate of vocational rehabilitation acceptance: Revisited. *Journal of Rehabilitation, 67*(3), 35–41.

World Health Organization. (2001). *International Classification of Functioning, Disability and Health.* Geneva, Switzerland: Author.

World Health Organization. (2011). *World report on disability 2011.* Geneva, Switzerland: Author.

Wortman, C. B., & Silver, R. C. (1989). The myths of coping with loss. *Journal of Consulting and Clinical Psychology, 57*(3), 349–357.

Wright, B. A. (1960). *Value changes in acceptance of disability.* Washington, DC: American Psychological Association.

Wright, B. A. (1983). *Physical disability: A psychosocial approach.* New York, NY: HarperCollins.

Wright, B. A. (1988). Attitudes and the fundamental negative bias: Conditions and corrections. In H. E. Yuker (Ed.), *Attitudes toward people with disabilities* (pp. 3–21). New York, NY: Springer Publishing.

Yoshida, K. K. (1993). Reshaping of self: A pendular reconstruction of self and identity among adults with traumatic spinal cord injury. *Sociology of Health & Illness, 15*(2), 217–245.

Yuker, H. E. (Ed.). (1988). The effects of contact on attitudes toward disabled persons: Some empirical generalizations. In H. E. Yuker (Ed.), *Attitudes toward persons with disabilities* (pp. 262–274). New York, NY: Springer Publishing.

Zeluf, G., Dhejne, C., Orre, C., Mannheimer, L. N., Deogan, C., Höijer, J., & Thorson, A. E. (2016). Health, disability and quality of life among trans people in Sweden—A web-based survey. *BMC Public Health, 16*(1), 903.

Zola, I. K. (1988). Aging and disability: Toward a unifying agenda. *Educational Gerontology: An International Quarterly, 14*(5), 365–387.

3

Human Growth and Development

Malachy Bishop and Bradley McDaniels

In the almost a century since its creation, the professional scope of rehabilitation counseling has expanded considerably beyond its original focus on the employment-related issues of working-age adults with disabilities. In response to demographic and sociological shifts in the United States and global population and the evolving experiences and needs of Americans with disabilities, rehabilitation counselors are working with people of all ages in an expanding range of rehabilitation counseling settings. As a result, effective and comprehensive rehabilitation counseling requires knowledge and understanding of theories, systems, processes, and issues of human growth and development across the lifespan. In this chapter we review the following topics related to human growth and development:

- Debates and important issues in early developmental processes
- Genetic testing and genetic counseling
- Key theories of personality development
- Individual and family response to disability
- Rehabilitation counseling with older Americans
- Human sexuality and disability
- Learning styles and strategies

Debates and Important Issues in Early Developmental Processes

Learning Objectives

By the end of this unit you should be able to:

1. Describe the nature versus nurture debate in human development.
2. Discuss the differences between continuous or discontinuous theoretical perspectives on human growth and development.
3. Identify the purpose of genetic testing and genetic counseling.

Key Concepts

Rehabilitation counselors are increasingly working with younger clients in a range of professional settings but primarily in the context of transition from school to work or postsecondary education. This is particularly evident in the 2014 passage of the Workforce Innovation and Opportunities Act (WIOA), which mandates that each state's vocational rehabilitation (VR) agency have an increased role in transition services. Effective and comprehensive rehabilitation counseling across the lifespan increasingly means that rehabilitation counselors have an understanding of a number of processes and issues associated with human growth and development. In this section we review some of the key theories, debates, and ideas associated with personal and physical development.

I. The Nature Versus Nurture Debate in Human Development

The nature versus nurture debate concerns the question of the degree to which innate characteristics and environmental factors influence development. The **nativist (nature) perspective** suggests that hereditary, genetic, or biological factors are the primary influence on development. One implication of this perspective is that modifying the environment will have little effect on development. Evidence supporting the nativist perspective includes evidence from twin studies (monozygote identical twins and dizygote fraternal twins) that there is a genetic component to the development of specific speech and language disorders, autism spectrum disorders, and personality attributes such as happiness, loneliness, timidness, aggression, and hostility.

The **nurturist perspective** suggests that the environment shapes behavior and can modify genetic inclinations. Evidence for this perspective suggests that an enriched environment, a supportive or adaptive environment, and early and appropriate interventions can promote language and cognitive development, whereas a stimulus-deprived environment has negative consequences for social and cognitive development.

The **combined perspective** suggests that both nature and nurture have relative influence on human development. The interactional model suggests that genotype (genetic inheritance) defines a range of capacity or sets absolute limits on phenotype (the observed characteristics). In other words, the genotype defines maximum limits that, without a supportive and positive environment, cannot be achieved. Although the debate continues for some, currently the majority of developmental psychologists view development as resulting from a combination of hereditary (i.e., genetics) and environmental (e.g., cultural, societal, familial) factors (Sternberg, 2011). The area of study associated with the interaction of genetics and the environment is referred to as *epigenetics.*

II. Continuous and Discontinuous Development

Depending on the theoretical orientation, human development has been conceived in terms of continuous or discontinuous patterns. Theories proposing **continuous** development (see e.g., Skinner, Bandura) suggest that development occurs as a process of smooth, gradual, and incremental quantitative change (e.g., a small frog becomes a big frog; degree of change), whereas, theories proposing **discontinuous** development (see e.g., Freud, Erikson) describe development as a series of stages with clear-cut, qualitative changes occurring from one phase to the next (e.g., a tadpole becomes a frog; kind of change). Recent studies have shown that development demonstrates some stage-like properties and some consistency across domains. Table 3.1 summarizes key concepts in this section.

TABLE 3.1   Key Concepts in Developmental Ideas and Debates

Key Concept	Summary
Nativist perspective	Hereditary, genetic, or biological factors are the primary influence on development.
Nurturist perspective	The environment shapes behavior, and can modify genetic inclinations.
Combined perspective	Both nature and nurture have relative influence on human development.
Continuity	Development occurs as a process of smooth, gradual, and incremental change.
Discontinuity	Development is a series of steps with clear-cut, qualitatively different changes occurring from one phase to the next.

III. Genetic Testing and Genetic Counseling

Genetic testing and prenatal diagnostic testing are fast becoming topics of significant interest and concern among disability advocates and professionals as increasingly complex ethical questions emerge from our growing understanding and capacities in genetics and prenatal testing. With increasing capacity for prenatal detection of genetic conditions, difficult questions arise for parents and society. Rehabilitation counselors should be prepared with cursory knowledge of genetic counseling and prenatal testing. Moreover, rehabilitation counselors should be aware that genetic counselors have completed a specific educational curriculum, typically have a master's degree in genetic counseling or genetics, and are board certified. Genetic counselors assist in determining the likelihood of genetic/biological conditions and in making decisions about ordering genetic testing or recommendations based on the results of completed tests. Genetic counselors obtain information about the couple's genetic background and history, including family diseases and genetic conditions and disorders, and evaluate laboratory tests. They counsel people about genetic conditions, advise on the probability of transmitting a genetic condition, and promote informed decision making.

People may seek genetic counseling at different times and for different reasons, including before or during pregnancy to learn about factors that might increase the chance for having a child with a genetic condition or after ultrasound or other prenatal testing indicates an increased risk for a genetic condition. Families might seek genetic counseling after a child is born with a genetic disease, condition, or disorder to better understand the condition and associated developmental issues. Adults may visit a genetic counselor to discuss the probability of developing a hereditary condition that occurs later in life, particularly if they have a parent or older relative with a genetic condition.

Theories of Personality Development

Learning Objectives

By the end of this unit you should be able to:

1. Identify and distinguish between major theories of social, cognitive, and personality development.

2. Understand key theoretical constructs in the major theories of social, cognitive, and personality development.

Key Concepts

Many theories of development have been proposed over the course of the past century to explain and describe the development of personality, behavior, motivation, and environment. Some of these theories have been based on the concept of critical physical, social, or emotional developmental tasks or stages throughout the lifespan; others are based on the impact of environmental influences, and still others on specific learning and cognitive processes (Vander Zanden, Crandell, & Crandell, 2007). In this section we review the key concepts of several major theories of personality development.

I. Psychoanalytic Theories

In the late 19th and throughout the 20th century, Sigmund Freud and other psychoanalytically oriented theorists introduced a number of ideas that changed the way children and childhood were viewed. Key ideas in child and personality development introduced by Freud include (a) the idea that personality develops progressively as individuals pass through various stages, during which they are faced with specific developmental tasks that must be mastered or with conflicts that must be resolved before advancing to the next stage; and (b) the importance of the first six years of life as a critical social developmental period and precursor to later personality.

Psychosexual stages of development. Freud's theory of development is described in terms of psychosexual stages. Each stage is dominated by the development of sensitivity in a particular erogenous or pleasure-giving zone of the body. Each stage presents a unique conflict that must be resolved before passing to the next stage. Unsuccessful resolution of conflict associated with any psychosexual stage prevents normal development to the next stage. Frustration or overindulgence of needs at any of the early developmental stages (e.g., parental overprotectiveness or rejection) or the occurrence of a traumatic event may result in fixation at that stage and adversely influence later personality development (Livneh & Bishop, 2012). The psychosexual stages and the key elements of each are presented in Table 3.2.

TABLE 3.2 Psychosexual Stages of Development: Stages and Key Elements

Stage	Age	Key Elements
1. Oral stage	Birth to 2	Focus The mouth and digestive tract. Interaction with the world is through activities associated with the mouth and digestive tract (eating, nursing, pleasure associated with oral stimulation, satisfaction).
		Conflict or challenge Issues in this stage involve the need to rely on and trust caregivers to provide nurturance and satisfaction and to move toward weaning and independence.
		Resolution Develop trust that the world will fulfill needs and that one can achieve satisfaction.
		Fixation If an infant gets too much or too little satisfaction during this stage, he or she may become fixated, with either oral receptive (dependent, gullible [e.g., willing to swallow anything, overly concerned with obtaining goods, information, or knowledge] or oral aggressive (conversationally aggressive, sarcastic, biting, possessive of others) tendencies and characteristics of personality.

(continued)

TABLE 3.2 Psychosexual Stages of Development: Stages and Key Elements (*continued*)

Stage	Age	Key Elements
2. Anal stage	2–3	Focus Satisfaction and tension release through bowel movements and control.
		Conflict or challenge Self-control over bowels and toilet training; conflicts with parents over control and power, played out in toilet training. The reactions and responses of parents at this stage affect one's personal view (e.g., if parent/caregiver is supportive and encouraging, the child is likely to experience self-esteem).
		Fixation Anal retentive—stingy, saving; orderly anal expulsive—messy, sloppy, prone to tantrums, and outbursts.
3. Phallic stage	4–5	Focus Satisfaction through genital stimulation; awareness of the presence or absence of a penis develops at this stage.
		Conflict or challenge Sexuality and relationships with same-sex and opposite sex parent. This stage introduces the Oedipal complex (boy wants to possess mother and father is seen as rival) and Electra complex (girl wants to possess father, mother is seen as rival); the concepts of castration anxiety and penis envy are associated with this stage. Formation of introjected superego also occurs at this stage; the superego is formed from father's/mother's interpretation of society's rules.
		Resolution Identification with same-sex parent.
4. Latency stage	6–12	Focus This stage is associated with a decrease, or repression of, sexual interest, and energies are redirected to more personally and culturally acceptable objects.
		Conflict or challenge Development of social skills, communication skills, and self-confidence.
5. Genital stage	12 to maturity	Focus Genitals, sexuality.
		Conflict or challenge Sexual energy is increasingly invested in mature sexual relationships, friendship, leisure, career development, and psychological balance.

Criticisms of Freud's psychosexual stages. Many criticisms have been aimed at Freud's concept of psychosexual development. Among these are that few of Freud's proposals about developmental processes can be tested using the scientific method and that the theory reflects the social structures and biases of the era in which Freud lived, which are no longer relevant. In addition, aspects of the theory have been criticized for being sexist.

II. Erik Erikson: Psychosocial Stages of Development

Erik Erikson proposed eight stages of psychosocial development, each of which confronts the individual with a major conflict that must be successfully resolved if healthy development is to occur. Compared with Freud, Erikson (a) placed less emphasis on sexual urges as drivers of development and focused more on social influences, (b) focused less on the unconscious and irrational id and more on the rational ego, and (c) extended development beyond adolescence. Table 3.3 identifies Erikson's psychosocial stages and key developmental issues associated with each stage.

TABLE 3.3   Erikson's Psychosocial Stages and Key Developmental Issues

Stage/Age	Issue
1. Birth to 1	Trust vs. mistrust The emphasis in this stage is on the degree to which physical and emotional needs are met by parents or caregivers. Trust, optimism, and confidence develop if basic needs are met.
2. 2–3	Autonomy vs. shame and doubt With increased mobility and motor development, the child explores and experiments with environment and learns and develops new skills and abilities. Children develop autonomy as parents/caregivers allow them to explore their abilities in an encouraging environment to lerant of failure.
3. 4–5	Initiative vs. guilt With increased social interaction and play, child begins to plan and initiate activities with others, ask questions, and develop a view of self. Support, valuing, and encouragement allow the child to develop a sense of initiative and security in abilities.
4. 6–11	Industry vs. inferiority Period of expanding interaction with the social world and school, school-aged peer group, and teachers becomes an important source of the child's self-esteem. By demonstrating competencies in skills (academic, sex-role, social) valued by peers and society, the child develops pride in the ability to set and reach goals.
5. Adolescence	Identity vs. role confusion In the transitional period between childhood and adulthood, the adolescents learn and explore sexual, occupational, and social identity roles and future career, social, and family roles, as well as the way that they will define self and fit in.
6. Young adulthood	Intimacy vs. isolation The adult explores adult relationships and strives to form intimate relationships beyond family members, leading to longer term commitments.
7. Middle age	Generativity vs. stagnation Period of establishing career, family, and role in community and of evaluating dreams and expectations and achieved reality; the adult strives to be productive at work, involved in and giving back to community activity, and avoid becoming stagnant and unproductive.
8. Later life	Integrity vs. despair Period of slowing productivity and increased contemplation of one's life and accomplishments. If adults see life as unproductive or feel guilt or regret about the past and goal achievement, they become dissatisfied and develop despair and depression. Alternately, viewing life as worthwhile, productive, and lived with integrity leads to a sense of completeness and acceptance.

III. Jean Piaget: Cognitive Stages in Development

Jean Piaget was a psychologist and developmental theorist who proposed that each individual progresses through several distinct stages in the course of intellectual development. These stages are not necessarily age specific, but the sequence is invariant for all children. According to Piaget, children are born with the requisite mental structure (e.g., genetics) on which subsequent learning and knowledge is built (Dansen, 1994). As a result, children build schema (i.e., patterns of behavior or thinking) and the processes of adjusting these schema (e.g., assimilation, accommodation), allowing them to interact with and make sense of their environment. The process of constructing new schema results in the child's ability to handle the imbalance (i.e., disequilibrium) resulting from new information or experiences, which leads to newly developed or altered schemata to create balance (i.e., equilibrium). This reoccurring assimilation and accommodation is commonly referred to as *constructivism*, the process through which children actively construct new understandings of the world based on personal experiences.

Piaget posited that the mind is a systematic repository for knowledge, which is described as being (a) constructed (i.e., knowledge is achieved through one's experiential struggle), (b) organized (i.e., the mind follows a predictable pattern), (c) and changed over time (e.g., assimilation, accommodation). Children, Piaget believed, actively construct a more accurate understanding of the world through curiosity and exploration. In this process, known as *discovery learning*, children are capable of individualized learning strategies. Moreover, the essence of Piagetian learning is that knowledge is garnered through active construction and is initiated by the learner rather than by the teacher. The key terms and concepts associated with Piaget's theory are listed in the following paragraphs, and Table 3.4 identifies Piaget's stages of cognitive development and associated developmental characteristics. Terms associated with Piaget's theory are provided as follows:

Schema. Schema is a cognitive structure, or set of related ideas or concepts, that people use to function in and respond to situations in their environment. In Piaget's theory, cognitive development is a stage-based process of adaptation involving alternating processes of assimilation and accommodation of schemata.

Assimilation. Assimilation is the process of taking in new knowledge and information and interpreting it so that it fits in the existing schema or view of world. People generally stretch a schema as far as possible to fit new observations before accepting that the existing schema requires modification.

Disequilibrium. Disequilibrium is considered the result of awareness that current observations cannot be made to fit within the existing schema.

Equilibrium. Equilibrium is the adaptation of new schemas or the adaptation of existing schemas to create balance.

Accommodation. Accommodation is the development or evolution of new schemata to fit existing and new information, resulting in a new understanding of the world.

TABLE 3.4   Piaget's Stages of Cognitive Development

Stage and Age Period	Characteristics of Developmental Stage
1. Sensorimotor: birth to 2	Characterized by: • Increasing awareness of sensory-motor integration • Object permanence—the understanding that objects not within the visual field do not cease to exist. • Cause-and-effect understanding
2. Pre-operational: 2–7	Characterized by: • Capacity to use symbols to portray the external world internally (especially language) • Egocentrism—the belief that the child's own point of view is the only point of view
3. Concrete operations: 7–11	Characterized by: • Mastery of logical operations, math, hierarchical structures, quantity, and shape • Rule-based operation in environment
4. Formal operations: 11 and older	Characterized by: • Capacity for abstract thinking • Capacity for understanding scientific principles

IV. Bandura's Social Cognitive Theory

The cognitive learning theory, formerly referred to as the *social learning theory*, of Albert Bandura stresses the value of the motivating and self-regulating role of cognition in human behavior (Bandura, 1986). Before Bandura's introduction of social cognitive theory (SCT), researchers had focused on learning through the consequences of one's behavior. However, in SCT, Bandura demonstrated that the tedious process of trial-and-error learning could be minimized through social modeling. Bandura referred to this type of modeling as *observational learning*, which he operationalized as learning by observing the behaviors of other people (i.e., models). In his famous experiment using the "Bobo doll," Bandura demonstrated the concept of vicarious learning, in which learners are more or less likely to perform a behavior based on the consequences experienced by the model they observe. There are four necessary conditions for effective modeling: (a) attention to the model, (b) retention (i.e., remembering what one paid attention to), (c) reproduction (i.e., ability to reproduce the behavioral image), and (d) motivation (i.e., having a good reason to imitate; Bandura, 1977). SCT explains behavior as a continuous and reciprocal interaction among cognitive, behavioral, and environmental influences (i.e., reciprocal determinism). Finally, SCT places heavy reliance on information processing, the way that children and adults cognitively process social experiences, and the way that these mental operations in turn influence their behavior.

V. Vygotsky's Social Development Theory

Lev Vygotsky's theory of cognitive development shares some concepts with Piaget's theory (e.g., learning does not take place in a vacuum void of personal contact), but Vygotsky offers the differentiating perspective that cognitive growth occurs in a sociocultural context and evolves from the child's social interactions. Vygotsky's theory focuses on culture, language, and the zone of proximal development. The impact of one's culture facilitates learning through specific interactional processes but also through symbolic representations of the given culture (e.g., song, art, play). Development reflects and internalizes the culture to which the child belongs; therefore, culture provides the framework through which the child constructs meaning (Daniels, 2007). Another important Vygotskian concept central to learning and culture is the child's interaction with a skillful tutor (i.e., mentor, more knowledgeable other) who can model behavior and provide verbal instructions (i.e., cooperative or collaborative dialogue; Vygotsky, 1978).

Although culture is considered paramount to one's cognitive development, language, which is directly derived from culture, is no less important. Vygotsky (1978) stressed three forms of language: (a) social speech (i.e., external communication with others), (b) private speech (i.e., self-directed speech), and (c) silent inner speech (i.e., inaudible private speech that serves a self-regulating function). Vygotsky saw a definite relationship between language and thought, which he also believed directed behavior. Vygotsky further believed that cognitive development resulted from conversations with parents, others, and society as a whole (Smith, Cowie, & Blades, 1998).

Although culture and language development are hallmarks of Vygotsky's sociocultural theory, the concept of the "zone of proximal development" is arguably his most important contribution. Foundational to this concept is the idea that, at any given time, a child functions at a particular level of development and that further development comes through the guidance and support of others. Vygotsky (1978) describes the zone of proximal development as the distance between a learner's actual developmental level, as evidenced by problem-solving abilities, and the potential level of development determined by problem-solving abilities under the guidance of a more knowledgeable other. A key factor in this theory is that an experienced other fulfills the vital role of guiding the child, making suggestions and offering strategies. Another concept that Vygotsky introduced relates to how this process unfolds: scaffolding. The term *scaffolding* is used to describe the temporary support and assistance that a more knowledgeable other provides to help a child complete new tasks (Gindis, 1995).

Individual and Family Response to Disability

Learning Objectives

By the end of this unit you should be able to:

1. Identify major theories and perspectives on psychosocial adaptation.
2. Understand rehabilitation counseling issues in working with families responding to disability and chronic illness.

Key Concepts

Psychosocial adaptation to chronic illness and disability (CID) is one of the most important and extensively researched topics in rehabilitation counseling (Parker, Schaller, & Hansmann, 2003). Understanding how people adapt to the changes associated with the onset of CID aids clinicians in effectively helping persons cope with these changes and maintaining their quality of life (QOL). Over the past several decades, rehabilitation researchers have applied a wide variety of theoretical frameworks to the understanding of the psychosocial adaptation process.

Psychological and psychosocial distress are commonly associated with CID onset and are associated with factors such as the crisis nature of CID onset; chronicity, or the idea of permanence; the uncertain prognosis frequently associated with CID; the sometimes prolonged course of treatments; interference (sometimes increasing) with one's ability to perform life roles and activities; and the impact on family, friends, and social network. Understanding the role and response of the family in adapting to the onset and experience of living with CID and understanding the potential impact of the family on rehabilitation are important components of the rehabilitation counselor's role.

I. Assessment of Psychosocial Adaptation and Research Findings

In rehabilitation counseling, psychosocial adaptation has been defined in terms of a number of functional and psychosocial outcomes. Some of these include the capacity to manage pain and symptoms and master skills associated with functional changes; participation in health care regimens; the presence, absence, or level of significant psychological clinical disorders such as depression, anxiety, and adjustment disorder; sense of mastery; self-esteem; functional status and role-related behavior in work, school, or social domains; social participation; well-being, QOL, and satisfaction in domains of life; and various coping frameworks.

Research on the adjustment and adaptation to disability has revealed that (a) no overriding personality type is associated with a specific disability, (b) there is no simple or direct relationship between adjustment and the severity of the disability, and (c) adjustment to disability is an individual reaction and similar people with similar disabilities react differently.

Some of the factors that psychosocial adaptation and coping research has associated with more positive psychosocial outcomes are the ability to develop resources (internal and external) to cope with change, social support, and finding of positive consequences or meaning in CID.

Coping styles and strategies and personal characteristics associated with more positive psycho-social outcomes include higher levels of optimism, an active and problem-focused coping style (person's attention focused on what can be done to change the situation [manage the source of the problem; actively plan, seek information and social support, and express feelings]), information seeking, and the presence of an internal locus of control. Research also supports the idea that people often initially experience high levels of psychological distress with CID, but for most people, this distress appears to be a temporary state that diminishes over time.

II. Models and Frameworks of Adjustment or Adaptation to Chronic Illness and Disability

Models and conceptual frameworks of adaptation to CID have been part of the field of rehabilitation counseling for well over half a century and incorporate a wide spectrum of views on the nature of CID and the processes of adapting to the changes associated with living with a CID. In this section we provide an overview of key models or categories of models of adaptation to CID.

Wright's somatopsychological approach and acceptance of disability. Beatrice Wright and other researchers in the somatopsychological tradition proposed a number of perspectives on adaptation to CID that continue to influence the field of rehabilitation counseling. These include the importance of recognizing the influence of the environment in understanding the individual's response (Barker, Wright, & Gonick, 1946; Wright, 1960, 1983); the distinction between the insider (i.e., individual experiencing the CID) and outsider (e.g., professionals, family members, persons in social network, society perspectives); and the transformation of values following the onset of CID (Dembo, Leviton, & Wright, 1956; Wright, 1960, 1983). The transformation of values framework describes the following changes associated with accepting disability: (a) enlarging the scope of values (realizing values other than those affected by disability); (b) containing disability effects (limiting the impact of the condition); (c) subordinating physique (seeing body image as other than a symbol of worth and desirability) and reconceptualizing physical attributes; and (d) transforming comparative status values into asset values (focusing on one's assets versus comparing oneself to others).

Stage/phase models. In stage or phase models, the process of adjustment is seen as a gradual, developmental process of assimilating the changes in body, self-concept, and person–environment interaction. Theories propose that the individual passes through a series of stages or phases of response, typically including reactions such as shock, denial, anger, depression, and eventually, acceptance and adjustment. Criticisms of the various stage or phase models include (a) that the proposed reactions to CID are not universally experienced, (b) that a state of final adjustment is not in reality experienced but that the process of adjustment is cyclical or recurring, and (c) that the concept of unavoidable stages may lead professionals to withhold or delay interventions while waiting for the client to experience some stage or level of adjustment. Many clinicians and researchers do, however, support the existence of observable phases of reaction, although they may not be temporally ordered and discrete (i.e., one following the other in established and well-defined order).

Ecological or integrative models. Ecological or integrative models of adaptation suggest that adjustment depends on the balance between the individual's available personal, social, and environmental resources and the demands on resources in the person's environment. The process of adjustment is seen as being mediated by characteristics inherent in the individual, the event or transition, and the environment. Ecological or integrative models suggest that in considering the personal impact of CID, professionals must consider characteristics of the individual, including personal, economic, psychological, and social resources; the sociocultural and physical environment; and the condition or disability.

Individual variables to be considered include the person's gender, age, ethnicity, assets and resources, and education. Also considered are personality variables, level of family and social support, and coping style (e.g., emotion focused—focus is on alleviating emotional distress and changing the meaning of the problem; avoidant—disengagement, denial, wishful thinking; or active and problem focused). Environmental variables to be considered include one's family response and relationships within the family, family support, social support, community and financial resources, availability of assistive technology and resources for modification, and the physical environment in which the individual lives and works. Variables associated with the disability or illness include time and type of onset, course and prognosis, level of controllability or predictability, treatability, visibility, perceived cause and stigma associated with the condition, severity, functions impaired, pain, lethality, and prognosis (Livneh, 2001; Livneh & Antonak, 1997; Smart, 2009).

Quality of life models. Finally, several researchers have proposed QOL-based models of adaptation to disability (Bishop, 2005; Devins et al., 1983; Devins, Bezjak, Mah, Loblaw, & Gotowiec, 2006; Livneh, 2001; Livneh, Bishop, & Anctil, 2014; Schwartz & Sprangers, 2000). Generally, these models suggest that adaptation can be assessed and understood in terms of the effect of CID on QOL and the processes by which one attempts to restore or maintain QOL. Livneh (2001), for example, proposed that successful adaptation is reflected in the ability to effectively re-establish and manage both the external environment and one's internal experiences to attain improved QOL.

III. Family Response to Disability and the Rehabilitation Counseling Process

The client undergoing rehabilitation counseling is generally a member of family and social systems that may both affect and be affected by the rehabilitation counseling process. As part of a holistic approach, rehabilitation counselors have an ethical responsibility, with consent from the client, to enlist the support of family members as a positive resource in the rehabilitation counseling process, if appropriate. Research has demonstrated the influence of a client's family on the rehabilitation process and outcomes. For example, research shows that attending to the emotional health of the family is positively correlated with the client's functional level (Hart et al., 2007) and employability (Sander et al., 2002), feelings of independence and competence, adherence to treatment, and adaptation. Alternatively, failure to address family issues or dysfunctional dynamics can have a negative influence on the client, which may result in unproductive rehabilitation efforts and hinder psychosocial adaptation. Rehabilitation professionals also know that families can have a powerful influence in the lives and development of children with disabilities (Lustig, 2002). Therefore, an important aspect of the rehabilitation counselor's role includes "a thorough understanding of the family stress and coping process" (Kosciulek, McCubbin, & McCubbin, 1993, p. 41).

To assess the client's family situation, in addition to demographic information, the counselor might discuss family communication patterns, the division of labor within the family, family health or illness, the impact of the CID on the family and the family's reaction to the disability, and the family's attitude toward the rehabilitation counseling process (Power & Dell Orto, 1980). In addition, the family's resilience, coping processes, and adaptation can be assessed using a wide variety of inventories designed for the purpose (Frain, Bishop, Frain, Tansey, & Tschopp, 2007).

Almost one in three Americans care for a family member with CID, and this number will likely rise due to an aging population and medical advances that prolong life. With the onset of CID, family members may experience a range of adverse physical and psychosocial effects, including depression, anxiety, stress associated with changes in family roles and available social support, substance use, communication difficulties, and health problems

(Frain et al., 2007). For families of a child with a disability, adjustment involves coping with the educational implications of the disability, dealing with the reactions of peer groups, accessing community resources, adjusting emotionally to the chronicity of the CID, adjusting family roles, dealing with the financial implications and caregiving requirements, planning for future vocational development, and arranging for socialization opportunities in the community (Frain et al., 2007; Lustig, 2002).

The process of family adaptation to CID encompasses the ways in which the family responds to stress or crisis in light of available resources and coping strategies. The family's response may be affected by factors such as (a) characteristics of, and prior experiences with, the disability; (b) the client's immediate and ongoing response to living with the disability; and (c) the existing and historical characteristics of the family, including demographic and sociocultural variables, the physical and social environment in which the family lives, and the nature and patterns of relationships and communication among family members (Frain et al., 2014).

To successfully adapt to the caregiving role, families may use coping strategies to help alleviate the increased burden and stress commensurate with this new dynamic. Inadequate coping strategies have been found to relate to increased distress and decreased caregiver QOL, including interpersonal, intrapersonal, and extrapersonal functioning (Chronister & Chan, 2007). When a person is confronted with a situation appraised as stressful, coping mediates emotional responses, which ultimately allows for more adaptive outcomes (Folkman & Lazarus, 1988). Much research on coping delineates two primary coping strategies: problem-focused and emotion-focused coping. Problem-focused coping (e.g., making of a plan of action, problem solving) is viewed as directly addressing the issue that causes distress, whereas emotion-focused coping (e.g., denial, reframing) is focused on decreasing the negative emotions associated with the stressor. Although the research is mixed, problem-focused coping appears to be associated with more positive long-term outcomes.

A variety of coping techniques have been found to be effective in handling the stresses associated with family adjustment to CID. Cognitive beliefs that positively affect family adjustment include a shared commitment and purpose, a positive reframing of life and events, and social comparisons that enhance self-esteem (Lustig, 2002). Receiving assistance from friends, extended family, support groups, and professionals has also been found to promote effective coping. Other factors predicting positive coping include the capacity to balance various roles (e.g., spouse, employee, parent), religious beliefs, and the ability to get periods of rest and breaks from caregiving responsibilities (Lustig, 2002).

Rehabilitation Counseling With Older Americans

In this section we discuss rehabilitation counseling issues associated with aging and older Americans. We discuss employment trends and changing health circumstances that affect the professional practice of rehabilitation counselors working with this population.

Learning Objectives

By the end of this unit you should be able to:

1. Describe the current status and trends in employment among older Americans.
2. Identify key rehabilitation counseling issues associated with CID among older Americans.

Key Concepts

I. Older Americans: Overview

The proportion of the United States and world population of persons aged 65 and over is rapidly growing. In 2014, there were 46.2 million Americans in this age group, aproximately 10 million more than in 2004, and the current number is expected to double to about 98 million by 2060 (Administration on Aging, 2015). Older Americans represent approximately 14.5% of the U.S. population, or about one in seven Americans. By 2040, this percentage is expected to reach about 21%, or more than one in five Americans (Administration on Aging, 2015).

As the United States' population ages, the older adult population will become more culturally and ethnically diverse. Between 2014 and 2030, the population of White non-Hispanics aged 65 and over is expected to increase by 46% compared with 110% for older ethnic minority populations, including Hispanics (137%), African Americans (90%), American Indian and Native Alaskans (93%), and Asians (104%) (Administration on Aging, 2015). By 2050, older non-Hispanic White adults will represent only about 58% of the U.S. population aged 65 or older, whereas between 2010 and 2050, the proportion of Hispanics is expected to almost triple from 7% to almost 20%, Asian Americans to increase from 3.3% to 8.5%, and African Americans to increase from 8.3% to 11.2% (Centers for Disease Control and Prevention [CDC], 2013).

Americans in the Baby Boom generation, which includes the large section of the U.S. population, who were born between 1945 and 1964, are currently reaching or approaching traditional retirement age. This population shift, frequently referred to as "'the graying of America'" is having, and will continue to have, an important impact on U.S. employment and health demographics.

II. Older Americans and Employment

Between 2000 and 2018, the number of workers in the 55–64 age group will have roughly doubled (from 14.4 to around 28.8 million; U.S. Census Bureau, 2011). As a result, older workers are one of the fastest growing subsets of the U.S. labor market. Because the likelihood of having a disability increases with age (Tishman, Van Looy, & Bruyere, 2012), older workers with disabilities are predicted to become and remain a greater proportion of VR caseloads (Barros-Bailey, Fischer, & Saunders, 2007). An increasing number of older Americans with disabilities depend on employment for financial independence, particularly those affected by dwindling or depleted savings, non-participation in Social Security, shifts in company pension and insurance benefits, and public health care systems that have not accommodated the growing population of older Americans (Wadsworth, Estrada-Hernandez, Kampfe, & Smith, 2008).

A number of barriers face older workers with disabilities in obtaining and retaining employment. In addition to barriers facing persons with disabilities, older workers may face negative employer and coworker attitudes and age-related discrimination, limiting workplace (e.g., inflexible work schedules) and social environments, and increasingly challenging and increasingly complex workplace conditions (Kettaneh, Kinyanjui, Slevin, Slevin, & Harley, 2015).

In the rehabilitation counseling literature, the focus on issues related to older adults with disabilities has been very limited (Kettaneh et al., 2015), and there is, as yet, little information in the way of evidence-based or effective practices specific to this population, rehabilitation counselors working with older clients should be aware of and prepared to educate clients and employers about relevant legislation and accommodations, including assistive technology that may ameliorate functional barriers to employment.

Relevant pieces of legislation that protect older people with disabilities from discrimination and address health and employment supports for older Americans include the Civil Rights Act of 1964, the Older Americans Act of 1965, the Age Discrimination in Employment Act of 1967 (Pub. L. No. 90–202), the Americans with Disabilities Act of 1990 and Americans With Disabilities Act Amendments Act (ADAAA) of 2008, and the Patient Protection and Affordable Care Act of 2010. Familiarity with Medicaid, Medicare, and Social Security disability programs is also necessary for rehabilitation counseling with older Americans.

III. Older Americans, Health, and Disability

As people age, the probability of acquiring a disability or chronic illness increases dramatically (Barros-Bailey et al., 2007). According to 2010 U.S. Census data, among Americans between the ages 65 and 69 the incidence of disability is 35.0%, between 70 and 74 the incidence is 42.6%, between 75 and 80 the incidence is 53.6%, and among people 80 and older the incidence is 70.5% (Brault, 2012). The likelihood of having multiple disabilities or chronic conditions also increases with age. Approximately two thirds of older Americans have multiple chronic conditions.

According to 2010 U.S. Census data, approximately 11% of Americans aged 65 and older had difficulty hearing; 18% had difficulty seeing, hearing, or speaking; and about 40% had difficulty with ambulatory activities. With the continued aging of the Baby Boom generation, along with the significant increase in life expectancies for all Americans (Wickert, Dresden, & Rumrill, 2013), the rate of hearing loss in America has grown 160% since the early 1980s (Roessler, Rubin, & Rumrill, 2016). Other chronic illnesses and health conditions prevalent among older Americans include hypertension and other cardiovascular diseases, mental illness, diabetes, arthritis, cancer, and stroke.

An important component in the rehabilitation counselor's ability to effectively serve older individuals is understanding the significant impact of mental health on employment-related and general functioning (Swett & Bishop, 2003). Because of the prevalence of mental health disorders among older Americans and the potential impact of these disorders on function and rehabilitation, it is vital that rehabilitation counselors be prepared to recognize and deal with mental health problems.

Mental illness, particularly depression and anxiety, is a significant problem for older adults. Approximately 25% of adults aged 65 years or older report some type of mental health problem, with the most common conditions including anxiety, severe cognitive impairment, and mood disorders (CDC, 2013; CDC & National Association of Chronic Disease Directors [NACDD], 2008). About 15% of Americans aged 65 or older have been told by a health professional that they have a depressive disorder (including depression, major depression, dysthymia, or minor depression; United Health Foundation, 2016). Most important, prevalence rates of mental illness among older adults are lower for individuals living in the community compared with those of residents of nursing or long-term medical and residential care facilities.

It is important that rehabilitation counselors, and their older clients, understand that depression is not a normal part of aging and that is a treatable condition. Research suggests that older adults with depression and anxiety generally benefit from both counseling and psychotropic medications. Unfortunately, depression and related conditions are under-recognized and often untreated or under-treated among older adults (American Psychological Association [APA], 2016; CDC & NACDD, 2008). Furthermore, there is an insufficient number of adequately trained professionals to provide mental and behavioral health services to older adults (APA, 2016).

Chronic medical disorders commonly occur with psychiatric disorders (e.g., depression and anxiety) and are an established risk factor. The high co-occurrence of medical with mental health issues in the elderly population may be attributable to a number of precipitating factors, including multiple personal losses, chronic insomnia, risk factors of heart disease and stroke, neurodegenerative diseases, progressive reduction in the number of social supports, diminished role functioning, and limited access to adequate treatment (Reynolds, Alexopoulos, Katz, & Lebowitz, 2001).

In summary, recent and expected sociodemographic changes have led to an increased need for awareness among rehabilitation counselors of the employment and disability issues of older Americans with disabilities. Trends toward increased labor force participation and increased disability among older Americans will translate into opportunities for rehabilitation counselors to increasingly serve older consumers. Based on their comprehensive training in case management, disability, and employment issues, rehabilitation counselors have a combination of knowledge and skills that enable them to effectively address the needs of older adults (Bishop, Boland, & Sheppard-Jones, 2008; Swett & Bishop, 2003).

Disability and Sexuality

Learning Objectives

By the end of this unit you should be able to:

1. Describe the historical issues and current perspectives on sexuality and disability.
2. Describe the importance of sexuality to consumers of rehabilitation counselors.
3. Discuss the rehabilitation counselor's roles related to clients' sexuality and disability.

Key Concepts

Sexuality has been recognized as one of the most significant psychosocial factors in an individual's life. Sexual adjustment has been recognized as one of the key components of overall rehabilitation success (Kazukauskas & Lam, 2010). Sexuality is important to the rehabilitation process because of its close relationship to self-esteem, body image, and overall well-being (Juergens, Smedema, & Berven, 2009).

I. Historical and Current Perspectives on Disability and Sexuality

Historically, the sexuality of individuals with disabilities has been disregarded and stigmatized by society (Esmail, Darry, Walter, & Knupp, 2010). Reasons for this failure to recognize individuals with disabilities as having sexual needs stemmed from lack of public education and limited exposure to topics related to sexuality and disability (Esmail et al., 2010). Prior to the 1970s, there was limited research conducted on sexuality and disability. The research that was conducted during this era was derived from the medical model, which was also the key model for research related to disability studies (Esmail et al., 2010).

Traditional models of sexual response focus on a linear, staged sequence of physiological functioning. In Masters and Johnson's model (1966), which remains a widely accepted model of sexual functioning, "normal" sexual response moves through four stages: excitement, plateau, orgasm, and resolution. Use of these types of physiological models of sexual response can be problematic for addressing the sexual health and sexuality issues of individuals with disabilities because the healthy functional sexual response may be more varied, although this does not make the sexual functioning any less satisfying (Di Giulio, 2003).

Over the past 20 years, the social model (see Table 3.5) has become the predominant model used for both sexuality and disability studies (Esmail et al., 2010; Sakellariou, 2006). Current research is looking at the public's response to individuals with disabilities and society's inability to remove attitudinal and environmental barriers. Because of the increased shift toward the social model, sexual development is now recognized as a multidimensional process that is greatly influenced by society. Societal barriers are one of the key issues individuals with disabilities face in regard to sexuality. In the United States, a new view of sexuality is developing, with sexuality being recognized as more than just physical performance and as also including emotional closeness and pleasure (Esmail et al., 2010).

II. Sexuality in Rehabilitation Counseling

Sexuality is one of the most significant psychosocial factors in a person's life; this is true for individuals with and without disabilities (Kazukauskas & Lam, 2010). Sexual adjustment is predictive of overall disability adjustment, QOL, body image, and self-esteem (Juergens et al., 2009; Kazukauskas & Lam, 2010). Sexual adjustment is also increasingly being seen as an important part of the overall rehabilitation process. The presence of a disability affects an individual's ability to find a partner and personal confidence levels in the area of sexuality (Esmail et al., 2010). Taleporos, Dip, and McCabe (2002) found that sexual esteem and sexual satisfaction were strong predictors of self-esteem in individuals with physical disabilities and that individuals with physical disabilities had a lower likelihood of feeling depressed if they felt good about their bodies and were satisfied sexually (Taleporos et al., 2002).

III. Rehabilitation Counselors' Roles in Clients' Sexuality and Disability

Sexuality is a topic that is commonly left out of the rehabilitation process (Kazukauskas & Lam, 2009). Reasons for this range from limited staff knowledge and training, negative attitudes about disability and sexuality and discomfort in discussing sexuality issues with consumers (Kazukauskas & Lam, 2009). Certified rehabilitation counselors (CRC® counselors [CRCs]) can play a key role in helping consumers acquire knowledge about sexuality and disability. As part of the holistic rehabilitation counseling process, sexuality is an issue that consumers may feel comfortable discussing with CRCs (Kazukauskas & Lam, 2009). Topics that CRCs should be prepared to discuss include the areas of fertility, sexual expression, prevention of unwanted pregnancy, prevention of sexual abuse, establishment of a sexual relationship with a partner, dating, and sexual orientation (Juergens et al., 2009). CRCs should be prepared to conduct a detailed interview when sexuality issues arise. Information that can be gathered during the interview process with the client may include sexual expectations, sexual knowledge, and more specific questions related to the disability and sexuality (Juergens et al., 2009). Clients may seek information about the sexual response cycle, sexual anatomy, ways that the individual's specific disability may affect sexual functioning, and ways that various treatments and medications may affect sexuality. Along with providing information to consumers, CRCs should also be prepared to make relevant resources available to clients so that referrals can be made to other professionals trained in the area of sexuality (Jeurgen et al., 2009).

TABLE 3.5   Key Concepts in Disability and Sexuality

Key Concept	Summary
Sexuality	Sexuality is a collection of characteristics that identify and communicate the sexual nature of an individual (Dombrowski, Petrick, & Strauss, 2000).
Social model of disability	Disability is the result of a social structure that excludes certain people from accessing employment, social resources, and positive identities. It is not an individual possessive trait, but rather an external, socially mediated phenomenon (Esmail et al., 2010).

Learning Styles

Learning Objectives

By the end of this unit you should be able to:

1. Define *learning styles*.
2. Discuss what rehabilitation counselors can do to assist consumers with different learning styles.

Key Concepts

Learning styles refer to the idea that individuals learn in different ways. Individuals have different ways of instruction and studying that are more effective for them (Pashler, McDaniel, Rohrer, & Bjork, 2009). Learning styles are described as an aspect of individual's personality and, because of this, learning styles are not expected to change in the short term (Serife, 2008). The idea of learning styles has been gaining increased influence over the years in the United States. Educators and psychologists have embraced the idea of learning styles, while educational psychologist and teachers are being taught that students have different learning and are urged to accommodate through varied instructional methods (Pashler et al., 2009).

I. Learning Styles

Although several models of learning styles (Entwistle, 1981; Felder & Silverman, 1988; Honey & Mumford, 1982; Kolb, 1984; Pask, 1976) have been developed, each model describes different aspects of how people prefer to learn. For example, Felder and Silverman describe learning styles in terms of four dimensions, combining major learning style models (Liu & Graf, 2009). In broad strokes, the styles include (Felder & Silverman, 1988):

1. Active/reflective learners. Active learners retain and understand information best through activity, such as discussing, applying, or explaining the information. Reflective learners prefer to think through the material and tend to prefer working alone.
2. Sensing/intuitive learners. Sensing learners prefer learning facts, whereas intuitive learners prefer discovering possibilities and relationships.
3. Visual/verbal learners. Visual learners remember best what they see. Verbal learners remember words, both written and spoken, best.

4. Sequential/global learners. Sequential learners gain understanding in logical, linear steps. Global learners absorb material in terms of the big picture.

Dunn and Dunn (as cited in Heiman, 2006; Honigsfeld & Dunn, 2006) described five factors that influence an individual's learning style. These include environmental situation, personal–emotional characteristics, sociological preferences for learning, physiological characteristics, and global aspects. In addition, individuals have preferred strategies of learning, which include visual, tactual, auditory, and kinesthetic (Honigsfeld & Dunn, 2006).

II. Assisting Consumers With Different Learning Styles

Learning style theorists recommend that CRC students explore their own individual learning styles. As a result, they will be better able to deal with the academic goals they are striving to meet and will better able to handle the stress associated with entering the academic world (Heiman, 2006). However, researchers have recently suggested that using learning styles to deliver educational material has a number of limitations (e.g., Riener & Willingham, 2010; Scott, 2010). Although there is ample evidence of individual learning preferences, few studies have found any validity in using learning styles in education (Willingham, Hughes, & Dobolyi, 2015).

Multiple-Choice Questions

1. Which of the following theories of human development is best supported by studies involving both monozygotic and dizygotic twins?

   A. Nurturist perspective

   B. Combined perspective

   C. Nativist perspective

   D. Studies with twins have not been conducted in this regard

2. What is the correct order of Freud's stages of psychosexual development?

   A. Anal, oral, latency, phallic, genital

   B. Oral, anal, phallic, latency, genital

   C. Phallic, oral, anal, latency, genital

   D. Genital, oral, anal, phallic, latency

3. During Freud's stage of psychosexual development, there is a repression of sexual interest and energy, which are replaced with more personally acceptable objects.

   A. Phallic stage

   B. Anal stage

   C. Genital stage

   D. Latency stage

4. Which of the following differentiates Erikson's psychosocial stages of development from Freud's psychosexual stages?

   A. Erikson's psychosocial stages extended beyond adolescence.

   B. Erikson's psychosocial stages are empirically validated.

   C. Erikson's psychosocial stages did not include infancy.

   D. Erikson's psychosocial stages focused on unconscious processes.

5. Concepts critical to Piaget's stages of cognitive development include all of the following *EXCEPT*:

   A. Age-specific stages

   B. Assimilation

   C. Schema

   D. Accommodation

6. Bandura's theory of development is best known as:

   A. Social development theory

   B. Behavioral development theory

   C. Social cognitive theory

   D. Sociocultural theory

7. According to Wright's somatopsychological approach to adaptation, which of the following is not included in the transformation of values framework?

   A. Transforming comparative status values into asset values

   B. Subordinating the physique

   C. Accepting one's disability and what has been lost

   D. Enlarging the scope of values

8. According to the research, which coping strategy appears to be associated with more positive long-term outcomes?

   A. Reframing

   B. Problem focused

   C. Emotion focused

   D. Denial

9. Rehabilitation counselors need to be particularly aware of the significant impact of _____ on employment and general functioning of older Americans.

   A. Physical health

   B. Fatigue

   C. Mental health

   D. Ambivalence

10. Sexuality is considered important in the rehabilitation counseling process due to its close relationship with all of the following *EXCEPT*:

A. Overall well-being

B. Self-esteem

C. Body image

D. All of the above

Answer Key

1C, 2B, 3D, 4A, 5A, 6C, 7C, 8B, 9C, 10D

Advanced Multiple-Choice Questions

1. An individual who learns best by discussing concepts with another uses which learning style?

A. Sensing/intuitive learning

B. Active/reflective learning

C. Sequential/global learning

D. Visual/verbal learning

2. When considering the nature versus nurture debate, the majority of developmental psychologists believe development is most likely based on _____.

A. Nature

B. Nurture

C. A combination of both

D. There is no clear consensus

3. Which of the following is not considered a criticism of Freud's theory of psychosexual development?

A. Freud developed his theory late in life.

B. His theory lacks appropriate scientific rigor.

C. His theory was based on the biases of the era in which he lived.

D. His theory is highly sexist.

4. Billy has learned to feed himself with a spoon. When his mother gives him a fork, he immediately begins to use it appropriately. Billy has _____ the fork into his schema for eating utensils.

A. Appropriated

B. Initiated

C. Assimilated

D. Accommodated

5. Which of the following are true regarding adjustment and adaptation to chronic illness and disability?

   A. No specific personality types are associated with various disabilities.

   B. No direct relationship exists between one's adjustment and the severity of the disability/illness.

   C. Adjustment is an individual process—all may react differently.

   D. All of the above

6. Which of the following is true regarding the stage/phase models of adaptation to chronic illness and disability?

   A. All individuals progress through an ordered sequence of reactions in the same way.

   B. Adaptation occurs quicker if the disability or illness is less severe.

   C. The process of adjustment is a gradual, individualized developmental process of assimilation to changes.

   D. Treatment should be withheld until the individual reaches the appropriate stage.

7. Adequately enlisting the involvement of an individual's family and/or support system has been shown to _____.

   A. Impede the process of adaptation

   B. Result in higher paying employment opportunities

   C. Be positively correlated with the individual's functional level

   D. None of the above

8. Factors associated with effective family coping techniques include:

   A. Positive reframing

   B. Religious beliefs

   C. Respite

   D. All of the above

9. Which of the following groups will be one of the fastest growing populations in the labor market in the coming years?

   A. Hispanics

   B. Women

   C. Older workers

   D. Youth

10. For older adults, which of the following is considered the primary concern in terms of functional limitations?

    A. Changes in eyesight

    B. Hearing loss

    C. Mobility limitations

    D. All of the above

Answer Key and Explanation of Answers

1B: Active learners have a preference for developing an understanding for new information through active discussion, application, or explanation of novel concepts. Although active/reflective is a combined learning strategy, reflective learners, on the contrary, prefer to contemplate new material and often like to work independently. An important note is that although individuals may have a preferred learning style, he/she may appreciate alternative styles in different situations.

2C: The nature versus nurture debate has existed for decades, and proponents of each continue to provide evidence for the developmental approach of their choosing. Although this debate continues, the majority of developmental psychologists agree that development can be described as a combination of nature (e.g., heredity, genetics) and nurture (e.g., cultural, familial). This view has spawned the research area known as *epigenetics*.

3A: Although many of Freud's concepts greatly influenced the field of clinical psychology, debate continues regarding the soundness of his theory of psychosexual development. Little of Freud's psychosexual theory can be validated through the use of rigorous scientific methods. Moreover, many question the validity of his theory because there is a lack of generalizability, meaning that his subjects (Victorian-era women) were quite different from those of today's society. Finally, supporters of feminist theory believe Freud's theory to be sexist and overly reliant on a male perspective.

4C: Piaget called the schema the basic building block of intelligent behavior—a way of organizing knowledge. Indeed, it is useful to think of schemas as "units" of knowledge, each relating to one aspect of the world, including objects, actions, and abstract concepts. Assimilation entails using an existing schema (e.g., using a spoon to eat) to deal with a new object (e.g., fork) or situation. Accommodation, however, is when an existing schema does not work and needs to be changed in order to deal with a new object or situation.

5D: There exist a number of theories conceptualizing the process of adjustment to chronic illness and disability. All of these theories seem to agree on a few key factors: (a) There is no overriding personality type associated with given disability, (b) there is no direct relationship between adjustment and the severity of the disability, and (c) adjustment to disability is a highly individual process, so similar people with similar disabilities may react quite differently.

6C: In stage/phase models of adjustment, the process is best explained as a gradual, developmental process of assimilating changes in body, self-concept, and the person–environment interaction. Although it is proposed that individuals with disabilities experience a variety of responses (e.g., shock, denial, anger, depression, acceptance), not every individual experiences all reactions, nor are experiences necessarily orderly.

7C: Rehabilitation counseling emphasizes a holistic approach to working with clients, and as such, rehabilitation counselors have an ethical responsibility to enlist family members as positive resources. The emotionally healthy family's influence on the rehabilitation process has been shown to positively correlate with the client's functional level, employability, feelings of competence, adherence to treatments, and ultimate adaptation. However, the family's influence can also be counterproductive to the rehabilitation process if internal issues fail to be addressed.

8D: As part of the caregiving role and support system, families undoubtedly use various coping strategies to allow them to deal with the increased stress associated with the new dynamic. A number of coping strategies have proved effective for families as they begin the adjustment process. These include positive reframing of life and events, social comparisons that enhance self-esteem, support groups, religious beliefs, and periods of rest from new responsibilities.

9C: The proportion of the U.S. population aged 65 and over is rapidly increasing. By 2018, workers aged 55–64 will approach 29 million, so older workers will be one of the fastest growing subsets in the labor market. Moreover, older workers are predicted to become an even greater proportion of vocational rehabilitation caseloads.

10D: As individuals live longer, the chances of acquiring a disability increases dramatically. Hearing loss, poor eyesight, and mobility issues are particularly prevalent among older individuals. However, one of the most significant issues for the aged is mental illness (e.g., depression, anxiety). Considering the rapid growth in older adults remaining in or reentering the workforce, understanding the potential complications that occur in the older population is critical for rehabilitation counselors.

References

Administration on Aging. (2015). A profile of older Americans: 2015. Retrieved from https://www.acl.gov/sites/default/files/Aging%20and%20Disability%20in%20America/2015-Profile.pdf

American Psychological Association. (2016). Mental and behavioral health and older Americans. Retrieved from http://www.apa.org/about/gr/issues/aging/mental-health.aspx

Bandura, A. (1977). *Social learning theory.* New York, NY: General Learning Press.

Bandura, A. (1986). *Social foundations of thought and action: A social cognitive theory.* Englewood Cliffs, NJ: Prentice Hall.

Barker, R. G., Wright, B. A., & Gonick, M. R. (1946). *Adjustment to physical handicap and illness: A survey of the social psychology of physique and disability.* New York, NY: Social Science Research Council.

Barros-Bailey, M., Fischer, J., & Saunders, J. L. (2007). Age, work, and disability: Rehabilitation at the end of the worklife. *Journal of Applied Rehabilitation Counseling, 38*(1), 20–31.

Bishop, M. (2005). Quality of life and psychosocial adaptation to chronic illness and acquired disability: A conceptual and theoretical synthesis. *Journal of Rehabilitation, 71*(2), 5–13.

Bishop, M., Boland, E. A., & Sheppard-Jones, K. (2008). Human growth and development: Educational and professional challenges and opportunities. *Rehabilitation Education, 22*(4), 267–276.

Brault, M. W. (2012). *Americans With Disabilities: 2010 current population reports, household economic studies* (Report Number P70-131). Washington, DC: U.S. Census Bureau.

Centers for Disease Control and Prevention. (2013). *The state of aging and health in America 2013.* Atlanta, GA: Centers for Disease Control and Prevention, US Department of Health and Human Services.

Centers for Disease Control and Prevention and National Association of Chronic Disease Directors. (2008). *The state of mental health and aging in America, Issue Brief 1: What do the data tell us?* Atlanta, GA: National Association of Chronic Disease Directors.

Chronister, J., & Chan, F. (2007). Hierarchical coping: A conceptual framework for understanding coping within the context of chronic illness and disability. In E. Martz & H. Livneh (Eds.), *Coping with chronic illness and disability* (pp. 49–71). New York, NY: Springer.

Daniels, H. (2007). Pedagogy. In J. W. Daniels & M. Cole (Eds.), *The Cambridge companion to Vygotsky* (pp. 307–332). New York, NY: Cambridge University Press.

Dansen, P. (1994). Culture and cognitive development from a Piagetian perspective. In W. J. Lonner & R. S. Malpass (Eds.), *Psychology and culture* (pp. 145–149). Boston, MA: Allyn & Bacon.

Dembo, T., Leviton, G. L., & Wright, B. A. (1956). Adjustment to misfortune: A problem of social-psychological rehabilitation. *Artificial Limbs, 3*, 4–62.

Devins, G. M., Bezjak, A., Mah, K., Loblaw, D. A., & Gotowiec, A. P. (2006). Context moderates illness-induced lifestyle disruptions across life domains: A test of the illness intrusiveness theoretical framework in six common cancers. *Psycho-Oncology, 15*, 221–233.

Devins, G. M., Blinik, Y. M., Hutchinson, T. A., Hollomby, D. J., Barre, P. E., & Guttmann, R. D. (1983). The emotional impact of end-stage renal disease: Importance of patients' perceptions of intrusiveness and control. *International Journal of Psychiatry in Medicine, 13*(4), 327–343.

Di Giulio, G. (2003). Sexuality and people living with physical or developmental disabilities: A review of key issues. *Canadian Journal of Human Sexuality, 12*(1), 53–68.

Dombrowski, L. K., Petrick, J. D., & Strauss, D. (2000). Rehabilitation treatment of sexuality issues due to acquired brain injury. *Rehabilitation Psychology, 45*(3), 299–309.

Entwistle, N. J. (1981). *Styles of learning and teaching.* New York, NY: Wiley.

Esmail, S., Darry, K., Walter, A., & Knupp, H. (2010). Attitudes and perceptions towards disability and sexuality. *Disability & Rehabilitation, 32*(14), 1148–1155. doi:10.3109/09638280903419277

Felder, R. M., & Silverman, L. K. (1988). Learning and teaching styles in engineering education. *Engineering Education, 78*(7), 674–681.

Folkman, S., & Lazarus, R. S. (1988). Coping as a mediator of emotion. *Journal of Personality and Social Psychology, 54*(3), 466–475.

Frain, M., & Bishop, M., Frain, J., Tansey, T., & Tschopp. M. K. (2014). The family role in progressive illness. In M. Millington & I. Marini (Eds.), *Families in rehabilitation counseling: A community-based rehabilitation approach* (pp. 171–191). New York, NY: Springer Publishing.

Frain, M. P., Lee, G. K., Berven, N. L., Tansey, T., Tschopp, M. K., & Chronister, J. (2007). Use of the resiliency model of family stress, adjustment and adaptation by rehabilitation counselors. *Journal of Rehabilitation, 73*(3), 18–25.

Gindis, B. (1995). The social/cultural implication of disability: Vygotsky's paradigm for special education. *Educational Psychologist, 30*(2), 77–81.

Hart, T., O'Neil-Pirozzi, T., Williams, K., Rapport, L., Hammond, F., & Kreutzer, J. (2007). Racial differences in caregiving patterns, caregiver emotional function, and sources of emotional support following traumatic brain injury. *Journal of Head Trauma Rehabilitation, 22*, 122–131.

Heiman, T. (2006). Assessing learning styles among students with and without learning disabilities at a distance-learning university. *Learning Disability Quarterly, 29*(1), 55–63.

Honey, P., & Mumford, A. (1982). *The manual of learning styles.* Maidenhead, UK: Peter Honey.

Honigsfeld, A., & Dunn, R. (2006). Learning-style characteristics of adult learners. *Delta Kappa Gamma Bulletin, 72*(2), 14–31.

Juergens, M. H., Smedema, S. M., & Berven, N. L. (2009). Willingness of graduate students in rehabilitation counseling to discuss sexuality with clients. *Rehabilitation Counseling Bulletin, 53*(1), 34–43. doi: 10.1177/0034355209340587

Kazukauskas, K. A., & Lam, C. S. (2009). Importance of addressing sexuality in certified rehabilitation counselor practice. *Rehabilitation Education, 23*(2), 127–140.

Kazukauskas, K. A., & Lam, C. S. (2010). Disability and sexuality: Knowledge, attitudes, and level of comfort among certified rehabilitation counselors. *Rehabilitation Counseling Bulletin, 54*(1), 15–25. doi: 10.1177/0034355209348239

Kettaneh, A. A., Kinyanjui, B., Slevin, J. R., Slevin, B., & Harley, D. A. (2015). Inclusion of aging in rehabilitation counseling journals 2000–2012: A content analysis. *Rehabilitation Research, Policy, and Education, 29*(1), 75–87.

Kolb, D. A. (1984). *Experiential learning: Experience as the source of learning and development.* Englewood Cliffs, NJ: Prentice Hall.

Kosciulek, J. F., McCubbin, M. A., & McCubbin, H. I. (1993). A theoretical framework for family adaptation to head injury. *Journal of Rehabilitation, 59,* 40–45.

Liu, T., & Graf, S. (2009). Coping with mismatched courses: Students' behaviour and performance in courses mismatched to their learning styles. *Educational Technology Research & Development, 57*(6). 739–752.

Livneh, H. (2001). Psychosocial adaptation to chronic illness and disability: A conceptual framework. *Rehabilitation Counseling Bulletin, 44*(3), 151–160.

Livneh, H., & Antonak, R. F. (1997). *Psychosocial adaptation to chronic illness and disability.* Gaithersburg, MD: Aspen.

Livneh, H., & Bishop, M. (2012). Psychosocial impact of chronic illness and disability. In R. M. Parker & J. B. Patterson (Eds.) *Rehabilitation counseling: Basics and beyond* (5th ed., pp. 167–198). Austin, TX: Pro-Ed.

Livneh, H., Bishop, M., & Anctil, T. (2014). Modern models of psychosocial adaptation to chronic illness and disability as viewed through the prism of Lewin's field theory: A comparative review. *Rehabilitation Research, Policy, and Education, 28*(3), 126–142.

Lustig, D. C. (2002). Family coping in families with a child with a disability. *Education and Training in Mental Retardation and Developmental Disabilities, 37*(1), 14–22.

Parker, R. M., Schaller, J., & Hansmann, S. (2003). Catastrophe, chaos, and complexity models and psychosocial adjustment to disability. *Rehabilitation Counseling Bulletin, 46,* 234–241.

Pashler, H., McDaniel, M., Rohrer, D., & Bjork, R. (2009). Learning styles: Concepts and evidence. *Psychological Science in the Public Interest, 9*(3), 105–119. doi:10.1111/j.1539-6053.2009.01038.x

Pask, G. (1976). Styles and strategies of learning. *The British Journal of Educational Psychology, 46,* 128–148.

Power, P., & Dell Orto, A. (1980). *Role of the family in the rehabilitation of the physically disabled.* Baltimore, MD: University Park Press.

Reynolds, C. F., Alexopoulos, G. S., Katz, I. R., & Lebowitz, B. D. (2001). Chronic depression in the elderly. *Drugs and Aging, 18,* 507–514.

Riener, C., & Willingham, D. (2010). The myth of learning styles. *Change, 42*(5), 32–35.

Roessler, R. T., Rubin, S. E., & Rumrill, P. D. (2016). *Foundations of the vocational rehabilitation process* (7th ed.). Austin, TX: Pro-Ed.

Sakellariou, D. (2006). If not the disability, then what? barriers to reclaiming sexuality following spinal cord injury. *Sexuality & Disability, 24*(2), 101–111. doi:10.1007/s11195-006-9008-6

Sander, A., Caroselli, J., High, W., Becker, C., Neese, L., & Scheibel, R. (2002). Relationship between family functioning in a post-acute rehabilitation program following traumatic brain injury. *Brain Injury, 8,* 649–657.

Schwartz, C. E., Sprangers, M. A. G. (2000). *Adaptation to changing health: Response shift in quality of life research.* Washington, DC: American Psychological Association.

Scott, C. (2010). The enduring appeal of learning styles. *Australian Journal of Education, 54*(1), 5–17.

Serife, A. K. (2008). A conceptual analysis on the approaches to learning. *Educational Sciences: Theory and Practice, 8*(3), 707–720.

Smart, J. (2009). *Disability, society, and the individual* (2nd ed.). Austin, TX: Pro-Ed.

Smith, P. K., Cowie, H., & Blades, M. (1998). *Understanding children's development* (3rd ed.). Oxford, UK: Blackwell.

Sternberg, R. J. (2011). Individual differences in cognitive development. In U. Goswami (Ed.), *The Wiley-Blackwell handbook of childhood cognitive development* (2nd ed., pp. 749–774). Hoboken, NJ: Wiley-Blackwell.

Swett, E. A., & Bishop, M. (2003). Mental health and the aging population: Implications for rehabilitation counselors. *Journal of Rehabilitation, 69*(2), 13–18.

Taleporos, G., Dip, G., & McCabe, M. P. (2002). The impact of sexual esteem, body esteem, and sexual satisfaction on psychological well-being in people with physical disability. *Sexuality & Disability, 20*(3), 177–183.

Tishman, F. M., Van Looy, S. V., & Bruyere, S. M. (2012). *Employer strategies for responding to an aging workforce.* New Brunswick, NJ: National Technical Assistance and Research Center to Promote Leadership for Increasing the Employment and Economic Independence of Adults with Disabilities.

United Health Foundation. (2016). America's health rankings: Depression in the United States. Retrieved from http://www.americashealthrankings.org/ALL/depression_sr

U.S. Census Bureau. (2011). *Statistical abstract of the United States: 2011* (130th ed.). Section 12: Labor force, employment, and earnings. Washington, DC: U.S. Government Printing Office. Retrieved from https://www2.census.gov/library/publications/2010/compendia/statab/130ed/tables/labor.pdf

Vander Zanden, J. W., Crandell, T. L., Crandell, C. H. (2007). *Human development* (8th ed.). New York, NY: McGraw-Hill.

Vygotsky, L. S. (1978). *Mind in society: The development of higher psychological processes.* Cambridge, MA: Harvard University Press.

Wadsworth, J. S., Estrada-Hernandez, N., Kampfe, C. M., & Smith, S. M. (2008). Economic outcome of employment for older participants in rehabilitation services funded by the Rehabilitation Services. *Rehabilitation Counseling Bulletin, 51,* 107–117.

Wickert, K., Dresden, D., & Rumrill, P. (2013). *The sandwich generations' guide to eldercare.* New York, NY: Demos.

Willingham, D. T., Hughes, E. M., & Dobolyi, D. G. (2015). The scientific status of learning styles theories. *Teaching of Psychology, 42*(3), 266–271.

Wright, B. A. (1960). *Physical disability: A psychological approach.* New York, NY: Harper & Row.

Wright, B. A. (1983). *Physical disability: A psychosocial approach.* New York, NY: Harper & Row.

4

Employment and Career Development

CONNIE SUNG, JESSICA M. BROOKS, VERONICA MULLER, DAVID STRAND, KANAKO IWANAGA, AND FONG CHAN

Work is fundamental to the well-being of people with or without disabilities (Chan, Shaw, McMahon, Koch, & Strauser, 1997; Dutta, Gervey, Chan, Chou, & Ditchman, 2008). Compared with persons who are employed, those who are unemployed tend to experience a higher prevalence of depression and anxiety disorders, use alcohol more frequently, and report lower scores on self-esteem and quality of life measures (Dutta et al., 2008). Recognizing its importance, rehabilitation counselors have consistently advocated for work as a fundamental human right of people with disabilities (Chan et al., 1997). Therefore, job placement at the highest level possible has been central to the professional practice of rehabilitation counseling (Chan et al., 1997).

Quality job placements result from quality vocational assessment, counseling, and planning services in the early rehabilitation phases. To facilitate vocational decision making, a rehabilitation client must be exposed systematically to the world of work; develop insights for skills, abilities, interests, and physical functioning; and be sensitive to labor market constraints (Chan et al., 1997). This, in turn, requires the skilled rehabilitation counselor to be knowledgeable about: (a) career-development theories, (b) community resources, (c) medical and psychosocial aspects of disability, (d) vocational implications of different disabling conditions, (e) work demands and requirements of different occupations, (f) job trends and training opportunities in the local and national economy, (g) availability of job accommodation methods and assistive devices for people with disabilities, and (h) job-placement techniques. This chapter reviews occupational information and job analysis, career-development theories, and job-placement models and techniques.

In addition, with the passage of the Workforce Innovation and Opportunity Act of 2014 and the accompanying amendments to the Rehabilitation Act of 1973 (U.S. Department of Labor, 2014), state vocational rehabilitation (VR) agencies are required to focus their efforts on mitigating the barriers to employment faced by individuals with disabilities, with special attention placed on the career development of youth. This legislation mandates that 15% of federal VR funding be allocated to preemployment transition services to improve the employment outcomes and career development of youth with disabilities. These preemployment services represent an investment in the "important connection between education and career preparation" (U.S. Department of Education, 2016). In addition, the Workforce Innovation and Opportunity Act (WIOA) of 2014 calls for "research related to meeting the education and employment needs of eligible youth," and specifically mandates the "development of alternative, evidence-based programs and other activities that enhance the choices available to eligible youth," including youth with disabilities (U.S. Department of Labor, 2016, section. 129).

Given the spirit of legislation mandating expanded transition services to improve outcomes for youth with disabilities, this chapter reviews the components of employment and career development in rehabilitation, occupational information systems, theories related to career development, job analysis and placement strategies, and supported employment. Specific topics include the following:

- Labor market information for career exploration
- Occupational information systems for vocational planning
- Job analysis
- Career-development and specific focus theories
- Career counseling
- Vocational consultation and job placement
- Job-placement assistance and supported employment

Labor Market and Occupational Information for Vocational Planning and Career Decision Making

Overview

Accurate labor market information is one of the essential ingredients of career decision making. Rehabilitation counselors play an influential role in helping people gather, analyze, and use this information. This section discusses current labor market trends and the importance of using labor market and occupational information systems for vocational planning and career decision making.

Learning Objectives

By the end of this unit you should be able to:

1. Understand the current employment situation of people with disabilities.
2. Understand the role of labor market and occupational information systems.

Key Concepts

I. Labor Market Information

The employment rate for individuals with disabilities continues to be unacceptably low. A recent U.S. Bureau of Labor Statistics (BLS) Employment Situation report estimated the employment rate of individuals with disabilities to be 18.0% compared with 63.9% for people without disabilities (BLS, U.S. Department of Labor, 2010). Similarly, the unemployment rate of workers with disabilities is 16.4%, which is significantly higher than the 9.5% rate for workers without disabilities (BLS, U.S. Department of Labor, 2010). Moreover, the recent recession had a disproportionate impact on workers with disabilities. Notably, the number of employed workers with disabilities declined at a rate more than three times that of workers without disabilities, and the unemployment rate rose dramatically to levels exceeding that of other workers (Kaye, 2010). Without a doubt, lack of employment opportunities excludes people with disabilities from full community participation, significantly affecting the quality of their lives.

Dunn (1974) suggested that job placement should be viewed as a program goal instead of a discrete set of activities (helping clients find jobs) that occur in the final stage of the VR process. Rehabilitation counselors must be familiar with labor market information, job requirements, and employer demands in order to help consumers develop appropriate vocational goals consistent with their job performance and capacity early in the VR process. More important, employment demand is changing and is projected to shift because of fundamental structural economic changes (Chan, Strauser, Gervey, & Lee, 2010). The organizational structures of American companies are also changing, so organizations are now flatter and team based, and the emphasis is on flexibility, productivity, and workplace socialization skills. Therefore, rehabilitation professionals must have a thorough understanding of employers' concerns about the hiring and retention of persons with disabilities and be able to address these concerns effectively. Helping people with disabilities develop flexible, versatile, and adaptable work skills to meet employer expectations and requirements for jobs in the new economy will improve their odds of obtaining employment.

Employers are less risk averse in occupations in which the demand is high and the supply of qualified workers is low. Preparing people with disabilities for these occupations will increase their chance of being hired. As a result, a demand-side employment approach is gaining considerable attention in VR. To improve employment rates and employment quality for individuals with disabilities, rehabilitation counselors must be able to identify the largest or fastest growth areas of employment opportunities and be knowledgeable about the skill sets needed for these in-demand occupations. It is important for rehabilitation counselors to be familiar with occupational information and analysis.

Occupational Information Systems

Overview

A variety of systems have been developed for classifying occupational information. Classification generally refers to industries, occupations, and/or instructional programs. This section provides a description of several major job classification systems that are important to the professional practice of rehabilitation counseling.

Learning Objectives

By the end of this unit you should be able to:

1. Understand the function of occupational information systems.
2. Identify commonly used occupational information systems and their designated purposes and features.

I. *Dictionary of Occupational Titles*

The revised fourth edition of *Dictionary of Occupational Titles (DOT)* (www.occupationalinfo .org) was published as two volumes by the U.S. Department of Labor (1991) and included additional information related to the O*NET database (see the next section for more information about O*NET). It is a very comprehensive occupational information resource, covering over 12,000 different types of jobs representative of the U.S. labor market.

The *DOT* uses a nine-digit code to classify occupations. The first digit provides information on one of the nine broad *occupational categories* (see Table 4.1, column 1). *Occupational divisions* (83 divisions) within each of the occupations are denoted by the first two digits, whereas the *occupational groups* (564 groups) within each division are defined by the first three digits. The middle three digits provide information on the worker function (functional demand) ratings for tasks performed in the occupation. The fourth digit refers to worker functions in relationship to *data*; the fifth digit refers to worker functions in relationship to *people*; and the sixth digit refers to worker functions in relationship to *things*. The numerical assignments for each of these relationships are shown in Table 4.1, columns 2 to 4. Finally, the last three-digit set aids in discriminating among closely related jobs within the same occupational group. Note that no two occupations have the same nine-digit code.

Each occupation in *DOT* is analyzed based on job analysis. *DOT* variables are analyzed in terms of necessary or desirable characteristics of the worker that derived from job analysis schedules that include (a) worker functions; (b) vocational aptitudes (see Table 4.2 for the 11 aptitude levels); (c) temperaments (see Table 4.2 for the 11 temperaments); (d) interests; (e) physical demands; (f) working conditions; (g) general educational development, and (h) specific vocational preparation (Mayall, 1994). The physical demands factor is particularly important in job-matching as it provides information about the extent that impairments/functioning can affect job performance and the kinds of accommodations that are needed to enable the person with a disability to perform the essential functions of a particular job. There are seven basic parts to an occupational definition; they present data about a job in a systematic fashion (U.S. Department of Labor, 1991). The parts are listed in the order in which they appear in every definition: occupational code number, occupational title, industry designation, alternate titles (if any), body of the definition, undefined related titles (if any), and definition trailer. Table 4.3 provides an example to illustrate the structure of *DOT* coding.

TABLE 4.1 Categories of Occupations and Worker Function Ratings (Data–People–Things)

Category (first digit)	Data (fourth digit)	People (fifth digit)	Things (sixth digit)
0/1 Professional, technical, and managerial	0 Synthesizing	0 Mentoring	0 Setting up
	1 Coordinating	1 Negotiating	1 Precision working
2 Clerical and sales	2 Analyzing	2 Instructing	2 Operating—controlling
3 Service	3 Compiling	3 Supervising	3 Driving—operating
4 Agricultural, fishery, forestry, and related	4 Computing	4 Diverting	4 Manipulating
5 Processing	5 Copying	5 Persuading	5 Tending
6 Machine trades	6 Comparing	6 Speaking—signaling	6 Feeding—offbearing
7 Benchwork	7 Serving	7 Handling	
8 Structural work		8 Taking instructions—helping	
9 Miscellaneous			

TABLE 4.2   Vocational Aptitudes and Temperaments

(G) General learning ability	(D) Directing, controlling, or planning activities of others
(V) Verbal aptitude	(R) Performing repetitive or short-cycle work
(N) Numerical aptitude	(I) Influencing people in their opinions, attitudes, and judgments
(S) Spatial aptitude	(V) Performing a variety of duties
(F) Form perception	(E) Expressing personal feelings
(Q) Clerical perception	(A) Working alone or apart in physical isolation from others
(K) Motor coordination	(S) Performing effectively under stress
(F) Finger dexterity	(T) Attaining precise set limits, tolerances, and standards
(M) Manual dexterity	(U) Working under specific instructions
(E) Eye-hand-foot coordination	(P) Dealing with people
(C) Color discrimination	(J) Making judgments

TABLE 4.3   Sample *DOT* Code and Its Coding Structure

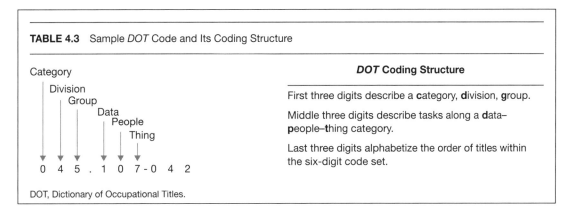

Category	*DOT* Coding Structure
	First three digits describe a **c**ategory, **d**ivision, **g**roup.
	Middle three digits describe tasks along a **d**ata–**p**eople–**t**hing category.
	Last three digits alphabetize the order of titles within the six-digit code set.

DOT, Dictionary of Occupational Titles.

II. Occupational Information Network (O*NET)

Developed in 1998, O*NET is a database of occupational and worker characteristics and attributes that uses a modern, empirically based framework and methodology for obtaining occupational information. It was developed as a replacement for the *DOT*. O*NET describes occupations in terms of skills and knowledge requirements, the way the work is performed, and typical work settings. The O*NET database is a comprehensive source of descriptors, with ratings of importance, level, relevance, or extent, for more than 1,000 occupations that are key to the U.S. economy. The conceptual foundation of O*NET is the content model, which provides a framework that identifies the most important types of information about work and integrates them into a theoretically and empirically sound system. It embodies a view that reflects the character of occupations (via job-oriented descriptors) and people (via worker-oriented descriptors). The content model also allows occupational information to be applied across jobs, sectors, or industries (cross-occupational descriptors) and within occupations (occupational-specific descriptors). These descriptors are organized into six major domains that enable the user to focus on areas of information that specify the key attributes and characteristics of workers and occupations (see Figure 4.1). O*NET descriptors for jobs include skills, abilities, knowledge, tasks, work activities, work context, required experience levels, job interests, work values/needs, and work styles. New tools and technology (T2) data provide information on machines, equipment, tools, and software that workers may use for optimal functioning in a high-performance workplace.

III. Standard Occupational Classification System

The 2010 Standard Occupational Classification (SOC) is used by federal statistical agencies to classify workers into occupational categories for the purpose of collecting, calculating, or disseminating data. All workers are classified into one of 840 detailed occupations according to their occupational definition. To facilitate classification, detailed occupations are combined to form 461 broad occupations, 97 minor groups, and 23 major groups. Detailed occupations in the SOC with similar job duties, and in some cases skills, education, and/or training, are grouped together. There are, at the most specified level, 840 *detailed occupations*. Each worker is classified into only one of the 840 detailed occupations based on the tasks performed. Each item in the SOC is designated by a six-digit code. The hyphen between the second and third digits is used only for clarity (BLS, U.S. Department of Labor, 2011). Table 4.4 provides an example of an SOC code to illustrate the structure of coding.

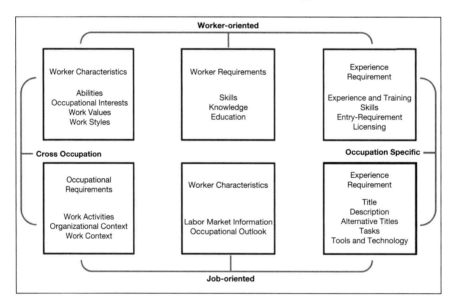

FIGURE 4.1 Content model of O*NET.

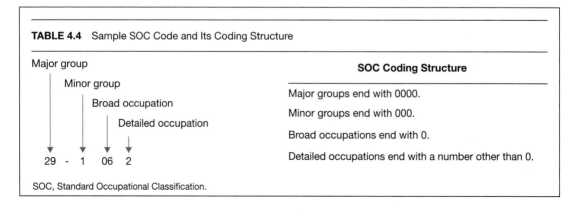

TABLE 4.4 Sample SOC Code and Its Coding Structure

				SOC Coding Structure
Major group				
	Minor group			Major groups end with 0000.
		Broad occupation		Minor groups end with 000.
			Detailed occupation	Broad occupations end with 0.
29	- 1	06	2	Detailed occupations end with a number other than 0.

SOC, Standard Occupational Classification.

The U.S. Department of Labor's BLS produces employment and wage estimates using the SOC system. Similarly, each O*NET occupational title and code is based on the updated O*NET-SOC 2009 taxonomy. This ensures that O*NET information links directly to other labor market information, such as wage and employment statistics that are important to rehabilitation counselors.

IV. North American Industry Classification System

North American Industry Classification System (NAICS) is the standard used by federal statistical agencies in classifying business establishments for the purpose of collecting, analyzing, and publishing statistical data related to the U.S. business economy. It was developed under the auspices of the Office of Management and Budget (OMB) and adopted in 1997 to replace the Standard Industrial Classification (SIC) system. NAICS is based on a production-oriented concept. The first two digits designate a *major economic sector* [formerly *division*], the third digit designates an *economic subsector* [formerly *major group*], the fourth digit designates an industry group, and the fifth digit designates the *specific industry*. Table 4.5 provides an example of an NAICS code to illustrate the structure of coding. Table 4.6 contains a list of all 20 NAICS sectors and their codes.

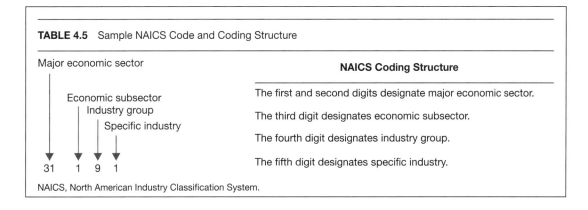

TABLE 4.5 Sample NAICS Code and Coding Structure

Major economic sector

Economic subsector
Industry group
Specific industry

31 1 9 1

NAICS Coding Structure

The first and second digits designate major economic sector.

The third digit designates economic subsector.

The fourth digit designates industry group.

The fifth digit designates specific industry.

NAICS, North American Industry Classification System.

TABLE 4.6 Economic Sectors Under NAICS

Code	Title
11	Agriculture, forestry, fishing, and hunting
21	Mining
22	Utilities
23	Construction
31-33	Manufacturing
41-43	Wholesale trade
44-46	Retail trade
48-49	Transportation and warehousing
51	Information

(*continued*)

TABLE 4.6 Economic Sectors Under NAICS (*continued*)

Code	Title
52	Finance and insurance
53	Real estate and rental and leasing
54	Professional, scientific, and technical services
55	Management of companies and enterprises
56	Administrative and support and waste management and remediation services
61	Educational services
62	Health care and social assistance
71	Arts, entertainment, and recreation
72	Accommodation and food services
81	Other services (except public administration)
91-93	Public administration

NAICS, North American Industry Classification System.

V. *Occupational Outlook Handbook*

The *Occupational Outlook Handbook (OOH)* (www.bls.gov/ooh) was developed by the U.S. Department of Labor, and its latest edition was revised and updated in 2016 (BLS, U.S. Department of Labor, 2016). It provides information for over 250 different occupations, which are clustered into 19 broad occupational categories. Information contained in the *OOH* includes nature of work; typical functions; working conditions; employment prospect; education preparation, training, and other qualifications; employment outlook; wage or salary levels; related occupations; and sources of additional information (BLS, U.S. Department of Labor, 2016). The information is obtained from trade associations, professional associations, educational institutions, and governmental agencies. The *OOH* is an excellent resource for rehabilitation counselors to provide job requirement information to their clients to help them make informed vocational decisions (Rubin & Roessler, 2008)

Job Analysis

Overview

Job analysis is a commonly used assessment and vocational process for gathering information and recommending work accommodation in rehabilitation counseling. This section discusses the purpose of job analysis and introduces the key elements of job analysis.

Learning Objectives

By the end of this unit you should be able to:

1. Understand the purpose and process of a job analysis.
2. Identify key elements and steps involved in a job analysis.
3. Identify possible resource for conducting a job analysis.

Key Concepts

The U.S. Department of Labor (1972) defined *job analysis* as a systematic study of the worker in terms of job duties, the methods and techniques one used to do the job, the resulting products or services one produces, and the traits necessary to accomplish the job. It is an important skill set used by rehabilitation counselors to analyze the essential functions of a job in order to determine transferable skills, job accommodation needs, and job placement (selective placement) of people with disabilities (Rubin & Roessler, 2008). Job analysis involves breaking the total job down into tasks and/or subtasks and determining how the job is performed, what is accomplished, where it is performed, and why it is performed. It also involves determining the tools, equipment, machines, work aids, and materials used in performing the job. The analysis also involves determining the physical requirements, environmental conditions, and special vocational preparation required to perform the job. Specifically, a comprehensive job analysis involves a careful analysis of the following factors associated with performing the job well: (a) purpose, (b) *DOT* data, (c) hiring requirements, (d) salary, (e) tasks and elements, (f) vocational aptitudes, (g) temperaments, (h) physical demands, (i) interests, (j) working conditions, (k) general educational development, (l) specific vocational preparation, (m) tools and machines used, (n) interpersonal interactions, (o) unscheduled demands, and (p) architectural barriers. To compare different occupational options, the *Worker Traits Data Book* can be used to provide ratings on every job found in the *DOT* in regard to minimal vocational aptitudes, physical demands, environmental conditions, and worker temperaments associated with performing the job well (e.g., temperament for adapting to a variety of work situations (Mayall, 1994).

Career-Development Theories

Overview

Rehabilitation counselors are involved in providing career assessment, counseling, and planning services to people with disabilities. Career counseling can help people with disabilities crystallize their vocational goals and obtain career-based occupations consistent with their interest and abilities. This section provides an overview of career-development theories and their applications in rehabilitation counseling.

Learning Objectives

By the end of this unit you should be able to:

1. Gain a basic understanding of the theories related to career development.
2. Identify the commonly used assessment instruments and other applications related to each specific theory.

Key Concepts

I. Career Development

Rehabilitation counselors provide career-development services such as career assessment, counseling, and planning. Theory-driven, career-development activities can help people with disabilities to crystalize their VR goals and find careers consistent with their interest and abilities.

Career-development theories address occupational choice, work adjustment, and the progression of career-related goals and behaviors (Super, 1990, 1994; Szymanski, Enright, Hershenson, & Ettinger, 2010). This section provides an overview of a number of career-development theories and their applications in rehabilitation counseling.

II. Person–Environment Interaction Theory

Parsons (1909) is regarded as the founder of the career-development movement. He developed trait and factor theory. Parsons described *trait* as an operational characteristic of the person and *factor* as an environmental characteristic necessary for successful job performance. Parsons outlined three career-development stages that counselors should support clients to accomplish: self-understanding, awareness of work requirements and conditions, and reasoning on the interaction of self-knowledge and vocational information. These trait and factor concepts strongly influenced other trait and type theories.

Parsons's (1909) conceptualization of trait and factor theory is now described as a person–environment interaction theory (Szymanski et al., 2010). The original theoretical underpinnings were that persons have stable traits, occupations require specific characteristics, and matches can be found between the person and job (Brown, 1990). Yet the current person–environment interaction theory is based on new assumptions: Persons seek out and create environments, the degree of fit between person and environment is related to outcomes that can significantly impact the individual and environment, and the process of the person–environment fit is reciprocal (Szymanski et al., 2010).

According to Parsons (1909), it is imperative for the career-selection process to include an evaluation of the client's self-awareness. To assess a client's self-understanding, clinicians can select from an array of assessment instruments. These instruments can evaluate five basic traits and factors: values, personality, interests, aptitudes, and achievement. Table 4.7 provides assessment samples for four of the traits and factors. Achievement samples are not provided because these tests are typically provided after classes or training programs to assess the level of information learned (Aiken, 2003). Specific examples of aptitude tests designed to reveal a person's expected future ability and performance are listed in Table 4.7.

TABLE 4.7   Instruments Used in the Person–Environment Interaction Theory

Area of Measurement	Assessment Instrument
Values	Study of Values Values Scale
Personality	California Psychological Inventory Sixteen Personality Factor Questionnaire
Interests	Kuder Career Search Strong Interest Inventory California Occupational Preference Survey
Aptitudes	Differential Aptitude Tests U.S. Employment Service General Aptitude Test Battery

The second critical factor of the person–environment interaction theory is to assess the environment through occupational information. Occupational information can be obtained on working conditions, salary, and job duties (Szymanski et al., 2010). Several classification systems can enable counselor and client to acquire this information. The *OOH* (U.S. Department of Labor, 2016) has detailed information for over 250 occupations. The handbook is available in print or online. However, the most comprehensive information can be found within the *DOT* published in 1991 by the U.S. Department of Labor. This classification system describes approximately 12,000 occupations. Designed as a substitute to the *DOT*, the O*NET was created as an online occupational classification system. Although the O*NET currently has information for over 1,000 occupations, new occupations continue to be added.

The third and final step in the person–environment interaction theory is to synthesize information derived from client and occupation assessments into a job analysis (Brown, 1990). If the occupational information is related to a client's traits, an optimal match may be found between person and career environment.

III. Work-Adjustment Theory

The Minnesota Theory of Work Adjustment (TWA) was originally developed in the 1960s to improve the work adjustment of VR clients. Lofquist and Dawis (1969, 1991) defined *work adjustment* as a dynamic, ongoing process by which the worker seeks to achieve and maintain congruity with the environment. Thus, work adjustment underscores job tenure and performance, differentiating work-adjustment theory from other trait and type theories (Sharf, 2006).

There are two predicting factors of work adjustment, satisfaction and satisfactoriness (Dawis & Lofquist, 1984). *Satisfactoriness* refers to the employer's satisfaction with the employee's performance. In contrast, *satisfaction* describes employees' satisfaction with their own work performance. Satisfaction is a key indicator of work adjustment because employees who are satisfied demonstrate better overall performance and longer job tenure. Similarly, a worker must demonstrate the abilities to meet the demands of the job requirements in order to achieve job tenure. Congruence between job satisfaction and job satisfactoriness, therefore, combine to predict job tenure.

Like other trait and type theories, work-adjustment theory focuses on assessments of the person's abilities, values, personality, and interests (Sharf, 2006). Dawis, Lofquist, and colleagues have developed, or are working on, the development of a variety of assessment instruments described in Table 4.8. However, because Dawis and Lofquist (1984) interpreted a person's interests as an expression of abilities and values, the primary focus is on ability and value assessment.

TABLE 4.8   Instruments Used in Work-Adjustment Theory

Area of Measurement	Assessment of Individuals	Assessment of Occupations
Abilities	General Aptitude Test Battery	Occupational Aptitude Patterns
Values	Minnesota Importance Questionnaire	Minnesota Job Description Questionnaire
Personality	Instruments are being developed	Instruments are being developed

The next step of work-adjustment theory is measuring the abilities and values needed for particular occupations. The Minnesota Job Description Questionnaire (MJDQ; Borgen, Weiss, Tinsley, Dawis, & Lofquist, 1968) was developed to assess how much an occupation reinforces the value patterns of individuals. For instance, certain people may prefer environments where they are busy all of the time. Therefore, a job that fosters this value system would reinforce similar personal values. Last, measurements of abilities are available through the Occupational Aptitude Patterns developed by the U.S. Department of Labor (1980) to define abilities needed for a broad range of jobs.

When matching the person's abilities and values to vocational abilities and values, clinicians have a variety of tools available to them (listed in Table 4.8). If a close match is formed, a person has an increased chance for job satisfaction and satisfactoriness (Lofquist & Dawis, 1984). The main objective of work-adjustment theory is to help the person with a disability find permanent and satisfying work.

IV. INCOME Framework

The INCOME framework was originally developed by Beveridge, Craddock, Liesener, Stapleton, and Hershenson (2002) to conceptualize the career development of people with disabilities. It was later expanded by Hershenson (2010) as a culturally inclusive and disability-sensitive framework for organizing career-development concepts and interventions. The framework encompasses concepts from a range of career-development theories and empirical research findings to inform of the selection of career interventions tailored to diverse segments of the population (e.g., gender, race, cultural background, sexual orientation, disability status). It also uses the Helms (1995) multicultural construct of statuses, defined as "mutually interactive dynamic processes by which a person's behavior could be explained" (Helms, 1995, p. 183), to address how the INCOME statuses may occur or recur in any order or combination in the career-development process (Hershenson, 2005). Hershenson suggests that persons experiencing a particular status may require specific career assessment and counseling interventions. The framework is referred to by the acronym INCOME in order to highlight the six statuses: Imagining, INforming, Choosing, Obtaining, Maintaining, and Exiting.

In the Imagining status, persons with disabilities become aware that there are occupations in the world of work and that there are jobs that may be a good match for them. This status includes three types of imagining: (a) awareness (e.g., becoming aware of the concept of work and its relevance to oneself), (b) fantasy imagining (e.g., visualizing having a different job), and (c) reality-based imagining (e.g., imagining only occupations or jobs consistent with one's capacities, resources, and opportunity structure) (Beveridge et al., 2002; Hershenson, 2005).

The iNforming status encompasses having a clear understanding of one's abilities, interests, ambitions, resources, and limitations and a good knowledge of the requirements and conditions of success, pros and cons, compensation, opportunities, and prospects in different lines of work. In this status, people gain knowledge of their work competencies (e.g., work habits, physical and mental skills that are applicable in work) and work-related interpersonal skills (Hershenson, 1996, 2005). After obtaining career information about the self and work, a person with a disability can determine whether a job will be a good match.

The Choosing status occurs when a job seeker has internalized career knowledge about the self and work and then selects a job or educational program (Hershenson, 2005). People in this status engage in a process of reasoning to determine which occupations are congruent with their values, interests, personality, abilities, and needs (Parsons, 1909). For example, a person may be interested in a career as a nurse because personality and values align with the helping profession. However, this person may not have the ability to work as a nurse without formal training. The individual decides not to enter an educational program because of being a single parent and instead chooses to find a clerical job in a hospital setting.

In the **O**btaining status, people seek and obtain an occupation or a job, preferably the occupation of their choice or a closely related one. This status includes preparing for, implementing, and successfully concluding the job-search process (i.e., job finding, networking, resume preparation, employment interviewing skills, and negotiating; Hershenson, 2005). The environment and the economy are contextual factors in this status that can impact the type of employment a person obtains.

The **M**aintaining status involves the process of adapting to, performing in, and sustaining an occupation or a job. It involves the dynamic interaction between the person and the environment that is the focus of person–environment interaction theories (Rounds & Tracy, 1990; Strauser, 2014), which makes work-adjustment theories particularly applicable to this status. According to Hershenson (1996, 2005), work adjustment comprises three components: (a) work role behavior (the interaction between people's work personality and behavioral expectations of the work setting), (b) task performance (the interaction between people's work competencies and the skill requirements of the work setting), and (c) worker satisfaction (the interaction between people's work goals and the rewards and opportunities offered by the work setting). The match between the needs of the person and the work environment influences successful outcomes. The length of time a person stays on a job is based on the quality of the job match.

Finally, the **E**xiting status involves the process of thinking about leaving or actually leaving one's current job. Exiting a position includes not only getting fired or retiring, but also incorporates getting promoted or departing voluntarily (Hershenson, 2005). A person may leave a position involuntarily if job performance is poor, the employer is downsizing, or mandatory retirement age is reached. On the other hand, voluntary exiting may occur when a person is not satisfied with the current position, the company lacks opportunities for advancement, or there are intolerable workplace conditions. A person with a disability may be in this status a number of times during a career and may consider exiting while in other statuses (e.g., while maintaining one job they are thinking about or imagining another job) but decide not to act on it.

V. Work-Personality Theory

Holland's (1966, 1973, 1985, 1992, 1997) theory proposes that an individual's career choice is based on personality type. He also believes that a person's beliefs, worldviews, generalizations, and stereotypes are usually accurate. By investigating these beliefs and stereotypes, Holland assigns both people and work environments to specific work personality category types (Sharf, 2006).

Holland proposes that personality types and environments in which people live and work can resemble six types of categories: realistic, investigative, artistic, social, enterprising, and Conventional. People who associate with the realistic personality and work environment tend to like to work with their hands, enjoy working with machines, like building things, enjoy technical or mechanical activities, and prefer work environments that allow them to engage in these activities. People who associate with the investigative personality and work environment enjoy analysis, problem solving, and intellectual activities and are interested in math and science. Artistic individuals enjoy creative activities, and tend to prefer work environments that allow individual expression and creativity, and generally enjoy activities related to art, music, creative writing, and similar creative activities. People who associate with the social personality tend to enjoy social engagement and group-based activities, and are concerned with helping and promoting the welfare of others and solving interpersonal issues, and many people associating with this category are employed in helping professions (counselors, psychologists, social workers) and education. Enterprising individuals tend to enjoy activities that allow them to persuade, sell, or influence others, and are often found in sales, marketing, and management occupations. Conventional individuals like to engage in well-defined, clearly organized tasks that allow them to use their skills in organizing, entering, and managing data, and are often engaged in office-based occupations involving record keeping, data management, and structure.

A person's personality generally will not reflect only one of these categories (e.g., only artistic). People generally associate more closely with two or three or more of Holland's personality types. Holland developed a hexagonal model that represents the relationships between the personality types and environments in which those that are more alike and tend to go together are closer to each other, and those that are more different are farther away from each other in the model. Those that are opposite each other (e.g., realistic and social, artistic and conventional, investigative and enterprising) are generally inconsistent with each other and are depicted as opposites in the model. The coupling of individuals and environments allows for a prediction of vocational, social, and educational outcomes (Holland, 1997).

Assessment instruments can be included in Holland's approach to career counseling to provide additional vocational assistance to individuals. The Self-Directed Search (SDS; Holland, Fritzsche, & Powell, 1994) and the Vocational Preference Inventory (VPI; Holland, 1985) provide objective assessments of personality types. The Career Attitudes and Strategies Inventory (CASI; Holland & Gottfredson, 1994) and the Environmental Identity Scale (EIS; Gottfredson & Holland, 1996) assesses work attitudes. Finally, the Position Classification Inventory (PCI; Gottfredson & Holland, 1991) classifies positions by Holland personality types. These assessment instruments can provide objective information to clinicians when assessing persons with disabilities and their environments.

Special Focus Theories

Overview

A number of theories describe career development in distinctive ways. Many of these theories have applied psychological theory or constructs to the career decision making process. This section reviews three special focus theories.

Learning Objectives

By the end of this unit you should be able to:

1. Understand the other special focus theories related to career development.
2. Identify the assessment instruments and intervention strategies developed for each specific theory.

Key Concepts

I. Social Learning Theory

Krumboltz's social learning theory reflects one of the earlier applications of Bandura's (1977) social learning concepts to career development (Hackett & Lent, 1992). This social learning theory describes how individuals make career decisions based on cognition and behavior. The following four categories of factors influence career decision making: genetic endowment, environmental conditions and events, learning experiences, and task approach skills. The subsequent outcomes of learning experiences may include self-observation generalizations, worldview generalizations, task approach skills, and actions (Mitchell & Krumboltz, 1990, 1996). Although many other career-development theories emphasize abilities and environmental events, social learning theory emphasizes the significance of learning experiences and task approach skills (Mitchell & Krumboltz, 1996).

In recent work, Krumboltz and associates have emphasized the change within the person and environment. Thus, the second part of the theory is that clients need to expand their capabilities and interests, clients need to prepare for changing work tasks, clients need to be empowered to take a stance, and counselors need to provide vocational counseling at all career-development stages (Mitchell & Krumboltz, 1996). Therefore, Krumboltz (1996) believes that career counselors should implement initial, ongoing, and follow-up vocational services. Cognitive and behavioral strategies have been developed to assist clients with career development (Sharf, 2006). Behavioral strategies may integrate the following techniques: reinforcement, role models, role-playing, and simulation (Krumboltz, 1970). Cognitive strategies may include goal clarification, reframing, resolution of discrepancies, and cognitive rehearsal (Krumboltz, 1996). Krumboltz's theory suggests that counselors integrate cognitive and behavioral interventions into career counseling to assist clients with career development.

II. Social Cognitive Career Theory

Social cognitive career theory (SCCT) was advanced by Lent, Brown, and Hackett (1994) to explain how job seekers develop career interests, set goals, gain competence, and persist in achieving career goals. It is an extension of Bandura's social cognitive theory (SCT), which focuses on how people accomplish goals and tasks successfully (Bandura, 1986, 2004). Lent and associates (Lent & Brown, 2006; Lent, Brown, & Hackett, 2000) emphasized self-efficacy, outcome expectancies, and goal-making as essential in an interaction system of personal attributes, background contextual factors, and overt behaviors. A number of career assessment instruments can be used to evaluate these dynamic constructs (Sharf, 2006). Relationships among key constructs of the SCCT are depicted in Figure 4.2.

As shown in the figure, self-efficacy beliefs and outcome expectations are seen as jointly promoting career-related interests in a SCCT model (Lent & Brown, 2006). Career-related interests foster corresponding career choice goals (e.g., intentions to pursue a given career path), which in turn, motivate individuals to take actions designed to implement their goals (e.g., enrolling in a particular course of training; Lent & Brown, 1996). SCCT postulates that when people perceive themselves as competent and when they anticipate that performing a target behavior will produce valued outcomes, they form enduring interests in an activity and form career goals for sustaining or increasing their involvement in the activity. These goals, in turn, increase the likelihood of subsequent activity practice. Practice efforts give rise to a particular pattern of goal attainments (e.g., successes vs. failures), which serve to revise self-efficacy beliefs and outcome expectations in an ongoing feedback loop (Lent & Brown, 1996).

III. Lifespan Theory

Super's research (1970, 1994) has explained the career-development stages of the lifespan and infiltrated most of the current career counseling literature in the United States (Szymanski et al., 2010). The key tenets of this developmental theory for adults capture two major concepts: life roles and life stages.

The six major life roles are child, student, leisurite, citizen, worker, and homemaker (see Figure 4.3). Super (1990) hypothesizes that persons identify the importance of work differently

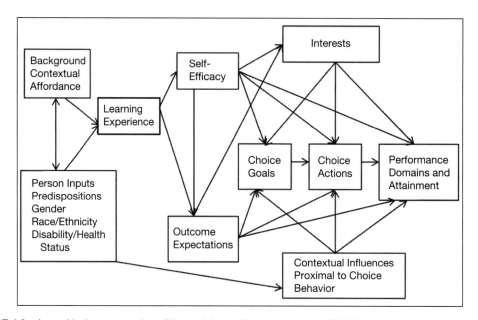

FIGURE 4.2 A graphical representation of the social cognitive career theory (SCCT).

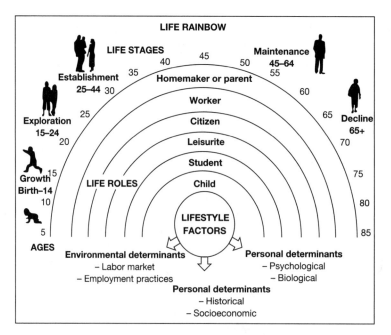

FIGURE 4.3 The life roles rainbow.

at varying periods in their lives. Clinicians can administer the Salience Inventory (SI; Super & Nevill, 1986) to assess the saliency of roles at any given point in time.

Roles change not only because of saliency, but also because of the nature of involvement. Involvement can be assessed by participation, commitment, knowledge, and values expectations. Super and associates developed specific assessment instruments to measure knowledge and values expectations. The *Career Development Inventory* (CDI; Super, Thompson, Lindeman, Jordan, & Myers, 1981) measures knowledge about work roles, and the *Values Scale* (VS; Super & Nevill, 1986) and the SI (Super & Nevill, 1986) measure values expectations for work roles.

The concept of life stages is the second component of Super's lifespan theory (1990). The life stages are age related; individuals typically go through a temporal order of the stages of growth, exploration, establishment, maintenance, and decline or disengagement. Yet it is possible that an individual can experience a stage at any time in life. The Adult Career Concerns Inventory (ACCI; Super, Thompson, Lindeman, Myers, & Jordan, 1986) can assist counselors in identifying life stages. After life stages and roles assessment, counselors are able to provide appropriate and individualized career-development services.

Career Counseling

Overview

This section provides rehabilitation counselors with a framework for the implementation of career-development theories and suggests strategies for providing career counseling to individuals with disabilities.

Learning Objectives

By the end of this unit you should be able to:

1. Identify important considerations when providing career counseling to individuals with disabilities.
2. Identify the stages of the career-development process and their relationship to career counseling.

Key Concepts

I. Applications for Individuals With Disabilities

Person–environment interactions, the fundamental components of trait and type theory, have long been a focus of assessment and planning approaches to VR (e.g., Rubin & Roessler, 1994). More recently, trait and type theories and other career-development theories have been described as having great potential for people with disabilities (Szymanski et al., 2010). However, clinicians should not solely use career-development theoretical approaches when providing VR services to people with disabilities. Although career-development theories have been suggested to be applicable to individuals with disabilities, these theories must be applied with an understanding of the limitations resulting from disability and possible need for accommodations. These theoretical approaches and related assessment instruments can be included in a rehabilitation counselor's toolkit, but counselors should still consider the whole person, including the impact of disability.

Salomone (1988) suggested strategies for providing career counseling to people with disabilities and delineated the career-development process in ordinal stages. He suggested adding two stages to Parsons's (1909) original three. This career counseling approach posits helping clients reach the following steps: understanding self, understanding work and work environments, understanding the decision-making process, implementing career and educational decisions, and adjusting and adapting to the world of work and school. These stages may provide rehabilitation counselors with a framework for the implementation of career-development theories. Rehabilitation interventions may need to combine career-development theories and psychosocial adaptation strategies to assist clients in developing coping skills, increasing community participation, and achieving work adjustment.

Vocational Consultation and Job Placement

Overview

Job development and placement are important services in rehabilitation counseling. This section provides an overview of job placement and discusses the essential skills sets to be considered.

Learning Objectives

By the end of this unit you should be able to:

1. Understand the concept of job placement.
2. Identify the difference between specific employability, general employability, and placeability skills needed for job placement.

Key Concepts

I. Job Placement

To obtain and retain competitive employment in integrated settings, individuals with disabilities must develop appropriate specific employability, general employability, and placeability skills (Chan et al., 1997; Chan, Leahy, & Saunders, 2005). *Specific employability skills* (e.g., intelligence, aptitudes, temperament, physical capacity, job knowledge, skills) are job specific and vary from one job class to another. Vocational behaviors and skills in specific employability are important in predicting job performance. Conversely, *general employability skills*, also known as *general work personality*, are not job specific. General employability skills are required in every job. Examples of these behaviors include grooming and hygiene, attendance, punctuality, safety consciousness, interpersonal relationships, frustration tolerance, work stamina, and productivity (Chan et al., 1997). General employability behaviors and skills are important in the prediction of job-maintenance behavior. *Placeability* is often referred to as the degree of sophistication in job-acquiring skills. Although placeability has little to do with the person's ability to perform a job, it is an important factor to evaluate in rehabilitation because it addresses a person's ability to obtain a job. Job-seeking behaviors are evaluated in terms of, for example, the client's resourcefulness, motivation, skills in writing resumes and cover letters, and interview behaviors (Chan et al., 1997; Chan et al., 2005). As a process, *job placement* is referred to as a set of activities involved in locating a suitable job for VR consumers and getting them hired for the job (Rubin & Roessler, 2008). Specifically, job-placement assistance includes job-seeking skills training, direct placement, job development, supported employment, and demand-side job placement.

II. Job-Seeking Skills Training

Rubin and Roessler (2008) indicated that poor job-seeking skills is the main culprit for poor quality employment outcomes for people with disabilities. Some of these deficits include (a) lack of awareness of techniques needed to secure job leads; (b) difficulty explaining the significance of educational background, job skills, and job history to the interviewer; (c) inability to appropriately discuss disability-related issues and accommodation needs in job interviews; (d) deficiency in completing job applications and preparing job resumes; and (e) failure to look for work frequently and dress appropriately for job interviews. Job-seeking skills training is designed to provide practice opportunity and to teach clients to:

- Determine job suitability
- Identify vocational strengths and limitations
- Prepare a resume
- Perform in a job interview
- Secure job leads

One of the most successful training programs for job-seeking skills is the "Job Club" approach. In addition to providing clients with typical job-seeking skills training, the Job Club seeks to enhance motivation by using techniques such as the buddy system, family support, role models, and ample practice in completing job applications, writing resumes, and performing job interviews. In their experimental study, Azrin and Philip (1979) reported that 95% of Job Club members were employed compared with 28% of rehabilitation clients in a traditional job-seeking skills program. However, a high dropout rate (70%) for people with severe mental illness was reported as a problem by Corrigan, Reedy, Thadani, and Ganet (1995).

III. Direct-Placement Intervention

Selective placement is defined as the precise and detailed matching of the person's abilities with the work environment and the requirements of the job. Direct-placement intervention requires the aggressive marketing of the benefits of hiring people with disabilities to employers and the ability to supply employers with qualified candidates with disabilities using selective placement. Job analysis is essential to successful selective placement and is used to determine person–job fit and the modifications that can be used to enhance the appropriate fit. However, Salamone (1996) advocated the use of client-centered placement because the selective placement approach may impair the dignity, independence, and self-confidence of clients. He indicated that it is more effective to teach clients job-seeking and job-retaining skills. Client-centered placement is a subset of psychoeducational counseling with the goal of helping clients become self-directed, self-motivated individuals with a can-do attitude. It is an empowerment model that encourages clients to take charge of their own lives and to develop the requisite attitudes and skills needed to succeed in obtaining and maintaining meaningful employment. Client-centered placement is not independent job seeking but is required frequent meetings with the counselor to develop effective job-search strategies. Nonetheless, clients are responsible for acting as their own agents in making contacts with employers and setting up job interviews.

Job-Placement Assistance

Overview

Job-placement assistance includes job-seeking skills training, direct placement, job development, supported employment, and demand-side job placement. This section provides an overview of various job-placement assistance strategies and discusses different supported employment approaches.

Learning Objectives

By the end of this unit you should be able to:

1. Identify various types of job-placement assistance and the difference between direct placement and client-centered placement.
2. Understand concepts related to the supported employment model.
3. Identify the major components of various supported employment approaches, such as the train–place–train–follow-up and the place–train–follow-up approaches.
4. Understand the relationship of disability and job analysis and placement.

Key Concepts

I. Supported Employment

The supported employment model is a wide-ranging selective placement approach (Salomone, 1996). This type of placement highlights job preparation for individuals with severe disabilities (e.g., schizophrenia, mental retardation) in competitive employment settings and continued follow-up of services during the course of employment. Rubin and Roessler (2001) state that supported employment's focus with on-job training, advocacy, long-term job retention, and follow-up services is what distinguishes this work model from other job-placement approaches. The supported work approach permits placement of clients who do not have all the needed work and social skills necessary for immediate job success. This is a noteworthy variation from conventional placement approaches, which focus on work and social skill development before placement can occur (Wehman & Kregel, 1985).

There are a number of variations of the supported employment model; among the most prevalent are the train–place–train–follow-up (TPTF; Lagomarcino, 1986) and the place–train–follow-up (PTF; Wehman, 1986) approaches. The TPTF approach is composed of four major parts: (a) surveying potential employers to establish significant vocational and social survival skills that require training, (b) training individuals with the purpose of performing such skills, (c) placing trainee clients in competitive employment settings, and (d) supplying long-term follow-up training (Lagomarcino, 1986). The first part of this approach stresses the identification of prospective job placements within the community and conducting a job analysis for the available positions. The second part focuses on training by means of time-limited preemployment training programs. Individuals are placed, for no longer than 6 months, within community-based training programs in local industries, where they learn the necessary and required skills for competitive employment. The third part of the approach (placement) provides clients with the necessary services to transition from training to competitive employment. The last part centers on providing follow-up services and has a shorter duration than the training phase.

The PTF approach is composed of four major components: job placement, job-site training, (c) ongoing assessment, and job retention (Wehman, 1986). In job placement, staff activities should include structuring job-search attempts for the client and matching strengths to the job's needs, interacting with the employer on behalf of the client, arranging transportation or travel related to training, and encouraging the client's family to help identify suitable jobs. During job-site training, staff activities should include providing clients with training in necessary behavioral and social skills at the job site, working with the client's employer and coworkers to provide help to the client, and aiding the client and coworkers in their adjustment to each other. In on-going assessment, staff activities should include attaining employer feedback on the client's development, supervising the client's progress in learning the job through direct observation, and occasionally assessing client and family satisfaction with the program. In the last component, job retention, staff activities should include systematically reducing staff intervention at the job placement, following up with the client's employer, and helping the client find a new job if needed (Wehman, 1986).

In both of these approaches, and all other approaches with selective placement orientation, job analysis plays a fundamental role. The TPTF approach emphasizes job training before placement of the client in a permanent competitive job. The PTF approach focuses on placing the client at a specific job setting where on-the-job training and long-term employment can be attained (Rubin & Roessler, 2001).

II. Customized Employment

Customized employment is a new option for supported employment reauthorized through the WIOA of 2014 (Wehman et al., 2016). The U.S. Department of Labor, Office of Disability & Employment Policy (ODEP), in the *Federal Register* (2002), first defined *customized employment* as "individualizing the employment relationship between employees and employers in ways that meet the needs of both. It is based on an individualized determination of the strengths, needs, and interests of the person with a disability, and is also designed to meet the specific needs of the employer" (2002, p. 43154). Although customized employment is a natural extension of supported employment, it departs from traditional supply-side and demand-side employment practices (Griffin, Hammis, Geary, & Sullivan, 2008). Customized employment is a flexible approach in which a job seeker with a disability and an employment specialist partner with a potential employer create a job description that matches the abilities of the job candidate with the business needs of the employer (Wehman et al., 2016).

Customized employment consists of four main components: discovery, job-search planning, job development and negotiation, and postemployment support (Harvey, Szoc, Dela Rosa, Pohl, & Jenkins, 2013). Employment specialists start the process of customized employment with an assessment phase called *discovery* (Griffin et al., 2008), which helps the employment specialist better understand the strengths, needs, and interests of the person with the disability; this is accomplished through meetings with the individual, family, and friends; observations; and other evaluations. The person with disability is therefore considered a primary source of information for work goals, reasonable accommodations, and other needs. That information is used to develop a *job-search plan*, including a list of potential employers (Harvey et al., 2013). After the assessment and planning stages, the employment specialist and the job seeker with a disability work on *job development* and *negotiation*. Individualized job options are either self-employment or competitive employment through negotiation with an employer. The customized employment process concludes with *postemployment support* through on-going supports and monitoring to ensure job satisfaction for both the employee and the employer.

Internet Resources

Occupational Information
American's Career InfoNet
www.acinet.org

O*NET Online
www.onetonline.org

Labor Market Information
Bureau of Labor Statistics—Employment Projections (Occupational Data)
www.bls.gov/emp/ep_data_occupational_data.htm

The Riley Guide - Employment and Industrial Trends
www.rileyguide.com/trends.html#gov

Career Development
National Career Development Association
http://associationdatabase.com/aws/NCDA/pt/sp/home_page

Minnesota State CAREERwise Education
www.iseek.org

Quintessential Careers: College, Careers, and Jobs Guide
www.quintcareers.com

Job Placement
Career & Job News, Work, & Employment Salary Trends
http://online.wsj.com/public/page/news-career-jobs.html

Susan Ireland's Resume Site
http://susanireland.com

The Riley Guide - Using Employment Kiosks and Online Job Applications
www.rileyguide.com/kiosk.html

Job Banks
America's Job Bank Transition
www.ajb.dni.us

Job Search, Employment, & Career Sites
www.careerbuilder.com
http://monster.com
www.gettinghired.com
www.indeed.com

Multiple-Choice Questions

1. The founder of the vocational guidance movement was:
   A. Super
   B. Parsons
   C. Bandura
   D. Holland

2. According to Parsons's theory, what is a necessary characteristic for successful job performance?
   A. Trait
   B. Factor
   C. Personality
   D. Awareness
   E. Knowledge

3. The first step of a successful career-selection process is to have an understanding of oneself. Parsons suggested that counselors use instruments to assess a client's self-understanding. These instruments must be able to evaluate five basic traits and factors. Which of the following is *NOT* one of them?
   A. Dexterity
   B. Personality
   C. Interests
   D. Aptitude
   E. Achievement

4. The second factor of the person–environment interaction theory is to assess the environment through occupational information. Which of the following is *NOT* one of the most commonly used occupational information systems?
   A. *Occupational Outlook Handbook*
   B. *Dictionary of Occupational Titles*
   C. Occupational Information Network (O*Net)
   D. Self-Directed Search

5. Which of the following assessment instruments would be considered a measure for personality?
   A. California Psychological Inventory
   B. Kuder Career Search
   C. Strong Interest Inventory
   D. General Aptitude Test Battery
   E. None of the above

6. The *Dictionary of Occupational Titles* covers over ___ jobs in the U.S. economy.

    A. 800

    B. 1,000

    C. 5,000

    D. 12,000

7. The North American Industry Classification System (NAICS) is the standard used by federal statistical agencies in classifying business establishments. NAICS covers how many business sectors?

    A. 15

    B. 20

    C. 30

    D. 40

8. What theory originally described the career-development process in three stages that involve self, work, and the interaction between self and work?

    A. Lifespan theory

    B. Work-adjustment theory

    C. Trait and factor theory

    D. Social learning theory

    E. None of the above

9. Which of the following life stages does *NOT* belong to the lifespan theory?

    A. Growth

    B. Contemplation

    C. Establishment

    D. Maintenance

    E. Decline

10. What is the correct sequence of the five life stages of the lifespan theory?

    A. Growth, exploration, establishment, maintenance, decline

    B. Birth, growth, exploration, maintenance, disengagement

    C. Growth, exploration, establishment, maintenance, death

    D. Birth, growth, education, construction, retirement

    E. Growth, exploration, establishment, decline, death

11. Choose the correct six life roles of the lifespan theory.

    A. infant, toddler, student, citizen, worker, senior

    B. child, student, citizen, worker, leisurite, senior

    C. child, student, leisurite, worker, homemaker, senior

D. child, student, leisurite, citizen, worker, homemaker

E. infant, toddler, student, citizen, worker, leisurite

12. What is the definition of *satisfaction* in the Minnesota Theory of Work Adjustment?

A. The employer's satisfaction with the person's performance

B. An individual's satisfaction with personal work performance

C. The employee's overall productivity compared with the average

D. The congruence between salary and job duty

13. Who proposed that a person's career choice is based on their personality type?

A. Parsons

B. Dawis

C. Holland

D. Super

E. Krumboltz

14. On which theory did Krumboltz build his theory?

A. The trait and factor theory

B. The social learning theory

C. The scaffolding theory

D. The theory of multiple intelligence

E. Freud's psychoanalysis

15. Which of the following is *NOT* true concerning the social learning theory?

A. It emphasizes that clients need to expand their capabilities and interests.

B. It emphasizes that clients need to prepare for changing work tasks.

C. It emphasizes that clients need to be empowered to take a stance.

D. It emphasizes that counselors need to provide vocational counseling at all career-development stages.

E. None of the above

16. According to the social cognitive career theory, career interests are affected by several elements. One of them, called_____, refers to individuals' beliefs about whether they can successful at performing a particular task.

A. Goals

B. Facilitators

C. Self-efficacy

D. Knowledge

E. Outcome expectancy

17. Salomone has suggested five strategies that help clients to reach their career counseling goals in five steps. Which of the following is NOT one of the steps?

    A. Understand self

    B. Understand work and the work environment

    C. Understand the decision-making process

    D. Understand government policy

    E. Adjust and adapt to the world of work and school

18. To obtain and maintain competitive employment in integrated settings, individuals with disabilities must develop the following skills *EXCEPT*:

    A. Specific employability skills

    B. General employability skills

    C. Placeability

    D. Creativity

19. Which of the following is *NOT* an example of job-placement assistance?

    A. Job-seeking skills training

    B. Direct placement

    C. Monthly allowance to purchase appropriate attire

    D. Job development

    E. Support employment

20. *Place–train–follow-up* is composed of four major components. Which one of the following is *NOT* one of the components?

    A. Job placement

    B. Job-site training

    C. Ongoing assessment

    D. Long-term follow-up training

21. *Train–place–follow-up* is composed of the following major parts except:

    A. surveying potential employers to establish significant vocational and social survival skills that require training

    B. training individuals with the purpose of performing such skills

    C. placing trainee clients in competitive employment settings

    D. supplying 30-day follow-up training

22. Job-seeking skills training is designed to provide practice opportunity and to teach clients to:

    A. Determine job suitability

    B. Identify vocational strengths and limitations

    C. Secure job leads

D. Perform in a job interview

E. All of the above

23. What is *Job Club*?

A. One of the most unsuccessful job-seeking skills training programs

B. A routine that includes daily physical training to enhance clients' stamina

C. An approach to enhance clients' motivation by using various techniques, such as the buddy system

D. A famous 12-steps program to help clients to obtain competitive job placement

E. A place clients gather together to critique each other's resumes and give feedback

24. Which is most essential to successfully placing and ensuring the most appropriate fit between a person and a placement?

A. Job Club

B. Job analysis

C. Job training

D. Job posting

25. Customized employment involves which one of the following job-placement strategies?

A. Carving out a job solely based on the job seeker's interests and needs

B. Finding a job for a person with a disability based on the demand of the job market

C. Creating a new job through self-employment

D. Locating a job based on the needs of both the employer and job seeker

E. Both C and D

F. All of the above

Answer Key

1B, 2B, 3A, 4D, 5C, 6D, 7B, 8C, 9B, 10A, 11D, 12B, 13C, 14B, 15C, 16C, 17D, 18D, 19C, 20D, 21D, 22E, 23C, 24B, 25E

Advanced Multiple-Choice Questions

1. Person–environment interaction and work-adjustment theories are BOTH what kind of career-development theory?

A. Lifespan theory

B. Developmental theory

C. Social learning theory

D. Trait and type theory

2. The *train–place–train–follow-up* is composed of four major parts. Which of the following components is *NOT* a component?

   A. Identifying prospective job placements within the community and conducting a job analysis

   B. Providing time-limited preemployment training programs in which clients learn the necessary and required skills for competitive employment

   C. Structuring job-search attempts for clients and matching their strengths to the job's needs

   D. Teaching clients to act as their own agent in making contacts with employers and setting up job interviews

   E. Providing clients with the necessary services to transition from training to competitive employment

3. Based on Holland's personality hexagon, which of the following is *NOT* considered a personality type?

   A. Conventional

   B. Investigative

   C. Realistic

   D. Enterprising

   E. Creative

   F. Social

4. Based on the INCOME model, which of the following involves "the process of career decision-making by understanding the relations between self-knowledge and knowledge about occupations or jobs and selecting a job or occupation program"?

   A. Selecting status

   B. Imaging status

   C. Obtaining status

   D. Informing status

   E. Choosing status

5. Which of the following is *NOT* one of the four factors that influence career decision making based on the social learning theory?

   A. Genetic endowment

   B. Environmental conditions and events

   C. Learning experiences

   D. Task approach skills

   E. Personality type

6. Which of the following is *NOT* true regarding the social cognitive theory?

   A. Self-efficacy beliefs refer to individuals' beliefs about whether they can be successful at performing a particular task.

   B. Outcome expectations refer to individuals' beliefs regarding what consequences are most likely to ensue if particular behaviors are performed.

   C. Enhancement of self-efficacy beliefs can lead to an increase in outcome expectancy.

D. *Personal goals* refer to individuals' intention to engage in a certain activity or to produce a particular outcome.

E. All of the above

7. What are the two major concepts of social cognitive career theory?

A. Trait and factor

B. Satisfaction and satisfactoriness

C. Self-efficacy beliefs and outcome expectations

D. Life role and life stages

E. Person and environments

8. Social cognitive career theory was advanced by Lent, Brown, and Hackett as an extension of Bandura's _____.

A. Social cognitive theory

B. Self-determination theory

C. Stage of change theory

D. Hope theory

E. Attachment theory

9. Two types of strategies have been developed to assist clients with career development, according to Krumboltz's social learning theory: cognitive and behavioral strategies. Which of the following is an example of *COGNITIVE* strategies?

A. Reinforcement

B. Role models

C. Simulation

D. Reframing

E. Role-playing

10. According to the social learning theory, which of the following is an example of *BEHAVIORAL* strategies that have been developed to assist clients with career development?

A. Goal clarification

B. Reinforcement

C. Reframing

D. Resolution of discrepancies

E. Cognitive rehearsal

11. Lifespan theory has two major concepts: life role and life stage. What is the age range for the maintenance stage?

A. 25–44

B. 45–64

C. 65+

D. 15–24

12. Which of the following statements best describes *job placement*?

    A. Process or set of activities involved in locating a suitable job for vocational rehabilitation clients and getting them hired for the job

    B. Techniques such as the buddy system, family support, role models, and ample practice in completing job applications, writing resumes, and performing job interviews

    C. Identification of a client's vocational interests and goals

    D. Use of various assessments to understand a client's strengths and limitations

13. What is the main feature of Job Club that is different from other job-seeking skills programs?

    A. The use of a buddy system

    B. The use of vocational assessment

    C. The use of career counseling

    D. The use of selective placement

    E. The use of client-centered placement

14. What is the main culprit for poor quality employment outcomes for people with disabilities?

    A. Failure to meet the educational requirement

    B. Cost of the accommodation

    C. Transportation issues

    D. Lack of computer skills

    E. Poor job-seeking skills

15. There are two types of employability skills, specific employability skills and general employability skills. Which is an example of a specific employability skill?

    A. Personal hygiene

    B. Intelligence

    C. Attendance and punctuality

    D. Interpersonal relationships

    E. Productivity

16. Which of the following is *NOT* one of the trait and type theories of career development?

    A. Lifespan theory

    B. Person–environment interaction theory

    C. Minnesota Theory of Work Adjustment

    D. Work-personality theory

17. A Self-Directed Search score can determine:

    A. The client's three highest personality types based on Holland's theory

    B. The fastest-growing occupation in the United States

    C. The highest paying job in the area

    D. The client's current life stage

18. What should rehabilitation counselors be aware of when applying career-development theories?

    A. Most of the theories are outdated and need revision.

    B. Theories must be applied with an understanding of the limitations resulting from disability and possible need for accommodations.

    C. Asian Americans with disabilities are still focusing on math-related jobs.

    D. Career-development theories are the only tools a rehabilitation counselor can use in the career decision-making process.

19. What is *NOT* true concerning job analysis?

    A. It is a systematic study of job duties, the methods and techniques used to do the job, the resulting products or services one produces, and the traits necessary to accomplish the job.

    B. It includes analysis of the essential functions of a job to determine transferable skills, job accommodation needs, and job placement (selective placement) of people with disabilities.

    C. It involves determining the tools, equipment, machines, work aids, and materials used in performing the job.

    D. It involves determining the physical requirements, environmental conditions, and special vocational preparation required to perform the job

    E. All of the above

20. Which of the following is *NOT* part of a job analysis?

    A. Breaking the job down into tasks

    B. Determining how the job is performed

    C. Determining what tasks are accomplished

    D. Calculating the hourly rate

    E. Determining where the job is performed

21. The *Dictionary of Occupational Titles* uses a nine-digit code to classify each occupation, with each digit bearing a specific meaning. What does the first digit mean?

    A. Category

    B. Geographic location

    C. Division

    D. Group

    E. Department

22. According to Salamone, the negative consequences of selective placement include:

    A. Increased client dependence

    B. Decreased self-confidence

    C. Impaired dignity

    D. All of the above

23. Among specific employability skills, general employability skills, and placeability, which is the most important in predicting job-maintenance behavior?

    A. Specific employability skills

    B. General employability skills

    C. Placeability

    D. All of the above

    E. None of the above

24. Which of the following is important in predicting a client's ability to obtain a job?

    A. Specific employability skills

    B. General employability skills

    C. Placeability

    D. All of the above

    E. None of the above

25. Which of the following is NOT how a client's job-seeking behaviors are evaluated?

    A. Financial plans

    B. Resourcefulness

    C. Motivation

    D. Interview skills

    E. All of the above

Answer Key and Explanation of Answers

1D: Both the person–environment interaction and the work-adjustment theories are trait and type theories, which assess traits of individuals to match these traits to specific job requirements.

2D: The *train–place–train–follow-up* is composed of four major parts: (a) surveying potential employers to establish significant vocational and social survival skills that require training, (b) training individuals with the purpose of performing such skills, (c) placing trainee clients in competitive employment settings, and (d) supplying long-term follow-up training.

3E: The hexagon consists of six different personality types: realistic, investigative, artistic, social, enterprising, and conventional.

4E: The choosing status occurs when a job seeker has internalized career knowledge about the self and work and then selects a job or educational program. People in this status engage in a process of reasoning in order to determine which occupations are congruent with their values, interests, personality, abilities, and needs.

5E: Krumboltz's social learning theory describes how individuals make career decisions based on cognition and behavior. The following four categories influence career decision making: genetic endowment; environmental conditions and events; learning experiences; and task approach skills. Personality type does not influence career decision making in Krumboltz's theory.

6E: All of the statements are described in Bandura's social cognitive theory.

7C: In the social cognitive career theory, self-efficacy beliefs and outcome expectations are seen as jointly promoting career-related interests.

8A: The social cognitive career theory is an extension of Bandura's social cognitive theory, which focuses on how people acquire and maintain certain behavioral patterns. Self-efficacy and outcome expectancy are two of the most prominent determinants of the social cognitive theory.

9D: Reframing is an example of a cognitive strategy. The rest of the choices are examples of behavioral strategies.

10B: All choices are examples of cognitive strategies except reinforcement which is an example of a behavioral strategy.

11B: The exploration age is from age 15–24, the establishment stage is from age 25–44, the maintenance stage is from age 45–64; and the decline stage is age 65 and above.

12A: Job placement is a process or a set of activities involved in locating a suitable job for vocational rehabilitation clients and getting them hired for the job. Answer B is a description of Job Club, answer C is a description of interest/goal exploration, and answer D is a description of vocational assessment.

13A: Job Club has a strong emphasis on motivational factors, including the use of a buddy system, family support, and role models.

14E: Poor job-seeking skills is the main reason for poor quality employment outcomes for people with disabilities.

15B: Intelligence is a specific employability skill; the rest of the skills are characterized as general employability skills.

16A: Super's lifespan theory is considered a developmental theory, and it has two major concepts: life roles and life stages.

17A: Self-Directed Search is designed based on Holland's six personality types.

18B: Although it has been suggested that career-development theories are applicable to individuals with disabilities, these theories must be applied with an understanding of the limitations resulting from disability and the possible need for accommodations. These theoretical approaches and related assessment instruments can be included in a rehabilitation counselor's toolkit, but counselors should still consider the whole person, including the impact of the disability on the individual.

19E: All of the statements describe what a job analysis is and how it is performed.

20D: The correct sequence of the job analysis should be breaking the job down into tasks and/or subtasks and determining how the job is performed, what is accomplished, where it is performed, and why it is performed.

21A: The first three digits in the *Dictionary of Occupational Titles* describe category, division, and group; the middle three digits describe data, people, and thing; and the last three digits alphabetize the order of titles within the six-digit code set.

22D: Selective placement is commonly used to connect vocational rehabilitation consumers to employment. The basic assumption is that the skills and aptitudes of workers and the job requirements could be measured accurately and reliably, allowing the rehabilitation counselor to use a match or selling approach to connect people with disabilities to employment. However, selective placement fosters dependency and discourages skill building, leading the client to return to the counselor for additional selective placement services.

23B: General employability behaviors and skills are important in predicting job maintenance behavior.

24C: Although placeability has little to do with the person's ability to perform a job, it is an important factor to evaluate in rehabilitation because it addresses a person' ability to obtain a job.

25A: A client's job-seeking behaviors are evaluated in terms of resourcefulness, motivation, skills in writing resumes and cover letters, and interview behaviors.

References

Aiken, L. R. (2003). *Psychological testing and assessment* (11th ed.). Boston, MA: Allyn & Bacon.

Azrin, N. H., & Philip, R. A. (1979). Job Club method for the handicapped: A comparative outcome study. *Rehabilitation Counseling Bulletin, 23,* 144–155.

Bandura, A. (1977). *Social learning theory.* Englewood Cliffs, NJ: Prentice Hall.

Bandura, A. (1986). *Social foundations of thought and action: A social cognitive theory.* Englewood Cliffs, NJ: Prentice Hall.

Bandura, A. (2004). Health promotion by social cognitive means. *Health Education & Behavior, 312,* 143–164.

Beveridge, S., Craddock, S. H., Liesener, J., Stapleton, M., & Hershenson, D. (2002). INCOME: A framework for conceptualizing the career development of persons with disabilities. *Rehabilitation Counseling Bulletin, 454,* 195–206.

Borgen, F. H., Weiss, D. J., Tinsley, H. E., Dawis, R. V., & Lofquist, L. H. (1968). *Minnesota Job Description Questionnaire.* Minneapolis: University of Minnesota, Psychology Department, Vocational Psychology Research.

Brown, D. (1990). Trait and factory theory. In D. Brown & L. Brooks (Eds.), *Career choice and development: Applying contemporary theories to practice* (2nd ed., pp. 13–36). San Francisco, CA: Jossey-Bass.

Bureau of Labor Statistics, U.S. Department of Labor. (2010). The employment situation: July 2010 [Press release]. Retrieved from http://www.bls.gov/schedule/archives/empsit_nr.htm#2010

Bureau of Labor Statistics, U.S. Department of Labor. (2011). Standard occupational classification, 2010 edition. Retrieved from http://www.bls.gov/soc

Bureau of Labor Statistics, U.S. Department of Labor. (2016). *Occupational outlook handbook, 2016–2017.* Retrieved from http://www.bls.gov/ooh

Chan, F., Leahy, M. J., & Saunders, J. L. (Eds.). (2005). *Case management for rehabilitation health professionals* (2nd ed.). Osage Beach, MO: Aspen Professional Services.

Chan, F., Shaw, L., McMahon, B. T., Koch, L., & Strauser, D. (1997). A model for enhancing consumer-counselor working relationships in rehabilitation. *Rehabilitation Counseling Bulletin, 41,* 122–137.

Chan, F., Strauser, D., Gervey, R., & Lee, E. (2010). Introduction to demand-side factors related to employment of people with disabilities. *Journal of Occupational Rehabilitation, 204,* 407–411.

Corrigan, P. W., Reedy, P., Thadani, D., & Ganet, M. (1995). Correlates of participation and completion in a job club for clients with psychiatric disability. *Rehabilitation Counseling Bulletin, 39,* 42–53.

Dawis, R. V., & Lofquist, L. H. (1984). *A psychological theory of work adjustment.* Minneapolis: University of Minnesota Press.

Dunn, D. J. (1974). *Placement services in the vocational rehabilitation program.* Menomonie: University of Wisconsin–Stout, Department of Rehabilitation & Manpower Services, Research & Training Center.

Dutta, A., Gervey, R., Chan, F., Chou, C. C., & Ditchman, N. (2008). Vocational rehabilitation services and employment outcomes of people with disabilities: A United States study. *Journal of Occupation Rehabilitation, 18,* 326–334.

Federal Register, June 26, 2002, Vol. 67, No. 123, pp. 43154–43149.

Gottfredson, G. D., & Holland, J. L. (1991). *Position Classification Inventory professional manual.* Odessa, FL: Psychological Assessment Resources.

Gottfredson, G. D., & Holland, J. L. (1996). *Dictionary of Holland occupational codes* (3rd ed.). Odessa, FL: Psychological Assessment Resources.

Griffin, C., Hammis, D., Geary, T., & Sullivan, M. (2008). Customized employment: Where we are; where we're headed. *Journal of Vocational Rehabilitation, 28*(3), 135–139.

Hackett, G., & Lent, R. W. (1992). Theoretical advances and current inquiry in career psychology. In S. D. Brown & R. W. Lent (Eds.), *Handbook of counseling psychology* (2nd ed., pp. 419–451). New York, NY: Wiley.

Harvey, J., Szoc, R., Dela Rosa, M., Pohl, M., & Jenkins, J. (2013). Understanding the competencies needed to customize jobs: A competency model for customized employment. *Journal of Vocational Rehabilitation, 38*(2), 77–89.

Helms, J. E. (1995). An update of Helms's White and People of Color racial identity models. In J. G. Ponterotto, J. M. Casas, L. A. Suzuki, & C. M. Alexander (Eds.), *Handbook of multicultural counseling* (pp. 181–198). Thousand Oaks, CA: Sage.

Hershenson, D. B. (1996). Work adjustment: A neglected area in career counseling. *Journal of Counseling and Development, 74*(5), 442–446.

Hershenson, D. B. (2005). INCOME: A culturally inclusive and disability-sensitive framework for organizing career development concepts and interventions. *Career Development Quarterly, 54*(2), 150–161.

Hershenson, D. B. (2010). Career counseling with diverse populations: Models, interventions, and applications. In E. M. Szymanski & R. M. Parker (Eds.), *Work and disability: Contexts, issues, and strategies for enhancing employment outcomes for people with disabilities* (3rd ed., pp. 163–202). Austin, TX: Pro-Ed.

Holland, J. L. (1966). *The psychology of vocational choice.* Waltham, MA: Blaisdell.

Holland, J. L. (1973). *Making vocational choices: A theory of careers.* Englewood Cliffs, NJ: Prentice Hall.

Holland, J. L. (1985). *Making vocational choices: A theory of vocational personalities and work environments* (2nd ed.). Englewood Cliffs, NJ: Prentice Hall.

Holland, J. L. (1992). *Making vocational choices: A theory of vocational personalities and work environments.* Odessa, FL: Psychological Assessment Resources.

Holland, J. L. (1997). *Making vocational choices: A theory of vocational personalities and work environments* (3rd ed.). Odessa, FL: Psychological Assessment Resources.

Holland, J. L., Fritzsche, B. A., & Powell, P. G. (1994). *The Self-Directed Search (SDS) technical manual.* Odessa, FL: Psychological Assessment Resources.

Holland, J. L., & Gottfredson, G. D. (1994). *The Career Attitudes and Strategies Inventory.* Odessa, FL: Psychological Assessment Resources.

Kaye, S. H. (2010). The impact of 2007–09 recession on workers with disabilities. *Monthly Labor Review, 133,* 19–30.

Krumboltz, J. D. (1970). *Job experience kits.* Chicago, IL: Science Research Associates.

Krumboltz, J. D. (1996). A learning theory of career counseling. In M. L. Savickas & W. B. Walsh (Eds.), *Handbook of career counseling theory and practice* (pp. 55–80). Palo Alto, CA: Consulting Psychologists Press.

Lagomarcino, T. (1986). Community services. In F. Rusch (Ed.), *Competitive employment issues and strategies* (pp. 65–75). Baltimore, MD: Brookes.

Lent, R. W., & Brown, S. D. (1996). Social cognitive approach to career development: An overview. *Career Development Quarterly, 44*(4), 310–321.

Lent, R. W., & Brown S. D. (2006). On conceptualizing and assessing social cognitive constructs in career research: A measurement guide. *Journal of Career Assessment, 14,* 12–35. doi:10.1177/1069072705281364

Lent, R. W., Brown S. D., & Hackett G. (1994). Toward a unifying social cognitive theory of career and academic interest, choice, and performance [Monograph]. *Journal of Vocational Behavior, 45*, 79–122. doi:10.1006/jvbe.1994.1027

Lent, R. W., Brown S. D., & Hackett G. (2000). Contextual supports and barriers to career choice: A social cognitive analysis. *Journal of Counseling Psychology, 47*, 36–49.

Lofquist, L. H., & Dawis R. V. (1969). *Adjustment to work: A psychological view of man's problems in a work-oriented society.* New York, NY: Appleton-Century-Crofts.

Lofquist, L. H., & Dawis R. V. (1991). *Essentials of person-environment correspondence counseling.* Minneapolis: University of Minnesota Press.

Mayall, D. (1994). *The worker trait data book.* Indianapolis, IN: JIST.

Mitchell, L. K., & Krumboltz, J. D. (1990). Social learning approach to career decision making: Krumboltz's theory. In D. Brown & L. Brooks (Eds.), *Career choice and development: Applying contemporary theories to practice* (2nd ed., pp. 145–196). San Francisco, CA: Jossey-Bass.

Mitchell, L. K., & Krumboltz, J. D. (1996). Krumboltz's learning theory of career choice and counseling. In D. Brown & L. Brooks (Eds.), *Career choice and development* (3rd ed., pp. 233–280). San Francisco, CA: Jossey-Bass.

Parsons, F. (1909). *Choosing a vocation.* Boston, MA: Houghton Mifflin.

Rounds, J. B., & Tracy, T. J. (1990). From trait-and-factor to person-environment fit counseling: Theory and process. In W. B. Walsh & S. H. Osipow (Eds.), *Career counseling: Contemporary topics in vocational psychology* (pp. 1–44). Hillsdale, NJ: Erlbaum.

Rubin, S. E., & Roessler, R. T. (1994). *Foundations of the vocational rehabilitation process* (4th ed.). Austin, TX: Pro-Ed.

Rubin, S. E., & Roessler, R. T. (2001). *Foundations of the vocational rehabilitation process* (5th ed.). Austin, TX: Pro-Ed.

Rubin, S. E., & Roessler, R. T. (2008). *Foundations of the vocational rehabilitation process* (6th ed.). Austin, TX: Pro-Ed.

Salomone, P. R. (1988). Career counseling: Steps and stages beyond Parsons. *Career Development Quarterly, 36*, 218–221.

Salomone, P. R. (1996). Career counseling and job placement: Theory and practice. In E. M. Szymanski & R. M. Parker (Eds.), *Work and disability: Issues and strategies in career development and job placement* (pp. 365–420). Austin, TX: Pro-Ed.

Sharf, R. S. (2006). *Applying career development theory to counseling.* Belmont, CA: Brooks/Cole.

Strauser, D. R. (2014). Introduction to the centrality of work for individuals with disabilities. In D. R. Strauser (Ed.), *Career development, employment and disability in rehabilitation: From theory to practice* (pp. 1–10). New York, NY: Springer Publishing.

Super, D. E. (1970). *Work Values Inventory.* Boston, MA: Houghton Mifflin.

Super, D. E. (1990). A life-span, life-space approach to career development. In D. Brown & L. Brooks (Eds.), *Career choice and development: Applying contemporary theories to practice* (2nd ed., pp. 197–261). San Francisco, CA: Jossey-Bass.

Super, D. E. (1994). A life span, life space perspective on convergence. In M. L. Savickas & R. W. Lent (Eds.), *Convergence in career development theories: Implications for science and practices* (pp. 63–74). Palo Alto, CA: Consulting Psychologists Press.

Super, D. E., & Nevill, D. D. (1986). *The Salience Inventory.* Palo Alto, CA: Consulting Psychologists Press.

Super, D. E., Thompson, A. S., Lindeman, R. H., Jordan, J. P., & Myers, R. A. (1981). *The Career Development Inventory.* Palo Alto, CA: Consulting Psychologists Press.

Super, D. E., Thompson, A. S., Lindeman, R. H., Myers, R. A., & Jordan, J. P. (1986). *Adult Career Concerns Inventory.* Palo Alto, CA: Consulting Psychologists Press.

Szymanski, E. M., Enright, M. S., Hershenson, D. B., & Ettinger, J. (2010). Career development theories and constructs: Implications for people with disabilities. In E. M. Szymanski & R. M. Parker (Eds.), *Work and disability: Contexts, issues, and strategies for enhancing employment outcomes for people with disabilities* (3rd ed., pp. 87–132). Austin, TX: Pro-Ed.

U.S. Department of Education. (2016). RSA: Workforce Innovation and Opportunity Act. Retrieved from http://www2.ed.gov/about/offices/list/osers/rsa/wioa-reauthorization.html#overview

U.S. Department of Labor. (1972). *Handbook for analyzing jobs.* Washington, DC: U.S. Government Printing Office.

U.S. Department of Labor. (1980). *Manual for the USES General Aptitude Test Battery. Section II-A: Development of the occupational aptitude pattern structure.* Washington, DC: U.S. Government Printing Office.

U.S. Department of Labor. (1991). *Dictionary of occupational titles* (4th ed.). Washington, DC: U.S. Government Printing Office.

U.S. Department of Labor. (2014). Career guide to industries. Retrieved from https://www.bls.gov/ooh/about/ooh-faqs.htm#info4

U.S. Department of Labor. (2016). Workforce Innovation and Opportunity Act; Joint rule for unified and combined state plans, performance accountability, and the one-stop system joint provisions; final rule. Retrieved from https://www.doleta.gov/wioa/Final_Rules_Resources.cfm

Wehman, P. (1986). Competitive employment in Virginia. In F. Rusch (Ed.), *Competitive employment issues and strategies* (pp. 23–33). Baltimore, MD: Brookes.

Wehman, P., Brooke, V., Brooke, A. M., Ham, W., Schall, C., McDonough, J., … Avellone, L. (2016). Employment for adults with autism spectrum disorders: A retrospective review of a customized employment approach. *Research in Developmental Disabilities, 53,* 61–72.

Wehman, P., & Kregel, J. (1985). A supported work approach to competitive employment of individuals with moderate and severe handicaps. In P. Wehman & J. Hill (Eds.), *Competitive employment for persons with mental retardation* (pp. 20–45). Richmond: Rehabilitation Research and Training Center, Virginia Commonwealth University.

5

Counseling Theories, Skills, and Principles of Practice

Sandra Fitzgerald and Julie Chronister

This chapter reviews contemporary and traditional counseling theories and models, basic counseling skills, competencies, and practice principles related to confidentiality, crisis counseling, trauma-informed care (TIC), conflict resolution, distance counseling, and counseling supervision. The counseling theories and models reviewed include contemporary approaches (multicultural counseling, empowerment approach, solution-focused, motivational interviewing [MI]), humanistic theories (person-centered, existential, gestalt), behavioral and cognitive behavioral related theories (behavioral, cognitive behavioral, rational–emotive behavior therapy [REBT], trait–factor); and psychodynamic theories (drive theory, ego-psychology, object relations, self-psychology, Adlerian, and Jungian).

Learning Objectives

By the end of this unit you should be able to:

1. Know counseling theories and models.
2. Know basic counseling skills and competencies.
3. Understand practice principles related to confidentiality, crisis management and disaster relief, TIC, conflict resolution, distance counseling, and counseling supervision.

Contemporary Approaches

I. Solution-Focused Brief Therapy

Conceptualized by de Shazer and Berg (1997), solution-focused brief therapy (SFBT) is a short-term, strength-based approach to counseling that has empirical support (Bannink, 2007; Kim, 2008; T. F. Lewis & Osborn, 2004; Stams, Dekovic, Buist, & de Vries, 2006). SFBT is based on social constructivism theory (SCT) which assumes that information does not exist separate from the self or the environment. Thus, SFBT counselors work to understand the client's subjective experience within their sociocultural context and view a client's future as one that can be created and negotiated versus fixed due to history, social status, or diagnosis (G. Corey, 2013; de Shazer et al., 2007). SFBT counselors view people as healthy and capable with the innate ability to formulate their own solutions to problems (Biggs & Flett, 2005). More specifically, people have experiences from which they can draw to overcome present challenges and change behavior if provided a supportive environment that activates their capabilities to allow them to reconstruct their perspective on life (Burwell & Chen, 2006). Thus, SFBT counselors view clients as having the necessary ingredients to recreate themselves, change their worldviews, and alter behaviors to experience a more satisfying life.

The SFBT counseling process is time limited, and thus, the primary focus is to find positive solutions for resolving problems that come from within the individual. The focus is not on cause, diagnosis, or limitations (Burwell & Chen, 2006); it is a collaborative process whereby the counselor assists the client in identifying personal solutions by evaluating their perception of reality to reconstruct a different perspective on the problem—all within a few counseling sessions. Simply put, the source of the solution is within the client, and the counseling process assists in identifying what currently works, doing more of what works, and stopping what does not work (Bannink, 2007). SFBT views incremental behavior change as the most effective and efficient approach to improvement (Seligman & Reichenberg, 2010), and counseling ends when clients put into action effective personal solutions.

Fundamental to the SFBT approach is asking intentional present and future-oriented questions, including coping, exception, miracle, scaling, and relationship questions. **Coping questions** are designed elicit from clients the status of the problems and how they coped in spite of them. For example, "How have you managed to keep your problems from getting worse?" The answer reflects whether the problem has become more or less manageable (Trepper et al., 2012). **Exception questions** elucidate times when problems are not present and the reasons why the situation did not cause a problem (Seligman & Reichenberg, 2010). Answers to exception questions increase client awareness related to the frequency of problems and exceptions to problems (Biggs & Flett, 2005). Examples of exception questions include, "In what situation do you feel better already?" (Bannink, 2006, p. 156) and "What was different about that moment?" (Bannink, 2006, p. 157). **Miracle questions** are used to assist clients in articulating a desired future in which problems do not exist (Bannink, 2006).

Commonly used in the first counseling session, miracle questions are designed to encourage the client to reflect on how life would look if the problem no longer existed. For example, "Imagine that a miracle occurred and the problem that brought you here disappeared tomorrow. What would tomorrow look like? How would it be different from today?" Answers typically shed light on counseling goals and tasks as it elucidates where the client wants to be in the future (Berg & Dolan, 2001). For example, if a client responds that they would not be living with the spouse and employed at a different law firm, then the solution-based goal may be taking steps toward separation and applying for a new job. **Scaling questions** are designed to measure progress, asking clients to rate how they are doing using a 10-point scale. For example, "On a scale of 1 to 10 (1 = problem is the worst and 10 = problem is resolved), where are you today?" Answers that reflect progress facilitate discussions about exceptions and ways to score higher on the scale, assessing the client's level of self-determination (Burwell & Chen, 2006). **Relationship questions** are designed to elicit dialogue around how the client views the perception of significant others on resolving the problem and whether these viewpoints influence if and how the client succeeds in solving the problem (de Jong & Berg, 2002). Relationship questions assume that significant others would be aware of changes in the client once the problem is resolved. Examples include, "What will your husband notice that is different about you once you solve this problem?" and "What will your coworkers think of you when this problem is no longer present?"

The SFBT approach is used to treat persons with various mental health conditions, including depression, alcohol and substance abuse, posttraumatic stress disorder (PTSD), and personality disorders (Bakker & Bannink, 2008; Berg & Dolan, 2001; Berg & Miller, 1992; de Jong & Berg, 1997), as well as work-related stress, domestic violence, loss, or family conflict (de Jong & Berg, 1997). SFBT is effective with children and adolescents (Berg & Steiner, 2003), adults (Berg & Miller, 1992), and couples and families (de Shazer, 1985) and can be combined with other therapeutic modalities such as MI (T. F. Lewis & Osborn, 2004).

II. Motivational Interviewing

MI was developed by Rollnick and Miller (1995) as an alternative to traditional addictions treatment that focused on confrontation. MI is a nonconfrontational, yet directive counseling approach designed to elicit positive behavioral change by addressing the individual's level of ambivalence to change (Rollnick & Miller, 1995). MI gained popularity in rehabilitation counseling settings because of its brief, strength-based intervention that fit well into contemporary rehabilitation settings (Manthey, Brooks, Chan, Hedenblad, & Ditchman, 2015). MI is not based on one particular theory, but several psychological constructs and theories, including **conflict and ambivalence** (Orford, 1985), **reactance** (Brehm & Brehm, 1981), **person-centered** (C. R. Rogers, 1957), **cognitive dissonance** (Festinger, 1957), **self-determination** (Ryan & Deci, 2002), **self-efficacy** (Bandura, 1999), **value theory** (Rokeach, 1973), **self-affirmation** (Steele, 1988), **and strength-based approaches** (Manthey et al., 2015; Saleebey, 2006).

The **goal** of MI is to develop a positive, collaborative counseling relationship that evokes reasons for change and strengthens personal motivation and commitment to a specific goal. The basic principles that underlie MI include **empathic understanding, acceptance** and **affirmation, identification of discrepancies, "rolling" with resistance**, and **facilitation of self-efficacy** to help achieve goals. MI techniques include the strategic use of particular counseling microskills such as **o**pen-ended questioning, **a**ffirmation, **r**eflection, and **s**ummary statements—also known as OARS (Miller & Rollnick, 2002). These skills are used to explore motivation to change and uncover competing interests, values, and conflicts related to achieving rehabilitation goals (Manthey et al., 2015).

III. Multicultural Counseling

Multicultural counseling emerged to address the diverse landscape of our society and more effectively respond to the experiences of historically marginalized communities. Multicultural counseling is also a response to the large number of Western/European theories formulated through the cultural lens of the White majority. Indeed, the experiences and values of clients from nondominant cultural groups, including those from oppressed racial, ethnic, gender, sexual, religious, disability, geographic, or heritage communities, do not align with many of the traditional counseling theories (Sue & Sue, 2003). This approach is also aligned with a pluralistic framework that reflects an ethical and political commitment to respecting, valuing and being inclusive toward others—their culture, worldview, values, beliefs, religion, and identities (M. Cooper & McLeod, 2007). As such, multicultural counseling is necessarily woven into the fabric of all counseling approaches by embracing and understanding difference, responding to clients' needs and wants through their cultural lens, respecting clients' multiple and intersecting cultural identities, and naturally broaching culture in counseling relationships. This approach views the counseling process, communication and social patterns, and presenting issues as culture bound and considers dimensions such as cultural identities, intersectionality, social justice, advocacy, power, prejudice, discrimination, and microaggressions as fundamental areas to broach with clients. Although initially established as a separate, unique counseling theory, multicultural counseling has evolved into **culturally competent counseling** and, much like Rogers' (1957) common factors, is integrated into all counseling relationships irrespective of counselor orientation or client–counselor cultural differences.

Culturally competent counseling approaches the counseling process with the awareness, skills, and knowledge necessary for working within the context of the client's culture (Sue, Arrendondo, & McDavis, 1992), and requires the counselor to be aware of personal cultural values and biases and the influence of these beliefs on the counseling relationship (Sue & Sue, 2003). Culturally competent counselors are aware of personal assumptions about human behavior, values, preconceived notions, limitations and biases; have an understanding of the worldview of clients who are culturally different without imposing negative judgments; and have the skills to practice appropriately with culturally different clients (Sue et al., 1992). Sue et al. (1992) identified three strategies for developing cultural competency: (a) acquiring specific race, ethnic and other cultural group information; (b) improving awareness, knowledge, and skill; and (c) using multicultural organizational development to address systemic factors beyond the individual. Sue et al. (1992) expanded on these three areas, developing 31 specific multicultural competencies which were then operationalized (see Arredondo et al., 1996). Cultural competency requires rehabilitation counselors to commit to a life-long process of open-mindedness, respect, and valuing toward cultural differences. The Code of Professional Ethics for Rehabilitation Counselors requires counselors to ensure that their own cultural values and biases do not result in a disregard of the cultural values of their clients and that ethical decision making occurs within diverse cultural contexts (American Counseling Association [ACA], 2014).

Culturally competent counseling is particularly important given the changing landscape of the United States and the high proportion of persons with disabilities who identify with other historically marginalized communities. According to the U.S. Census Bureau (2000), by the end of 2050, one in two citizens in the United States will be non-White compared with one in five in 1999. Specifically, in 2050, 50.1% of the total U.S. population is projected to be non-Hispanic Whites, 24% Hispanics, 15% African Americans, and 8% Asians. For Native Americans, there is an anticipated increase from 0.9% in 1997 to 1.1% by 2050 (A. Lewis, Bethea, & Hurley, 2009). Parallel to the U.S. population's increase in racial and ethnic diversity, the disability community has also become more culturally diverse. In fact, racial and ethnic minority communities have a disproportionally high rate of disability compared with Whites, with African Americans and Hispanics being particularly over-represented in all health and mental health conditions (Bradsher, 1996; Smart & Smart, 1997).

Aligned with a pluralistic and cultural competency approach is a **social justice** and **advocacy** orientation. "Within the counseling profession, the cutting edge is exemplified by the social justice counseling paradigm" (J. A. Lewis, Ratts, Paladino & Toporek, 2011, p. 6). This paradigm uses advocacy and activism as tools for addressing unjust and unequal economic and sociopolitical conditions that negatively impact the work, social, and educational lives of individuals, families, and communities (Ratts, 2009). Social justice–oriented counselors view client difficulties from an individual *and* contextual perspective and thus rely on advocacy to eliminate oppressive environmental barriers (J. A. Lewis et al., 2011). The goal of social justice counseling is to ensure that all individuals have the opportunity achieve their goals and potential without facing barriers. This orientation is based on the belief that every individual has a right to a quality education, to health care services, and to employment opportunities regardless of race, ethnicity, sex, sexual orientation, gender identity, gender expression, economic status, and creed, to list a few. The process for achieving social justice is collaborative; clients participate in the process and contribute to the therapeutic process, promoting client awareness, knowledge, and skills needed to navigate their world successfully. Traditional counseling theories are grounded in basic assumptions that implicitly perpetuate social injustices (Prilleltensky, 1994). The social justice counseling paradigm, in concert with culturally competent counseling, offers a paradigmatic shift that responds to the needs of client, counselors, and communities today (J. A. Lewis et al., 2011).

One of the major roles and functions of the social justice paradigm is **advocacy**. Advocacy is a core, fundamental component of counseling. At its most basic level, advocacy means to help or assist; counselors are advocates when they work on behalf of a client or a social cause (Lee, 1998a). Counselor advocacy is a form of social justice action because it occurs in the social contexts in which client problems occur and involves action to eliminate social problems, such as poverty, lack of access, prejudice, and discrimination, that negatively affect clients (Lee, 1998b). Similarly, a social justice approach to counseling involves using counseling tools and methods to confront injustice and inequality in society (Jackson, 2000; Mays, 2000; Strickland, 2000).

Collectively, advocacy and social justice counseling work involves "helping clients challenge institutional and social barriers that impede academic, career, or personal-social development" (Lee, 1998a, pp. 8–9). These approaches require that counselors leave their offices and work in settings such as a client's home or school, recreational centers, churches, local agencies, and offices of policy makers and government administrators.

Rehabilitation counselors have an ethical obligation to address the oppression and discrimination of oppressed communities in an affirmative manner (Blackwell, Martin, & Scalia, 1994). The Code of Professional Ethics for Rehabilitation Counselors (Commission on Rehabilitation Counselor Certification, 2010) provides a framework for critical thinking related to a counselors' ethical obligation to their clients in the areas of advocacy and accessibility. The Code includes six standards related to advocacy, including attitudinal barriers, advocacy in one's own agency and with cooperating agencies, areas of knowledge and competency, knowledge of benefit systems, and confidentiality. In addition, three standards focus on accessibility, including accessibility in counseling practice, barriers to access, and referral accessibility. These ethical standards emphasize the significant need for rehabilitation counselors to implement advocacy and accessibility strategies when counseling individuals with disabilities to ensure equitable opportunities to become fully participating members of their communities.

Empowerment Counseling Approach

Empowerment is defined as a process of increasing personal, interpersonal, or political power to allow individuals to act to improve their life situation (Gutierrez, 1990). Basic tenets of empowerment include every individual has worth and dignity, every individual should have the same opportunity to maximize personal potential, people generally strive to grow and change in positive directions, and individuals should be free to make personal decisions about managing life (Kosciulek, 2000). To facilitate an empowering counseling relationship, rehabilitation and mental health counselors focus on client capabilities, capacities, and opportunities rather than deficits (Sales, 2005). In addition, rehabilitation counselors value unique client experiences and recognize that clients come with different levels of control over their lives and their environments (Sales, 2005).

An empowerment approach is reflected by counselors who (a) focus on strengths rather than deficits; (b) think about and interact with the person, not the label or the diagnosis; (c) respect the client's right to self-determination; (d) consider the "whole" person, including quality of life and environmental factors; (e) respect the skills and knowledge that the client brings to the relationship; (f) trust that clients are internally motivated to learn and direct their own lives; and (g) respect each person's unique qualities, values and needs. In addition, rehabilitation and mental health counselors must (a) be empowered and model empowerment for their clients; (b) support client informed choice and self-determination; (c) view clients as a resource for, not the owner of, problems; (d) use effective therapeutic skills to develop a working alliance; (e) facilitate client self-understanding; (f) increase clients' knowledge about their world; (g) provide clients with sufficient opportunities, information, and perspectives to enable informed choice; (h) continuously update their knowledge of community resources, agencies, and opportunities in order to effectively support clients; and (i) provide client training in communication, assertiveness, self-advocacy, and problem-solving skills (Sales, 2005). Client empowerment approaches are associated with clients' greater consciousness of themselves as individuals with disabilities; reduced self-blame and recognition of anger as a catalyst for change; increased personal responsibility for changing themselves and society; and increased personal responsibility for decision making, actions and consequences (Sales, 2005).

Humanistic Approaches

I. Person-Centered Theory

Person-centered theory (PCT), also known as the Rogerian or client-centered theory, reflects the essence of the **humanistic** approach, which assumes that humans are fundamentally positive and striving toward **self-actualization** (process of moving toward one's greatest potential). Humanistic counselors are **phenomenological** (understanding a client's world as they see it) and **present focused** (Halbur & Halbur, 2006), which in turn allows access to a person's psychological experience (Halbur & Halbur, 2006; C. R. Rogers, 1961). The **primary goal** of PCT counseling is to facilitate growth and movement toward self-actualization which at times, is hindered by a distorted view of one's self (Halbur & Halbur, 2006). Thus, **self-concept**, or individuals' belief about themselves, includes their attributes and who and what the self is, plays a significant role in PCT. C. R. Rogers (1959) conceptualized self-concept as having three components: self-image, self-esteem, and ideal self. *Self-image* refers to how people view themselves; it is shaped by life experiences and, at times, is not always an accurate perception. Those experiencing distorted self-images (e.g., exaggerating their strengths or flaws) experience low **self-esteem**, or the value people have toward their self. The **ideal self** is who the individual desires to become; at times, individuals experience a discrepancy between their ideal self-concept and their real self-concept, resulting in a state of **incongruence**. Healthy functioning therefore occurs when there is **congruency** between a person's real self-concept and ideal self-concept (C. R. Rogers, 1961). Notably, a state of total congruence is rare; most people experience some degree of incongruence, and healthy individuals recognize that congruency and actualization are a never-ending process (C. R. Rogers, 1959). Indeed, congruence exists on a continuum rather than on an all-or-nothing basis (G. Corey, 1986).

Accordingly, PCT proposes that personality is formed through an individual's self-concept. Specifically, individuals with negative self-concepts do not like, trust, or appreciate themselves and view the world as untrustworthy and hostile, whereas individuals with positive self-concepts appreciate and like who they are, trust themselves and the world, are open to experiences, and look to themselves—rather than to others—for approval or disapproval (C. R. Rogers, 1959). Self-concept is shaped by levels of **genuineness**—also referred to as congruency, **unconditional positive regard,** and **accurate empathic understanding** from primary people in one's life. According to C. R. Rogers (1977), these conditions form the core of the therapeutic relationship and are considered **necessary and sufficient** for the development of a positive, congruent self-concept grounded in the individual's **organismic valuing process** or internal locus of evaluation. See Table 5.1 for definitions.

Notably, when individuals experience enduring conditional regard (vs. unconditional positive regard), barriers toward the organismic valuing process, congruency, and self-actualization occur. Individuals in this situation conform in order to obtain love and acceptance and thus live according to "**conditions of worth,**" or values introjected by others. Social norms and rules, and messages from other primary figures, become part of the self-concept, so conditions of worth cause people to operate "on an external locus of evaluation (because their values are not self-generated) rather than an internal locus of evaluation (the organismic valuing process)" (Murdock, 2016, p. 158). Conditions of worth therefore reflect a denial of one's own self-actualizing tendency and an inability to determine one's likes, dislikes, interests, talents, and overall uniqueness. In the extreme, individuals living with enduring conditions of worth become conforming, authoritarian, with rigid self-concepts (Halbur & Halbur, 2006).

The **primary PCT counseling technique** is the **therapeutic relationship** that is based on the six necessary and sufficient conditions outlined in Table 5.2. If these conditions are met, constructive personality change will occur (C. R. Rogers, 1957).

TABLE 5.1   Definitions of Basic Conditions

Genuineness/congruence is the most important counseling condition and requires the counselor to be genuine, open, integrated, and authentic during client–counselor interactions. Counselors' internal and external experiences must be congruent as this models the process of working toward greater authenticity and congruency. Although counselors are not expected to be fully self-actualized, they need to be genuine and congruent in the counseling relationship to facilitate effective counseling and change (G. Corey, 1986).

Unconditional positive regard refers to counselors' acceptance, caring, and valuing of the client. Counselors may not approve of clients' actions, but counselors always approve and value their clients. PCT counselors hold the attitude of "I'll accept you as you are." It is however, not possible for counselors to possess unconditional positive regard at all times (G. Corey, 1986).

Accurate empathic understanding refers to counselors' ability to understand sensitively and accurately (but not sympathetically) clients' experience and feelings in the here and now. Empathic understanding occurs when the counselor experiences client feelings as if they were their own without becoming lost in the feelings (G. Corey, 1986).

TABLE 5.2   Six Necessary and Sufficient Conditions for Counseling

Condition	Counselor	Client
1. Two persons are in psychological contact.	To have sufficient training to understand the role of the facilitative conditions, including the person-centered philosophy behind them	To be cognitively and emotionally capable of making psychological contact
2. The client is in a state of incongruence, being vulnerable or anxious.	To have no role except to recognize what propels the client into the therapeutic relationship	To recognize the client's own psychological state and to seek relief
3. The therapist is congruent or integrated in the relationship.	To enter the relationship as the genuine self (within professional boundaries), not hiding behind professional or personal facades	To be in the relationship

(continued)

TABLE 5.2 Six Necessary and Sufficient Conditions for Counseling (*continued*)

Condition	Counselor	Client
4. The therapist experiences unconditional positive regard for the client.	To extend nonpossessive love, acceptance, or caring to the client, valuing the client as a person regardless of behaviors that may be unattractive	To be in the relationship
5. The therapist experiences an empathic understanding of the client's internal frame of reference and endeavors to communicate this experience back to the client.	To accept the centrality of the client in the relationship, to experience the client's subjective inner world as if being the client (without losing sight of the "as if" quality), and through attentive and spoken behaviors, to demonstrate this understanding to the client	To be in the relationship
6. Communication to the client of the therapist's empathic understanding and unconditional positive regard is to a minimal degree achieved.	To have sufficient training to communicate these things and to monitor the relationship for indications that the communication is successful	To have the capacity and to be active enough in the relationship to perceive the communications of the therapist

Within this context, PCT counselors view clients as experts on their own lives and thus offer minimal advice or directives (Halbur & Halbur, 2006). PCT counseling applies as much to the relationships between counselors and their clients as it does to relationships between parents and children or teachers and students. In whatever context, if the goal is self-actualization, then the means to that end is the therapeutic relationship, as defined by the facilitative conditions of genuineness, unconditional positive regard, and empathic understanding (See & Kamnetz, 2015). PCT counseling is practiced in different ways. At one extreme is the classical form of counseling, which is long-term, is nondirective, and adheres closely to the necessary and sufficient facilitative conditions set forth by C. R. Rogers (1957). At the other end, is a more contemporary form of counseling where in the conditions are taught to counselors and paraprofessionals in various settings (e.g., agencies, schools) as a tool for facilitating brief intervention and behavior change. In these situation, when clients are focused on their inner subjective world and feelings, the practitioner more deliberately applies the facilitative conditions; when the focus moves to concrete skill development or knowledge attainment, the facilitative conditions give way to a more pedagogical orientation associated with education and training (See & Kamnetz, 2015). Irrespective of the counseling setting or theoretical orientation, research shows that Rogers' facilitative conditions account for the largest proportion of client gain than any other counseling theory technique, accounting for up to 70% of the outcome variance in counseling (Wampold, 2001). As such, these conditions have been labelled "common factors," as they are important to all credible counseling approaches and complement, if not facilitate, the working alliance to create the therapeutic relationship (See & Kamnetz, 2015).

II. Existential Theory

Existential theory is based on the fundamental issues related to the human condition, including death, isolation, and existence (Yalom, 1995). Anxiety is therefore related to coping with these human conditions. Specifically, the unknown related to death is believed to be the most fundamental issue that people are facing (Yalom, 1995). This approach focuses on facilitating meaning and purpose in life. The primary **goal of therapy** is awareness (G. Corey, 2004). Similar to person-centered counseling, existential counseling focuses on moving toward actualization. However, existentialists also believe that it is important to assist clients in confronting issues associated with existence, meaning, and the human condition (Hansen, Rossberg & Cramer, 1993). More specific goals include understanding the freedom to choose, taking responsibility for personal choices, acknowledging the limitations and barriers associated with freedom, and increasing awareness around available possibilities (Halbur & Halbur, 2006). The primary **technique** associated with this approach is the counseling relationship. The counselor uses acceptance, authenticity (genuineness), and empathy. It is critical that the counselor facilitate empathy by entering the client's world and understanding the client's worldview (G. Corey, 2004). In addition, the counselor's role is to be present while clients confront issues, to assist clients in accepting responsibility for their choices, and to problem-solve (G. Corey, 2004). Existential counseling is not technique oriented; it is relationship focused but may use techniques from other supporting counseling approaches.

III. Gestalt Theory

The Gestalt approach was founded by Fritz Perls and has strong roots in German philosophy and perceptual psychology. **Gestalt**, which refers to a unified whole, is the basis of this approach. A fundamental assumption of this approach is that the whole is greater than the sum of the parts and humans function best as a whole. Thus, the Gestalt approach understands humans as products of the interrelationship between thoughts, feelings, perceptions, mind, soul, and sensations as opposed to understanding each separate part of an individual. Gestalt counselors also believe that individuals have the capability to shape reality and make their own choices (Coven, 1979; Halbur & Halbur, 2006). Emotional difficulties occur when people, who begin as whole individuals, lose their integrated self. As such, therapeutic change includes gaining insight and reintegrating aspects of the self. The **major goals of therapy** are to increase awareness and self-responsibility to facilitate integration (Halbur & Halbur, 2006).

Gestalt **techniques** include focusing on the here and now, as the past is relevant only because it facilitates bringing the individual to the present. In addition, like other humanistic schools, the Gestalt counselor uses a phenomenological approach to see the world as the client sees it. Athough Perls is known for a variety of techniques, he did not believe that a counselor should be wed to any one particular technique. Some of Perl's most popular techniques include **empty chair**, which assists clients in moving beyond any "unfinished business" with another person and requires the client to imagine that the other individual is sitting in the other chair so that the client can have a dialogue with the person. Typically, the counselor instructs the client to assume both roles—moving to the other (empty) chair at times. **Pronouns** is a technique that involves assisting clients in using personal pronouns such as "I" or "me" versus third person such as "you" when talking about themselves. This technique facilitates personal growth by allowing clients to become more aware of their particular feelings and thoughts versus detaching themselves. **Sharing hunches** is a technique in which the counselor shares the potential meaning of nonverbal messages or helps clients share a possible meaning of nonverbal messages to help them gain greater self-awareness. Finally, **dream work** involves a client playing out roles or completing conversations that occurred in a dream (Halbur & Halbur, 2006).

Behavioral and Cognitive Behavioral Related Theories

The **behavioral approach** posits that human behavior is shaped by environmental conditioning and reinforcement. Although traditional behavioral approaches are grounded in empiricism and focus primarily on tangible behaviors, goals, and techniques, contemporary variations also attend to emotions and the counseling relationship (Halbur & Halbur, 2006).

I. Behavioral Therapy

Behavioral therapy is a compilation of approaches and techniques used to reduce maladaptive behaviors and increase adaptive behaviors (Stoll, 2004). Behavioral therapy emphasizes current rather than past behavior and relies on scientific methods to assess the effectiveness of the techniques through objective, measurable goals (G. Corey, 2001). Behavioral therapies use multiple assessments throughout treatment (Corrigan & Liberman, 1994) and view behavioral problems as a consequence of learning negative behaviors (Halbur & Halbur, 2006). There are two major theoretical underpinnings that describe traditional behavioral approaches: **classical conditioning** and **operant conditioning**.

    Classical conditioning, founded by Ivan Pavlov, is a learning process that occurs through associations between an environmental stimulus and a naturally occurring stimulus. Through the following experiment, Pavlov showed that a stimulus that should not cause an automatic reaction could be made to cause an automatic reaction: Pavlov rang a bell, he provided dogs with food, and the dogs salivated. He repeated this process until the dogs salivated when the bell rang but the dogs were given no food. The food therefore is the **unconditional stimulus** (US), meaning that it caused an automatic reaction (salivation), which is the **unconditional response** (UR). When a **neutral stimulus** (the bell) was repeatedly paired with the US (food), the bell became a conditional stimulus (CS) that elicited a response on its own, or the **conditioned response** (CR). Thus, learning occurred (Halbur & Halbur, 2006). More important, once the CS and CR relationship is established, the association will disappear if the CS is repeatedly presented without the US. This process is referred to as classical **extinction** (Schloss & Smith, 1994).

    Operant conditioning was founded by E. L. Thorndike and B. F. Skinner (Wilson, 1995). Thorndike developed the **law of effect** which posits that behaviors leading to satisfaction are reinforced, whereas behaviors leading to dissatisfaction are not reinforced. In the same vein, Skinner believed that complex behaviors resulted from how an organism interacted with or operated on the environment because of the consequences (G. Corey, 2001). The key components of operant conditioning are **reinforcement** and **punishment**. Reinforcement is anything that increases the frequency of a behavior, and punishment is anything that reduces the frequency of a behavior (Craighead, Craighead, Kazdin, & Mahoney, 1994). Reinforcement and punishment involve the provision of a positive reward for adaptive behavior (Craighead et al., 1994), and negative reinforcement occurs when the frequency of behavior increases through the elimination of a negative stimulus (Papajohn, 1982). Punishers may also be positive or negative; positive punishment occurs when an undesired behavior decreases after the provision of a particular stimulus, and negative punishment occurs when a positive stimulus is removed after an undesired behavior (Kiernan, 1975).

    There are two types of reinforcers: primary reinforcers, which are inherently reinforcing, and secondary reinforcers, which are reinforcing through learning and experience (e.g., tokens earned in a token economy). For operant conditioning to be effective however, reinforcers must be meaningful to the client (Mueser, 1993). In addition, reinforcers can be delivered through a variety of reinforcement schedules, including (a) a continuous schedule (reinforcement after each occurrence of the desired behavior); (b) a fixed interval schedule (reinforcement after a consistent time interval regardless of how many times the desired behavior occurred within the interval); (c) a fixed ratio schedule (reinforcement after the client makes a specified number of the desired responses); (d) a variable interval schedule (reinforcement after an unpredictable period of time); and (e) finally, a variable ratio schedule (reinforcement after a client demonstrates a variable number of desired responses) (Halbur & Halbur, 2006; Stoll, 2004). Operant conditioning can also include **extinction**, which occurs when reinforcement is withheld from a previously reinforced behavior to decrease the undesired behavior (Wilson, 1995).

The **goals of behavioral therapy** include helping clients change their environment and reinforce more adaptive behaviors. The focus of behavior therapy is corrective learning, which involves developing new coping skills, improving communication, and overcoming maladaptive emotional issues (Wilson, 1995). Many operant **techniques**, including shaping, differential reinforcement, behavioral contracts, token economies, and social skills training, are used to increase the frequency of adaptive behavior (Stoll, 2004). **Shaping** involves reinforcing closer approximations of the desired target behavior until the target behavior is shown. **Differential reinforcement** occurs when all behaviors except the target behavior are positively reinforced. **Behavioral contracts** are agreements between the counselor and the client (Kazdin, 1994) and include behaviors that need to be changed and the reinforcers and punishers needed for behavior change. **Token economies** are typically implemented in structured environments where desirable behaviors (e.g., taking medication, participating in activities) are reinforced with tokens, which can then be used to "buy" more desired reinforcers (Corrigan & Liberman, 1994). Finally, **social skills training** is used to enhance communication, assertiveness, problem solving, and other desired social skills (Corrigan & Liberman, 1994).

II. Cognitive Behavioral Therapy

Cognitive behavioral therapy (CBT), which is attributed primarily to Beck (1976, 1991), views emotional and behavioral consequences as a result of cognitions. Specifically, this approach posits that people's feelings and behaviors are based on how they think (cognitions). As such, psychological distress is largely due to one's thought processes that are based on faulty ineffective thinking. From this approach, personality is seen as an enduring set of behavioral and emotional responses to stimuli that stem from ingrained, idiosyncratic ways of thinking. CBT holds that individuals have innate dispositions that interact with the environment to shape their responses and worldviews (Beck & Weishaar, 2000). The primary **goal of therapy** is to teach clients about how they think so that they can correct faulty reasoning (Nelson-Jones, 2000). The **primary technique** is psychoeducation, and the emphasis is on developing skills for managing specific problems (Hanson et al., 1993). Five common CBT techniques include (a) identification of dysfunctional and distorted cognitions; (b) self-monitoring of negative thoughts, or "self-talk"; (c) identification of the relationships between thoughts, underlying beliefs, and feelings; (d) identification of alternate thinking patterns; and (e) personal hypothesis testing regarding the validity of basic assumptions about the self, world, and future (Craighead et al., 1994). Other popular techniques include skills training, assertiveness training, relaxation techniques, and training in areas such as life skills, social skills, communication, role-play, systematic desensitization, flooding, thought-stopping, and cognitive modification (Halbur & Halbur, 2006). CBT counselors typically work collaboratively with clients and develop a mutual relationship with therapeutic rapport. Although therapeutic alliance, empathic understanding, genuineness, and unconditional positive regard are all considered necessary for change, they are not sufficient; techniques are needed as well.

III. Rational–Emotive Behavior Therapy

Developed by Ellis (1962), REBT is an active–directive form of counseling in which practitioners use cognitive, behavioral, and emotive techniques to assist people in obtaining and maintaining positive change (Bishop & Fleming, 2015). This change occurs through an educational counseling process designed to help clients understand the following principles: (a) People create their own psychological disturbances and problems; (b) people do this by maintaining irrational beliefs; and (c) people can learn to address and overcome problems by learning to detect, question, challenge, and reject their irrational beliefs as illogical and unhelpful and by developing rational beliefs that are "true, sensible, and constructive" (Bishop & Fleming, 2015; Dryden, 2005). The fundamental tenet of REBT is that the events, incidents, or adversities themselves do not lead to emotional difficulties; rather, the irrational beliefs, dogmatic musts, and imperative demands that people hold about these events cause distress and lead people to engage in self-defeating emotions and problematic behaviors that thwart goal attainment. Conversely, people who take primary responsibility for their emotional difficulties and work to rid themselves of irrational thinking experience minimal self-defeating barriers and have a higher probability of experiencing happiness and satisfaction (Bishop & Fleming, 2015; Yankura & Dryden, 1994).

REBT is based on the premise that humans are fundamentally inclined toward growth, actualization, and rationality; yet, at the same time, humans experience opposing irrational and dysfunctional tendencies (Ellis, 1962). Both of these conflicting tendencies are considered to stem from biological, social and psychological influences (Bishop & Fleming, 2015). According to REBT, **rational** is that which helps a person achieve their goals or purposes and leads to healthy results. **Irrational** is that which prevents a person from achieving their goals and leads to unhealthy outcomes (Dryden, 2012, 2013). Given that people have unique goals and purposes, the meaning of *rationality* varies given the individual and their situation (Bishop & Fleming, 2015).

According to REBT, rational beliefs are considered to be the core of **psychological health**; as such, the primary goal of REBT is to assist clients to change irrational beliefs into rational beliefs (Dryden, 2013). Rational beliefs are characterized as being logical, flexible, consistent with reality, and consistent with one's long-term goals. A rational belief or expectation is expressed in terms of what we want or would like to happen, or as a preference, while recognizing that we may not have, and do not have to get, what we want. People who hold rational beliefs and expectations experience positive feelings of satisfaction when they get what they want and experience healthy negative feelings, such as disappointment, sadness, healthy anger, or regret when they do not (Dryden, 2012). These healthy negative feelings may motivate continued efforts toward the eventual attainment of goals or desires.

REBT is based on the premise that **irrational beliefs** become ingrained at an early age and manifest later in life (Gilliland & James, 1998). Irrational beliefs are rigid, illogical, inconsistent with long-term goals, and unhealthy. Irrational beliefs are expressed as demands (e.g., "Things *have to* work out the way I think they should"), as musts (e.g., "I *must* have what I want"), or as all-or-nothing absolutes (e.g., "I am *always* treated unfairly" or "I will *never* succeed"). Because these unhealthy negative emotions are probably associated with behaviors, such as withdrawal, isolation, procrastination, inactivity, escapism, or substance abuse, that negatively affect the health of the person's relationships, they hinder rather than promote the person's long-term goal pursuit and achievement. The distinction between rational and irrational beliefs is a central focus of REBT (e.g., Dryden, 2013; Weinrach, 2006). Ellis (1962) proposed a specific set of irrational beliefs that he viewed as the most frequent causes of emotional distress. These are presented in Table 5.3.

Ellis (1962) believed that humans can change these irrational thoughts by "attacking" the beliefs to reduce self-defeating, irrational thinking. Thus, the primary **goal of therapy** is to change the way people think because thoughts (vs. events and emotions) cause emotional problems (Gilliland & James, 1998). The goals and process of REBT are often summarized using the ABC method: **A** refers to the activating event or adversity; **B** is the individual's beliefs about the event, which may be rational and helpful or irrational and maladaptive; **C** refers to the emotional and behavioral consequences of those beliefs; **D** refers to the responsibility of the counselor to dispute the irrational beliefs and assist the client in obtaining more rational, adaptive beliefs; and **E** refers to the client developing new behavioral and emotional consequences (Gilliland & James, 1998). REBT attempts to change the client's basic value system (Hansen et al., 1993) and the ultimate consequence is for the client to live a rational life independent from the counselor (Halbur & Halbur, 2006).

The most common REBT **technique** is to teach. Counselors teach clients about REBT assumptions and the ways in which consequences of irrational beliefs impact functioning. Common techniques include **confrontation, disputing irrational beliefs**, and **bibliotherapy** (Halbur & Halbur, 2006). Affective and behavioral aspects are also addressed and may include techniques such as **imagery, role-playing, homework assignments, and skills training** (Gilliland & James, 1998). REBT is an active, directive, and problem-focused counseling approach that can be brief and uses tools such as **questionnaires, self-help forms, and homework**

TABLE 5.3 Irrational Beliefs

1. The idea that it is a dire necessity for an adult human being to be loved or approved by virtually every significant person in the community

2. The idea that one should be thoroughly competent, adequate, and achieving in all possible respects in order to be considered worthwhile

3. The idea that certain people are bad, wicked, or villainous and that they should be severely blamed and punished for their villainy

4. The idea that it is awful and catastrophic when things are not the way one would very much like them to be

5. The idea that human unhappiness is externally caused and that people have little or no ability to control their sorrows and disturbance

6. The idea that if something is or may be dangerous or fearsome, one should be terribly concerned about it and should keep dwelling on the possibility of its occurring

7. The idea that it is easier to avoid than to face certain life difficulties and self-responsibilities

8. The idea that one should be dependent on others and should need someone stronger than oneself on whom to rely

9. The idea that one's history is an all-important determiner of one's present behavior and that because something once affected one's life, it should indefinitely have a similar effect

10. The idea that one should become quite upset over other people's problems and disturbances

11. The idea that there is invariably a right, precise, and perfect solution to human problems and that it is catastrophic if this solution is not found

(e.g., reading of or listening to psychoeducational materials). Altough it is common for REBT counselors to convey unconditional acceptance, a warm relationship is not considered necessary and certainly not sufficient for change. Like CBT, techniques are considered paramount for change.

IV. Trait–Factor Approach

The **trait–factor approach** defines human behavior through **traits**, which are categories of aptitudes, interests, values, achievements, and personalities that are integrated in a variety of ways to form constellations of characteristics called **factors**. Based on these traits and factors, a scientific problem-solving method is applied to statistically predict outcomes that could be applied differently to individuals (Williamson & Biggs, 1979). This approach is based on the assumption that people have different traits, occupations require a particular combination of worker characteristics, and trait–factor counselors should match a person's traits with particular job characteristics (Kosciulek, Phillips & Lizotte, 2015). Parsons (1909) believed that choosing a career requires (a) knowledge of self, aptitudes, interests, ambitions, resources, and limitations; (b) knowledge of the requirements and conditions of success, advantages and disadvantages of specific jobs, compensation, opportunities, and prospects in different lines of work; and (c) accurate reasoning on the relation of these two groups of facts (Kosciulek et al., 2015; Parsons, 1909). In addition, the trait–factor counseling approach posits that (a) clients have traits that position them for a few correct occupations; (b) clients need vocational counseling to avoid choosing an inappropriate occupation; (c) correct occupations influence other personal decisions; (d) life is predictable and occupational decisions are constant; and (e) trait–factor counseling facilitates comparisons between individual traits and job tasks.

The trait–factor theory evolved from a vocational perspective and was designed for student personnel programs in university settings. As such, many of its **techniques and practices** are based on vocational and educational counseling of students experiencing typical developmental problems, and it is grounded in preventive counseling, information services, testing, and teaching (Gilliland & James, 1998). Trait–factor counseling focuses on the total development of the individual across the lifespan. Short-term goals are to help client's stop irrational, nonproductive thinking and behaviors and learn rational problem-solving skills for effective decision making (Lynch & Maki, 1981). Long-term goals are to provide the client with decision-making skills formulated jointly by the client and society. The counselor–client relationship is characterized by teaching, mentoring, and influencing, and measurement tools are fundamental to determining client characteristics.

Williamson (1965, 1972) viewed trait–factor counseling as facilitating self-understanding, realistic planning, and decision-making skills (Chartrand, 1991). He described the process as including analysis, synthesis, diagnosis, prognosis, counseling, and follow-up. Analysis, synthesis, and diagnosis entail gathering demographic and clinical information, synthesizing information to determine client strengths and limitations, making inferences based on strengths and needs, and determining a diagnosis from the type and cause of the vocational decision-making problem (Brown, 1990). A prognosis is made by estimating the probability of client adjustment given specific conditions or choice options and is followed by a rational, problem-solving approach to counseling that includes follow-up after the client makes a vocational decision. Trait–factor counselors act as tutors or advisors, assisting clients in obtaining data about self or jobs, presenting and discussing alternate options and actions, and attempting to help the client reach the best choice or decision (Rounds & Tracey, 1990). Basic assumptions of the trait–factor counseling theory are list in Table 5.4.

TABLE 5.4 Trait–Factor Basic Principles

1. Each individual has a specific pattern of traits that are stable over time and measurable.

2. Specific trait patterns are necessary for successfully performing specific vocational tasks.

3. Individual traits can be matched to the necessary vocational traits rationally and statistically.

4. Vocational success is highly probable if individual traits match vocational trait requirements.

5. Individual traits are best understood within the context of their environmental fit (e.g., geographical area, culture, community, family, socioeconomic status, educational/vocational setting).

6. Vocational counseling and its focus on person–environment fit can also be applied to daily living tasks related to school, family, and aging.

Source: Adapted from Gilliland and James (1998).

The trait–factor approach aligns with rehabilitation counseling in many ways. For example, job-matching systems, analysis of transferable skills, and ecological assessment processes used in supported employment are examples of trait–factor theory in rehabilitation counseling practice. Consistent with empowerment and consumer choice rehabilitation philosophies, the trait–factor approach to rehabilitation counseling attempts to improve client problem-solving and decision-making skills, promoting self-determination (Kosciulek, 1999). Assessment of client interests, aptitudes, and skills is fundamental to rehabilitation counseling and a core of component of the trait–factor approach (Lynch & Maki, 1981).

A. Minnesota Theory of Work Adjustment

Minnesota Theory of Work Adjustment (MTWA), which was developed specifically for persons with disabilities, is strongly aligned with the trait–factor approach (Dawis & Lofquist, 1984). Lofquist and Dawis (1969) define *work adjustment* as the "continuous and dynamic process by which the individual seeks to achieve and maintain correspondence with the work environment" (p. 46). The MTWA provides rehabilitation counselors with an organized and reliable model for applying trait–factor counseling methods. Specifically, the MTWA is designed to determine job satisfactoriness (i.e., the extent to which the person is able to perform the job) by correctly matching the person's abilities and work-related needs with the ability requirements and reinforcement structure of the work environment. The MTWA also provides a way to conceptualize disability within the context of work, identify needed vocational assessment information, facilitate vocational counseling procedures, and evaluate the effectiveness of rehabilitation counseling (Dawis & Lofquist, 1984).

During the 1990s, the trait–factor approach expanded to a Person × Environment (P × E) interaction model, moving away from focusing solely on person-centered traits to considering the person and environment in predicting behavior (Chartrand, Strong, & Weitzman, 1995). The P × E model explains how people fit into the world of work and moves the approach from a static matching orientation to a more dynamic analysis of how persons select and shape their environments (Hershenson, 1996; Tansey, Mizelle, Ferrin, Tschopp, & Frain, 2004). From a P × E perspective, the guiding questions in counseling are, "What kinds of personal and environmental factors are relevant to predicting vocational choice and adjustment" and "How is the process of person and environment interaction best characterized?" (Kosciulek, 1993). The contemporary

P × E counseling approach is a useful model for the provision of vocational counseling in a variety of settings, including rehabilitation and mental health counseling.

Chartrand (1991) described three basic assumptions of the P × E model originating from trait–factor counseling: (a) People are capable of making rational decisions through a cognitive approach that emphasizes learning but does not ignore affect (Kosciulek, 1993); (b) although people and work environments differ in reliable, meaningful, and consistent ways, important work behaviors, skill patterns, and working conditions can be identified to facilitate successful matches between people and work environments; and (c) the stronger the congruence between personal characteristics and job requirements, the greater the likelihood of success. Accordingly, person and environmental knowledge patterns inform people about the probability of satisfaction and adjustment to various job settings (Kosciulek, 1993). More important, the P × E approach extends beyond the assumption of congruence, or a good match, to include **dynamic reciprocity**, with individuals shaping the environment and the environment influencing individuals (Rounds & Tracey, 1990).

The P × E counseling approach is characterized by a supportive teaching style, with treatment and intervention recommendations based on the client's information-processing abilities. This approach is appropriate for clients who are motivated but lack the skills, understanding, ability, or confidence to effect change (Chartrand, 1991). P × E counseling is typically brief and is well suited for group counseling (Lunneborg, 1983). A Job Club—which is a group-oriented job-development and job-placement service, is an example of a rehabilitation-related P × E group counseling approach (Azrin & Besalel, 1980). Athough trait–factor counseling is generally considered a vocational and educational approach, the P × E approach is applicable to a broader range of problems (Rounds & Tracey, 1990). For example, studies show that the P × E problem-solving framework also influences nonvocational outcomes such as improved self-concept, positive attitudes, increased internal locus of control, and decreased levels of anxiety (Blustein & Spengler, 1995).

Psychodynamic Theories

Psychodynamic theory posits that humans are basically driven by psychic energy and impulses, and unconscious desires and conflicts stemming from childhood experiences are the root of psychological difficulties. Although there are various iterations of psychodynamic approaches (e.g., drive theory, ego psychology, object relations, and self-psychology), a core concept that permeates across all psychodynamic theories is **hedonism**, or striving for pleasure and avoiding pain. Classic psychoanalytic techniques and procedures are used less today because more contemporary psychodynamic approaches offer a wider assortment of interventions and explanations of human functioning. For example, although Freud's drive theory views impulses as solely sexual and aggressive, other psychodynamic theorists view impulses as stemming from socialization and individuation (the process of becoming whole).

I. Freud's Psychoanalytic Drive Theory

Psychoanalytic theory is based on sexual and aggressive urges formed in the early part of life through bodily and family experiences (Livneh & Siller, 2004). Fantasies are experienced as dangerous and result in anxiety, guilt, shame, inhibition, symptom formation, and unhealthy personality traits. Early bodily and family experiences influence personality and according to

Siller (1976), can be particularly salient to the development of persons with health and mental health conditions. For example, bodily changes related to a health condition may contribute to different impulses and desires that result in anxiety, guilt, and shame; the family environment may shape how an individual with a disability manages these impulses, potentially resulting in difficulties later in life. Freud viewed psychological functioning to be composed of three parts: **id**, **ego**, and **superego**. The **id** is driven by the **pleasure principle**—or one's "biological baby"— in which hunger, sleeping, and sex need immediate gratification. The **ego** is driven by the **reality principle**, which attempts to deal with the realities of the world and limited resources. The ego also serves to mediate between the id and the superego. The **superego** strives to be perfect and is a person's moralistic component. Accordingly, these three components drive every behavior and need to be mastered for health adult functioning. For example, the id is present at birth, and thus, needs are expected to be met immediately; when these needs are not met consistently by parental figures, mastery of this stage may be compromised, and unconscious conflicts and impulses may influence healthy development. As the child develops, the superego emerges through adult messages of what is right and wrong, and the child learns to negotiate between the id needs and the developing superego. This negotiation or mediation between the id and superego contributes to the development of a health or unhealthy ego (Halbur & Halbur, 2006).

Freud viewed **anxiety** as the fundamental problem of neurosis. He expanded the concept of anxiety from solely being the discharge of a repressed libido to being a signal of danger to the ego. He identified three types of anxiety: reality, neurotic, and moral. Defenses were considered functions of the ego, and thus psychoanalytic treatment expanded from focusing on the repressed libido to bringing **id** forces into consciousness and analyzing the defenses protecting the ego from anxiety (S. Freud, 1926/1959). Defense mechanisms such as **projection, repression, rationalization, sublimation, reaction formation, regression, and compensation** keep anxiety from interrupting a person's conscious life (Halbur & Halbur, 2006; Livneh & Siller, 2004). A major contribution of psychoanalysis to the understanding of how health and mental health conditions affect an individual is the study of ego defense mechanisms. Defense mechanisms are broadly viewed as unconscious processes used when the ego is unable to manage anxiety and other negative emotions or to cope with intolerable impulses (A. Freud, 1936/1946). To alleviate these distressing internal states, the ego resorts to a number of psychological defense mechanisms. See Table 5.5 for definitions.

TABLE 5.5 Definitions of Defense Mechanisms

Repression: Expelling conscious awareness of those intrapsychic conflicts and painful experiences (e.g., the person with a visible, congenital disability repressing feelings of shame triggered by early-life reactions of significant others).

Projection: Casting out or externalizing unconscious forbidden and unacceptable wishes, needs, and impulses and attributing them to others (e.g., the person with a recently acquired disability who attributes lack of progress during rehabilitation to medical staff incompetence rather than to own lack of effort; the individual who blames environmental conditions for the onset of lung cancer rather than to long-term smoking).

Rationalization: Using after-the-fact, false justifications for engaging in unacceptable or embarrassing behaviors so that negative emotions or consequences can be prevented (e.g., the person with hearing loss who attempts to attribute lack of participation in a conversation to boredom or fatigue).

(continued)

TABLE 5.5   Definitions of Defense Mechanisms (*continued*)

Denial: Among the plethora of definitions of denial, a leading contender among the psychoanalytically derived ones is an amalgam of affective and cognitive processes that seek to defuse, distort, or repudiate an encounter with both internal or external painful (anxiety-provoking, threat-inducing) stimuli (e.g., the person with spinal cord injury who, after many years of being a wheelchair user, still insists that he will be soon walking again). More often, however, rather than blatant reality-defying denial, it is the minimization of chronic illness and disability (CID) implications or the apprehension associated with the anticipated attitudes of others that is being denied.

Sublimation: Adopting beneficial and socially sanctioned behaviors to express forbidden and socially unacceptable wishes and impulses (e.g., a person with sudden-onset orthopedic disability whose anger toward, and wishes to retaliate against, an indifferent society are channeled into artistic endeavors or to benevolent behaviors toward other people, including those with CID).

Reaction formation: Substituting and expressing responses and feelings that are opposites of those that are forbidden (e.g., parents who demonstrate extreme manifestations of loving behaviors or overprotectiveness, rather than feelings of aversion and rejection, toward their child who was born with a severe physical deformity).

Regression: The reverting to childlike behaviors first exhibited by the individual during an earlier developmental stage (e.g., a recently disabled individual whose temper tantrums are activated when wishes are not immediately gratified).

Compensation: Seeking to excel in functionally related (direct or primary compensation) or mostly unrelated (indirect or secondary compensation) activities or behaviors to make up for disability-triggered loss (e.g., the person who lost sight at an early age and became a successful musician).

Source: Livneh and Siller (2015).

Character change is typically the goal of psychoanalytic counseling; it occurs through bringing the unconscious forward and increasing self-understanding, repair or removal of unhealthy defense mechanisms, developmental distortions, conflicts, and arrested development. Symptom relief is not a priority, only a by-product of character change. The **techniques** commonly used include **free association**, which brings the unconscious forward (Livneh & Siller, 2004) and procedures including **confrontation, clarification, interpretation**, and **working through** (Greenson, 1967). See Table 5.6 for definitions.

Transference and **countertransference** are also hallmark psychoanalytic therapeutic processes. Transference is not a conscious experience, occurring when the client unknowingly projects a needed aspect of a previously experienced or desired relationship onto the counselor. Because the relationship is "transferred," the client and counselor are expected to take complementary roles. For example, a client who is afraid of having a health condition, may take on a helpless child-like role and project a protective parent-like attribute onto the counselor, who is then expected to resolve the situation. Conversely, countertransference is the counselor response elicited by the client's unconscious transference communication. Countertransference responses include feelings, thoughts, and behaviors.

Ego psychology moved away from the three-part structure of the mind (id, ego, superego) and focused on strengthening the ego to facilitate reality-testing, impulse control, judgment, affect regulation, and defenses. Hartmann (1964) proposed that a healthy ego is one that functions independently from the conflicting personality structures (id and ego) and is the primary source for withstanding pressures associated with the personality as a whole and the interaction between the ego and the environment. Thus, ego psychology interventions focus on the development of an autonomous ego—separate from that which emerges from the id and superego—by strengthening the ego's ability to reality-test, make good judgements, control impulses and regulation emotions irrespective of intrapsyche conflict.

TABLE 5.6 Analytic Procedures

Confrontation is the first step in analyzing a psychic phenomenon. The phenomenon in question has to be made explicit to the patient's awareness. Greenson (1967) provides, as an example, failure to show up for a session, which was interpreted by the analyst as related to a general tendency to avoid unpleasantness. In the previous session, "controversial" material had been discussed that made her feel that the analyst was angry at her (supposed) misbehavior. The specific fear, embedded in a general avoidance of possible unpleasantness, was then confronted in the next session. "You missed your last session not because you 'forgot' but you were frightened that I was going to be angry with you!"

Clarification refers to those activities that aim at placing the psychic phenomenon being analyzed in sharp focus. Significant details have to be identified and separated from extraneous matter. The particular variety or pattern of the phenomenon in question has to be singled out and isolated. Greenson used his patient's characteristic avoidance of her anger by projecting it on to others as shown by invoking instances in which she feared retaliation from her own "boldness" (hostility). The clarification demonstrated how she projected her anger onto others, and her subsequent fear of rejection.

Interpretation is the "procedure which distinguishes psychoanalysis from all other psychotherapies because in psychoanalysis interpretation is the ultimate and decisive instrument. . . . To interpret means to make an unconscious phenomenon conscious. . . . To make conscious the unconscious meaning, source, history, mode, or cause of a given psychic event" (Greenson, 1967, p. 39). In the instance of the cited patient, the interpretation offered was that she was transferring (repeating) toward the analyst complex feelings of ambivalence toward her father, based on both correct and distorted images of him. Specifically, she had the unconscious belief that opposition toward him would lead to rejection and even abandonment. Her family history and personal recollections suggested that, although her father was somewhat authoritarian with the children, she greatly distorted the extent of his wrath. Typically, an indication of a correct and timely interpretation is the response of the person, such as the flow of associations.

Working through is the final step of the analyzing process. "Working through refers to a complex set of procedures and processes which occur after an insight has been given. The analytic work, which makes it possible for an insight to lead to change, is the work of working through. It refers in the main to the repetitive, progressive, and elaborate explanations of the resistances which prevent an insight from leading to change" (Greenson, 1967, p. 42). Change actually occurs through the working through. For the aforementioned patient, one aspect of working through involved demonstrating the many situations wherein hostile feelings on her part were projected onto others, particularly parental figures. The expectation of retaliatory punishment and rejection could then be seen as her own childlike fear of abandonment for noncompliance and willfulness. Insight regarding her use of projection as a resistance against contacting her own hostile feelings was followed up as its many guises were revealed. Self-affirmation began to be distinguished from hostility and selfishness as fears of abandonment abated.

Source: Livneh and Siller (2015).

Object relations theory, another iteration of psychoanalytic theory, emphasizes interpersonal relations, primarily in the family and particularly between mother and child. *Object* refers to an internal image of a person and, more specifically, to a person that is the object or target of the client's feelings or intentions. Objects can be represented as "good," or satisfying one's needs and desires, or "bad," or not satisfying one's needs. *Relations* refer to prior relationship experiences that influence the person in the present. **Object relations** therefore consists of memories based on feelings and desires experienced at the time of the prior event and are typically dominated by experiences with the individual's primary objects or attachment figures. What the person experiences in the present, however, is not a "true" representation of the present-day relationship but is the subjective psychological memory of a prior relationship. As such, object relations theorists focus on the internal images of these object relations and how they manifest themselves in current interpersonal situations. Indeed, new experiences are not experienced as entirely novel because they are experienced through internal images based on childhood experience. As with ego psychology, object relations theory aligns with classical psychoanalytic theory through its reliance on early childhood relationships, subjective internal states and development, and transference and countertransference.

Developed by Kohut (1971, 1977), **self-psychology** is related to object relations but focuses more on the emotional investment in the self, or an individual's subjective state, particularly around issues of differentiation, boundaries, continuity, esteem, and reactions to imbalances in that subjective state. **Narcissism** is central to this theory because the person deals with objects as if they were part of the self versus the other and thus performs an essential function for the self. Kohut conceptualized the narcissistic self as one that arises from severe, developmentally inappropriate, and/or enduring frustration by a child when the need for a "good-enough" parent represented as an idealized role model and a symbol of grandiosity is not met. Minor failures of "good-enough" parents, can however, lead to healthy development.

Developed by Carl Jung, **analytic theory** is based on the premise that people are holistic individuals who are connected at an ancestral level. Although Jung agreed with Freud that people possess physical drives, he viewed humans as positive and believed all people move intentionally toward individuation or wholeness. Even though Jung did acknowledge that people's past influenced their current situation, he was less deterministic than Freud, proposing that people actively moved toward their potential and that development occurs throughout the lifespan. Jung coined the term **psyche**, which is composed of three components: **ego**, **personal unconscious**, and **ancestral collective unconscious**. The ego, or people's current thoughts, feelings, and reflections, is readily accessible and contains current experiences. The personal unconscious holds difficult-to-access memories and thoughts, but it is ultimately accessible. The collective unconscious is the psyche's deepest level and most difficult to access. Jung believed that all cultures have common themes and stories that compose a deeper, ancestral level of a person's psyche. He posited that the ancestral collective unconscious contains **archetypes**, which are the basis of personality and include **shadow, wise one, healer, anima (female side), animus (male side)**, and **hero images**. Life experiences therefore build on these archetypes to shape their personality (Halbur & Halbur, 2006). The main **goal of therapy** is to integrate the psychic components—the ego, personal unconscious, and ancestral collective unconscious—which allows individuals to fully function. Jungian techniques include a warm client–counselor relationship, dream analysis, and archetypal analysis.

II. Individual Psychology

Founded by Alfred Adler, **individual psychology** assumes that humans are motivated primarily by socialization. **Gemeinschaftsgefühl**, typically translated as **social interest**, is the core tenet of individual psychology (Halbur & Halbur, 2006). Social interest is goal-directed behavior toward a sense of belonging and the feeling that one is recognized and valued by others (Ansbacher & Ansbacher, 1964). Social interest is driven by an innate capacity and desire for communion with others and formed through early life experiences and socialization. Adler saw people as **teological**, or goal-directed organisms who have free will, free choice, and a **creative power** to choose their own goals and behaviors. **Fictional finalism**, the ultimate, yet unobtainable goal, is the driving force behind becoming who one strives to be. Like Freud, Adler believed that personality is determined at an early age. However, his theory differs in its focus on people's experience within their family (e.g., parenting style, sibling relationships, and childhood stressors) and its impact on their social interest. These early experiences "write" the roles played later in life. For example, overprotective or critical parenting may hinder a child's ability to fully realize their innate capacity for social interest (Halbur & Halbur, 2006). Thus, Adler's theory of personality is based on four types of people according to their degree of social interest and level of goal-directed activity (Manaster & Corsini, 1982). The **socially useful** psychological type looks toward the needs of others and the improvement of society and contributes to the community without distractions from their own needs. The **ruling type** acts aggressively and dominantly and exhibits hostility toward others or, internalizes their aggression, resulting in maladaptive behaviors such as substance abuse, suicide ideations/attempts, or other forms of self-abuse. The **avoiding type** has limited interaction with others and withdraws from problems rather than approaching them. Finally, the **getting type**, which is the most common personality type, is characterized by a heavy dependence on others, without engaging in prosocial behaviors. These individuals are anxious and fearful and direct their efforts toward convincing others to give them what they want (Ansbacher & Ansbacher, 1964). The latter three types are considered **socially useless** because of the inability to behave in a manner that benefits the common interest. Adler also posited that people are born **inferior**, or a feeling of being "less than," which motivates a drive toward **superiority** to compensate for inferior feelings. Those who do not achieve a healthy sense of superiority are at risk for developing an **inferiority complex** or, conversely, a **superiority complex** (grandiose opinions of oneself) by overcompensating for inferiority feelings (Halbur & Halbur, 2006).

The primary **goal of therapy** is to increase the social interest of clients by changing disruptive private logic, resolving inferiority/superiority complexes, altering misguided goals to healthy goals to accomplish tasks in socially responsible ways. The **primary techniques** include a therapeutic alliance and lifestyle assessments, which allows the counselor to learn about the client's family constellation, private logic, and fictional finalism. In addition, Adlerians focus on gathering early recollections and look at these recollections to find patterns and themes (Halbur & Halbur, 2006).

Counseling Skills and Competencies

Counseling encompasses a therapeutic relationship in which a professionally trained counselor interacts with one or more individuals seeking assistance to manage difficulties and to make changes in their lives. In the context of rehabilitation and mental health counseling, the individuals seeking assistance have health or mental health conditions and disabilities (Berven, Thomas, & Chan, 2015). Counseling occurs in a variety of settings, including traditional office settings, as well as in educational institutions, community agencies, and state or federal agencies. Counseling as a treatment intervention is defined as:

> The application of cognitive, affective, behavioral, and systemic counseling strategies which include developmental, wellness, pathologic, and multicultural principles of human behavior. Such interventions are specifically implemented in the context of a professional counseling relationship and may include, but are not limited to, appraisal; individual, group, marriage, and family counseling and psychotherapy; the diagnostic description and treatment of persons with mental, emotional, and behavioral disorders or disabilities; guidance and consulting to facilitate normal growth and development, including educational and career development; the utilization of functional assessments and career counseling for persons requesting assistance in adjusting to a disability or handicapping condition; referrals; consulting; and research. (Commission on Rehabilitation Counselor Certification [CRCC], n.d., p. 2)

The effectiveness of counseling depends on establishing a counseling relationship with the individuals served; communicating with individuals in facilitative, helpful ways; obtaining information from individuals in a comprehensive and thorough manner; helping clients tell their stories and explain their problems and needs; understanding and conceptualizing behavior and problems in ways that will facilitate treatment and service planning; and facilitating follow-through on commitments and compliance with treatment and service plans that individuals have decided to pursue (Berven et al., 2015).

I. Basic Therapeutic Conditions

Rogers' person-centered approach has been foundational to the essential therapeutic ingredients necessary for therapeutic change, thus assuming the name **common factors**. Common factors are aspects of the therapeutic conditions that all forms of counseling share in common and are also referred to as Rogers' **facilitative conditions**, or genuineness, unconditional positive regard and empathic understanding. According to C. R. Rogers (1957), empathy is a unique type of understanding that requires the counselor to fully grasp clients' frames of reference in order to understand their perceptions of their experiences, or to "sense the client's private world as if it were your own, but without ever losing the 'as if' quality" (p. 99) Unconditional positive regard is being nonjudgmental and nonevaluative at all times and "experiencing a warm acceptance of a client's experience as being part of that client ... neither approval nor disapproval of the client ... simply acceptance." (Rogers, 1957, p. 98). Genuineness on the part of counselors is being "within the confines of this relationship, a congruent, genuine, integrated person ... not presenting a façade" and not denying personal own feelings to themselves. These facilitative conditions not only must be experienced by counselors, but also must be communicated effectively so that clients are able to perceive the empathy and acceptance that counselors feel toward them.

Common factors have also been found to include **goal setting, allegiance**, and the **working alliance** (Wampold, 2001). *Goal setting* refers to a collaborative process in which the client and counselor identify therapeutic goals and objectives, which guide the counseling process and intervention. Goal setting that relies on an outcome orientation is central to effective counseling and requires counselors to help clients set goals and envision them as future outcomes (Ridley, Mollen, & Kelly, 2011). *Allegiance* refers to the degree to which the counselor is committed to the belief that counseling will benefit the client. The therapeutic or working alliance is the client's effective relationship with the counselor, the client's motivation and ability to accomplish work collaboratively with the counselor, the counselor's empathic response to and involvement with the client, and the client and counselor's agreement about the goals and tasks of therapy (Wampold, 2001). There is substantial empirical evidence to support the importance of the therapeutic alliance to success in counseling across many different types of interventions and treatments (Norcross & Wampold, 2011).

Studies examining the efficacy of counseling conclude that at least 70% of psychotherapeutic effects is due to common factors, whereas only 8% is due to specific theoretical techniques; the remaining 22% is attributed to client differences (Wampold, 2001). Although studies empirically demonstrate a link between common factors and counseling outcomes, theoretical techniques, which account for significantly less of the variance in counseling outcomes, are still fundamental to the formulation of hypotheses, treatment planning, and goal setting. To maximize the effects of the common factors, counseling interventions need to be customized for each client, and treatment modalities used should be based on the client's needs, context, expectations, personality, and difficulties, as well as counseling approaches. Thus, the effectiveness of counseling depends on the application of counseling techniques in the appropriate manner and the counselor's ability to change style and approach according to the needs of the client (e.g., directive, reflective, neutral, supportive, confrontive, formal, or informal).

II. Microskills

The communication to which the therapeutic conditions, intake interviews, assessment and clinical intervention are conveyed occur, to some extent, in the form of **microskills**. Basic microskills include listening skills such as **attending, questioning, using minimal encouragers, paraphrasing, reflecting feelings, and summarizing**. These skills are important in the early phases of counseling, which focuses on building the therapeutic alliance and understanding a client's story. In addition, these skills are used in intake interviews and other types of clinical assessments and interviews (Berven, 2008, 2010). **Attending skills** are the verbal and nonverbal counseling skills communicating that the counselor is focused on clients and the information they are sharing, encourage and support client communication, and communicate the basic facilitative conditions (Hill, 2014; Ivey, Ivey, & Zalaquett, 2014). **Nonverbal communication** includes eye contact, body language, response latency, and voice qualities of volume, pitch, pace, and fluency. Indeed, communication, particularly of emotions, often occurs nonverbally (Berven et al., 2015). Nonverbal skills involve the physical orientation of the counselor toward the client as a means of showing attentiveness and availability (Chan, Berven, & Thomas, 2004). Effective posturing of counselors is usually achieved through an open and nondefensive body position, with a slight lean forward. Eye contact with a steady gaze, not staring, is also important. However, the normative standard for eye contact varies, depending on the client's cultural background. Moments of silence that give the client time to focus thoughts and experience emotions is also another commonly used nonverbal skill. Paying attention to the client's non verbal cues is an important way of showing attentiveness (Chan et al., 2004).

Response latency refers to the delay from the time a client finishes talking until the counselor responds. Latency varies from no delay to a short or very long delay and includes interrupting the client. Interruptions and short delays in communication may often be perceived as aggressiveness, whereas very long delays may be perceived as passivity. In addition, if counselors frequently interrupt clients or demonstrate very short response latencies, they may be perceived as more concerned with what they themselves have to say than what the client has to say. Longer latencies in responding may be particularly important with clients who tend to speak slowly and with long pauses, perhaps pondering before speaking, because the counselor may miss additional important things that the client wants to say (Berven et al., 2015). Silence can cause anxiety for counselors and clients. It is not unusual for counselors to break the silence too quickly; however, clients who are thinking or contemplating need continued silence by the counselor. In addition, counselors, particularly novice counselors, are often thinking about how they will respond, which prevents active listening and places them at risk for missing client communication (Berven et al., 2015). **Verbal tracking** occurs when counselors respond in a manner that is related to what the client is communicating at present versus introducing a new topic or referring back to a previously discussed topic. Verbal tracking contributes to organization in sessions and communicates to the client that they are being heard. Verbal tracking also can also provide space for exploring topics or stories at a deeper level (Berven et al., 2015).

Questions are an integral part of counseling and interviewing. However, the use of questions and the way in which questions are formulated can significantly influence the therapeutic rapport and client response (Ivey et al., 2014). Questions include closed-ended and open-ended types; closed-ended questions (e.g., "Do you like baseball?") can be answered with a few words, whereas open-ended questions (e.g., "What things are most important to you at your job?") are intended to facilitate longer responses. At times, this principle does not hold true, and closed-ended questions result in long responses, and vice versa. Open-ended questions may also be direct (e.g., "What is work like for you?") or indirect (e.g., "Tell me about school."). At times, broad open-ended questions (e.g., "Tell me about yourself.") are anxiety provoking and difficult to answer. Closed-ended questions tend to provide very specific direction to a client and are thus highly efficient in eliciting specific information. In general, questions are often used to open a session, obtain information, clarify facts, or follow up to explore a topic more in depth, seek elaboration, or gather greater detail (Berven et al., 2015; Ivey et al., 2014). Notably, a session composed entirely of questions is likely not effective in building the therapeutic alliance or facilitating basic conditions, particularly if the questions are close ended (Ivey et al., 2014). People generally tend to be more skilled in asking closed- rather than open-ended questions and tend to automatically phrase questions in a closed-ended format, so work is needed to build skill in using open-ended questions as a part of the repertoire of questioning skills (Berven et al., 2015).

Active listening responses focus on an aspect of what the client has communicated and reveals to the client that the counselor has heard the client. Active listening responses may focus on the content of a client response or on the affective component of what the client has communicated (Ivey et al., 2014). **Encouragers** are minimal nonverbal and verbal signals such as head nods, "Uh huhs," repetitions of key words, and other similar gestures. They convey warmth, which allow the client to open up and gain comfort (Ivey et al., 2014) but do not provide feedback to clients about what the counselor heard. **Paraphrases** are short summaries that reflect back to the client the content that was just shared using the counselor's words (Ivey et al., 2014). A paraphrase does not "parrot" a client statement but expresses the essence of the meaning using new words with the intention of providing more clarification and meaning for the client. A paraphrase may capture the essence of an entire client response or focus on one aspect of the response, encouraging the client to further expand. Accurate paraphrasing can facilitate deeper exploration and clarity, but if it is too disconnected from the content or the client's awareness, the client may not benefit or become defensive. **Reflections of feeling** focus on the affective component of client responses, encouraging the exploration of feelings as opposed to the content (Ivey et al., 2014). Because the communication of feelings often occurs through nonverbal channels, the verbal components of a client response may or may not explicitly state the feeling being communicated, so a client may not be fully aware of the feelings being expressed. The exploration of feelings is often a major component of counseling, as they may play important roles in concerns brought to counselors. For example, clients may often talk about needing to "sort out" their feelings in attempting to resolve a conflict or make a decision, and reflections of feeling may play an important role in understanding those concerns and the surrounding context. In addition, dysfunctional feelings, such as fear and anxiety, can pose major barriers to pursuing and achieving goals and may even be primary concerns brought to counselors. Reflections encourage clients to continue talking and exploring the feelings communicated in greater depth. Reflections of feeling may have different degrees of inference in the extent to which they go beyond the feelings explicitly communicated in the words spoken by clients but perhaps communicated through nonverbal channels. Going beyond what has been communicated explicitly may facilitate greater depth of exploration, or clients may not accept the reflections or react defensively, particularly if they are not aware of the feelings they are communicating implicitly or if the reflection is not particularly accurate. **Summarizations** provide a more comprehensive summary of client responses and typically occur at the end of the session, summarizing what has occurred and emphasizing areas that the counselor considers to be particularly important for the client to remember and reflect on before the next session (Ivey et al., 2014). Summaries are also used at the beginning of a session, summarizing what occurred in the previous and or sessions and then using this summary to move in the current session. Summarizations are also used before transitioning to a new topic or when a client is disorganized and rambling. The microskills repertoire includes advanced microskills as well as skills such as self-disclosure, interpretation, reframing, and empathic confrontation (Ivey et al., 2014). Ridley et al. (2011) suggest that the range of microskills be expanded to a variety of other counseling competencies (e.g., leveraging resources, working with other systems of care, self-appraising, consulting other sources, surmounting obstacles), including not only counseling behaviors, but also cognitive and affective skills. See Table 5.6 for definitions of key counseling skills and techniques.

Counseling termination is an important counseling skill. According to the Code of Professional Ethics for Rehabilitation Counselors (CRCC, 2010), rehabilitation counselors may not abandon clients and must make appropriate referrals for clients terminated by counselor. Appropriate reasons for termination include the following: The client is not benefitting from counseling, the client no longer needs counseling, counseling may harm the client or persons related to the client, and the client is not paying the agreed-upon fees (CRCC, 2010). If a counselor is transferring a client, the transfer must be done in a timely manner, and procedures should be in place to ensure that communication occurs with both the client and the new counselor. In addition, in the case of a counselor's incapacitation, death, or leaving/resignation, a note should be placed in the client's records and another professional should communicate with the client regarding the situation; the transfer process should occur immediately (CRCC, 2010).

Termination with an individual client should be a collaborative process between the client and the counselor and should loosely follow the following steps. First, the counselor should discuss termination with the client well before the termination date to emotionally prepare the client for the transition or cessation of the client–counselor relationship. Second, a discussion with the client of the positive changes that have occurred since the start of counseling, any memorable moments or obstacles in the counseling process, and a general expression of positive feelings regarding the client is important to communicate. Third, limitations associated with the parameters of counseling should be acknowledged, as should a review of resources available to the client to address any areas that were not adequately addressed within the counseling context. Fourth, the client should be provided with information about the process of returning for services if needed. Finally, limits of the counselor-client relationship should be addressed. For example, if the client wants to be friends (e.g., Facebook), the boundaries related to the client–counselor relationship with a former client should be clarified (Teyber, 2006).

Termination in a group setting also includes addressing the issue of termination prior to the last meeting of the group. Group members may be anxious about termination and the loss of an established social network. Group members should be reassured that the type of connections formed in the group can be replicated outside the group (M. S. Corey & Corey, 2006). In addition, rehabilitation counselors should recognize their own feelings related to endings and separation (M. S. Corey & Corey, 2006). According to M. S. Corey and Corey, (2006), the following specific termination tasks should be performed. First, the facilitator discusses any unfinished business related to the group and completes what can be accomplished and discusses what cannot be accomplished. Second, the facilitator should review what has been learned and acknowledge behavioral changes. Third, the facilitator should discuss ways in which group members can bring new, learned behaviors and knowledge to the outside world. Fourth, the group should be asked to provide concrete feedback to the facilitator and to specific individual members.

Practice Principles

I. Confidentiality

Confidentiality provides clients with assurance that personal information shared in the counseling session will remain only with the counselor (Woody, 2001). In fact, most clients assume that everything shared with counselors will remain confidential (Shaw & Tarvydas, 2001). Nonetheless, information is often shared with physicians and allied health professionals, supervisors, parents or guardians, case audits by regulatory bodies, third-party payors such as insurance companies, and other treatment team members (Campbell, 1994; Cobia & Boes, 2000; C. C. Cooper, 2000; Tarvydas, 1995). **Permission** to provide and receive client information must be obtained in writing and clearly articulate what information will be released, to whom it will be released, and for what reason. In addition, the document should specify a time frame for how long permission is granted and include the client's signature. **Breaking confidentiality** may occur (a) when a counselor needs to share information with parents/guardians of a minor or a person with an intellectual or psychiatric disability; (b) when a counselor has a **duty to protect** a client at risk of harming the self (suicide) or others (homicide), including the risk of exposing another to a life-threatening disease; (c) when a counselor is **legally mandated** to release information by a court order (CRCC, 2010); and (d) as a response to **mandatory reporting laws** related to abuse toward children, older adults, and persons with disabilities. In these situations, rehabilitation and mental health counselors are legally mandated to break confidentiality, and if a counselor fails to report abuse toward these vulnerable populations, they are in violation of state law.

The **Tarasoff decision** is based on the controversial malpractice case, *Tarasoff v. Regents of the University of California* (1976). In this case, a psychologist at UC-Berkeley was treating a graduate student, Prosenjit Poddar, who became obsessed with an undergraduate student, Tatiana Tarasoff. Poddar reported to the psychologist that he intended to kill Tarasoff and the psychologist reported the information to the police; the police detained Poddar, but after questioning him, he was released. Shortly after, Poddar murdered Tarasoff. The court decided that the duty to protect supersedes confidentiality when there is a foreseeable victim of harm perpetrated by the individual with whom the helping professional has a counseling relationship, defining the duty as "the duty to exercise reasonable care to protect the foreseeable victim of that danger" (*Tarasoff v. Regents of the University of California*, 1976; p. 345). As a result, the California Supreme Court adopted the principles regarding duty and limitations on confidentiality as a rule of law and other states adopted "duty" laws, each of which vary in the interpretation and definition of "foreseeability."

Privileged communication or **testimonial privilege** is the clients' right to confidential communication with their rehabilitation or mental health counselor. In many states, this right is extended to client–counselor relationships in recognition of the importance of confidentiality in the counseling relationships. Privileged communication is owned by the client, not the counselor, and in situations where confidentiality cannot be protected, counselors are required to inform clients of potential situations in which confidentiality may be breached. Breaking confidentiality always poses a risk to the client/counselor relationship. When breaking confidentiality, counselors should disclose the minimum amount of information required. In addition, counselors should be aware that the boundaries of confidentiality may differ from culture to culture. If the counselor is unfamiliar with the boundaries of another culture, the counselor should seek consultation from someone knowledgeable of the culture. Finally, counselors are responsible for keeping accurate and up-to-date client records in a confidential and safe environment, including records of deceased clients unless there is a legal mandate to disclose (CRCC, 2010).

II. Crisis Counseling

Suicide is the most common crisis concern. Suicide is the second leading cause of death among college students and is a serious risk among high school students and older adults (Granello & Granello, 2007). Common myths regarding suicide include the following: (a) Discussing suicide will cause the client to attempt it; (b) clients who talk about suicide will not attempt suicide; (c) suicide increases around Christmas and New Year's Eve; (d) only insane people attempt suicide; (e) when a suicidal client improves, it signals that the danger is over; (f) suicide is more prevalent among people of low socioeconomic status; and (g) suicide generally happens without warning (Sommers-Flanagan & Sommers-Flanagan, 1999). Many counselors believe they could trigger a suicide attempt by saying the wrong thing; fortunately, this is also a myth, yet it often prevents counselors from talking about suicide directly (Captain, 2006; Granello & Granello, 2007; Sommers-Flanagan & Sommers-Flanagan, 1999). Clients in crisis are typically relieved when an inquiry about suicide ideation (thoughts of suicide) occurs. Relief is likely related to having the space to finally express a deeply and painfully held secret. Most clients considering suicide are actually relieved to discuss the topic and are generally appreciative of being asked. An essential question in the mind of the client in crisis is likely, "Can this counselor help me through my crisis?" The ACA Code of Ethics (ACA, 2014) addresses the issues of suicide and client welfare. Specifically, the Code states that the general requirement that counselors keep information confidential does not apply when disclosure is required to protect clients or identified clients from serious and foreseeable harm or when legal mandates demand that confidential information be revealed. Counselors consult with other professionals when in doubt as to the validity of an exception (Section B.2). State laws also mandate that counselors and other professionals (e.g., psychologists, nurses, and physicians) breach confidentiality when the issue of self-harm arises (Remley & Herlihy, 2014).

Counselors must be prepared to conduct a risk assessment, consult with a supervisor, notify appropriate parties, document actions taken, and schedule an immediate follow-up session. In many cases, the client may be temporarily hospitalized, depending on a variety of factors such as a suicide plan, insurance, and hospital availability. **Suicide assessment** is not an exact science; thus counselors should apply a broad approach by addressing the client's **plan, intent, means, prior attempts, and substance use**. Verbalizing a plan suggests lethality; the more detailed and specific the plan, the greater the potential for lethality. The stated intent to follow through on a suicide plan also suggests higher lethality. The means the client plans to use in a suicide attempt suggests lethality; the deadlier the means (e.g., gun), the greater the lethality. Notably, women attempt suicide three times the rate of men, but men commit suicide approximately four times the rate of women (American Foundation for Suicide Prevention, 2013). The difference is due to men's use of more lethal means. Previous suicide attempts also suggest the client has considered suicide as a possible option. Typically, clients must work up to making a suicide attempt, and previous attempts indicate the client is beginning to again consider the option of suicide. Finally, a history of substance abuse, particularly alcohol, increases lethality, because those who use substances often have poorer coping skills and more difficulty managing crisis situations. As such, using a standard alcohol and drug assessment is suggested. McGlothen, Rainey, and Kindsvatter (2005) also suggest the following general guidelines in gauging lethality:

1. **Low lethality.** Suicidal ideation (thoughts of suicide) is present but intent is denied and the client does not have a concrete plan and has never attempted suicide in the past.

2. **Moderate lethality.** More than one general risk factor for suicide is present; suicidal ideation and intent are present but a clear plan is denied and the client is motivated to improve the psychological state.

3. **High lethality.** Several general risk factors for suicide are present; the client has verbalized suicidal ideation and intent and has communicated a well-thought-out plan with immediate access to the resources needed to complete the plan.

4. **Very high lethality.** The client verbalizes suicidal ideation and intent, has communicated a well-thought-out plan with immediate access to the resources needed to complete the plan, demonstrates cognitive rigidity and hopelessness for the future, denies any available suicide support, and has attempted suicide in the past.

Suicide assessment is unique to each person, is an ongoing process that relies on multiple perspectives, seeks to predict probable risk, relies on clinical judgement, and *is* treatment. In addition, counselors must err on the side of caution, considering all threats, warning signals, and risk factors as serious. Counselors must ask the tough questions, such as "I'm wondering if you might be considering suicide," and try to uncover underlying messages. Suicide assessment must be conducted in a culturally competent and collaborative manner (Hodges, 2015).

Suggestions for discussing suicide with a client include:

1. Do not panic or show signs of discomfort. Clients need to believe the counselor is calm in the face of their crisis.

2. If concerned a client may be suicidal, ask: "I'm wondering if you might be considering suicide."

3. Do not argue with the client about the plan or give them minimizing advice (e.g., "It'll get better," "It's really not that big a deal," "What will your family think?").

4. Focus on the therapeutic alliance and basic facilitating skills. It is critical that the client feel "heard" and not judged. Suicidal clients feel isolated and may first disclose their intent for self-harm to counselors. Empathy may help resolve the immediate crisis.

5. Most clients in crisis have thought of suicide but have not made a plan. If this is the case, reschedule the client as soon as possible. Provide the client with a 24-hour crisis number.

6. When a client discloses suicidal ideations, that client is saying, "Help me," to the counselor. Client admission to suicidal thoughts or intent offers the counselor a good chance of stopping the attempt.

Similar to suicide assessment, **assessing violence toward others** is also not an exact science (Granello & Granello, 2007; Sommers-Flanagan & Sommers-Flanagan, 1999). Facilitating a strong therapeutic alliance through the use of basic facilitative skills (Duncan, Miller, Wampold, & Hubble, 2010) is critical in crisis counseling, including assessing for violence. Anger, hostility, retaliation, and agitation can, at times, be most effectively addressed through empathic understanding and positive regard. In addition, proactive approaches for violence assessment include gathering information in the intake interview and reviewing case records. A few structured assessments, including the Structured Assessment of Violence Risk in Youth (SAVRY; Borum, Bartel, & Forth, 2002), the Suicide Assessment Checklist (SAC; J. R. Rogers, Lewis, & Subich, 2002), and the SAD PERSONS Scale (Patterson, Dohn, Bird, & Patterson, 1983) are available for determining the risk level for violence. However, formal, valid assessments are limited. Act of violence toward others occur more frequently that commonly recognized. In fact, research suggests that approximately 20% of emergency department patients are violent and 40% of psychiatrists are assaulted at least once in their careers (Tardiff, as cited in Shea, 1988). Sample questions counselors may use to determine the level of risk for violence include:

1. Does the client have a history of violence (bullying, cruelty to animals, domestic violence, and workplace violence)?

2. Does the client make references to violence and see violence as a means to meet personal needs?

3. Does the client tend to get physically or verbally aggressive when abusing substances such as alcohol or other drugs?

4. Does the client have a prevalence of violent ideation? Such clients may idealize violence and are likely more prone to commit acts of violence.

5. Does the client have a history of mental illness? Although mental illness alone is not a predictor of violence, mental illness plus substance abuse can be a significant factor.

6. Does the client have a history of being the victim of violence? Clients who have been the victims are more likely to be perpetrators of violence.

7. Does the client have a history of using physical and verbal violence to control people?

8. Does the client have a documented history of cruelty to animals or bullying?

9. Has the client made threats of violence to third parties?

10. Does the client have access to weapons?

11. Does the client belong to a social group that advocates and encourages violence?

The highest level is related to the degree to which the threat is direct, plausible, and specific; the threat poses imminent and serious danger to the self and others; the client implies that specific steps have been taken toward violence (e.g., stalking, acquisition of a weapon; National Association of School Psychologists, n.d.); the client has a documented history of violent acts; and the client is male. Guidelines for developing a plan of intervention include:

1. If the danger does not seem imminent (e.g., no specific plan for violence, no access to weapons), then continue with counseling.

2. Ask the client to participate in disclosing the information to third parties (provided the client agrees to do so). Express that the police may need to be notified and ensure the client is not surprised by the disclosure to the authorities.

3. Get the client screened for medication or medication change, if necessary, and arrange to get lethal weapons taken away from the client.

4. Keep up-to-date and accurate records. Record the name of the threatened party, date of the threat, and nature of the threat (be specific, e.g., the client threatened he would "get his ex by slashing her car"). In addition, explain the course of action taken.

5. Disclose the minimal amount of information needed to the intended victim.

6. Inform a supervisor of any and all issues related to the case

7. Monitor the case until the danger has passed. Monitoring activities should include follow-up with the police, the intended victim, the client, and other pertinent agencies such as parole, probation, child protection, and so forth (Appelbaum, 1985)

III. Trauma-Informed Care

TIC is a service delivery framework that acknowledges the pervasiveness of trauma in the lives of all persons (Keesler, 2014). TIC recognizes the enduring nature of trauma as an influencing factor on a person's present biopsychosocial functioning. As such, TIC institutions, agencies and services are prepared for trauma-related issues to present, irrespective of whether clients enter services with a trauma-related diagnosis or a record of such (Bloom, 2010; Butler, Critelli, & Rinfrette, 2011). TIC is woven into the fabric of the organization and considers clients, families and service providers using a common language and approach that reduces the likelihood of retraumatization (Bath, 2008; Brown, Baker, & Wilcox, 2012; Butler et al., 2011). TIC is based on a culture that emphasizes safety, trustworthiness, choice, collaboration, and empowerment among service providers and clients (Fallot & Harris, 2009). These values are integrated into an organization in a manner that aligns with the needs and characteristics of the population. Notably, organizations based on the medical model have been identified as a significant barrier to implementing widespread TIC in health care agencies—given its focus on the individual versus adverse, environmental experiences. Individuals with trauma-related backgrounds and symptoms often access multiple rehabilitation and other health care related services within a fragmented service-delivery system. These access points can often be retraumatizing, and thus, accessing care comes with a high personal and social cost (Fallot & Harris, 2009)

IV. Conflict Resolution

Conflict takes place when an individual's actions or goals are perceived as incompatible with the actions or goals of another individual (Fisher & Brown, 1988). Conflicts may occur when rehabilitation counselors and clients experience discrepancies between their expectations and their perceptions (Koch, McReynolds, & Rumrill, 2004). For example, conflicts surrounding expectations of roles and responsibilities, client eligibility, service-delivery methods and timeliness, and program policies and counselor error may occur (Holmes, Hall & Karst, 1989; Koch et al., 2004). Addressing conflict and facilitating resolution at the early stages of counseling communicates to clients their value as a member of the rehabilitation team and that they will receive quality services (Koch et al., 2004).

Conflict resolution involves the following steps: (a) myths about "good" working relationships must be addressed; (b) conflict needs to be accurately defined and reframed as differences related to interests and goals versus a negative will (Koch et al., 2004); (c) misperceptions should be clarified and the way that information has been interpreted should be discussed to prevent miscommunications (Koch et al., 2004); (d) individuals should discuss ideas that will contribute to the development of a set of shared expectations by reconciling differences; and (e) conflict resolution involves implementing and evaluating resolutions that involve agreement on what the roles and responsibilities of each will be, as well as written agreement outlining the roles and responsibilities of each. The best working relationship occurs when no discrepancies are present, individuals in the relationship have shared values and expectations, and the goal of the relationship is to avoid conflict. Working relationships work best when individuals deal with conflict, try to understand the other's values and perceptions of the situation, and work through the disagreements in a way that works for both parties (Koch et al., 2004). While reconciling differences, it is important for rehabilitation counselors to clearly delineate the guidelines and boundaries within which the team works (Koch et al., 2004). Individuals should review and revise the agreement throughout the counseling relationship to reduce the risk of future conflicts (Koch et al., 2004; Curl & Sheldon, 1992).

V. Supervision

Supervision is an essential component of the counseling discipline and involves qualified, experienced, and trained rehabilitation and mental health counselors to oversee supervisees' clinical experiences and to ensure that supervisees demonstrate satisfactory knowledge and skills in performing the fundamental duties of rehabilitation and mental health counselors. Herbert (2004) defined *clinical supervision* as a process by which supervisors use clinical techniques to provide supervision, focus on supervisee professional and personal development, and direct the clinical work of front-line staff so that client services can be provided to meet organizational goals and professional standards. Herbert (2004) identified how rehabilitation and mental health counselor supervision differs from supervision in other helping professions because it fosters skill development in psychosocial interventions, encourages personal growth and self-efficacy, and establishes supervisees' case conceptualization skills around health, mental health, and disability issues. Herbert (2004) emphasizes that psychosocial aspects of health, mental health, and disability should be a primary focus of rehabilitation and mental health counseling supervision.

Supervisory activities include support, consultation, counseling, training and instruction, and evaluation (Bradley & Ladany, 2001). Supervisors **support** supervisees by creating a safe environment to process anxiety, fears, uncertainty, and confusion. *Consultation* refers to supervisors and supervisees working collaboratively to determine diagnoses, interventions, and treatment plans. *Counseling* refers to the use of basic facilitative conditions (e.g., empathy, genuineness, positive regard) with supervisees within a professional context. **Training** and **instruction** involves supervisors determining the best approach when educating supervisees on skills, knowledge, and theories. Training and instruction must be tailored to meet supervisees' needs and developmental level. **Evaluation** occurs when supervisors provide supervisees with constructive feedback and professional development.

Herbert (2004) recognized five basic **formats of clinical supervision**—self-supervision, individual supervision, team supervision, group supervision, and peer supervision. In **self-supervision**, counselors review their own clinical work, assess for needs, and intervene when necessary; however, this approach poses problems as issues may be overlooked without reviews from peers. **Individual supervision** is a widely used approach in mental health settings, where experienced professionals monitor, evaluate, and mentor counselors-in-training. In **team supervision**, professionals from multiple disciplines consult about clients. **Group supervision** consists of professionals consulting with others from the same discipline, affording supervisees the opportunity to present cases and receive feedback about their clinical work and possible interventions. For professionals with advanced knowledge, experience, and skills, **peer supervision** is used for consultation and evaluation of clinical work with peers with whom no power differential exists. Peer supervision is often used among professionals who own their own private practice.

Methods for evaluating supervisee development include assessment of the competencies of counselors-in-training and evaluation of client–counselor interactions (Herbert, 2004). Herbert describes four methods for evaluating supervisee development—indirect delayed, direct delayed, direct present, and indirect present. The **indirect delayed method** includes self-reports of client progress, case conceptualizations, and reflections of interactions between supervisees and their clients through written documentations, such as process notes, case presentations, and case reviews. **Direct delayed methods** directly monitor counselor–client interactions through the use of audio and video recordings, which allow supervisors to make inferences about counselor–client interactions, assess how supervisees attend to presenting issues during the session, examine supervisee interventions, and formulate supervisory interventions tailored to improve supervisee skills and competence with clients (Herbert, 2004).

Direct present methods involve "live" supervision in which supervisors evaluate sessions in real time and intervene and work with the counselor as necessary. Supervisors and supervisees provide counseling services collaboratively in co-counseling, so supervisees have the opportunity to observe experienced counselors. **Live supervision** occurs with clients present. **Indirect present methods** include direct observations of counselor–client interactions with less intrusiveness. The most popular technique involves supervisees wearing a "bug-in-the-ear" while counseling sessions are in progress. Supervisors provide input and feedback for adjustments without disrupting the session.

Supervisee developmental level. Supervision outcomes depend on the degree to which supervisors adjust their roles and behaviors to match the developmental level of supervisees. Herbert (2004) states that beginning supervisees generally prefer encouragement, support, and space to examine personal concerns that may impact client interactions and a structured framework in which direct and clear suggestions are provided. In contrast, experienced counselors prefer greater autonomy, space to address personal issues such as countertransference, increased self-efficacy, and a structured framework devoted to case consultation (Herbert, 2004). The Integrated Developmental Model (IDM) provides a structured framework to better understand the developmental process of counseling trainees to become competent, experienced, and skilled professionals (Herbert, 2004). The IDM structure is based on supervisory interventions that are chosen based on the supervisee's affective and cognitive needs. The primary supervisory activities cover eight dimensions (Herbert, 2004), including assessment techniques, case conceptualization, individual differences, interpersonal assessment, intervention skills competence, professional ethics, theoretical orientation, and treatment plans and goals. In the IDM, supervisees continuously progress from level 1, counselors with limited experience, to level 3 integrated, counselors who successfully move through the eight dimensions. Growth and successful movement across the eight dimensions are assessed within each level by evaluating supervisees on three basic structures—awareness, motivation, and autonomy (Herbert, 2004; Maki & Delworth, 1995).

VI. Distance Counseling

Counseling through Internet-based (Internet-supported) or distance counseling media are becoming increasingly popular. Internet-based or distance counseling is diverse in presentation and format. For example, websites may provide static information, online software programs allow for confidential e-therapy, asynchronous email exchanges offer communication tools for clients and practitioners, and social media, blogs, chat rooms, and online peer-led support groups are additional Internet-based sources of help and support. Advantages of distance counseling include (but are not limited to) accessible counseling services to individuals who live in geographically remote areas, who do not have adequate transportation, or who have physical or mental health conditions that prevent in-person counseling (Barak & Grohol, 2011). Distance counseling may be particularly well suited for those who experience anxiety, social phobia, or agoraphobia; for adult children of parents with substance and alcohol abuse; for those with body image or shame/guilt issues; and for those more comfortable with anonymity (Alleman, 2002; Barnett, 2005). Studies suggest that online counseling is more cost effective and accessible for historically oppressed and disenfranchised communities (Barak & Grohol, 2011). Online counseling may also allow for less inhibition and increased personal and emotional expression. Although not a replacement for in-person counseling, online counseling can supplement in-person services or serve as a gateway to future in-person meetings (Barak & Grohol, 2011).

Limitations associated with Internet-based or distance counseling media include the following. Communication through email or distance counseling lack verbal and nonverbal cues that shed light on a client's experience and presentation. Clients may compensate for the lack of socioemotional cues with lexical variations and language intensity (Barnett, 2005). As such, rehabilitation counselors should attend to variations in texts, ensure clients understand the text, and be cautious of emotions portrayed through online communication. For example, bolded texts or the use of exclamations or capital letters may signify emotional intensity or urgency. Counselors should provide clients with a list of emoticons to use and check in regularly to be certain of their meaning (Barnett, 2005). Distance counseling may not be appropriate for clients in crisis, clients experiencing psychosis, or clients with borderline personality disorder or for diagnostic purposes when physical presentation is important to the assessment (e.g., anorexia nervosa; Alleman, 2002).

The Code of Professional Ethics for Certified Rehabilitation Counselors (CRCC, 2010), section J (Technology and Distance Counseling), and the code of ethics from the ACA (2014), section H (Distance Counseling, Technology, and Social Media), should be consulted before engaging in distance counseling or e-communication (e.g., emails, social media). Common ethical considerations include the following. First, an informed consent process that is specific to distance counseling must occur (ACA, 2014; CRCC, 2010). For example, the risks and benefits of distance counseling, including the possibility of technology failure, realistic response time from counselors, emergency protocol when the counselor is not immediately available, time zone differences, and cultural or language differences, should be covered. Second, the client's use of technology, including adequate access, must be sufficient for the distance counseling process. Third, the counselor and client should establish an alternative means of communication for emergencies and for identification of the client as the actual user of the technology. For example, client phone number and home address should be provided along with a code word for client verification. Websites and emails must be secure, messages should be encrypted, and confidentiality must be maintained. Counselors may also consider executing a formal waiver concerning the limitations of online counseling and must refer the client to traditional face-to-face services if the conditions are not met (Alleman, 2002). Finally, for licensed rehabilitation counselors (i.e., Licensed Professional Counselor [LPC], Licensed Professional Clinical Counselor [LPCC]), counseling should occur only with clients who reside in the state in which they are licensed; providing on-line counseling with clients in another state can result in legal violations (Barros-Bailey & Saunders, 2010).

Multiple-Choice Questions

1. Breaching client confidentiality must occur in which of the following situations?

   A. The client informs you that he is going to kill his girlfriend.

   B. The client tells you that he feels sad and depressed.

   C. The client tells you that he hit his son a couple times.

   D. A and C

2. Sexual relationships with former clients is prohibited for at least____years following termination.

   A. 2

   B. 5

   C. 10

   D. 20

3. *Irrational thinking* is most closely aligned with which counseling theory?

    A. Rational–emotive behavior therapy

    B. Existential

    C. Gestalt

    D. Client centered

4. Cultural competency includes all of the following *EXCEPT*:

    A. Understanding of one's own worldview.

    B. Understanding of one's attitudes and biases.

    C. Knowledge of cultural practices and worldviews different from one's own.

    D. A diverse workplace.

5. Rehabilitation counselor supervision differs from other types of clinical supervision in which of the following ways?

    A. Its primary focus is on psychosocial aspects of disabilities and chronic illness.

    B. It occurs in public vocational rehabilitation settings.

    C. It typically occurs in a group setting.

    D. It is often performed by multiple supervisors.

6. The empty chair technique is associated with which of the following counseling theories?

    A. Cognitive behavioral therapy

    B. Gestalt

    C. Client centered

    D. Psychodynamic

7. Reinforcement and punishment are key components of which form of learning?

    A. Classical conditioning

    B. Modeling

    C. Operant conditioning

    D. A and C

8. This occurs when reinforcement is withheld from a previously reinforced behavior to decrease the undesired behavior.

    A. Unconditional stimulus

    B. Law of effect

    C. Conditioned response

    D. Extinction

9. When the external stimulus, external reinforcement, and cognitive mediation processes interact to explain behavior, this is called:

    A. Social learning theory

    B. Reciprocal determinism

    C. Operant conditioning

    D. Cognitive behavioral therapy

Answer Key

1D, 2B, 3A, 4D, 5A, 6B, 7C, 8D, 9B

Advanced Multiple-Choice Questions

1. This counselor theory posits that humans are motivated primarily by socialization.

    A. Cognitive behavioral therapy

    B. Social learning theory

    C. Individual psychology

    D. Rational–emotive behavior therapy

2. Empathy, genuineness, and unconditional positive regard are considered necessary and sufficient for change to occur in which counseling theory?

    A. Client centered

    B. Gestalt

    C. Cognitive behavioral therapy

    D. Psychoanalysis

3. The "ABC" method was developed from which counseling theory?

    A. Cognitive behavioral therapy

    B. Existential

    C. Gestalt

    D. Rational–emotive behavior therapy

4. *Dual diagnosis* refers to:

    A. Comorbid physical and mental disorders

    B. Comorbid psychiatric and substance abuse disorders

    C. Differential diagnosis

    D. Coexisting physical disabilities

5. This is considered fundamental to the development of a counseling relationship and involves a "connection" or positive bond with clients and other treatment team members that involve mutual trust, respect, and acceptance.

   A. Empathy

   B. Working alliance

   C. Attending

   D. Reflection

6. A technique in motivational interviewing includes all of the following *EXCEPT*:

   A. Open-ended questioning

   B. Affirmation

   C. Confrontation

   D. Summary statements

7. The final step in conflict resolution is:

   A. Dispelling myths about "good" relationships.

   B. Defining the conflict.

   C. Generating options for resolving the conflict.

   D. Implementing solutions for resolving conflict.

8. Which of the following represents an appropriate reason to terminate a client–counselor relationship?

   A. Counselor has negative feelings toward the client.

   B. Client is resistant to counseling treatment.

   C. Client is not paying agreed-upon fees.

   D. Counselor is experiencing countertransference.

9. This approach to rehabilitation counseling requires a focus on a client's capabilities, capacities, and opportunities versus deficits and limitations.

   A. Ecological approach

   B. Empowerment approach

   C. Biopsychosocial approach

   D. Humanistic approach

Answer Key and Explanation of Answers

1C: Individual psychology, which is based on Alfred Adler's theory, posits that humans are motivated primarily by socialization. Alternatively, cognitive behavioral therapy believes that people's feelings and behaviors are based on how they think (cognitions), and personality is seen as an enduring set of behavioral and emotional responses to stimuli that stem from ingrained, idiosyncratic ways of thinking. Social learning theory posits that psychological functioning involves the reciprocal interaction between behavior, cognition, and the environment, and rational–emotive behavior therapy believes that individuals are constantly striving toward growth but are often stuck because of irrational thinking.

2A: The client-centered approach is based on the role of empathy, genuineness, and unconditional positive regard as the fundamental conditions necessary and sufficient for change to occur. Specific techniques above and beyond these conditions are not considered from this theoretical perspective. The Gestalt approach, while also humanistic, is known for a variety of techniques such as *empty chair, pronouns, sharing hunches*, and *dream work*. The cognitive behavioral therapy approach focuses primarily on psychoeducation and development of skills for managing specific problems and includes the use of a variety of techniques. Although empathy, genuineness, and unconditional positive regard are considered necessary for change, they are not considered sufficient. Finally, psychoanalysis relies heavily on free association, interpretation, confrontation, and working through as primary techniques.

3D: The goals and process of rational–emotive behavior therapy are often summarized using the ABC method: **A** refers to the activating event or adversity; **B** is the individual's beliefs about the event, which may be rational and helpful or irrational and maladaptive; **C** refers to the emotional and behavioral consequences of those beliefs; **D** refers to the responsibility of the counselor to dispute the irrational beliefs and assist the client in obtaining more rational, adaptive beliefs; and **E** refers to when a client develops new behavioral and emotional consequences.

4B: *Dual diagnosis* is reserved specifically for those who have both a psychiatric disability and a substance abuse disorder.

5B: Working alliance is considered fundamental to the development of a counseling relationship and involves a "connection" or positive bond with clients and other treatment team members that involve mutual trust, respect, and acceptance. *Empathy* is an act of knowing and understanding the experience of another. It is the ability to convey support and acceptance by understanding the client's experience via the client's perspective. *Attending* skills are nonverbal skills that involve the physical orientation of the rehabilitation counselor toward the client as a means of communication, with a goal of showing attentiveness and availability. *Reflection* of feeling is a verbal statement whereby there is recognition of the client's emotions by the counselor.

6C: The microskills counseling technique used in motivational interviewing can be remembered by the acronym, OARS: open-ended questioning, affirmation, reflection, and summarization. This technique supports the behavioral change process in a nonconfrontational way.

7D: The final step in conflict resolution is implanting solutions for resolving conflict. Specifically, the steps suggested for conflict resolution occurs in the following sequence: (a) Myths about "good" working relationship must be addressed such that the best working relationship occurs when no discrepancies are present, individuals in the relationship have shared values and expectations, and the goal of the relationship is to avoid conflict; (b) conflict needs to be accurately defined and reframed as differences related to interests and goals versus a negative will; (c) misperceptions should be clarified and the way that the information has been interpreted should be discussed to prevent miscommunications; (d) individuals should discuss ideas that will contribute to the development of a set of shared expectations by reconciling differences; and (e) conflict resolution involves implementing and evaluating resolutions that involve agreement on what the roles and responsibilities of each will be, as well as a written agreement outlining the roles and responsibilities of each.

8C: Client resistance, counselor countertransference, and counselor negative feelings toward a client are not sufficient reasons to terminate immediately. The later reasons do suggest the need for immediate consultation but not termination. If a client does not pay for agreed-upon fees, termination is an appropriate solution.

9B: The empowerment approach involves focusing on a client's capabilities, capacities, and opportunities versus deficits and limitations. *Empowerment* is defined as a process of increasing personal, interpersonal, or political power so that individuals can take action to improve their life situation. *Ecological approach* refers to considering the Person × Environment interaction in understanding disability and chronic illness; the biopsychosocial approach is an approach that emphasizes understanding the biological, psychological, and social aspects of health and disability used by all contemporary health and allied health professionals in response to the reliance on a biomedical explanation of illness. The humanistic approach generally posits that individuals are moving toward growth; this broad umbrella refers to a counseling school of thought that includes counseling theories such as client-centered, Gestalt, and existential theories of counseling.

References

Alleman, J. R. (2002). Online counseling: The internet and mental health treatment. *Psychotherapy: Theory, Research, Practice, Training, 39*(2), 199–209.

American Counseling Association. (2014). *ACA code of ethics*. Alexander, VA: Author.

American Foundation for Suicide Prevention. (2013). *Preventing suicide*. New York, NY: Author. Retrieved from http://www.afsp.org/preventing-suicide

Ansbacher, H. L., & Ansbacher, R. R. (1964). *The individual psychology of Alfred Adler: A systemic presentation in selections from his writings*. New York, NY: Harper & Row.

Appelbaum, P. S. (1985). Tarasoff and the clinician: Problems in fulfilling the duty to protect. *American Journal of Psychiatry, 142*(4), 425–429.

Arredondo, P., Toporek, R., Brown, S. P., Jones, J., Locke, D., Sanchez, J., & Stadler, H. (1996). Operationalization of the multicultural counseling competencies. *Journal of Multicultural Counseling and Development, 24*, 42–78.

Azrin, N. H., & Besalel, V. A. (1980). *Job Club counselor's manual: A behavioral approach to vocational counseling*. Austin, TX: Pro-Ed.

Bakker, J. M., & Bannink, F. P. (2008). Oplossingsgerichte therapie in de psychiatrische praktijk [Solution focused brief therapy in psychiatric practice]. *Tijdschrift voor Psychiatrie, 50*(1), 55–59.

Bandura, A. (1999). A social cognitive theory of personality. In L. A. Pervin & O. P. John (Eds.), *Handbook of personality: Theory and research* (2nd ed., pp. 154–196). New York, NY: Guilford Press.

Bannink, F. P. (2006). *1001 solution-focused questions*. New York, NY: W. W. Norton.

Bannink, F. P. (2007). Solution-focused brief therapy. *Journal of Contemporary Psychotherapy, 37*, 87–94.

Barak, A., & Grohol, J. M. (2011). Current and future trends in internet-supported mental health interventions. *Journal of Technology in Human Services, 29*(3), 155–196.

Barnett, J. E. (2005). Online counseling: New entity, new challenges. *The Counseling Psychologist, 33*(6), 872–880.

Barros-Bailey, M., & Saunders, J. L. (2010). Ethics and the use of technology in rehabilitation counseling. *Rehabilitation Counseling Bulletin, 53*(4), 255–259.

Bath, H. (2008). The three pillars of trauma-informed care. *Reclaiming Children and Youth, 17*(3), 17–21.

Beck, A. T. (1976). *Cognitive therapy and the emotional disorders*. New York, NY: International Universities Press.

Beck, A. T. (1991). Cognitive therapy: A 30-year retrospective. *American Psychologist, 46*, 368–375.

Beck, A. T., & Weishaar, M. E. (2014). Cognitive therapy. In D. Wedding & R. J. Corsini (Eds.), *Current psychotherapies* (10th ed., pp. 231–264). Belmont, CA: Brooks/Cole.

Berg, I. K., & Dolan, Y. (2001). *Tales of solutions: A collection of hope-inspiring stories.* New York, NY: W. W. Norton.

Berg, I. K., & Miller, S. D. (1992). *Working with the problem drinker: A solution focused approach.* New York, NY: W. W. Norton.

Berg, I. K., & Steiner, T. (2003). *Children's solution work.* New York, NY: W. W. Norton.

Berven, N. L. (2008). Assessment interviewing. In B. F. Bolton & R. M. Parker (Eds.), *Handbook of measurement and evaluation in rehabilitation* (4th ed., pp. 241–261). Austin, TX: Pro-Ed.

Berven, N. L. (2010). Clinical interviews. In E. Mpofu & T. Oakland (Eds.), *Assessment in rehabilitation and health* (pp. 158–171). Upper Saddle River, NJ: Merrill.

Berven, N. L., Thomas, K. R., & Chan, F. (2015). An introduction to counseling for rehabilitation and mental health professionals. In F. Chan, N. L. Berven, & K. R. Thomas (Eds.), *Counseling theories and techniques for rehabilitation and mental health professionals* (pp. 1–14). New York, NY: Springer Publishing.

Biggs, H. C., & Flett, R. A. (2005). Rehabilitation professionals and solution-focused brief therapy. In H. Biggs (Ed.), *Proceedings of the inaugural Australian Counseling and Supervision Conference: Integrating research, practice, and training.* Carseldine, Australia: Queensland University of Technology. Retrieved from http://eprints.qut.edu.au/3796/1/3796_1.pdf

Bishop, M., & Fleming, A. R. (2015). Rational emotive behavior therapy. In F. Chan, N. L. Berven, & K. R. Thomas (Eds.), *Counseling theories and techniques for rehabilitation and mental health professionals.* [Bookshelf Online]. Retrieved from https://bookshelf.vitalsource.com/#/books/9780826198686

Blackwell, T. L., Martin, W. E., & Scalia, V. A. (1994). *Ethics in rehabilitation: A guide for rehabilitation professionals.* Athens, GA: Elliott & Fitzpatrick.

Bloom, S. L. (2010). Organizational stress and trauma-informed services. In B. L. Levin & M. A. Becker (Eds.), *A public health perspective of women's mental health* (pp. 295–311). New York, NY: Springer.

Blustein, D. L., & Spengler, P. M. (1996). Personal adjustment: Career counseling and psychotherapy. In W. B. Walsh & S. H. Osipow (Eds.), *Handbook of vocational psychology: Theory, research, and practice* (2nd ed., pp. 295–329). Hillsdale, NJ: Erlbaum.

Borum, R., Bartel, P. A., & Forth, A. (2002). *SAVRY: Structured assessment of violence risk in youth.* Lutz, FL: Psychological Assessment Resources.

Bradley, L. J., & Ladany, N. (2001). *Counselor supervision: Principles, process and practice* (3rd ed.). Philadelphia, PA: Brunner-Routledge.

Bradsher, J. E. (1996). Disability among racial and ethnic groups. *Disability Statistics Abstract, 10*, 1–4.

Brehm, S. S., & Brehm, J. W. (1981) Psychological reactance: A theory of freedom and control. New York, NY: Academic Press.

Brown, D. (1990). Trait and factor theory. In D. Brown & L. Brooks, *Career choice and development: Applying contemporary theories to practice* (pp. 13–36). San Francisco, CA: Jossey-Bass.

Brown, S. M., Baker, C. N., & Wilcox, P. (2012). Risking connection trauma training: A pathway toward trauma-informed care in child congregate care settings. *Psychological Trauma: Theory, Research, Practice, and Policy, 4*(5), 507.

Burwell, R., & Chen, C. (2006). Applying the principles and techniques of solution-focused therapy to career counselling. *Counselling Psychology Quarterly, 19*, 189–203.

Butler, L. D., Critelli, F. M., & Rinfrette, E. S. (2011). Trauma-informed care and mental health. *Directions in Psychiatry, 31*(3), 197–212.

Campbell, T. W. (1994). Psychotherapy and malpractice exposure. *American Journal of Forensic Psychology, 12*, 4–41.

Captain, C. (2006). Is your patient a suicide risk? *Nursing, 36*(8), 43–47.

Chan F., Berven, N. L., & Thomas, K. R. (2004). *Counseling theories and techniques for rehabilitation health professionals*. New York, NY: Springer Publishing.

Chartrand, J. M. (1991). The evolution of trait-and-factor career counseling: A person × environment fit approach. *Journal of Counseling and Development, 69,* 518–524.

Chartrand, J. M., Strong, S. R., & Weitzman, L. M. (1995). The interactional perspective in vocational psychology: Paradigms, theories, and research practices. In W. B. Walsh & S. H. Osipow (Eds.), *Handbook of vocational psychology: Theory, research, and practice* (2nd ed., pp. 35–65). Hillsdale, NJ: Erlbaum.

Cobia, D. C., & Boes, S. R. (2000). Professional disclosure statements and formal plans for supervision: Two strategies for minimizing the risk of ethical conflicts in post-master's supervision. *Journal of Counseling & Development, 78,* 293–296.

Commission on Rehabilitation Counselor Certification. (n.d.). *Scope of practice for rehabilitation counseling*. Rolling Meadows, IL: Author.

Commission on Rehabilitation Counselor Certification. (2010). *Code of Professional Ethics for Rehabilitation Counselors*. Schaumburg, IL: Author.

Cooper, C. C. (2000). Ethical issues with managed care: Challenges facing counseling psychology. *Counseling Psychologist, 28,* 179–236.

Cooper, M., & McLeod, J. (2007) A pluralistic framework for counselling and psychotherapy: Implications for research. *Counselling and Psychotherapy Research, 7*(3), 135–143.

Corey, G. (1986). *A person-centered foundation for counseling and psychotherapy* (2nd ed.). Pacific Grove, CA: Brooks/Cole.

Corey, G. (2001). *Theory and practice of counseling and psychotherapy* (4th ed.). Pacific Grove, CA: Brooks/Cole.

Corey, G. (2004). *Theory and practice of counseling and psychotherapy,* (5th ed.). Pacific Grove, CA: Wadsworth.

Corey, G. (2013). *Theory and practice of counseling and psychotherapy*. Belmont, CA: Brooks/Cole.

Corey, M. S., & Corey, G. (2006). *Groups: Process and practice*. Belmont, CA: Thomson Brooks/Cole.

Corrigan, P. W., & Liberman, R. P. (1994). Overview of behavior therapy in psychiatric hospitals. In P. W. Corrigan & R. P. Liberman (Eds.), *Behavior therapy in psychiatric hospitals* (pp. 1–38). New York, NY: Springer Publishing.

Council on Rehabilitation Education. (2011). Professional standards. Retrieved from http://www .core-rehab.org

Coven, A. B. (1979). The Gestalt approach to rehabilitation of the whole person. *Journal of Applied Rehabilitation Counseling, 9,* 144–147.

Craighead, L. W., Craighead, W. E., Kazdin, A. E., & Mahoney, M. J. (1994). *Cognitive and behavioral interventions: An empirical approach to mental health problems*. Needham Heights, MA: Allyn & Bacon.

Curl, R. M., & Sheldon, J. B. (1992). Achieving reasonable choices: Balancing the rights and responsibilities of consumers with those of rehabilitation counselors. *Rehabilitation Education, 6,* 195–205.

Dawis, R. V., & Lofquist, L. H. (1984). *A psychological theory of work adjustment*. Minneapolis: University of Minnesota Press.

de Jong, P., & Berg, I. K. (1997). *Interviewing for solutions*. Pacific Grove, CA: Brooks/Cole.

de Jong, P., & Berg, I. K. (2002). *Interviewing for solutions* (2nd ed.). Pacific Grove, CA: Brooks/Cole.

de Shazer, S. (1985). *Keys to solution in brief therapy*. New York, NY: W. W. Norton.

de Shazer, S., & Berg, I. K. (1997). "What works?" Remarks on research aspects of solution-focused brief therapy. *Journal of Family Therapy, 19,* 121–124.

de Shazer, S., Dolan, Y., Korman, H., Trepper, T., McCollum, E., & Berg, I. K. (2007). *More than miracles: The state of the art of solution-focused brief therapy*. London, UK: Routledge.

Dryden, W. (2005). Rational emotive behavior therapy. In A. Freeman, S. H. Felgoise, C. M. Nezu, A. M. Nezu, & M. A. Reinecke (Eds.), *Encyclopedia of cognitive behavior therapy* (pp. 321–324). New York, NY: Springer.

Dryden, W. (2012). Rational emotive behavior therapy (REBT). In W. Dryden (Ed.), *Cognitive behaviour therapies* (pp. 189–215). London, UK: Sage.

Dryden, W. (2013). On rational beliefs in rational emotive behavior therapy: A theoretical perspective. *Journal of Rational-Emotive and Cognitive-Behavior Therapy*, *31*, 39–48.

Duncan, B., Miller, S. D., Wampold, B., & Hubble, M. (2010). *The heart and soul of change: Delivering what works in therapy* (2nd ed.). Washington, DC: American Psychological Association.

Ellis, A. (1962). *Reason and emotion in psychotherapy*. Secaucus, NJ: Lyle Stuart.

Fallot, R., & Harris, M. (2009). Creating Cultures of Trauma-Informed Care (CCTIC): A self-assessment and planning protocol. *Community Connections, 2*(2), 1–18.

Festinger, L. (1957). A theory of cognitive dissonance, Evanston, IL: Row & Peterson.

Fisher, R., & Brown, S. (1988). *Getting together: Building a relationship that gets to yes*. Boston, MA: Houghton Mifflin.

Freud, A. (1946). *The ego and the mechanisms of defense*. New York, NY: International Universities Press. (Original work published 1936)

Freud, S. (1959). Inhibitions, symptoms, and anxiety. In J. Strachey (Ed. & Trans.), *The standard edition of the complete psychological works of Sigmund Freud* (Vol. 20, pp. 75–173). London, UK: Hogarth Press. (Original work published 1926)

Gilliland, B. E., & James, R. K. (1998). *Theories and strategies in counseling and psychotherapy*. Boston, MA: Allyn & Bacon.

Granello, D. H., & Granello, P. F. (2007). *Suicide: An essential guide for helping professionals and educators*. New York, NY: Pearson/Allyn & Bacon.

Greenson, R. R. (1967). *The technique and practice of psychoanalysis* (Vol 1.). New York, NY: International Universities Press.

Gutierrez, L. M. (1990). Working with women of color: An empowerment perspective. *Social Work, 35*(2), 149–153.

Halbur, D. A., & Halbur, K. (2006). *Developing your theoretical orientation in counseling psychotherapy*. Boston, MA: Pearson.

Hansen, J. C., Rossberg, R. K., & Cramer, S. H. (1993). *Counseling: Theory and process* (5th ed.). Boston, MA: Allyn & Bacon.

Hartmann, H. (1964). *Essays on ego psychology: Selected problems in psychoanalytic theory* (Vol. 61). New York, NY: International Universities Press.

Herbert, J. H. (2004). Clinical supervision in rehabilitation settings. *Counseling Theories and Techniques for Rehabilitation Health Professionals, 21*, 405–422.

Hershenson, D. B. (1996). Work adjustment: A neglected area in career counseling. *Journal of Counseling & Development, 74*, 442–446.

Hill, C. E. (2014). *Helping skills. Facilitating exploration, insight, and action* (4th ed.). Washington, DC: American Psychological Association.

Hodges, S. (2015). *The counseling practicum and internship manual* (2nd ed.). New York, NY: Springer Publishing.

Holmes, G. E., Hall, L., & Karst, R. H. (1989). Litigation avoidance through conflict resolution: Issues for state rehabilitation agencies. *American Rehabilitation, 15*, 12–15.

Ivey, A. E., Ivey, M. B., & Zalaquett, C. P. (2014). *Intentional interviewing and counseling: Facilitating client development in a multicultural society* (8th ed.). Belmont, CA: Brooks/Cole.

Jackson, J. (2000). What ought psychology to do? *American Psychologist, 55*, 328–300.

Kazdin, A. E. (1994). *Behavior modification in applied settings* (5th ed.). Pacific Grove, CA: Brooks/Cole.

Keesler, J. M. (2014). A call for the integration of trauma informed care among intellectual and developmental disability organizations. *Journal of Policy and Practice in Intellectual Disabilities, 11*(1), 34–42.

Kiernan, C. (1975). Behaviour modification. In D. Bannister (Ed.), *Issues and approaches in the psychological therapies* (pp. 241–260). New York, NY: Wiley.

Kim, J. S. (2008). Examining the effectiveness of solution-focused brief therapy: A meta-analysis. *Research on Social Work Practice, 18*, 107–116.

Koch, L. C., McReynolds, C., & Rumrill, P. D. (2004). Basic counseling skills. In F. Chan, N. L. Berven, & K. R. Thomas (Eds.), *Counseling theories and techniques for rehabilitation health professionals* (pp. 227–243). New York, NY: Springer Publishing.

Kohut, H. (1971). *The analysis of the self*. New York, NY: International Universities Press.

Kohut, H. (1977). *The restoration of the self*. New York, NY: International Universities Press.

Kosciulek, J. F. (1993). Advances in trait-and-factor theory: A person × environment fit approach to rehabilitation counseling. *Journal of Applied Rehabilitation Counseling, 24*(2), 11–14.

Kosciulek, J. F. (1999). Consumer direction in disability policy formulation and rehabilitation service delivery. *Journal of Rehabilitation, 65*(2), 4–9.

Kosciulek, J. F. (2000). Implications of consumer direction for disability policy development and rehabilitation service delivery. *Journal of Disability Policy Studies, 11*(2), 82–89.

Kosciulek, J., Phillips, B., & Lizotte, M. C. (2015). Trait factor theory and counseling process. In F. Chan, N. L. Berven, & K. R. Thomas (Eds.), *Counseling theories and techniques for rehabilitation and mental health professionals*. [Bookshelf Online]. Retrieved from https://bookshelf.vitalsource.com/#/books/9780826198686

Lee, C. C. (1998a). Counselors as agents for social change. In C. C. Lee & G. R. Walz (Eds.), *Social action: A mandate for counselors* (pp. 3–16). Alexandria, VA: American Counseling Association.

Lee, C. C. (1998b). Professional counseling in a global context: Collaboration for international social action. In C. C. Lee & G. R. Walz (Eds.), *Social action: A mandate for counselors* (pp. 293–306). Alexandria, VA: American Counseling Association.

Lewis, A., Bethea, J., & Hurley, J. (2009). Integrating cultural competence in rehabilitation curricula in the new millennium: Keeping it simple. *Disability and Rehabilitation, 31*(4), 1161–1169.

Lewis, J. A., Ratts, M. J., Paladino, D. A., & Toporek, R. L. (2011). Social justice counseling and advocacy: Developing new leadership roles and competencies. *Journal for Social Action in Counseling and Psychology, 3*(1), 5–16.

Lewis, T. F., & Osborn, C. J. (2004). Solution-focused counseling and motivational interviewing: A consideration of confluence. *Journal of Counseling and Development, 82*, 38–48.

Livneh, H., & Siller, J. (2004). Psychodynamic therapy for rehabilitation professionals. In F. Chan, N. L. Berven, & K. R. Thomas (Eds.), *Counseling theories and techniques for rehabilitation health professionals* (pp. 20–52). New York, NY: Springer Publishing.

Livneh, H., & Siller, J. (2015). Psychodynamic therapy. In F. Chan, N. L. Berven, & K. R. Thomas (Eds.), *Counseling theories and techniques for rehabilitation and mental health professionals*. [Bookshelf Online]. Retrieved from https://bookshelf.vitalsource.com/#/books/9780826198686

Lofquist, L. H., & Dawis, R. V. (1969). *Adjustment to work: A psychological view of man's problems in a work-oriented society*. New York, NY: Appleton-Century-Crofts.

Lunneborg, P. W. (1983). Career counseling techniques. In W. B. Walsh & S. H. Osipow (Eds.), *Handbook of vocational psychology: Applications* (Vol. 2). Hillsdale, NJ: Erlbaum.

Lynch, R. K., & Maki, D. R. (1981). Searching for structure: A trait–factor approach to vocational rehabilitation. *Vocational Guidance Quarterly, 30*, 61–68.

Maki, D. R., & Delworth, U. (1995). Clinical supervision: A definition and model for the rehabilitation counseling profession. *Rehabilitation Counseling Bulletin, 38,* 282–303.

Manaster, G. J., & Corsini, R. J. (1982). *Individual psychology: Theory and practice* (Vol. 401). Itasca, IL: F. E. Peacock.

Manthey, T. J., Brooks, J., Chan, F., Hedenblad, L. E., & Ditchman, N. (2015). Motivational interviewing. In F. Chan, N. L. Berven, & K. R. Thomas (Eds.), *Counseling theories and techniques for rehabilitation and mental health professionals* (p. 246). New York, NY: Springer Publishing.

Mays, V M. (2000). A social justice agenda. *American Psychologist, 55,* 326–327.

McGlothen, J. M., Rainey, S., & Kindsvatter, A. (2005). Suicidal clients and supervisees: A model for considering supervisor roles. *Counselor Education and Supervision, 45,* 135–146.

Miller, W. R., & Rollnick, S. (2002). *Motivational interviewing: Preparing people for change* (2nd ed.). New York, NY: Guilford Press.

Mueser, K. T. (1993). Schizophrenia. In A. S. Bellack & M. Hersen (Eds.), *Handbook of behavior therapy in the psychiatric setting* (pp. 269–292). New York, NY: Plenum.

Murdock, N. L. (2016). *Theories of counseling and psychotherapy: A case approach.* Saddle River, NJ: Pearson.

National Association of School Psychologists. (n.d.). *Threat assessment: Predicting and preventing school violence.* Washington, DC: Author. Retrieved from http://www.nasponline.org/resources/factsheets/threatassess_fs.aspx

Nelson-Jones, R. (2000). *Six key approaches to counseling and therapy.* New York, NY: Continuum.

Norcross, J. C., & Wampold, B. E. (2011). Evidence-based therapy relationships: Research conclusions and clinical practices. In J. C. Norcross (Ed.), *Psychotherapy relationships that work: Evidence-based responsiveness* (2nd ed., pp. 423–430). New York, NY: Oxford.

Orford (1985). *Excessive appetites: A psychological view of additions.* New York, NY: Wiley.

Papajohn, J. C. (1982). *Intensive behavior therapy: The behavioral treatment of complex emotional disorders.* New York, NY: Pergamon.

Parsons, F. (1909). *Choosing a vocation.* Boston, MA: Houghton Mifflin.

Patterson, W. M., Dohn, H. H., Bird, J., & Patterson, G. A. (1983). Evaluation of suicidal patients: The SAD PERSONS scale. *Psychosomatics, 24*(4), 343–349.

Prilleltensky, I. (1994). *Morals and politics of psychology: The psychological discourse and the status quo.* New York, NY: SUNY Press.

Ratts, M. J. (2009). Social justice counseling: Toward the development of a fifth force among counseling paradigms. *Journal of Humanistic Counseling, Education and Development, 48*(2), 160–172. Retrieved from https://search.proquest.com/docview/212453687?accountid=13802

Remley, T. P., & Herlihy, B. (2014). *Ethical, legal and professional issues in counseling* (4th ed.). Upper Saddle River, NJ: Pearson.

Ridley, C. R., Mollen, D., & Kelly, S. D. (2011). Beyond microskills: Toward a model of counseling competence. *Counseling Psychologist, 39,* 825–864.

Rogers, C. R. (1957). The necessary and sufficient conditions of therapeutic personality change. *Journal of Consulting Psychology, 21,* 93–103.

Rogers, C. R. (1959). *A theory of therapy, personality, and interpersonal relationships: As developed in the client-centered framework* (Vol. 3, pp. 184–256). New York, NY: McGraw-Hill.

Rogers, C. R. (1961). *On becoming a person.* Boston, MA: Houghton Mifflin.

Rogers, C. R. (1977). *Carl Rogers on personal power.* New York, NY: Delacorte.

Rogers, J. R., Lewis, M. M., & Subich, L. M. (2002). Validity of the Suicide Assessment Checklist in an emergency crisis center. *Journal of Counseling and Development, 80,* 493–502.

Rollnick, S., & Miller, W. R. (1995). What is motivational interviewing? *Behavioural and Cognitive Psychotherapy, 23*(04), 325–334.

Rokeach, M. (1973). *The nature of human values.* New York, NY: Free Press.

Rounds, J. B., & Tracey, T. J. (1990). From trait-and-factor to person–environment fit counseling: Theory and process. In W. B. Walsh & S. H. Osipow (Eds.), *Career counseling: Contemporary topics in vocational psychology* (pp. 1–44). Hillsdale, NJ: Erlbaum.

Ryan, R. M., & Deci, E. L. (2002). Overview of self-determination theory: An organismic dialectical perspective. In R. M. Ryan & E. L., Deci (Eds.). *Handbook of self-determination research.* Rochester, NY: The University of Rochester Press.

Saleebey, D. (2006). Power in the people. In D. Saleeby, (Ed.), *The strengths perspective in social work practice* (4th ed.). Boston, MA: Pearson/Allyn & Bacon.

Sales, A. (2005). Rehabilitation counseling within an empowerment perspective. In R. M. Parker, E. M. Szymanski, & J. B. Patterson (Eds.), *Counseling: Basics and beyond* (4th ed., pp. 179–210). Austin, TX: Pro-Ed.

Schloss, P. J., & Smith, M. A. (1994). *Applied behavior analysis in the classroom.* Boston, MA: Allyn & Bacon.

See, J., & Kamnetz, B. (2015). Person-centered counseling. In F. Chan, N. L. Berven, & K. R. Thomas (Eds.), *Counseling theories and techniques for rehabilitation and mental health professionals.* [Bookshelf Online]. Retrieved from https://bookshelf.vitalsource.com/#/books/9780826198686

Seligman, L., & Reichenberg, L. (2010). *Theories of counseling and psychotherapy: Systems, strategies, and skills* (3rd ed.). Upper Saddle River, NJ: Pearson.

Shaw, L. R., & Tarvydas, V. M. (2001). The use of professional disclosure in rehabilitation counseling. *Rehabilitation Counseling Bulletin, 45,* 40–47.

Shea, S. C. (1998). *Psychiatric interviewing: The art of understanding: A practical guide for psychiatrists, psychologists, counselors, social workers, nurses, and other mental health professionals* (2nd ed.). New York, NY: Saunders.

Siller, J. (1976). Psychosocial aspects of disability. In J. Meislin (Ed.), *Rehabilitation medicine and psychiatry* (pp. 455–484). Springfield, IL: Charles C Thomas.

Smart, J. F., & Smart, D. W. (1997). The racial/ethnic demography of disability. *Journal of Rehabilitation, 63* (4), 9–15.

Sommers-Flanagan, R. S., & Sommers-Flanagan, J. S. (1999). *Clinical interviewing* (2nd ed.). New York, NY: Wiley.

Stams, G. J., Dekovic, M., Buist, K., & de Vries, L. (2006). Effectiviteit van oplossingsgerichte korte therapie: Een meta-analyse [Efficacy of solution focused brief therapy: A meta-analysis]. *Gedragstherapie, 39,* 81–95.

Steele, C. M. (1988). The psychology of self-affirmation: Sustaining the integrity of the self. *Advances in Experimental Social Psychology, 21,* 261–302.

Stoll, J. L. (2004). Behavior therapy. In F. Chan, N. L. Berven, K. R. Thomas, F. Chan, N. L. Berven, K. R. Thomas (Eds.), *Counseling theories and techniques for rehabilitation health professionals* (pp. 136–158). New York, NY: Springer Publishing.

Strickland, B. R. (2000). Misassumptions, misadventures, and the misuses of psychology. *American Psychologist, 55,* 331–338.

Sue, D. W. (2006). *Multicultural social work practice.* Hoboken, NJ: Wiley.

Sue, D. W., Arredondo, P., & McDavis, R. J. (1992). Multicultural counseling competencies and standards: A call to the profession. *Journal of Counseling and Development, 70,* 477–486.

Sue, D. W., & Sue, D. (2003). *Counseling the culturally diverse: Theory and practice.* New York, NY: Wiley.

Tansey, T. N., Mizelle, N., Ferrin, J. N., Tschopp, M. K., & Frain, M. (2004). Work related stress and the demand-control support framework: Implications for the p x e model. *Journal of Rehabilitation, 70,* 34–41.

Tarasoff v. Regents of the University of California, 13 Cal. 3d 177, 529 P.2d. 533 (1976).

Tarvydas, V. M. (1995). Ethics and the practice of rehabilitation counselor supervision. *Rehabilitation Counseling Bulletin*, *38*(4), 294–306.

Teyber, E. (2006). Interpersonal process in psychotherapy: An integrative approach. Belmont, CA: Brooks/Cole.

Trepper, T. S., McCollum, E. E., de Jong, P., Korman, H., Gingerich, W. J., & Franklin, C. (2012). Solution-focused brief therapy manual. In C. Franklin, T. Trepper, W. Gingerich, & E. McCollum (Eds.), *Solution-focused brief therapy: A handbook of evidence-based practice* (pp. 20–36). New York, NY: Oxford University Press.

U.S. Census Bureau. (2000). Overview of race and Hispanic origin: Census 2000 brief. Retrieved from https://www.census.gov/prod/2001pubs/c2kbr01-1.pdf

Wampold, B. E. (2001). *The great psychotherapy debate: Models, methods, and findings*. Mahwah, NJ: Erlbaum.

Weinrach, S. G. (2006). Nine experts describe the essence of rational-emotive therapy while standing on one foot. *Journal of Rational-Emotive & Cognitive-Behavior Therapy*, *24*, 217–232.

Williamson, E. G. (1965). *Vocational counseling*. New York, NY: McGraw-Hill.

Williamson, E. G. (1972). Trait–factor theory and individual differences. In B. Stefflre & W. H. Grant (Eds.), *Theories of counseling* (pp. 136–176). New York, NY: McGraw-Hill.

Williamson, E. G., & Biggs, D. A. (1979). Trait–factor theory and individual differences. In H. M. Burks, Jr., & B. Stefflre (Eds.), *Theories of counseling* (3rd ed., pp. 91–131). New York, NY: McGraw-Hill.

Wilson, G. T. (1995). Behavior therapy. In R. J. Corsini & D. Wedding (Eds.), *Current psychotherapies* (5th ed., pp. 197–228). Itasca, IL: Peacock.

Yalom, I. (1995). *Group psychotherapy*. New York, NY: Basic Books.

Yankura, J., & Dryden, W. (1994). *Albert Ellis*. Thousand Oaks, CA: Sage.

6

Group Work and Family Dynamics

Eun-Jeong Lee, Jinhee Park, and Kristin Kosyluk

The composition of groups in group counseling ranges from couples to families to large groups of individuals (Ditchman, Lee, & Huebner, 2015). Across this range of compositions, common goals include self-understanding, personal growth, and building on inner resources (Corey & Corey, 2013). Group counseling involves individuals who come together to form a social system with norms and expectations, who interact with each other as well as with the leader, who share needs and experiences, who exchange supports, and who form an identity as members of the group. In group counseling, the group context and the group process constitute the treatment intervention (Ditchman et al., 2015). The therapeutic effects originate within the group context and are based on the fundamental assumption that the presence of others provides a unique opportunity for self-exploration and learning that is not present in individual approaches (Corey & Corey, 2013; Ditchman et al., 2015). This chapter reviews the following issues related to group and family counseling:

- *Group dynamics and counseling theory*
- *Group process*
- *Group leadership styles and techniques*
- *Family dynamics and counseling theory*
- *Ethical and legal issues impacting group process*

Group Dynamics and Counseling Theory

Multiple theoretical approaches may apply to group counseling. Ditchman et al. (2015) reviewed four categories of therapeutic approaches in group counseling. In this section, those four broad categories of therapeutic approaches are briefly reviewed, and the fundamental differences between theoretical approaches are discussed. In addition, more contemporary group counseling approaches are introduced. Finally, common group therapeutic factors across all theories are discussed.

Learning Objectives

By the end of this unit you should be able to:

1. Understand the core assumptions and values of each theoretical approach.
2. Understand how each theoretical approach can be uniquely applied in group settings.
3. Understand general therapeutic factors in group settings.

Key Concepts

I. Psychodynamic Approaches

Psychodynamic approaches include psychoanalysis, object relations, and interpersonal theory. The goal of psychodynamic intervention is to provide a climate in which clients may reexperience relationship with others. The group process itself may elicit transference and defense mechanisms in group members. Transference elicits interaction patterns that may be dysfunctional in the current context. Through identification, analysis, and interpretation of such patterns in the group, members are provided the opportunity to develop insights into the origins of flawed psychological development and expectations in relationships (e.g., self-defeating, self-fulfilling, personal strengths, and weaknesses). Developing insight into the origins of dysfunctional patterns of interaction reduces the shame associated with recognizing weaknesses because weaknesses are understood as logical adaptive responses to experiences (Ditchman et al., 2015).

Application

Persons with disabilities experience the same life issues as individuals without disabilities such as relationship challenges, emotional distress, cultural issues, and abuse, to name a few (Patterson, McKenzie, & Jenkins, 1995). In addition, experiences with disability may elicit stereotypical responses, including misperceptions of abilities, the spread of disability to all aspects of life, lowered expectations for adaptation, and social isolation (Seligman & Marshak, 2004). Effective group leaders recognize that these expectations and stereotypical responses may be enacted in the group, providing opportunities to practice alternative responses for developing social competence and proper social skills.

II. Experiential and Humanistic Approaches

Gestalt therapy, logotherapy, existential therapy, and person-centered therapy are characterized as experiential approaches. The goal of these approaches is to develop a realistic and present-centered understanding of the self and to empower group members to change and take responsibility for their lives. The focus of group work is on present feelings and responses. Nonverbal behaviors are attended to as clues to masked feelings. The focus on the here-and-now experience is intended to increase awareness of emotions, provide catharsis, and develop congruence between actions and feeling (Ditchman et al., 2015).

Applications

Experiential groups may help individuals experience mourning or anger related to their disabilities or others. Role-playing, empathic group responses, reflection, modeling, use of the empty chair, and keeping of a journal of emotions and thoughts are some of the techniques typical of experiential group work (Ditchman et al., 2015).

III. Cognitive Behavioral Approaches

Cognitive behavioral approaches to group work include behavior therapy, rational–emotive therapy, cognitive therapy, reality therapy, stress inoculation, and solution-focused therapy.

The goal of cognitive behavioral approaches is to identify maladaptive behavior and patterns of thinking and to replace them with adaptive behavior and rational cognition (Ditchman et al., 2015). The group members and leader reinforce adaptive behavior and thoughts, seek to extinguish maladaptive responses, and promote direct and vicarious learning.

Applications

Group role-play, structured experiences, inoculation, reframing of cognitive distortion, and problem solving may help people with disabilities to redefine a disability and assist people in identifying and expanding adaptive strategies and strengths (Ditchman et al., 2015). Other techniques commonly used in the cognitive behavioral approaches include cognitive restructuring, systematic desensitization, relaxation, realization, meditation, assertiveness, time-management training, workbooks, and reading assignments. Positive reinforcement such as tokens or stickers can also be used to visualize progress (Ditchman et al., 2015).

IV. Psychoeducational Approaches

Educational groups, support groups, and self-help groups are included in these approaches. The goals are to impart and acquire knowledge, to develop pragmatic coping strategies, and to exchange social support with others who have similar experiences. The group leader may be very active in planning and running a support group. The leadership may rotate among members or there may be no formal group leader. Group membership may also vary from session to session. The level of self-disclosure and cohesiveness may vary as well. Group members function not only as a support and knowledge base for one another, but also as a source of practical solutions to problems and action planning (Ditchman et al., 2015).

Applications

Various psychoeducational groups exist within inpatient, outpatient, and vocational programs. Groups can be organized based on the goals and needs of group members. For example, an illness-awareness and illness-management group can provide specific health-related information and teach management skills, and Job Clubs can support individuals with chronic unemployment through structured and intensive job searches and training (Salomone, 1996); specific job-skill training for successful transition from school to work can also be provided as a group format (McWhirter & McWhirter, 1996).

V. Motivational Interviewing and Stages of Change

Motivational interviewing (MI) group interventions are used for members with substance abuse, chronic health conditions, and other behavioral issues (Wagner & Ingersoll, 2012). MI is a person-centered and goal-directed method of enhancing intrinsic motivation to change by exploring and resolving ambivalence (W. R. Miller & Rollnick, 2002). There are four key principles effective in facilitating change: rolling resistance rather than confronting it, expressing empathy, developing discrepancy between current behavior and a desired future, and supporting client self-efficacy. MI is commonly associated with the transtheoretical or stages-of-change model, because this model can provide a framework for understanding the process of behavior change. According to the stages-of-change model, people move through five stages when they try to make major life changes. These include precontemplation, contemplation, preparation, action, and maintenance (Prochaska & DiClemente, 1983). Group leaders can facilitate movement and possible behavior changes through the stages by using MI techniques (Leeman, 2013).

Applications

MI groups may help people with disability change their behaviors or lifestyle due to their functional limitation or health condition. *Change talk*, which is a client's desire, abilities, reasons, or needs for positive behavior change, is the most common technique through the use of microcounseling skills such as open-ended questions, affirmations, reflections, and summary (W. R. Miller & Rollnick, 2002).

VI. General Therapeutic Factors

Although different theoretical orientations can have an impact on facilitating a group in a certain manner, there also exist common factors associated with the effectiveness of group procedures that transcend a single orientation (Ditchman et al., 2015). Yalom and Leszcz (2005) identified these general therapeutic factors of group interventions based on a review of empirical data and clinical observations. These factors are as follows: (a) *group cohesion* that refers to the therapeutic relationships in the group context; (b) *universality*, or recognition of similar thoughts, feelings, and challenges shared with other members; (c) *instillation of hope* about personal progress by observing other members' success; (d) *altruism;* (e) *imparting of information;* (f) *imitative behavior* through vicarious learning and observation of other members' progress; and (g) *interpersonal learning* obtained from personal insight though feedback provided by other members.

Group Process

Group process refers to the ways in which a group develops or evolves over time from beginning to end. Group process is concerned with the dynamics among the members that go on within the group (Corey & Corey, 2013).

Learning Objectives

By the end of this unit you should be able to:

1. Understand the stages of group development and the typical characteristics of these stages.
2. Understand how a leader may facilitate the group in moving from one stage of development to the next.
3. Understand the different styles of leadership, which can be adopted during the group process.

Key Concepts

I. Stages of Group Development

Groups can be conceptualized as progressing through a series of stages from beginning to end. According to Corey and Corey (2013), group development is divided into four stages: initial, transition, working, and final. Groups may not progress through all stages and may get stuck at a particular stage, which they may never move beyond. Each stage may be characterized or differentiated according to several things: processes and tasks that members are going through or trying to accomplish, responses and behaviors of members, and leader behaviors (Corey & Corey, 2013; see Table 6.1).

Initial stage
The initial stage is a time of orientation and exploration when members are trying to find their way, learning how to relate and behave within the group, and beginning to trust the group

---

TABLE 6.1 Summary Table: Stages of Group Development

Stage of Group Development	Characteristic Activities, Thoughts, Feelings, and Behaviors	Leader Functions and Behaviors
Initial	• Getting acquainted • Learning how the group functions • Developing unspoken norms to regulate group behavior • Exploring fears and hopes related to the group and participation in the group • Clarifying expectations • Identifying personal goals • Determining the degree of safety that is present in the group	• Deciding on an optimal degree of sharing of leadership responsibility between group leader(s) and members • Deciding on an optimal degree of structuring on the part of the group leader(s) and the nature of that structuring
Transition	• Identification of, and dealing with, feelings, thoughts, and behaviors that may interfere with productive work on issues and problems in order to move into a more highly productive working stage of the group • Expression of feelings and difficulties as members work through the resistance, conflicts, mistrust that inhibit work	• Challenging the resistance that is a barrier to working on issues within the group • Encouraging more risk taking • Identifying and processing feelings, thoughts, and behaviors and facilitating self-expression in order to move forward with group work (working through the resistance)
Working	• Work on issues and attempts to accomplish goals • Commitment to deal with problems and attention to group dynamics • Trust, cohesion, and a sense of inclusion. • Open communication, self-disclosure, and taking risks • Shared leadership, with leaders carrying less of the leadership responsibility • Interpersonal conflict and control and power issues recognized and effectively dealt with • Direct communication among members, freely-given feedback, nondefensive acceptance of feedback, and constructive confrontation • Feelings of support and hopefulness • Willingness to work outside of the group to experiment and achieve behavioral changes	• Continuing to encourage facilitative norms and cohesiveness • Reducing activity in structuring and leading the group to allow for greater shared leadership • Modelling direct communication, self-disclosure, feedback, and constructive confrontation • Supporting direct communication, self-disclosure, feedback, and constructive confrontation • Identifying and exploring common themes to link the work of different members • Translating insight into action by encouraging the practicing of new behaviors, both in the group and outside through homework assignments

(continued)

TABLE 6.1 Summary Table: Stages of Group Development (*continued*)

Stage of Group Development	Characteristic Activities, Thoughts, Feelings, and Behaviors	Leader Functions and Behaviors
Final	• Possible feelings of anxiety, sadness, and separation • Concerns about unfinished business; things left "hanging" with little time to resolve them • Concerns about "what comes next"	• Dealing with member feelings surrounding the ending of the group • Asking, "What has this experience meant to you?" • Asking, "What are your thoughts or feelings as we begin to wrap up our time together?" • Recognizing and dealing with unfinished business • Identifying and reinforcing the growth, changes, and achievements of members • Helping members transfer changes and achievements to real life • Reemphasizing confidentiality • Evaluating member growth and change, along with the strengths and weaknesses of the group

and individual members. It is often characterized by tentativeness. This is the stage in which personal goals regarding what members will gain from participation are identified. The main theme in the initial stage is that members become acclimated to the group and get acquainted with one another.

Transition stage

The transition stage is characterized by beginning to challenge the resistance that is a barrier to working on issues within the group and to take more risks. It is a stage in which feelings, thoughts, and behaviors that may interfere with productive work on issues and problems are identified and dealt with in order to move into a more highly productive working stage. This stage is also characterized by the expression of feelings and difficulties as members work through the resistance, conflicts, or mistrust that inhibit work.

Working stage

This stage is characterized by work on issues and attempts to accomplish goals and by a commitment on the part of members to explore and deal with problems. It is also characterized by attention to the dynamics of the group.

Final stage

This stage is a time of clarifying the meaning of individuals' experiences in the group, consolidating what has been accomplished and working toward applying those accomplishments to change outside of the group.

II. Disability Considerations

Group counseling in rehabilitation involves members with various types of disabilities with varying degrees of function, which may require an adaptation of group procedure (Patterson et al., 1995). The following information provides several considerations related to disability and possible accommodations when forming a group.

Group heterogeneity

It is not unusual that group members come from different backgrounds (e.g., age, gender, socio-economic status [SES], and education level) with different functional abilities. Therefore, group leaders need to consider strategies for managing the heterogeneity of the group. Such accommodations could be a buddy system in which high-functioning group members assist lower-functioning group members, collaborative modifications to group procedures, and setting of individual goals within group goals (Seligman & Marshak, 2004).

Cognitive limitations

Members with limited cognitive abilities can benefit from the following accommodations: using a consistent structure and agenda with simple and brief instructions, using more visual cues and sensory/motor activities, and providing frequent feedback and concise examples (Seligman & Marshak, 2004; Stein, 1996).

Communication limitations

Because of the importance of verbal expression within the group process, a member's limited communication ability could be challenging. Various verbal and nonverbal activities may provide all parities with an opportunity to participate. Augmentative communication devices and alternative communication methods (e.g., sign language, body gestures, drawing, and writing) can be used (Seligman & Marshak, 2004).

Attention/behavioral difficulties and fatigue

Shorter but more frequent groups can be beneficial for members with short attention spans or who experience pain or fatigue. Members can be taught to control certain behaviors or to cope with fatigue. Members with attention/behavioral issues can also be encouraged to take over a portion of a group tasks to enhance group engagement (Seligman & Marshak, 2004).

Physical and sensory impairments

In rehabilitation settings, members need to use certain assistive devices such as wheelchairs, traction devices, or oxygen tanks. These devices must be accommodated to allow all group members to see and interact with one another (Seligman & Marshak, 2004). Looking directly at the group member with hearing loss while speaking, providing a summary of the group session, including a scribe or interpreter in the group, and using American Sign Language (ASL) can be effective accommodations for working with group members with hearing impairments (M. Miller & Moores, 1990). Providing assistive technologies to enlarge written materials or to enhance hearing could be useful for those with visual impairments (Livneh, Wilson, & Pullo, 2004).

Group Leadership Styles and Techniques

Group procedures demand that the leader be aware of all the members in the group, focus on the group dynamics, and possess group leadership skills. According to Corey and Corey (2013) and the Association for Specialists in Group Work (ASGW, 2008), group leaders need to have (a) knowledge of human behavior, behavior change, group process, group dynamics, therapeutic factors, ethical issues, and their own strengths and limitations as group leaders; (b) skill in assessing, understanding, and responding to the needs of group members and in using a variety of leader responses, styles, and roles; and (c) self-awareness of attitudes, values, beliefs, and ways in which they may influence personal behavior as group leaders.

Learning Objectives

By the end of this unit you should be able to:

1. Understand the problems and issues of group leaders.
2. Understand the skills and techniques of leadership at various stages of a group.
3. Be aware of the skills and competencies necessary to be an effective group leader.

Key Concepts

I. Leadership Styles

There are three general leadership styles: authoritarian, democratic, and laissez-faire. The leadership styles may be shifted from time to time based on the perceived needs of the group and the stage in which the group is currently operating. Each style has different strengths and limitations.

Authoritarian
Group leadership and control are concentrated in authoritarian leaders, who are likely to teach or direct. These leaders may be friendly and persuasive but are not necessarily "bad" leaders. Communications tend to be directed between leaders and members, who may be compliant or show little enthusiasm. Members may be productive, but not particularly satisfied, and may feel little responsibility for group accomplishments. Member participation may depend on "prodding" from leaders (Sampson & Marthas, 1981).

Democratic
In the democratic approach, leadership is shared between leaders and members, as is control of policies and decisions, which are matters for discussion. Leaders guide rather than direct the group, are receptive to member ideas, and leave most decisions up to the members. This style provides a problem-solving framework in which leaders attempt to create a safe environment and members express themselves freely. Communications are between leaders and members and among different members. Members may participate more actively

and may show more enthusiasm and motivation to accomplish goals. They may show more caring toward one another and feel a greater sense of belonging. They may also show more responsibility and initiative and have a greater sense of ownership of group accomplishments (Sampson & Marthas, 1981).

Laissez-faire

Laissez-faire group leadership is concentrated in the members, and leaders are essentially nonleaders. Leaders are nondirective, just letting the group "happen." Leaders may be very accepting but removed from the group process, serving more as resources for members. Leaders are just a member of the group, with communications occurring primarily between members. Some obstacles may be encountered in adopting this leadership style. Members may experience confusion and frustration due to lack of direction. Productivity may be low, although high-functioning members may do well with this leadership style. Participation may be uneven among members (Sampson & Marthas, 1981). Members may absolve themselves of any responsibility because of confusion and frustration.

II. Leader Characteristics and Functions

Lieberman, Yalom, and Miles (1973) identified four basic functions that group leaders should present in the group process. These include (a) executive function, which is related to setting up the parameters of the group, establishing rules and guidelines, and keeping the group on track; (b) caring for group members' well-being and the effectiveness of the intervention; (c) emotional stimulation to uncover and encourage expression of thoughts, emotions, and values among group members; and (d) meaning attribution that allows leaders to help members develop their own ability to understand themselves and others.

III. Leadership Techniques

There is a core set of basic skills and functions that are critical for successful group leadership. These skills are active listening, restating, clarifying, summarizing, questioning, interpreting, confronting, reflecting feelings, supporting, empathizing, facilitating, initiating, goal setting, evaluating, giving feedback, suggesting, protecting, self-disclosure, modeling, linking, blocking, and terminating (Corey & Corey, 2013).

IV. Coleadership Issues

Coleaders may divide responsibility for leadership and cover for each other. There is much to attend to as the group proceeds, and a coleadership approach allows two people to attend to all the interactions, discussions, and behaviors within the group. Coleaders can cooperate in planning and summarizing/processing group sessions and provide feedback to each other. Task and maintenance roles can provide a basis for conceptualizing coleader roles. Such leaders must function in a cooperative and close-working relationship—as a team (Corey & Corey, 2013).

Family Dynamics, Counseling Theories, and Interventions

Disability affects not only the person with a disability, but also the entire family system (Kosciulek, 2004). Coping with the impact of disability is one of the most difficult tasks that can confront a family (Power, 1995). Counselors need to have more awareness of the impact of disability on families and try to meet the needs of individual family members and entire family systems (Kosciulek, 2004). In this section, family dynamics, counseling theories, and interventions are reviewed to assist counselors in understanding the family systems.

Learning Objectives

By the end of this unit you should be able to:

1. Understand family dynamics.
2. Understand how each theoretical approach can be uniquely applied in family counseling.
3. Be able to differentiate between different theoretical approaches as they apply to family counseling.

Key Concepts

I. Family Dynamics

A "family" is a group of two or more persons related by birth, marriage, or adoption (U.S. Census Bureau, 2015). Also included in the concept of "family" are more nontraditional groups, such as people who never marry, who marry and never have children, who marry and divorce and people in various other nontraditional arrangements. According to Hill (1958), the family is not ideally set up to withstand stress, yet society has assigned to it the heaviest responsibility: the socialization of the young and the meeting of the major emotional needs of all citizens. Counselors shift perspective from trying to change individual behavior to focusing on the family system. This shift occurs in three key dimensions: transition from individual to systems dynamics, shift from linear to circular causality, and distinction between content and process dynamics (Worden, 2003).

Individual versus systems dynamics
The family is viewed as a whole that is greater than the sum of its parts, rather than a collection of individuals. The family becomes an entity of analysis in and of itself. Individual behavior is rooted within the larger family context. For example, an individual's problematic behavior is seen as an outcome of family interactions and is perceived as an expression of the family's dysfunctional transactional patterns (Worden, 2003).

Linear versus circular causality
Circular causality refers to the idea that everyone's behavior affects everyone else's behavior. Therapists examine the family's self-perpetuating cycles of interaction, rather than individual cause-and-effect relationships. Circular causality eliminates the family scapegoat (Worden, 2003).

Content versus process dynamics

Content refers to the concrete issue being discussed and *process* refers to how the issue is portrayed in the family's interactions. Attention should be given to process, not content (Worden, 2003).

II. Therapeutic Approaches to Family Therapy

Family system theory

Overall, *family system theory* is a term for conceptualizing a group of related elements that interact as a whole identity. It is more a way of thinking than a standardized theory. Problems might be a symptom of how the family functions. Problematic behavior may serve a function for the family, be a function of the family's inability to operate productively, and be a symptom of dysfunctional patterns handed down across generations.

Intergenerational family therapy

Intergenerational, multigenerational, or transgenerational family therapy was introduced by Bowen (1978), who saw that an individual's behavior depends on personal relations with an intergenerational network of family members. Therefore, analyzing the family from a three-generation perspective provides good understanding. This therapy model posits that to develop a mature personality, emotional fusion to the family must be addressed. Two of the key concepts central to Bowen's theory are differentiation of self and triangulation.

Differentiation of self. Differentiation of self originates from the idea that social groups tremendously influence the way an individual thinks. The less developed and differentiated the self, the more a person has an unhealthy dependence on others and is controlled by them.

Triangulation. A triangle is the smallest stable relationship system. A two-person system is unstable and forms into a three-person system under stress. The third person can be a substitute for conversation or a messenger.

Therapy under this theory focuses on helping each family member deal with unresolved emotional attachments transmitted from one generation to the next and obtain a balanced sense of self as well as family as a whole. Two of the main goals include decreasing anxiety and increasing the level of differentiation of self. Therapists must be aware of how they have been influenced by their own families. A commonly used technique for promoting thinking and reducing emotional reactivity is *process questions*, which encourage family members to talk about how they respond to others within the family as well as how they are involved in these interactions. Therapists should be cautious about not taking sides to reduce the risk of triangulation (Cruza-Guet, Williams, & Chronister, 2015).

Psychoanalytic family therapy

Nathan Ackerman (1938) is the founder of psychoanalytic family therapy. The foundation of his theory rests on the importance of identifying basic wants and needs that keep individuals from interacting in a mature way. According to this approach, problems are identified within people, rather than between people. The goal is to free family members from unconscious restrictions so that they will be able to interact with one another as a whole. Having insight is necessary for behaviors to change. Techniques include listening, empathy, interpretation, and analytic neutrality (Nichols & Schwartz, 2001).

Humanistic and experiential family therapy

Key figures of humanistic and experiential family therapy include Carl Whitaker and Virginia Satir (Napier & Whitaker, 1978). Emphasis is placed on the mutually shared experience of the therapist and the family. One major goal is to increase family members' capacity to experience their lives more fully by sharing their struggle with the here and now. The role of a therapist is to create turmoil and then coach family members through the experience (Napier & Whitaker, 1978). When a warm and nurturing experience is developed in therapy, family members can explore their deeper layers of emotions, communicate these emotions, and genuinely connect with one another (Cruza-Guet et al., 2015). According to this approach, planned techniques are not important. As a therapist, it is important to be with a family. Therapy is often conducted with two therapists.

Behavioral and cognitive behavioral family therapy

Key figures of behavioral and cognitive behavioral family therapy include Gerald Patterson and Neil Jacobson. The focus is on discrete problem areas defined by clear behavior patterns, rather than character change and insight. The goal is to modify the specific behavior or thought pattern to alleviate symptoms. Two key concepts are careful, detailed assessments and specific strategies designed to modify contingencies of reinforcement. Techniques include behavioral contracts, training in communication skills, active suggestion, and homework (Bowers, 1988).

Structural family therapy

The key figure for the structural family therapy orientation is Salvador Minuchin. The focus is on the interactions of family members as a way of understanding the structure of the family. Key concepts include the following: (a) family structure is the invisible set of rules that organize the way members relate to one another; (b) family subsystems, which refer to organized coalitions of two or more family members that distinguish themselves from the larger system, include spousal, parental, sibling, and extended family categories; (c) boundaries are emotional barriers that protect and enhance the integrity of families (disengagement–enmeshment); and (d) families and their subsystems are shaped in a hierarchical manner. The therapist attempts to create clear boundaries, to increase flexibility, and to modify a dysfunctional family structure. Techniques include family mapping, enactments, and reframing (Minuchin & Fishman, 1981).

Strategic family therapy

The key figure in strategic family therapy is Jay Haley. The focus is on solving problems in the present (Haley, 1976). The overall goal is to resolve a problem and to arrive at tangible changes by focusing on behavioral sequences, rather than insight. All family members are seen as responsible for this process of changes and outcome. The therapist acts as a consultant and is responsible for planning a strategy to resolve problems. Techniques include using directives (advice, suggestion, and coaching), ordeals, paradoxical injunctions, and reframing.

Narrative and constructivist family therapy

In narrative and constructivist family therapy, people are seen as actively shaping how they understand the world, what meanings they create to explain the world, and how these meanings are constructed. Therefore, therapy would be more beneficial if the focus were more on understanding the meaning that each family member attributes to familial events or problems, rather than on interpreting complex patterns of family interaction (Cruza-Guet et al.,

2015). The key concept in social constructivism is that meaning is constructed through a social interaction. The therapist is seen not as an expert but as a collaborator with the family (Nichols & Schwartz, 2001). The therapist may use questions about family relationships that will allow family members to share their views about familial issues and their unique experiences with each other. This questioning empowers each family member and gives each voice, as well as provides an opportunity to explore new possibilities and solutions for the family (Bitter & Corey, 1996).

Brief family therapy

Key figures of brief family therapy include Luigi Boscolo and Gianfranco Cecchin. Brief therapy is increasingly popular because of economic limitations of clients and clinicians and the introduction of managed care. The goal is solution focused and encourages clients to shift from talking about problems to talking about solutions (Talmon, 1993). Therapists and clients discuss resources, goals, and exceptions to the problem. Techniques include setting concrete, realistic, and achievable goals and an endpoint; reinforcing family strengths; and assigning homework. Therapists may ask the "miracle question."

III. Family Counseling Strategies

Marshak and Seligman (1993) introduced the five-level guidance for conceptualizing the intensity of counselor interface with family needs and preferences. The five levels are:

Level 1: Focus on the individual client

Level 2: Provide information for the family

Level 3: Provide emotional support for the family

Level 4: Provide structured assessment and intervention

Level 5: Provide family therapy (Kosciulek, 2004, pp. 275–276)

According to Roessler, Chung, and Rubin (1998), many counselors are able to provide high-quality intervention at levels 1 through 3. However, counselors must possess structural and relationship skills to provide effective family counseling at levels 4 and 5. *Structural skills* refer to the counselor's ability to identify problems or needs, define outcomes and alternatives, and confront family members' resistance. *Relationship skills* refer to the capacities to build rapport with and express empathic understanding to families.

Ethical and Legal Issues Impacting Individuals and Families

Knowledge of ethical issues is as essential as a solid base of psychological knowledge and skills. Rehabilitation professionals must be thoroughly familiar with the ethical standards of their professional specialization. They must learn to make ethical decisions, a process that can be taught in group courses and in practicum/internship supervisions. Groups designed around ethically and legally sound principles have a far greater chance of being effective than groups designed without these principles in mind. This section reviews some ethical issues in group settings (Corey & Corey, 2013).

Learning Objectives

By the end of this unit you should be able to:

1. Understand what constitutes an ethical consideration in a group setting.

2. Be aware of resources that certified rehabilitation counselors should consult with regard to ethical dilemmas and the way that one may plan for and resolve ethical concerns.

Key Concepts

I. Informed Consent

A sound policy regarding informed consent is to provide to group members a professional disclosure statement that includes information on a variety of topics, including (see Rule A.7 in ASGW Best Practice Guidelines: Thomas & Pender, 2008):

- Nature, purposes, and goals of group

- Confidentiality, including the limits of confidentiality

- Qualifications of the leader (may also include theoretical orientations)

- Services that can be provided

- Roles and responsibilities of members

- Right to withdraw from the group

- Potential risks and benefits associated with membership

II. Freedom to Withdraw From a Group

For groups that are voluntary, group members typically have the right to withdraw. It is important to specify any commitments expected of group members in terms of attending, arriving on time and not leaving early, and remaining in the group for a specified number of sessions. It is also important to specify anticipated risks of withdrawing from a group early. If someone really wants to withdraw, it may be best to let them go. However, the decision should be made with careful consideration and explanation. Otherwise, the consequences could be negative for remaining members (Corey & Corey, 2013).

III. Potential Risks for Group Members That May Require Attention

Self-disclosure may not be adequately addressed, and painful things might be disclosed that might be ignored by the group, resulting in additional feelings of hopelessness or pain. *Confidentiality* might be violated by group members. Group participants should be aware that confidentiality cannot be guaranteed, but group leaders should emphasize and regularly remind members about the importance of confidentiality among group members (Commission on Rehabilitation Counselor Certification, 2010; Ditchman et al., 2015). *Scapegoating* in which members may be singled out or "ganged up on," may occur.

Leaders may be inadequately prepared for the group and may find themselves operating beyond the bounds of their competence.

IV. Multicultural Issues

In group settings, there may be effects of shared values and beliefs within a culture in a person's view of the world and events. Stereotyping may lead to invalid perceptions and attributions, and as a result, it may have a negative impact on group dynamics. It is important to consider the effects of cultural differences on group dynamics and processes because cultural differences are the way that such problems can be conceptualized and solved. There are three issues to which rehabilitation counselors need to attend when working with clients from minority backgrounds (Mpofu, Beck, & Weinrach, 2004). First is knowledge of the culture or cultures with which the client identifies. The client's culture provides a process for conceptualizing the perceptual world. Second is an awareness of the client's worldview. Counselors need to listen and ask clients questions that educate them about their values and life meanings. Finally, as a group counselor, it is critical to be sensitive to clues such as values, rate of conversation, style of nonverbal cues, and expectations that members often give to indicate that they would like to talk about how their culture is affecting their participation in the group.

V. Resolving Ethical Dilemmas

When faced with an ethical question, it is essential that counselors look at the applicable professional code for guidance. For rehabilitation counselors, this is the professional code of ethics and the standards for certified rehabilitation counselors (www.crccertification.com/filebin/pdf/CRCCodeOfEthics.pdf). Consulting with a colleague is also important. The most important person to consult with is one's supervisor. The goal should be to correct the situation and not resort to recrimination or punishment. Finally, it is important to think about the situation in relation to the ethical principles of autonomy, beneficence, fidelity, justice, nonmaleficence, and veracity.

Internet Resources

American Counseling Association
www.counseling.org/Resources

American Counseling Association: Ethics Resources
www.counseling.org/knowledge-center/ethics/code-of-ethics-resources

Association for Specialists in Group Work
www.asgw.org

American Association for Marriage and Family Therapy
www.aamft.org/iMIS15/AAMFT

Multiple-Choice Questions

1. Thoughts, feelings, and behaviors characteristic of group members during the transition stage of the group process include:

    A. Defensiveness and resistance; anxiety and fear; struggle for control; conflict and confrontation

    B. Trust, cohesion, and a sense of inclusion; open communication, self-disclosure, and taking of risks; shared leadership; effectively managed interpersonal conflict, control, and power issues; direct communication among members; and freely given feedback

    C. Defensiveness and resistance; anxiety and fear; giving of feedback; and self-disclosure

    D. Anxiety, sadness, and fear; concerns about unfinished business; and questioning about what comes next

2. The leadership style characterized by control concentrated in the leader, with the leader functioning as a teacher/director is:

    A. Democratic

    B. Parental

    C. Dominant

    D. Authoritarian

3. A democratic leadership style is likely to impact the group by:

    A. Leading to group member compliance, little enthusiasm from group members, and no particular feelings of satisfaction or responsibility for accomplishments

    B. Resulting in more active participation, greater enthusiasm, more responsibility and initiative, and a greater sense of ownership of the group members

    C. Leading to group member compliance, greater feelings of caring about other group members, and feelings of confusion and frustration

    D. Causing feelings of confusion and frustration, lower productivity, and uneven participation among members

4. Some group-building and maintenance roles central to the group process are:

    A. Coordinating, energizing, opinion giving, elaborating, and orienting

    B. Information seeking, recording, encouraging, and harmonizing

    C. Compromising, standard setting, encouraging, and group observing

    D. Initiating, evaluating-criticizing, expediting of procedures, and harmonizing

5. The theory stating that problems within a group may serve a function for the group, may be a function of the group's inability to operate productively, and may be a symptom of dysfunctional patterns handed down across generations is:

    A. Bowen's family system theory

    B. Psychoanalytical family therapy

   C. Social constructionism

   D. Family system theory

6. The key figure in experiential family therapy is:

   A. Luigi Boscolo

   B. Nathan Ackerman

   C. Jay Haley

   D. Carl Whitaker

7. The ethical code to which all certified rehabilitation counselors are bound is the:

   A. Hippocratic oath

   B. Best Practice Guidelines of the Association for Specialists in Group Work

   C. The ethical code of their respective institution

   D. Code of Professional Ethics for Rehabilitation Counselors

8. One major goal of behavioral and cognitive behavioral family therapy is:

   A. To increase family members' capacity to experience their lives more fully by sharing their struggle with the here and now

   B. To modify the specific behavior or thought pattern to alleviate symptoms

   C. To decrease anxiety and increase the level of differentiation of self

   D. To encourage clients to shift from talking about problems to talking about solutions

9. Gestalt therapy, reality therapy, and person-centered therapy are examples of what type of approach to counseling?

   A. Experiential

   B. Cognitive behavioral

   C. Psychoeducational

   D. Psychodynamic

10. If you are involved in group work with a culturally diverse population, it will be important for you to:

   A. be an expert in each of the populations

   B. accept the challenge of modifying your strategies to meet the unique needs of the members

   C. be of the same ethnic background as the members in your group

   D. conduct empirical research on your groups to validate your effectiveness

Answer Key

1A, 2D, 3B, 4B, 5D, 6D, 7D, 8B, 9A, 10B

Advanced Multiple-Choice Questions

1. Resolving ethical dilemmas in group practice is best done by considering the following actions:

    A. Obtaining consultation from a colleague.

    B. Thinking about the situation in relation to the ethical principles of beneficence, nonmaleficence, autonomy, justice, and fidelity.

    C. Looking at the applicable professional code.

    D. A and C

    E. A, B, and C

2. Group counseling is most effective when leaders operate from the following theoretical orientations:

    A. Cognitive behavioral

    B. Existential

    C. Psychodynamic

    D. None of the above (An eclectic style is recommended, taking into consideration the composition, purpose, and issues of the group.)

3. The therapy that emphasizes the mutually shared experience of the therapist and the family and whose main goal is to increase family members' capacity to experience their lives more fully by sharing their struggle with the here and now is:

    A. Psychoanalytical family therapy

    B. Behavior and cognitive behavioral family therapy

    C. Structural family therapy

    D. Experiential family therapy

4. Which of the following is not one of the main advantages of a coleadership structure?

    A. Exchanging feedback about the group

    B. Sharing responsibilities

    C. Resolving conflicts among group members quicker

    D. Collaborating in planning and processing the group

5. Which of the following is NOT a key leader function/behavior during the transition stage of the group process?

    A. Challenging resistance

    B. Making decisions about the degree of shared leadership

    C. Identifying and processing feelings

    D. Increasing risk taking

6. You are leading a group that has been meeting for several weeks and has established a set of group rules and norms and identified some of the goals that they would like to address. Recently several of the group members have been very reluctant to speak in group, and the leader overheard a conversation between two members who are discussing how they do not want to speak in front of the group for fear of looking foolish. Within what stage of development is this group likely functioning?

   A. Initial stage

   B. Transition stage

   C. Working stage

   D. Final stage

7. The leader has received a referral to work with a same-sex couple who have a 5-year-old son and are currently experiencing some relationship problems after one of the partners lost a job. Their son has been having some behavioral problems at school, which the school feels is linked to the problems at home. The leader is a certified rehabilitation counselor who specializes in family dynamics. Based on this information, you would make the following statement:

   A. Based on the family dynamics specialization, the leader feels prepared to assist this family.

   B. Family dynamics applies only to traditional family structures, so these clients should be referred to someone who is prepared to handle their needs.

   C. These clients do not qualify for family therapy; instead the child should receive individual counseling, and the same-sex partners should pursue either couples counseling or individual therapy.

   D. None of the above

8. A group has begun to exhibit signs of trust, cohesion, and a sense of inclusion. Some individuals are trying to practice some of the things that they are learning in their homes and communities. Some members are taking on more of a leadership role. This group is most likely in the _____ stage of group development.

   A. Initial

   B. Transition

   C. Working

   D. End

9. The group has recently been exhibiting a great deal of resistance to discussing and dealing with common issues. There has been a lot of conflict between group members, who do not seem to trust one another. The leader's key roles at this time may include

   A. Recognizing and dealing with unfinished business

   B. Reducing the active role in the group to allow for greater shared leadership

   C. Identifying and processing feelings, thoughts, and behaviors

   D. B and C

10. A substance abuse group is in the working stage based on the level of trust and cohesion among its members and the presence of open communication, self-disclosure, and risk taking. The group operates from a democratic leadership style. At this point the leader should _____ the level of activity in structuring and leading the group and therefore decides to adopt the _____ leadership style.

   A. Maintain, democratic

   B. Reduce, authoritarian

   C. Increase, authoritarian

   D. Reduce, laissez-faire

Answer Key and Explanation of Answers

1E: Ethical dilemmas in rehabilitation counseling must be resolved in a sensitive and professional manner to ensure protection of both the client and the professional. Considering just one mode of ethical consultation in isolation may result in unsuccessful resolution of the problem.

2D: Adopting one specific counseling orientation and rigidly applying it to all clients and all groups is not the most effective way of facilitating personal exploration and achieving set goals. Instead, the counselor needs to be able to evaluate the needs of individual clients and the group as a whole and to apply different orientations in an eclectic manner. Flexibility and sensitivity to the clients'/group's needs are key.

3D: Humanistic and experiential family therapy, introduced by Carl Whitaker and Virginia Satir (Napier & Whitaker, 1978), emphasizes the mutually shared experience of the therapist and the family. When a warm and nurturing experience is developed in therapy, family members can explore their deeper layers of emotions, communicate these emotions, and genuinely connect with one another. One major goal of this approach is to increase family members' capacity to experience their lives more fully by sharing their struggle with the here and now.

4C: Some of the major benefits of a coleadership structure are the ability to obtain feedback about the group and the facilitation of the group from a partner and the opportunity to divide responsibilities among coleaders. Having two people share these tasks helps ensure that nothing is overlooked.

5B: Deciding on the degree of leadership to share is a role/function of the leaders in the initial stage of the group process. Challenging resistance, identifying and processing feelings, and increasing risk taking are all key roles and functions of leaders in the transition stage.

6B: This group has been meeting for several weeks, has developed a set of group norms and rules, and has decided on some mutual goals, which means that they have accomplished many of the key tasks of the initial stage. Judging by the resistance and the anxieties expressed by group members, this group is functioning in the transition stage.

7A: According to the definition of *family* under which certified rehabilitation counselors operate, a same-sex couple would be considered a family, and their son would be a part of this family. Therefore, a counselor whose training is in family dynamics would most likely feel prepared to work with this family unit. The fact that they are a same-sex couple does not exclude them from family therapy.

8C: This group is operating in the working stage of group development. The group is beginning to exhibit signs of trust, cohesion, and a sense of inclusion. In the initial stage of group development, members are unfamiliar with one another, so these signs are not yet present. It is during the working stage that these group elements are seen. Members are also taking on more of a leadership role. During the initial stages of group development, leaders take on most of the leadership responsibility as the members acclimate to the group environment and to one another. During the working stage, members begin to feel secure enough to take on more leadership responsibility. Based on these signs, one should deduce that this group is operating in the working stage of group development.

9C: Several key points which hint at the roles that the leaders should be occupying within this group's development: (a) The group is exhibiting a great deal of resistance to discussing and dealing with common issues, (b) there has been a lot of conflict between group members, and (c) the group exhibiting a lack of trust. This group needs a more active leadership role to assist with resolving the conflicts and to help members build trust in one another. Therefore, reducing the leadership role would not be helpful at this time. Recognizing and dealing with unfinished business is a leader's role during the final stage of group development. The best functions that the leader can perform would be to process the feelings, thoughts, and behaviors surrounding the conflict to assist the group in moving forward, developing trust, and working on common issues.

10D: Decreasing formal leadership and structure would be the best option at this time. By increasing control, the leader would be stifling the group's progress and inhibiting further development of a group operating from a democratic leadership style. The only leadership style that is less structured and exerts less control would be laissez-faire.

References

Ackerman, N. (1938). The unity of the family. *Archives of Pediatrics*, *55*, 51–62.

Association for Specialists in Group Work. (2008). ASGW Best Practice Guidelines 2007 revisions. *Journal for Specialists in Group Work*, *33*(20), 111–117.

Bitter, J. R., & Corey, G. (1996). Family systems therapy. In G. Corey (Ed.), *The theory and practice of counseling and psychotherapy* (5th ed., pp. 365–443). Pacific Grove, CA: Brooks/Cole.

Bowen, M. (1978). *Family therapy in clinical practice*. New York, NY: Aronson.

Bowers, W. A. (1988). Beck's cognitive therapy: An overview for rehabilitation counselors. *Journal of Applied Rehabilitation Counseling*, *19*, 43–46.

Commission on Rehabilitation Counselor Certification. (2010). *Code of professional ethics for rehabilitation counselors*. Schaumburg, IL: Author. Retrieved from https://www.crccertification.com/filebin/pdf/CRCCodeOfEthics.pdf

Corey, M. S., & Corey, G. (2013). *Groups: Process and practices* (9th ed.). Pacific Grove, CA: Brooks/Cole.

Cruza-Guet, M., Williams, R. A., & Chronister, J. A. (2015). A family systems and social-ecological perspective for rehabilitation health professionals. In F. Chan, N. L. Berven, & K. R. Thomas (Eds.), *Counseling theories and techniques for rehabilitation and mental health professionals* (pp. 299–334). New York, NY: Springer Publishing.

Ditchman, N., Lee, E-J., & Huebner, R. A. (2015). Group procedures. In F. Chan, N. L. Berven, & K. R. Thomas (Eds.), *Counseling theories and techniques for rehabilitation and mental health professionals* (pp. 279–298). New York, NY: Springer Publishing.

Haley, J. (1976). *Problem-solving therapy*. San Francisco, CA: Jossey-Bass.

Hill, R. (1958). Generic features of families under stress. *Social Casework*, *49*, 139–150.

Kosciulek, J. F. (2004). Family counseling. In F. Chan, N. L. Berven, & K. R. Thomas (Eds.), *Counseling theories and techniques for rehabilitation health professionals* (pp. 264–281). New York, NY: Springer Publishing.

Leeman D. G. (2013). Review of motivational interviewing in group: Applications of motivational interviewing. *Social Work with Groups: A Journal of Community and Clinical Practice*, *36*(4), 374–378.

Lieberman, M., Yalom, I. D., & Miles, M. (1973). *Encounter groups: First facts*. New York, NY: Basic Books.

Livneh, H., Wilson, L. M., & Pullo, R. E. (2004). Group counseling for people with physical disabilities. *Focus on Exceptional Children, 36*, 1–18.

Marshak, L. E., & Seligman, M. (1993). *Counseling for persons with physical disabilities*. Austin, TX: Pro-Ed.

McWhirter, P. T., & McWhirter, J. J. (1996). Transition-to-work group: University students with learning disabilities. *Journal for Specialists in Group Work, 21*, 144–148.

Miller, M., & Moores, D. (1990). Principles of group counseling and their application to deaf clients. *Journal of the American Deafness and Rehabilitation Association, 23*, 82–87.

Miller, W. R., & Rollnick, S. (2002). *Motivational interviewing: Preparing people for change* (2nd ed.). New York, NY: Guilford Press.

Minuchin, S., & Fishman, H. C. (1981). *Family therapy techniques*. Cambridge, MA: Harvard University Press.

Mpofu, E., Beck, R., & Weinrach, S. (2004). Multicultural rehabilitation counseling: Challenges and strategies. In F. Chan, N. Berven, & K. Thomas (Eds.), *Counseling theories and techniques for rehabilitation health professionals* (pp. 386–404). New York, NY: Springer Publishing.

Napier, A. Y., & Whitaker, C. A. (1978). *The family crucible*. New York, NY: Harper & Row.

Nichols, M. P., & Schwartz, R. C. (2001). *Family therapy: Concepts and methods* (5th ed.). Boston, MA: Allyn & Bacon.

Patterson, J. B., McKenzie, B., & Jenkins, J. (1995). Creating accessible groups for individuals with disabilities. *Journal for Specialists in Group Work, 20*, 76–82.

Power, P. W. (1995). Family. In A. E. Dell Orto & R. P. Marinelli (Eds.), *Encyclopedia of disability and rehabilitation* (pp. 312–326). New York, NY: Macmillan.

Prochaska, J. O., & DiClemente, C. C. (1983). Stages and processes of self-change of smoking: Toward an integrative model of change. *Journal of Consulting and Clinical Psychology, 51*, 390–395.

Roessler, R. T., Chung, W., & Rubin, S. E. (1998). Family-centered rehabilitation case management. In R. T. Roessler & S. E., Rubin (Eds.), *Case management and rehabilitation counseling: Procedure and techniques* (3rd ed., pp. 231–254). Austin, TX: Pro-Ed.

Salomone, P. R. (1996). Career counseling and job placement: Theory and practice. In E. M. Szymanski & R. M. Parker (Eds.), *Work and disability* (pp. 365–420). Austin, TX: Pro-Ed.

Sampson, E. E., & Marthas, M. S. (1981). *Group process for the health professions* (2nd ed.). New York, NY: Wiley.

Seligman, M., & Marshak, L. (2004). Group approaches for persons with disabilities. In J. DeLucia-Waack (Ed.), *Handbook of group counseling and psychotherapy* (pp. 239–252). Thousand Oaks, CA: Sage.

Stein, S. M. (1996). Group psychotherapy and patients with cognitive impairment. *Journal of Developmental and Physical Disabilities, 8*, 263–273.

Talmon, T. (1993). *Single session solutions: A guide to practical, effective, and affordable therapy*. Reading, MA: Addison-Wesley.

Thomas, R. V., & Pender, D. A. (2008). Association for Specialists in Group Work: Best practice guidelines 2007 revisions. *Journal for Specialists in Group Work, 33*(2), 111–117.

U.S. Census Bureau. (2015, August). Current Population Survey: Subject definitions. Retrieved from https://www.census.gov/programs-surveys/cps/technical-documentation/subject-definitions.html

Wagner, C. C., & Ingersoll, K. S. (2012). *Motivational interviewing in groups*. New York, NY: Guilford Press.

Worden, J. W. (2003). *Grief counselling and grief therapy: A handbook for the mental health practitioner* (3rd ed.). New York, NY: Springer Publishing.

Yalom, I., & Leszcz, M. (2005). *The theory and practice of group psychotherapy* (5th ed.). New York, NY: Basic Books.

7

Assessment and Evaluation

Eun-Jeong Lee and Nicole Ditchman

Assessment and evaluation are important aspects of rehabilitation across settings. Formal assessment approaches are often used to determine eligibility for services, provide diagnostic information, assist individuals with identifying and reaching career goals, assess program outcomes, evaluate the effectiveness of intervention strategies, and ultimately recommend a course of action (Rubin & Roessler, 2008). This chapter reviews the role and purpose of assessment in rehabilitation, psychometric concepts related to assessment, assessment tools and approaches, and ethical considerations. Specific topics include:

- *Role of assessment in rehabilitation*
- *Assessment procedures*
- *Basic measurement concepts and principles*
- *Client involvement in assessment planning*
- *Selection and administration of appropriate measures and approaches*
- *Ethical, legal, and cultural implications in assessment*

Role of Assessment in Rehabilitation

Overview

Assessment is the process of gathering in-depth information to identify a client's needs and develop a comprehensive rehabilitation plan (Rubin & Roessler, 2008). Comprehensive assessment approaches generally evaluate personality, intelligence, educational achievement, functional abilities, work experiences, personal and social adjustment, employment opportunities, environmental characteristics, and other relevant factors helpful in determining the nature and scope of the rehabilitation services needed to achieve successful vocational and independent living outcomes. The continual assessment and synthesis of this information form the basis of the plan for rehabilitation services. In this section, assessment is broadly defined, and the role of assessment in rehabilitation is discussed.

Learning Objectives

By the end of this unit you should be able to:

1. Define *assessment* and related concepts.
2. Understand the role of assessment in rehabilitation.

Key Concepts

Assessment is defined broadly as "any systematic method of obtaining information from tests and other sources, used to draw inferences about people, objects, or programs" (American Educational Research Association [AERA], American Psychological Association [APA], & National Council on Measurement in Education [NCME], 2014). *Test* is defined broadly as "an objective and standardized measure of a sample of behavior" (Anastasi & Urbina, 1997). Assessment is more complex than *testing*; it typically requires integrating information from multiple sources and clinical judgments that go beyond psychometric data. *Measurement* is defined as "the assignment of numbers to attributes of persons according to rule stated explicitly" (Bolton, 2001).

The purpose of assessment in rehabilitation is to integrate information from multiple sources to plan a course of action. Assessment is used for a range of purposes, including screening job applicants, evaluating work or academic performance, determining diagnoses, and evaluating the effectiveness of interventions. In rehabilitation, assessment is usually vocationally related. Vocational assessment and evaluation involve exploring a person's strengths, weaknesses, and preferences and discovering how the individual's potential for vocational adjustment can be enhanced. The scope of assessment is broad enough to include the identification of specific and potential problems relevant to achieving career goals, the development of career goals, and the planning of strategies to resolve problems and attain the established objectives (Berven, 1997). Assessment must be understood in a context of legislation, consumer advocacy and involvement, environmental demands and influences, professional collaboration, ethnically diverse client populations, and assistive technology (Power, 2013; Rubin & Roessler, 2008).

Specific uses of assessment in rehabilitation. Assessment can be used for a variety of purposes in rehabilitation. It is commonly used to (a) describe individuals and their functioning, often including a description of abilities, interests, and personality characteristics; (b) clarify or recommend goals and objectives for rehabilitation services; (c) evaluate responsiveness or likely responsiveness to intervention strategies; (d) determine eligibility for services, especially state-federal vocational rehabilitation services; and/or (e) identify supports to optimize the functioning (Power, 2013; Rubin & Roessler, 2008).

Vocational assessment is commonly used in rehabilitation. In vocational rehabilitation, it is important to apply a holistic perspective of the individual throughout the assessment process, considering the physical, intellectual, and emotional components of personality, as well as the influence of environment and contextual factors impacting the individual. The interrelationships among emotional well-being, mental functioning, physical capabilities, and environmental factors should always be considered. The most useful assessment approaches not only take into account all of these dimensions, but also recognize that the client's participation in the evaluation process is crucial to the success of any assessment approach (Rubin & Roessler, 2008).

Assessment Procedures

Overview

Information from a variety of measures and tools is incorporated into the assessment process. This section discusses common assessment procedures in rehabilitation.

Learning Objective

By the end of this unit you should be able to:

1. Identify recommended steps and procedures in rehabilitation assessment.

Key Concepts

Assessment procedures can include interviews, standardized tests, inventories, observations, job tryouts, simulated tasks, and medical examinations. Rubin and Roessler (2008) recommend a four-step assessment procedure for vocational rehabilitation assessment. First, the client's functional capacity is determined via information obtained directly from the client as well as from observations by others. The primary source of information from the individual with a disability is the rehabilitation counseling interview. Additional perspectives on the person's functioning can be obtained through reports from purchased services, such as medical, psychological, and vocational evaluations. As the process proceeds from one step to the next, each step yields different types of information, and knowledge of the person builds in a cumulative manner (Rubin & Roessler, 2008).

    Intake interview. A comprehensive assessment begins with the information-collection process, called an *intake* or *initial interview*. The intake interview generates a social-vocational history, which is useful in formulating the rehabilitation plan and in determining whether subsequent evaluations are needed based on questions that the client can answer directly. According to Rubin and Roessler (2008), the focus of intake interviews should be:

- Determining the person's reason for rehabilitation services

- Providing the individual with necessary information about the role and function of the agency

- Developing adequate rapport

- Initiating the diagnostic process

- Informing the client of any medical, vocational, or psychological evaluations that must be completed and the purposes of such evaluations

    Medical evaluation. A medical examination is required by all public state rehabilitation agencies when working with an individual with a physical disability or chronic illness. This evaluation is used to establish the presence and extent of the disability, provide information on the physical functioning of the client, determine the types of activities precluded by the disability, and identify additional medical evaluations necessary for achieving the first three purposes. The medical examination provides information (a) clarifying general health at present; (b) describing of the extent, stability, and prognosis of the present disability, as well as recommended treatments; (c) assessing present and future implications of the disability and its potential effects on the performance of essential job functions; and (d) reporting the presence of residual medical conditions that could impact the individual during the rehabilitation process (Rubin & Roessler, 2008). When working with individuals with physical disabilities, the counselor should refer the client to a physician for medical evaluation and inform the physician of the client's tentative vocational goals.

Psychological evaluation. Psychological assessments yield information regarding the clients' intelligence, aptitudes, achievement, personality, interests, and adjustment related to vocational functioning. Its results help determine the appropriateness of long-term vocational training, the need for adjustment services, and (c) any potential need to confront the client regarding unrealistic vocational choices (Rubin & Roessler, 2008). This evaluation can also be used to establish the presence of cognitive or psychiatric disability.

Vocational evaluation. Vocational evaluation provides reliable and valid data to (a) generate vocationally relevant information about the client's current levels of social, educational, psychological, and physiological functioning; (b) estimate the client's potential for behavior change and skill acquisition; (c) determine the client's most effective learning style; (d) identify possible jobs the client can perform without additional vocational services; (e) identify education or special training programs that might increase the client's vocational potential; (f) identify potentially feasible jobs for the client with further vocational services; and (g) identify the community support services that might augment job retention following successful job placement (Rubin & Roessler, 2008). This process consists of different techniques, focusing on assessing the relationship of the person's skills, abilities, personality characteristics, and physical tolerance to perform the required tasks associated with potential jobs.

Basic Measurement Concepts and Principles

Overview

When using standardized tests and work samples, rehabilitation professionals must determine each measure's appropriateness for a client. Certain standards for evaluating these methods should be used to choose the most appropriate measures. For example, an instrument must show some form of internal quality and consistency (reliability) before it can be expected to have external utility, or validity (Thorndike & Thorndike-Christ, 2008). In this section, key terms and concepts in measurement and assessment are introduced; salient features of standardized tests and basic types of standard scores are described.

Learning Objectives

By the end of this unit you should be able to:

1. Understand basic measurement and psychometric concepts related to assessment procedures.
2. Identify important considerations when interpreting test scores.

Key Concepts

Scales of measurement. Psychological measurement converts characteristics of people into quantifiable data or numbers. An ongoing concern in assessment and score interpretation is the extent to which test scores are meaningful. These measurement issues can be addressed through scaling techniques. Four measurements scales are generally recognized:

- **Nominal:** Classifies and assigns numerals but does not distinguish size or amount (e.g., any categorical variable, such as ethnicity or gender)
- **Ordinal:** Indicates an ordering but does not indicate distances between objects on the scale (e.g., placing first, second, and third)
- **Interval:** Indicates equal intervals on the scale (e.g., Celsius temperature scale)
- **Ratio:** Possesses a nonarbitrary zero point (e.g., measures of weight, Kelvin temperature scale)

I. Reliability and Validity

The concepts of reliability and validity are important when considering the appropriateness of a test for a particular use. A reliable procedure is one that produces similar results when repeated. Validity provides an estimate of how well a test measures what it purports to measure, and *reliability* refers to the dependability, consistency, and precision of an assessment procedure. Evidence for reliability and validity is often based on correlations, expressed by the coefficient r. Correlations show the degree of association between two measures and range from −1 to 1. A correlation coefficient of 0.8 or higher (or −0.8 or lower) is generally considered a very high correlation, whereas coefficients close to 0 represent little to no correlation.

    Reliability is a measure of consistency (*Is the test consistent, dependable, and precise?*). There are several ways to estimate a test's reliability:

- **Test–retest reliability:** Measure of consistency over time. Test–retest correlations indicate relationships between scores obtained by individuals within the same group on two administrations of the test.
- **Split-half reliability:** Measure of internal consistency. Split-half correlations indicate a consistency of scores obtained by individuals within the same group on two different parts of the test (e.g., odd vs. even items).
- **Parallel or alternate forms reliability:** Correlation that indicates a consistency of scores of individuals within the same group on two alternate but equivalent forms of the same test taken at the same time.
- **Cronbach's alpha:** Internal consistency reliability statistic calculated from the pairwise correlations between items on the measure.

    Validity can be understood as the extent to which meaningful and appropriate inferences can be made from the instrument (e.g., *Does the test measure what it says it measures?*). A measure cannot be valid if it is not also reliable; however, a reliable test may not be valid. There are several types of validity evidence:

- **Face validity:** Subjective appraisal of the extent to which the test's content covers the concept it was designed to measure (i.e., it "looks like" it is measuring what it is supposed to measure).
- **Content validity:** Evaluation by subject matter experts of test items' representativeness of the construct being measured.

- **Criterion or predictive validity:** Comparison of the test with another outcome measure.
- **Construct validity:** Extent to which the measure actually measures the theoretical construct.

II. Central Tendency and Normal Distribution

Central tendency indicates how scores tend to cluster in a particular distribution. Important concepts related to central tendency include the following:
- **Mean:** Sum of scores in a distribution divided by number of scores (i.e., *average*)
- **Median:** Midpoint when scores are placed from lowest to highest
- **Mode:** Most frequent score
- **Standard deviation:** Measurement of variability from the mean. High standard deviations (*SD*s) indicate data spread over a large range of values; low *SD*s indicate data points close to the mean.

   Normal distribution is a frequency distribution that results in a bell-shaped curve and indicates relative standing within a comparison group of interest. In a normal distribution, mean, median and mode all have the same value, since the curve is highest in the middle. Approximately, 68% of total cases are within one *SD* of the mean (see Figure 7.1).

   Types of scores. Every test typically yields a score or set of scores.

   Raw score is one's performance on a test (e.g., percentage of items correct). However, an individual's raw score is meaningless without additional knowledge concerning the instrument.

   Standard scores can be used to make norm-referenced interpretations. Standard scores are transformed scores with a specified mean (*M*) and standard deviation (*SD*) in relation to a comparison group (e.g., Z-scores: $M = 0$, $SD = 1$; T-scores: $M = 50$, $SD = 10$; IQ scores: $M = 100$, $SD = 15$).

   Percentiles are rank order scores indicating the percentage of persons in the comparison group who attained a lower score. For example, someone who scores in the 50th percentile

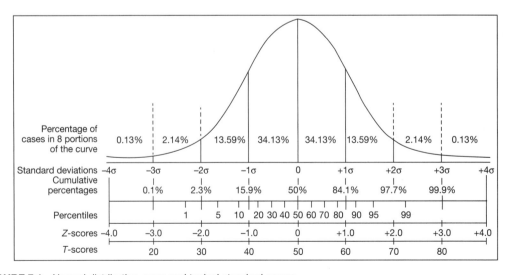

FIGURE 7.1 Normal distribution curve and typical standard scores.

performed better or equal to 50% of others. Percentiles should not be confused with the percentage correct, which is the raw score.

    Types of score interpretations. It is essential to have information about the nature and number of items composing the test, the response format used, and the range of possible scores to interpret what the score means. Raw scores are meaningless without additional reference information. There are three primary ways to interpret scores.

- **Self-referenced interpretation** is when a score is compared to an internal frame of reference, such as changes in an individual's performance on a test over time (e.g., *Sally improved her typing speed score from 40 to 60 words per minute*).

- **Criterion-referenced interpretation** is when a score is compared with an absolute standard, external frame of reference, such as a proficiency standard (e.g., *Sally's typing score of 60 words per minute met her employer's requirement*).

- **Norm-referenced interpretation** is when a score is compared with other individuals' scores, external frame of reference, typically through percentile comparison to a norm group (e.g., *Sally's score of 60 words per minute puts her in the 70th percentile compared with her same-age peers*).

Client Participation and Preparation in Assessment

Overview

Clients should be active participants and decision makers throughout the assessment process. This section overviews the steps recommended by Power (2013) to promote client empowerment.

Learning Objectives

By the end of this unit you should be able to:

1. Understand the role of the client in the assessment process.
2. Identify steps to promote client empowerment during the assessment process.

Key Concepts

Promoting client empowerment. Power (2013) provides the following steps for promoting client empowerment in the assessment process: (a) Establish a working relationship; (b) understand the needs, expectations, values, and goals of the client; (c) communicate information about the assessment process; (d) encourage active client involvement; and (e) allow the client to make informed choices and express self-determination when selecting evaluation approaches. The professional should monitor clients to ascertain their level of active participation in the assessment process.

    Preparing people for assessment involves two important steps. First, rehabilitation counselors should communicate to clients the importance of their input throughout the process.

Second, once a mutual decision is made regarding the assessment process, the client must be carefully prepared for it. The professional needs to explain the purpose of the assessment and the ways that the results can assist in achieving realistic rehabilitation goals.

To promote client involvement, rehabilitation professionals should orient the individual to the evaluation process itself. An effective orientation begins with a full explanation of the purpose and goals of the evaluation and a visit to the evaluation site before the person is scheduled for assessment. During the visit, the client should meet the evaluator and discuss prospective assessment measures, tools, and techniques (Grissom, Eldredge, & Nelson, 1990).

Selecting Appropriate Measures and Approaches

Overview

Several measurement tools and types of interviews are used in assessment. This section provides an overview of commonly used standardized tests, inventories, and work samples and describes situational and ecological assessments.

Learning Objectives

By the end of this unit you should be able to:

1. Identify commonly used tests, inventories, and assessment tools and their designated purposes, including computer and online assessment tools.
2. Gain a general understanding of psychometric properties and considerations of specific measurement tools.

I. Standardized Tests and Inventories

Standardized tests are frequently classified as falling into one of the following five areas: intelligence, aptitude, achievement, personality, and interests. Rehabilitation counselors must be familiar with these tests because their results and interpretations commonly appear in vocational evaluation reports used in service planning. In this section, commonly used tests and inventories are discussed. Table 7.1 lists tests and inventories that should be familiar to rehabilitation counselors.

II. Assessment of Intelligence

Many definitions have been offered for *intelligence,* and there remains considerable disagreement regarding its meaning and the best way to measure it. It is generally conceptualized as the ability to solve problems and to learn and retain new information (Power, 2013).

TABLE 7.1 Commonly Used Tests and Inventories in Rehabilitation by Assessment Construct

Title of Measurements	Abbreviation
Intelligence	
Wechsler Adult Intelligence Scale-IV	WAIS-IV
Stanford–Binet Intelligence Scales, Fifth Edition	SB5
Slosson Intelligence Test–Revised, Third Edition	SIT-R3
Peabody Picture Vocabulary Test, Fourth Edition	PPVT-4
Beta III	
Raven's Progressive Matrices	
Quick-Test	QT
Kaufman Brief Intelligence Test	KBIT
Luria–Nebraska Neuropsychological Battery	
Halstead–Reitan Neuropsychological Test Battery	
Test of Nonverbal Intelligence	TONI
Culture Fair Intelligence Test	
Wonderlic Personnel Test	
Haptic Intelligence Scale for Adult Blind	
Woodcock–Johnson Test of Cognitive Abilities	
Aptitude	
O*NET Ability Profiler	AP
General Aptitude Test Battery	GATB
Differential Aptitude Test, Fifth Edition, Form C	DAT
Armed Services Vocational Aptitude Battery	ASVAB
Bennett Mechanical Comprehension Test	BMCT
Minnesota Paper Form Board Test, Revised	MPFB-R
Career Ability Placement Survey	CAPS
Hand-Tool Dexterity Test	
Ability Explorer	AE
APTICOM	
Ball Aptitude Battery	BAB
CareerScope	CS
Career Planning Survey	CPS
Occupational Aptitude Survey and Interest Schedule, Third Edition	OASIS-3
PESCO 2001	
Detroit Tests of Learning Aptitude	
Short Tests of Clerical Ability	

(continued)

TABLE 7.1   Commonly Used Tests and Inventories in Rehabilitation by Assessment Construct (*continued*)

Title of Measurements	Abbreviation
Flanagan Aptitude Classification Tests	FACT
Minnesota Clerical Test	
Bennet Mechanical Comprehension Test	
Achievement	
Wide Range Achievement Test, Fourth Edition	WRAT-4
Adult Basic Learning Examination, Second Edition	ABLE-2
Peabody Individual Achievement Test–Revised	PIAT-R
California Achievement Test	
SRA Reading and Arithmetic Indices	
Woodcock–Johnson Tests of Achievement	
Wechsler Individual Achievement Test	WIAT
Personality	
Minnesota Multiphasic Personality Inventory, Second Edition	MMPI-2
Myers–Briggs Type Indicator	MBTI
Sixteen Personality Factor Questionnaire, Form E	16-PF
California Psychological Inventory, 1996 Revision	CPI
NEO Personality Inventory–Revised	NEO PI-R
Psychological Screening Inventory	PSI
Tennessee Self-Concept Scale	TSCS
Adult Personality Inventory	API
Jackson Personality Inventory–Revised	
Hogan Personality Inventory	
Millon Clinical Multiaxial Inventory-III	MCMI-III
Personality Assessment Inventory	PAI
Projective Measures	
Rorschach Test	
Thematic Apperceptions Test	TAT
Interests	
Geist Picture Interest Inventory, Revised	
Reading-Free Vocational Interests Inventory, Second Edition	R-FVII-2
Strong Interest Inventory	SII
Kuder Occupational Interest Survey	
Self-Directed Search (Form R)	SDS
Career Assessment Inventory	CAI
Occupational Aptitude Survey and Interest Schedule, Third Edition	OASIS-3

(*continued*)

TABLE 7.1 Commonly Used Tests and Inventories in Rehabilitation by Assessment Construct (*continued*)

Title of Measurements	Abbreviation
Ohio Vocational Interest Survey-2	OVIS-II
Career Decision-Making System–Revised	CDM-R
Campbell Interest and Skill Survey	CISS
Work Samples	
McCarron–Dial Evaluation System	MDES
Valpar Component Work Sample	
Micro-TOWER System of Vocational Evaluation	
Vocational Information and Evaluation Work Samples	VIEWS
Wide Range Employment Sample Test	WREST

Commonly used intelligence tests in the vocational rehabilitation process

The **Wechsler Adult Intelligence Scale-IV (WAIS-IV)** is an intelligence quotient (IQ) test to measure adult and adolescent intelligence. The original WAIS was published in 1955 and the fourth edition was released in 2008. Two broad scores are generated, which can be used to summarize general intellectual abilities: (a) Full Scale Intelligent Quotient (FSIQ), based on the total combined performance of four indexes (described in the following list), and (b) General Ability Index (GAI), based only on the six subtests that comprise the Verbal Comprehension Index (VCI) and the Perceptual Reasoning Index (PRI). The GAI can be used as a measure of cognitive abilities that are less vulnerable to impairment.

The WAIS-IV consists of 10 subtests and 5 supplemental subtests and generates 4 indices:

- **VCI** includes four subtests: similarities, vocabulary, information, and comprehension.

- **PRI** comprises five subtests: block design, matrix reasoning, visual puzzles, picture completion, and figure weights.

- **Working Memory Index (WMI)** is obtained from three subtests: digit span, arithmetic, and letter-number sequencing.

- **Processing Speed Index (PSI)** includes three subtests: symbol search, coding, and cancellation.

Scores on the WAIS-IV indexes and full scale are based on a mean of 100 and an *SD* of 15. According to Wechsler's (2008) qualitative score descriptions, composite scores between 90 and 109 are considered "average," while scores less than 70 are "extremely low" and scores higher than 129 are described as "very superior."

The **Stanford–Binet Intelligence Scales, Fifth Edition** (SB5; Roid, 2003) consists of 10 subtests (five verbal and five nonverbal). Nonverbal subtests can be used for people with hearing impairments, communication disorders, and limited English-language background. The SB5 yields FS IQ, verbal IQ and nonverbal IQ scores, and five factor indexes (fluid reasoning, knowledge, quantitative reasoning, visual-spatial reasoning, and working memory).

The **Peabody Picture Vocabulary Test, Fourth Edition** (PPVT 4; Dunn & Dunn, 2007) is an untimed, easily administered, oral test of intelligence. It can be administered in 10–15 minutes. Reading is not required and item responses are made by pointing. It can be used for people with intellectual disabilities.

The **Slosson Intelligence Test–Revised, Third Edition** (SITR-3; Slosson, Nicholoson, & Hibpshman, 1990) is an easily administered, individual, oral test of verbal intelligence. It can be administered in 15–20 minutes. It is a quick screening test of intelligence and can be used for individuals with visual impairments, reading difficulty, and physical disabilities.

The **Beta III** (Kellogg & Morton, 1999) is a nonverbal test for people who are relatively illiterate or do not speak English. It is designed for use with adults (aged 16–89) suspected of having literacy problems. The Beta III contains five subtests: coding, picture completion, clerical checking, picture absurdities, and matrix reasoning.

Raven's Progressive Matrices (Raven, 1986) measures the ability to perceive and use relationships between nonverbal materials and requires spatial aptitude, inductive reasoning, and perceptual accuracy. It is designed for use with children and adults (aged 5 and older). It may be applicable for people with physical or emotional disabilities.

III. Assessment of Aptitude

Although there is some disagreement in the literature over how *aptitude* differs from *achievement*, aptitudes are regarded as relatively stable abilities that are innate and developed over a long time (Power, 2013; Rubin & Roessler, 2008). Aptitude tests are used to (a) assess individuals' skills and abilities, (b) measure more specific or focused areas that predict the likelihood of learning and mastering knowledge or skills needed for success in a specific vocation, and (c) predict how successful an individual will likely be at learning different aspects of a formal training program.

Commonly used aptitude tests in the vocational rehabilitation process
The **O*NET Ability Profiler (AP)** is a freely available instrument for download from the O*NET website (a computerized occupational database of both job and worker characteristics, www.onetonline.org). It is based on the General Aptitude Test Battery (GATB; U.S. Department of Labor, 1970), although it is not a direct replacement. The AP uses 11 timed tests to measure 9 basic abilities related to the world of work, including verbal ability, arithmetic reasoning, computation, spatial ability, form perception, clerical perception, motor coordination, manual dexterity, and finger dexterity. Administration can range from 1.5–2 hours, depending on the number of subtests used.

The **Armed Services Vocational Aptitude Battery** (ASVAB) is the most widely administered multiple-aptitude battery to classify and select potential military recruits (Parker, 2001). The ASVAB consists of 10 subtests:

- General science
- Work knowledge
- Paragraph comprehension
- Electronics information
- Code speed
- Arithmetic reasoning
- Mathematics knowledge
- Mechanical comprehension
- Auto and shop information
- Numerical operations

The **Differential Aptitude Tests, Fifth Edition, Form C** (DAT; Bennett, Seasher, & Wesman, 1990) is used for vocational and education counseling guidance. It features two levels. Level 1 is used for students in grades 7–9 and level 2 is used for students in grades 10–12; both levels can also be used with adults. The testing time for the complete battery is approximately 3 hours. The DAT consists of eight subtests:

- Verbal reasoning

- Numerical reasoning

- Abstract reasoning

- Perceptual speed and accuracy

- Mechanical reasoning

- Space relations

- Spelling

- Language usage

IV. Assessment of Achievement

Achievement testing is used to provide an evaluation of the specific information that individuals have learned throughout their education and life. In this area, rehabilitation counselors are generally interested in assessment of the verbal and numerical skills of the client, since these skills are important areas related to job efficiency.

Commonly used achievement tests in the vocational rehabilitation process

The **Wide Range Achievement Test, Fourth Edition** (WRAT-4; Wilkinson & Robertson, 2006) is a brief measure of fundamental academic skills. It is helpful in assessing academic achievement when the client has had no recent educational experience and the rehabilitation professional wants to determine basic reading and arithmetic capabilities for possible training. The WRAT-4 has two equivalent forms (blue and green) and consists of four subtests: sentence comprehension, word reading, spelling, and math computation. It yields raw scores, grade equivalents, standard scores, and percentile ranks. It is brief to administer, taking 35–45 minutes.

The **Peabody Individual Achievement Test–Revised** (PIAT-R; Markwardt, 1998) is a wide-range screening measure of achievement in mathematics, reading, spelling, and general information. The test yields six final scores: mathematics, reading recognition, reading comprehension, spelling, general information, and a total score. It is administered individually and the total testing time required is 30–40 minutes.

The **Adult Basic Learning Examination, Second Edition** (ABLE-2; Karlsen & Gardner, 1986) is an achievement test used to determine the general educational level of adults who have not completed a formal eighth-grade education, to diagnose individual strengths, and to assist in the development of educational planning. It yields scores on vocabulary, reading, spelling, computation, and problem solving. This test contains three levels: level 1 (grades 1–4), level 2 (grades 5–8), and level 3 (grades 9–12). Total testing time is about 2.5 hours for level 1 and level 2 and 3 hours for level 3. When testing time is limited, the ABLE Screening Battery may be administered as an alternative to the full ABLE battery; it can be administered in about an hour.

V. Assessment of Personality

Personality broadly refers to individual differences in characteristic patterns of thinking, feeling, and behaving. Personality tests are designed to measure an individual's emotional, interpersonal, motivational, and attitudinal characteristics (Anastasi & Urbina, 1997). The purpose of such testing in rehabilitation is to identify personality strengths and weaknesses that might impact job acquisition and retention. In vocational evaluation, personality assessment should focus on behaviors necessary for employment or productive output (Power, 2013).

Commonly used personality tests in the vocational rehabilitation process

The **Minnesota Multiphasic Personality Inventory, Second Edition** (MMPI-2; Hathaway, McKinley, & Butcher, 1990) is the most widely used personality inventory. The MMPI-2 consists of 567 true–false statements that assess major psychological characteristics and is designed for adults aged 16 and older. The test provides *T*-scores (*M* = 50, *SD* = 10) on four validity scales ("Cannot Say," L, F, & K) and on the following 10 clinical scales:

- Hypochondriasis (Hs)
- Depression (D)
- Conversion hysteria (Hy)
- Psychopathic deviate (Pd)
- Masculinity femininity (MF)
- Paranoia (Pa)
- Psychasthenia (Pt)
- Schizophrenia (Sc)
- Hypomania (Ma)
- Social introversion (O or Si)

The **Myers–Briggs Type Indicator** (MBTI; Briggs Myers & Briggs, 1988) is based on Jung's concepts of perception and judgment. The MBTI is scored on eight scales yielding four bipolar dimensions:

- Extroversion (E) versus introversion (I)
- Sensing (S) versus intuition (N)
- Thinking (T) versus feeling (F)
- Judgment (J) versus perception (P)

The MBTI personality type is summarized in four letters; this combination indicates the direction of the person's preference on each of the four dimensions. All possible combinations of the four paired scales result in 16 different potential personality types. The MBTI has no good or bad scores or combinations of types. Each type combination has its own strengths. Although it remains a widely used measure, its validity and reliability have been called into question (Pittenger, 1993).

The **Sixteen Personality Factor Questionnaire, Form E** (16-PF) was designed to provide information about an individual's primary personality factors (Cattell, 1986). The 16-PF has 128

A: Warmth

B: Reasoning

C: Emotional stability

E: Dominance

F: Liveliness

G: Rule-consciousness

H: Social boldness

I: Sensitivity

L: Vigilance

M: Abstractedness

N: Privateness

Q: Apprehension

Q1: Openness to change

Q2: Self-reliance

Q3: Perfectionism

Q4: Tension

items and requires a third- to sixth-grade reading level. Final scores are given on 16 primary factors:

The **California Psychological Inventory, 1996 Revision** (CPI; Gough & Bradley, 1996) is designed for people aged 14 years and older to assess normal personality characteristics important in everyday life. It has 462 items and takes 45–60 minutes to complete. The test includes these basic scales:

- Interpersonal style and manner of dealing with others (dominance, capacity for status, sociability, social presence, self-acceptance, independence, and empathy)

- Cognitive and intellectual functioning (achievement via conformance, achievement via independence, and intellectual efficiency)

- Thinking and behavior (psychological mindedness, flexibility, and femininity/masculinity)

- Internalization and endorsement of normative convention (responsibility, socialization, self-control, good impression, communality, tolerance, well-being)

- Special scales and indexes (managerial potential, work orientation, leadership potential index, social maturity index, creative potential index)

The **NEO Personality Inventory–Revised** (NEO PI-R; Costa & McCrae, 1992) was developed to assess the Big Five personality factors and consists of five 48-item scales. Scores are obtained for the five broad personality domains (neuroticism, extraversion, openness, agreeableness, and conscientiousness), as well as for 30-facet subscales. A shortened version, the NEO Five-Factor Inventory (NEO FFI), is also available.

VI. Assessment of Vocational Interests

Vocational interest inventories help clients identify jobs in which they are likely to experience greater job satisfaction. Knowledge of the match between the client's aptitudes and abilities and the skill demands of a job enhance the likelihood of a client's satisfaction with a given job. However, it is also important to consider the match between the client's interests and the extrinsic and intrinsic rewards that can be acquired from the job (Rubin & Roessler, 2008). Interest inventories promote a client's vocational self-exploration.

Commonly used interest inventories in the vocational rehabilitation process
The **Strong Interest Inventory** (SII; Strong, Hansen, & Campbell, 1994) is one of the oldest and most scientifically developed interest surveys. It was developed (a) to give individuals information about themselves and their preferences to help them make sound career decisions, (b)

to provide information to professionals, and (c) to help in studying groups of individuals. The test consists of 291 items and 6 categories, including occupations, school subjects, activities, leisure activities, types of people, and your characteristics. It yields scores and scales based on the Holland R-I-A-S-E-C typology. The profile is divided into four major sections: 6 general occupational themes, 30 basic interest scales, 244 occupational scales, and 5 personal style scales. The test is easy to administer, requires at least sixth-grade reading level, and takes approximately 30 minutes to complete.

The **Self-Directed Search (Form R)** (SDS; Holland, 1994) is based on Holland's theory. It is a self-administered, self-recorded, and self-interpreted vocational counseling tool. It has two forms (Form R and E). Form R requires at least a seventh- to eighth-grade reading level, and form E requires at least a fourth-grade reading level. The SDS was developed to help students and employees find the occupations that best suit their interests and abilities, to provide a counseling tool that can be used to serve a wider population, and to help researchers with a psychometrically sound instrument that can be used to examine the validity of Holland's typology theory. It consists of an assessment booklet and an occupations finder. The booklet has five sections: occupational daydreams, activities, competencies, occupations, and self-estimates. The SDS yields a total score for each of the six personality types (Holland's theory: realistic, investigative, artistic, social, enterprising, and conventional). The highest three summary scores determine a three-digit personality type (e.g., a person with high investigative, social, and enterprising interests would be coded ISE).

The **Reading-Free Vocational Interest Inventory, Second Edition** (R-FVII-2; Becker, 2000) provides information about vocational preferences for people aged 13 and older with cognitive and learning disabilities. The R-FVII-2 consists of illustrated depictions of occupations in a forced-choice format presented in 55 triads throughout the booklet. It provides scores in 11 interest areas.

VII. Work Samples Assessment

Work samples are an assessment approach in which the client is observed performing a simulated or actual work activity, usually in a rehabilitation center or vocational evaluation unit. Work samples are designed to see whether the individual follows the procedures and appropriately uses the tools and materials involved in jobs (Rubin & Roessler, 2008). Work samples are used to measure a variety of constructs, including vocational aptitudes, worker temperament, vocational interests, hand dexterity, tolerance for standing or sitting, work habits and behaviors, learning styles, and understanding of written and oral instructions (Gice, 1985). A major advantages of work samples is that they can be used with populations for which valid measurement with paper and pencil tests is not possible. A disadvantage is that they may lack standardization and measure only a person's abilities at a specific moment in time within a contrived, time-pressured situation and not a real situation (Powers, 2013). Several commercially available systems are used by vocational evaluators.

The **McCarron-Dial Evaluation System** (MDES; McCarron & Spires, 1991) was developed to predict an individual's ability for community-based employment. A battery of tests consists of eight separate instruments that assess five factors (verbal-cognitive, sensory, motor, emotional, and integration). The basic battery takes approximately 3 hours to administer and the comprehensive battery takes 5 days to complete.

Valpar (Botterbusch, 1987) is a provider of vocational evaluation services that uses a criterion-referenced approach in accordance with the U.S. Department of Labor's (1991) job standards. Valpar analyzes most of its work samples using methods–time measurement (MTM) standards, which is an approach to analyzing tasks to determine how long it would take an experienced employee to repeatedly perform the exercise over an 8-hour workday.

VIII. Transferrable Skills Analysis and Computer-Based Matching Systems

Transferrable skills analysis is a procedure used by rehabilitation providers to determine new job positions when the client is no longer able to perform the previous job, often due to an injury. Transferrable skills analyses are integral to the job-matching process, which includes the following steps: (a) identifying jobs performed in a person's work history, (b) determining residual functional capacity following the injury, (c) searching for matching occupations, (d) revising occupational possibilities, (e) assessing the feasibility of selected occupations in a specific location, (f) assessing the employability of the individual, and (g) determining the placeability of the individual in a given location (Truthan & Field, 2013). A number of commercially available computer-based systems can assist with this process and provide access to the *Dictionary of Occupational Titles* and O*NET databases, including SkillTRAN-OASYS, McCroskey Vocational Quotient System (MVQS), Career A.I., and Software for Employment, Education, and Rehabilitation (SEER; Truthan & Field, 2013).

IX. Situational and Ecological Assessments

Situational assessments offer a work-assessment approach in which a client's job performance and work behaviors are systemically observed in a realistic but controlled working environment, such as in a rehabilitation facility or sheltered workshop (Bolton & Parker, 2008). The terms *situational assessment, community-based situational assessment, job tryouts, on-the-job evaluation (OJE),* and *supported employment evaluation* are often used interchangeably. Situational assessments can provide valuable insights regarding the client's general employability behaviors. These assessments focus on the client's work potential in regard to factors such as ability to (a) accept supervision, (b) get along with coworkers, (c) stay on task, (d) sustain productivity for 8 hours, and (e) tolerate frustration (Rubin & Roessler, 2008).

Ecological assessment occurs in the natural setting, such as actual work sites where the individual could be a long-term employee. The goal is to evaluate the individual's capacity to meet the productivity demands of that setting now or in the near future through the provision of training or on-the-job supports. Examples of ecological assessment include supported employment placements and OJEs (Rubin & Roessler, 2008).

Supported employment. Vocational evaluation in supported employment can occur *after* the person has assumed a particular job. This assessment predicts what a person can do in a specific job setting with the necessary social and vocational support systems in place (Rubin & Roessler, 2008). This assessment focuses on the need for worksite accommodations and supports, the level of the person's independent living skills, and the types of continuing services the person will need (McAlees & Menz, 1992). The ecological assessment in supported employment allows the counselor and the client to engage in a closer working relationship at the job site to identify job modifications, supports, and training required to enhance the person–job match.

OJEs assess the functioning of individuals with disabilities in actual work settings where they are involved in activities presumed to be compatible with their vocational interests and skills. OJEs can occur within work stations in institutions, rehabilitation facilities, or business and industries and focus on a variety of variables, including personality, attitudes, aptitudes, work traits, work skills, and physical capacities (Rubin & Roessler, 2008). The length of an OJE can range from a single day to a month or longer. An OJE may be helpful for considering jobs that may be more appropriate to fit the skills and preferences of the client, such when a client may not be meeting the demands of the current job and may better fit with a job requiring a lower level of the specific vocational aptitudes in question. OJEs are also helpful in determining appropriate on-site supports or training needed to enable the client to perform the job successfully (Rogan & Hagner, 1990).

Ethical, Legal, and Cultural Implications in Assessment

Overview

This section draws on established guidelines for assisting rehabilitation counselors with decision making strategies, such as the Commission on Rehabilitation Counselor Certification (CRCC) Code of Professional Ethics for Rehabilitation Counselors. Legal and ethical considerations are outlined, and considerations related to the selection, administration, and interpretation of measures for individuals with disabilities are discussed.

Learning Objectives

By the end of this unit you should be able to:

1. Identify the key legal and ethical issues in assessment.
2. Understand the relationship of disability effects on the selection, administration, and interpretation of assessment measures.

Key Concepts

I. Ethical and Legal Issues in Assessment

Test development and selection. Power (2013) offers several guidelines for addressing issues related to test selection and development:

- Caution must be exercised when depending on test instruments to provide information about client needs and traits. The selection of assessment measures should be carefully planned and tailored to the needs of the client to avoid overuse or indiscriminate use of testing.

- Vocational assessment may be used as both a descriptive appraisal of current levels of a client functioning and as an indicator of potential. It is imperative that the rehabilitation professional assesses the appropriateness of a test or assessment measure with regard to reliability, validity, and normative populations.

- Rehabilitation professionals should be aware of available assessment measures and the proper use of testing.

- Each test used should be defined according to what it measures, and the process of test development should be clearly outlined.

- When a test battery is selected, adequate interpretive strategies should be available.

Test fairness. The vocational evaluator is ethically obliged to report why a client may perform below average and suggest ways for remediating the deficiency (Matkin, 1980). It is also important to carefully consider the client's needs and reaction to the assessment process (e.g., environmental influences, client traits).

To promote test fairness, Power (2013) suggests that tests should be administered under the same conditions that were established in their standardization. When there is a need to modify tests to accommodate certain disability groups, attention should be given to ensure appropriate assessment methods so that the validity and reliability of the test are not compromised.

Types of testing accommodations include testing medium, time limits, and test content.

Test interpretation should incorporate all other relevant information about the client, such as educational history, motivation, and adjustment to disability (Bolton, 1982). Important decisions about clients should not be based on the results of a single test or testing session.

Test-taker rights in assessment. According the CRCC Code of Professional Ethics for Rehabilitation Counselors, test takers have the right to:

- Know in advance of testing why they are being tested, how the testing will benefit them, how the test data will be used, and how must time and money the test will cost them
- Participate in planning and scheduling of the testing
- Be free of unnecessary and outdated tests
- Be tested in an atmosphere that is free from distractions and conducive to positive test performance
- Be assessed via the most appropriate instruments and techniques available
- Have a complete, comprehensive, clear, and honest explanation, analysis and application of test results
- Discuss their test results with people competent to interpret the test protocols, relate test data to other available data, and answer questions
- Have their confidentiality protected
- Have further counseling or assessment, if indicated

Test privacy. The privacy of the client must be respected, and all information and materials obtained during the assessment process should be safeguarded. The confidentiality of test instruments and test data is of paramount importance in maintaining the integrity of the tests and the validity of test results.

Evaluator competencies. Vocational evaluators should demonstrate competencies by not only understanding and interpreting assessment results, but also by demonstrating competence in their knowledge of the world of work, familiarity with studies of human behavior, and awareness of the limitations of test interpretation.

II. Multicultural Issues

Culturally competent assessment requires recognition of the issues of test bias, criteria for cultural competence, and the unique considerations that are integral to ethnic minority clients who undergo vocational evaluation.

Test bias. Tests may be biased against a person or group of persons by containing items that favor one group over another, by using test results even if the criteria used for selection and prediction varies greatly among different groups, and by not considering test-related factors such as motivation, anxiety, and the test sophistication of those being assessed.

Cultural competence. Sensitivity and awareness of values, attitudes, and beliefs are essential components of cultural competence. Training for cultural competence includes (a) determining the acculturation status of client prior to the standard assessment approaches, (b) applying methodology and research findings throughout the assessment process, (c) using or appropriately adapting standard assessment instruments, and (d) developing an awareness of attitudes, beliefs, knowledge, and skills in working with culturally diverse groups. Response style, performance motivation, language, and acculturation can affect assessment results and make the test results less useful.

III. Disability Considerations in Assessment

Because standardized test instruments may not be the best way to assess factors such as motivation, work tolerance, or interest, observations of the client in various settings or trial work experiences may prove better methods for understanding rehabilitation potential. Test performance of persons with severe disabilities may be affected by emotional states or sensory or motor limitations.

Disability considerations in test selection. Disability-related considerations are important when selecting assessment measures because the nature of the disability could impact the intended use of the test (e.g., "What is the verbal level of the test?" or "How might impaired manual ability impact performance?"). Individuals with serious emotional or cognitive problems may have limited attention spans, so shorter tasks may be more appropriate (Power, 2013).

Disability considerations in test administration. Power (2013) suggests that to minimize client anxiety, less involved performance-based tests, such as interest or personality inventories, should be administered first. For some individuals with disabilities, tests administered in small blocks of time is preferable. Particular attention should be given to clients with visual or hearing impairments or issues related to fatigue. For clients with cognitive disabilities, it is usually preferable to administer the assessment measures individually rather than in a group setting to minimize distractions.

Disability considerations in test interpretation. It is important to communicate test results at the client's level of understanding. Rehabilitation practitioners should consider how the client's disability influences the test-taking process when interpreting and reporting findings.

Multiple-Choice Questions

1. An interpretation of a test score, such as a percentile score, that is based on the individual's performance relative to scores obtained by a group of individuals, would be considered a:

   A. Self-referenced interpretation

   B. Criterion-referenced interpretation

   C. Norm-referenced interpretation

   D. Not enough information provided

2. A scale that classifies variables based on categorical information without distinguishing size or amount would be classified as:

    A. Nominal

    B. Ordinal

    C. Interval

    D. Ratio

3. All of the following are best classified as vocational interest inventories, *EXCEPT*:

    A. Strong Interest Inventory

    B. Kuder Career Search

    C. Self-Directed Search (Form R)

    D. Wide Range Achievement Test, Fourth Edition

4. All of the following are among the four index scores generated by the Wechsler Adult Intelligence Scale-IV, *EXCEPT*:

    A. Clerical Perception Index

    B. Working Memory Index

    C. Perceptual Reasoning Index

    D. Verbal Comprehension Index

5. The Self-Directed Search can best be described as:

    A. A labor market survey

    B. A self-administered interest inventory based on Holland's career theory

    C. A standardized test measuring career motivation

    D. A work sample

6. A type of nonstatistical validity evidence based on a subjective appraisal of a test's content is:

    A. Face validity

    B. Predictive validity

    C. Construct validity

    D. Concurrent validity

7. Assume a set of scores are distributed as follows: 10, 10, 20, 25, 35. Which of the following statements is accurate regarding the indexes of central tendency?

    A. Mode = 10, median = 25, mean = 20

    B. Mode = 20, median = 25, mean = 10

    C. Mode = 10, median = 20, mean = 20

    D. Mode = 20, median = 10, mean = 25

8. All of the following statements are true about *reliability* and *validity* with regard to psychometric measurement, *EXCEPT*:

   A. Reliability is a measure of consistency, whereas validity is the extent to which meaningful and appropriate inferences can be made from the instrument.

   B. It is possible to have a test with high validity without reliability.

   C. Test–retest, parallel or alternate forms, and split-half are ways of estimating reliability correlation coefficients.

   D. A test with high reliability is relatively free from measurement error.

9. Performance on this test would be most impacted by a limited reading ability.

   A. Test of Nonverbal Intelligence

   B. Raven's Progressive Matrices

   C. Peabody Individual Achievement Test–Revised

   D. Geist Picture Interest Inventory, Revised

10. A standard score based on the normal distribution curve with a mean equal to 0 and a standard deviation equal to 1 ($M = 0$, $SD = 1$) is a:

    A. T-score

    B. Z-score

    C. Percentile

    D. Raw score

Answer Key

1C, 2A, 3D, 4A, 5B, 6A, 7C, 8B, 9C, 10B

Advanced Multiple-Choice Questions

1. During the assessment process in rehabilitation, test-taker rights include all of the following, *EXCEPT*:

   A. Knowledge in advance why they are being tested

   B. Assessment provided by a competent evaluator

   C. Protection of confidentiality and awareness of limits to confidentiality

   D. Immediate access to all testing materials and scoring manuals if requested

2. John is a consumer with a significant visual impairment who is referred for intelligence testing to determine his cognitive functioning. His rehabilitation counselor recommends that John take the verbal comprehension subtests of the Wechsler Adult Intelligence Scale-IV but is not sure how to measure performance-based intelligence. Of the following tests, which would you recommend?

   A. Raven's Progressive Matrices

   B. Stanford–Binet Intelligence Scales, Fifth Edition

C. Haptic Intelligence Scale

D. Processing Speed Index from the Wechsler Adult Intelligence Scale-IV

3. Your client scores in the 92nd percentile on a reading comprehension examination, meaning:

A. She answered 92 out of 100 answers correctly.

B. She received a score of 92% on the test, after the examination was curved.

C. She scored higher than 91% of the other test takers.

D. Both B and C

4. All of the following statements are true about assessment with individuals with disabilities *EXCEPT*:

A. It is important to consider how response style, performance motivation, disability effects, and language may affect test performance and consequently the usefulness of test results.

B. Only tests that have separate norms for individuals with disabilities are considered valid measures in assessment approaches in vocational rehabilitation.

C. Sensitivity and awareness of values, attitudes, and beliefs are considered the essential components of cultural competence in assessment.

D. Test bias is an important consideration when selecting tests and interpreting results.

5. Kelly is a 21-year-old consumer. She receives a Full Scale Intelligence Quotient score of 70 on the Wechsler Adult Intelligence Scale-IV. Her index scores are 65 on the Working Memory Index, 60 on the Verbal Comprehension Index, 60 on the Processing Speed Index, and 80 on the Perceptual Reasoning Index. Assuming that these scores are representative of her true performance and are valid, what inference could be made?

A. Kelly is considered to have a severe intellectual disability (or severe mental retardation).

B. Kelly's abstract verbal reasoning and verbal comprehension fall in the average range relative to her same-age peers.

C. Kelly's spatial reasoning and visual processing are relative strengths.

D. Nothing can be concluded from these scores.

6. All of the following are true regarding a true normal curve, *EXCEPT*:

A. Approximately 68% of total cases fall within two standard deviations of the mean.

B. Approximately 98% of cases are within three standard deviations of the mean.

C. The mean, median, and mode all have the same value.

D. The limits of the curve are infinite.

7. Teri is a 30-year-old woman who would like to find employment. She left high school in the 10th grade to raise her child and has never worked. She is interested in obtaining a GED and would like to pursue a college degree in elementary education. The rehabilitation counselor is interested in a brief measure to assess Teri's basic reading and arithmetic capabilities and would likely choose to administer the:

A. Wide Range Achievement Test, Fourth Edition

B. Wechsler Adult Intelligence Scale-IV

C. Armed Services Vocational Aptitude Battery

D. Beta III

8. A new consumer who reports that she took a test several years ago in which her scores were elevated on the Psychasthenia and Schizophrenia scales. She took the:

A. Myers–Briggs Type Indicator

B. Sixteen Personality Factor Questionnaire, Form E

C. Minnesota Multiphasic Personality Inventory, Second Edition

D. Raven's Progressive Matrices

9. According to the Commission on Rehabilitation Counselor Certification's Code of Professional Ethics for Rehabilitation Counselors regarding evaluation, assessment, and interpretation:

A. Rehabilitation counselors are not responsible for preventing the misuse of obsolete or outdated measures and assessment data by others.

B. Rehabilitation counselors are able to reproduce or modify published assessments without acknowledgement and permission from the publisher under some circumstances.

C. Prior to assessment, rehabilitation counselors are expected to explain the nature and purposes of assessment in the language and/or at the developmental level of the consumer, unless explicit exception has been agreed on in advance.

D. Since it may be necessary to accommodate consumers with disabilities, a test may not be administered under standard conditions. If this occurs, it is up to the rehabilitation counselor to decide whether to note this change in the interpretation of the test results.

10. E-S-F-P (Extroversion, Sensing, Feeling, Perception) is a possible score summary of a personality type on this well-known personality test based on the works of Jung:

A. Sixteen Personality Factor Questionnaire, Form E

B. Myers–Briggs Type Indicator

C. Minnesota Multiphasic Personality Inventory, Second Edition

D. NEO Personality Inventory–Revised

Answer Key and Explanation of Answers

1D: The Commission on Rehabilitation Counselor Certification's Code of Professional Ethics for Rehabilitation Counselors clearly protects the rights of test takers. It is the responsibility of the rehabilitation counselor to ensure that consumers are aware in advance as to why they are being tested so that they can provide informed consent, the assessment is provided by a competent evaluator, and confidentiality is protected. Because it is important to maintain the integrity and security of tests and other assessment techniques, rehabilitation counselors must comply with legal and contractual obligations even if a test taker requests access. Rehabilitation counselors are not able to appropriate, modify, or reproduce published assessments without explicit permission from the publisher.

2C: The Haptic Intelligence Scale for Adult Blind was specifically designed to parallel the performance based measures of the Wechsler Adult Intelligence Scale-IV (WAIS-IV) for individuals with visual impairments. Raven's Progressive Matrices, many of the subtests of the Stanford–Binet Intelligence Scales, Fifth Edition, and the Processing Speed Index subtests of the WAIS-IV all require vision.

3C: Percentiles are rank order scores that indicate the percentage of persons in the comparison group who the test taker has outperformed. It is important not to confuse percentile scores with raw scores (which usually represent the percentage correct). Although percentile ranks are reported frequently because of their ease of understanding, they exaggerate differences near the mean and collapse differences at the extremes. For example, the raw score difference between two individuals scoring at the 47th and 75th percentiles may only be a few points.

4B: Disability, cultural background, language, test bias, and motivation can affect an individual's test performance and results and should be considered during test selection, administration, and interpretation. In some cases it may be important to use comparison norms based on a specific disability population; however, this is not always the case. For example, a rehabilitation counselor assessing the clerical aptitude of an individual with a lower back injury would likely be interested in how this individual's performance compares with others successfully working in clerical occupations rather than a specific disability population.

5C: Kelly scored an 80 on Perceptual Reasoning Index of the Wechsler Adult Intelligence Scale-IV (WAIS-IV). Although this score falls in the low average range compared with her same-age peers, it is notably higher than her performance on the other scales and suggests that her spatial reasoning and visual processing are strengths relative to the other areas measured. Kelly's Full Scale Intelligent Quotient score of 70 would be classified as borderline intellectual functioning but is not indicative of a *severe* intellectual disability. The Verbal Comprehension Index provides an estimate of Kelly's abstract verbal reasoning and comprehension. Her score of 60 suggests that she falls in the extremely low range on this scale relative to the norm group, whereas a score of 90 to 109 would suggest average performance.

6A: Approximately 68% of the total cases fall within one standard deviation of the mean on a true normal curve; 95% fall within two standard deviations, and 98% are within three.

7A: The Wide Range Achievement Test, Fourth Edition (WRAT-4) is a commonly used brief measure of achievement level. The Beta III and the Wechsler Adult Intelligence Scale-IV are intelligence tests, and the Armed Services Vocational Aptitude Battery is an aptitude test. In addition to not measuring the construct of interest, these latter three tests are also more extensive and lengthier to administer than the WRAT-4.

8C: Psycasthenia and Schizophrenia are among the 10 clinical scales on the Minnesota Multiphasic Personality Inventory, Second Edition. Elevated scores on the clinical scales reflect maladjustment and psychological dysfunction. The Myers–Briggs Type Indicator and the Sixteen Personality Factor Questionnaire, Form E, are used to assess broad personality characteristics rather than psychopathology. Raven's Progressive Matrices measures nonverbal intelligence.

9C: The Commission on Rehabilitation Counselor Certification's Code of Professional Ethics for Rehabilitation Counselors clearly specifies that rehabilitation counselors are expected to communicate the nature and purpose of assessment to the consumer. In addition, rehabilitation counselors (a) are responsible for preventing the misuse of assessment data by others, (b) should never reproduce or modify published assessments without permission from the publisher, and (c) are expected to note any changes made to standardized testing conditions in the interpretation of test results.

10B: The Myers–Briggs Type Indicator was designed based on Jung's concepts of perception and judgment. It is scored on eight scales yielding four bipolar dimensions: extroversion (E) versus introversion (I), sensing (S) versus intuition (N), thinking (T) versus feeling (F), and judgment (J) versus perception (P). An individual's personality type is then summarized using four letters. Scores on the Sixteen Personality Factor Questionnaire, Form E, are given on 16 bipolar primary personality factors, scores on the Minnesota Multiphasic Personality Inventory, Second Edition, are based on elevations on specific clinical scales, and scores on the NEO Personality Inventory–Revised reflect the five-factor model of personality.

References

American Educational Research Association, American Psychological Association, & National Council on Measurement in Education. (2014). *Standards for educational and psychological testing.* Washington, DC: American Educational Research Association.

Anastasi, A., & Urbina, S. (1997). *Psychological testing* (7th ed.). Upper Saddle River, NJ: Prentice Hall.

Becker, R. (2000). *Reading-Free Vocational Interest Inventory-2.* Columbus, OH: Elbern.

Bennett, G. K., Seasher, H. G., & Wesman, A. G. (1990). *Differential Aptitude Tests–fifth edition.* New York, NY: Psychological Corp.

Berven, N. L. (1997). Professional practice: Assessment. In D. Maki & T. Riggar (Eds.), *Rehabilitation counseling* (pp. 151–169). New York, NY: Springer Publishing.

Bolton, B. (1982). *Vocational adjustment of disabled persons.* Austin, TX: Pro-Ed.

Bolton, B. (2001). *Handbook of measurement and evaluation in rehabilitation.* Belmont, CA: Aspen.

Bolton, B., & Parker, R. (2008). *Handbook of measurement and evaluation in rehabilitation* (4th ed.). Austin, TX: Pro-Ed.

Botterbusch, K. F. (1987). Commercial vocational evaluation systems. In B. Bolton (Ed.), *Vocational adjustment of disabled persons* (pp. 93–126). Baltimore, MD: University Park Press.

Briggs Myers, I., & Briggs, K. C. (1988). *Myers-Briggs Type Indicator.* Palo Alto, CA: Consulting Psychologists Press.

Cattell, R. B. (1986). *Sixteen Personality Factor Questionnaire.* New York, NY: Psychological Corp.

Costa, P. T., & McCrae, R. (2007). *NEO-PI-R professional manual.* Odessa, FL: Psychological Assessment Resources.

Dunn, L. M., & Dunn, L. (1997). *Peabody Picture Vocabulary Test–Fourth Edition.* Circle Pines, MN: American Guidance Service.

Gice, J. (1985). In search of…"The perfect vocational evaluation." *Vocational Evaluation and Work Adjustment Bulletin, 18*(1), 4–7.

Gough, H. G., & Bradley, P. (1996). *California Psychological Inventory.* Palo Alto, CA: Consulting Psychologists Press.

Grissom, J., Eldredge, G., & Nelson, R. (1990). Adapting the vocational evaluation process for clients with a substance abuse history. *Journal of Applied Rehabilitation Counseling, 21*(3), 30–32.

Hathaway, S., McKinley, C., & Butcher, J. (1990). *Minnesota Multiphasic Personality Inventory–Second Edition.* Minneapolis, MN: National Computer Systems.

Holland, J. (1994). *The Self-Directed Search.* San Antonio, TX: Psychological Corp.

Karlsen, B., & Gardner, E. F. (1986). *Adult Basic Learning Examination.* New York, NY: Psychological Corp.

Kellogg, C. E., & Morton, N. W. (1999). *Revised Beta examination-Beta III.* New York, NY: Psychological Corp.

Markwardt, F. C. (1998). *Peabody Individual Achievement Test–Revised*. Circle Pines, MN: American Guidance Service.

Matkin, B. (1980). Legal and ethical issues in vocational assessment. *Vocational Evaluation and Work Adjustment Bulletin, 13*, 57–60.

McAlees, D., & Menz, F. (1992). Consumerism and vocational evaluation. *Rehabilitation Education, 6*, 213–220.

McCarron, L. T., & Spires, H. P. (1991). *McCarron-Dial system vocational interest exploration instructor's manual*. Dallas, TX: McCarron-Dial Systems.

Parker, R. M. (2001). *Occupational Aptitude Survey and Interest Schedule–Third Edition*. Austin, TX: Pro-Ed.

Pittenger, D. J. (1993). Measuring the MBTI and coming up short. *Journal of Career Planning and Employment, 54*, 48–52.

Power, P. W. (2013). *A guide to vocational assessment* (5th ed.). Austin, TX: Pro-Ed.

Raven, J. C. (1986). *Raven's Progressive Matrices*. New York, NY: Psychological Corp.

Rogan, P., & Hagner, D. (1990). Vocational evaluation in supported employment. *Journal of Rehabilitation, 56*, 45–51.

Roid, G., (2003). *Stanford-Binet Intelligence Scale–Fifth Edition*. Itasca, IL: Riverside.

Rubin, S. E., & Roessler, R. T. (2008). *Foundations of the vocational rehabilitation process* (4th ed.). Austin, TX: Pro-Ed.

Slosson, R. L., Nicholoson, C. L., & Hibpshman, T. H. (1990). *Slosson Intelligence Test–Revised*. East Aurora, NY: Slosson.

Strong, E. K., Hansen, J. C., & Campbell, D. P. (1994). *Strong Interest Inventory*. Palo Alto, CA: Consulting Psychologists Press.

Thorndike, R. M., & Thorndike-Christ, T. (2008). *Measurement and evaluation in psychology and education* (8th ed.). Boston, MA: Pearson.

Truthan, J. A., & Field, T. F. (2013). Computer-based vocational guidance systems and job matching. In D. R. Strauser (Ed.), *Career development, employment, and disability in rehabilitation* (pp. 243–259). New York, NY: Springer Publishing.

U.S. Department of Labor. (1970). *Manual for USES general aptitude test battery*. Washington, DC: U.S. Government Printing Office.

U.S. Department of Labor. (1991). *The revised handbook for analyzing jobs*. Washington, DC: U.S. Government Printing Office.

Wechsler, D. (2008). *Manual for the Wechsler Adult Intelligence Scale–Fourth Edition (WAIS-IV)*. San Antonio, TX: Psychological Corp.

Wilkinson, G. S., & Robertson, G. J. (2006). *Wide Range Achievement Test 4 professional manual*. Lutz, FL: Psychological Assessment Resources.

8

Research Methods and Evidence-Based Practice

CHUNGYI CHIU AND PHILLIP RUMRILL

Knowledge of research methods enables rehabilitation professionals to critically review research articles and perceptively apply the evidence to support their clinical and ethical practices. Understanding research methods assists one in either conducting well-designed studies or in evaluating the effectiveness, efficacy, and efficiency of a rehabilitation program. This chapter reviews quantitative and qualitative research methods, program evaluation strategies, and research ethics.

Learning Objectives

By the end of this unit you should be able to:

1. Understand types of literature review, levels of evidence, types of research validity, and scientific writing guidelines.
2. Understand concepts related to psychometric tests and statistical analyses.
3. Understand characteristics of experimental and quasi-experimental designs, single-case research designs, developmental research methods, and qualitative research designs.
4. Understand key concepts related to program evaluation methodologies and designs.
5. Understand the basic principles and application of research ethics in practice.

Literature Review and Writing a Scientific Report

Overview

This section discusses literature reviews, evidence-based research hierarchy, evaluating the validity of research, and writing a research report.

Key Concepts

Systematic literature reviews involve a more comprehensive literature search that evaluates and synthesizes empirical or research-based evidence in order to make recommendations for answering future research questions (Dijkers, 2015). Systematic reviews differ from narrative literature reviews by defining the specific criteria for selecting the studies included in the review and by assessing the empirical robustness of the selected studies included in the review. A systematic review, however, does not empirically analyze the included studies, but describes narratively what the selected research body suggests. *Narrative literature reviews* summarize and synthesize the literature in a given content area (Centre for Reviews and Dissemination, 2009; Dijkers, 2015) to provide readers with background information related to a particular topic area. Literature reviews may be stand-alone papers or, more popularly, the first component of a research study paper. A *scoping literature review* is a more focused and systematic literature review that explores a particular research question by describing key concepts, available evidence, and gaps in the research. This type of literature review typically occurs prior to an empirical study in this chosen area (Colquhoun et al., 2014). A *meta-analysis* analyzes the empirical results of a group of similar quantitative studies using each study's effect size (Centre for Reviews and Dissemination, 2009; Dijkers, 2015).

Levels of evidence (also known as the hierarchy of evidence) provide a method for evaluating the quality, validity, and applicability of research studies to be applied in practice. Ackley, Swan, Ladwig, and Tucker (2008) suggested the following levels: **level 1**—evidence from a systematic review or meta-analysis of all relevant randomized controlled trials (RCTs) or evidence-based clinical practice guidelines based on systematic reviews of RCTs or three or more RCTs of good quality that have similar results; **level 2**—evidence from at least one well-designed RCT of an appropriate sample size (e.g., a large multisite RCT); **level 3**—evidence from well-designed controlled trials without randomization (i.e., quasi-experimental designs); **level 4**—evidence from well-designed case-control or cohort studies; **level 5**—evidence from systematic reviews of descriptive and qualitative studies; **level 6**—evidence from a single descriptive or qualitative study; **level 7**—evidence from the opinion of authorities and/or reports of expert committees.

Research validity generally refers to the degree to which the knowledge gleaned from a study can actually be attributed to the study itself. In other words, does the study truly investigate what it is claiming to investigate? There are four particular types of validity evidence that shed light on the overarching validity of the study: internal validity, external validity, construct validity, and statistical conclusion validity. *Internal validity* refers to the researcher's confidence that the independent and dependent variables have a cause-and-effect relationship (Cozby & Bates, 2015; Rumrill & Bellini, in press). Threats to internal validity include history (life events), maturation, instrumentation, sample selection, attrition (mortality), and the vagueness of the direction of causal influence (Heppner, Wampold, Owen, Thompson, & Wang, 2016). *External validity* refers to the extent to which the findings of a study can be generalized to other populations, settings, and conditions (Cozby & Bates, 2015). Examples of threats to external validity include participants' characteristics, specific features of the stimulus condition (e.g., a given intervention), contextual characteristics (e.g., experimental arrangements), and assessment characteristics of the variables under study (Kazdin, 2016; Rumrill & Bellini, in press). *Construct validity* refers to the degree to which the variables under study are operationalized and measured in a way that reflects what the study aims to investigate. In other words, are the constructs (e.g., self-esteem) under investigation defined and measured in a manner that most accurately represents self-esteem? Construct validity is often determined by an analysis of the quality and quantity of the items in the measure (Cozby & Bates, 2015; Kazdin, 2016; Rumrill & Bellini, in press). Threats to construct validity include inadequate explication and operationalization of constructs, single operations (e.g., are the findings actually due to the selected independent variable?) and narrow stimulus operations and narrow stimulus sampling (e.g., are there other effects that occur due to the independent variable beyond that identified by the researcher?), experimenter expectations (e.g., study effects may occur because of the researchers' expectations perceived by the research participants), and cues associated with the experimental situation (e.g., other factors related to information about the study that may influence research participant response) (Kazdin, 2016; Rumrill & Bellini, in press). *Statistical conclusion validity* refers to the appropriateness and accuracy of research conclusions about variable relationships based on the researcher's statistical tests used in a study (Heppner et al., 2016). Threats to statistical conclusion validity are low statistical power (the probability that the analyses correctly reject the null hypothesis when the research or alternative hypothesis is true) and violation of statistical assumptions such as normal distribution of data, data from multiple groups have the same variance, and data have a linear relationship. Fishing and error-rate issues occur when researchers conduct numerous statistical tests and are thus more likely to reject the null hypothesis when it is in fact true (type I error). Unreliable measures influence statistical validity because the scores/data from a particular measure have low levels of reliability (e.g., the scores will not be the same over time). Range restriction refers to when the data is limited to a particular criteria or a subset of data is used. Unreliable treatment implementation occurs when there is a lack of standardization in the implementation of an independent variable or treatment. Inaccurate effect size estimates occur when statistics overestimate or underestimate the size of an effect (Heppner et al., 2016).

In order to improve the precision and transparency of scientific reports, guidelines for writing research reports have been recommended. **PRISMA** (Preferred Reporting Items for Systematic Reviews and Meta-Analyses) provides a set of guidelines for reporting systematic reviews and meta-analyses (Moher, Liberati, Tetzlaff, Altman, & PRISMA Group, 2009). **CONSORT** (Consolidated Standards of Reporting Trials) is a framework for reporting randomized clinical trials (RCTs; Schulz, Altman, & Moher, 2010). **STROBE** (STrengthening the Reporting of OBservational studies in Epidemiology) is a guideline for reporting observational studies, specifically cohort, case-control, and cross-sectional studies (von Elm et al., 2014). **MOOSE** (Meta-analysis Of Observational Studies in Epidemiology) is a guideline used for reporting meta-analyses of observational studies (Stroup et al., 2000). **STARD** (STAndards for the Reporting of Diagnostic accuracy studies) is a guideline for reporting studies of diagnostic or prognostic accuracy (Bossuyt et al., 2003). **SPIRIT** (Standard Protocol Items: Recommendations for Interventional Trials) is a guideline for the reporting of scientific trial protocols (Chan et al., 2013).

Basic Measurement Concepts and Statistics Basics

Overview

This section discusses basic psychometric concepts and descriptive and inferential statistics.

Key Concepts

I. Measurement Scales

Variables are measured on four types of scales (Cozby & Bates, 2015). *Nominal scales* are used to identify an individual or a class by names or labels. Nominal scales are labeled, for example, by such categorical names as gender, race/ethnicity, political affiliation, and treatment conditions (e.g., labeling as a treatment group or a control group). These nominal categories cannot be ordered in any meaningful way. The arithmetic operation for nominal scales is counting the frequency of each category. Variables with *ordinal scales* are used to rank participants or scores, such as rankings of sports teams and percentile scores on standardized tests. For ordinal scales, the distance between scores or rankings is not equal units; the ranking or order of the data is most important. Methods used to rank ordinal data include such analyses as a frequency count or through the use of Spearman's rho correlation coefficients. *Interval scales,* also known as equal-unit scales, are based on the premise that any two consecutive numbers are equal in distance. For example, on a weight on Fahrenheit temperatures scale, the distance between 20 degrees and 30 degrees (10 degrees) is the same as the distance between 40 degrees and 50 degrees (10 degrees). As such, addition, subtraction, multiplication, and division are appropriate arithmetic calculations that can be done with this type of scale. Notably, interval scales are the most common type of scales used in research given the applicability of a broad range of arithmetic options. However, there is no real zero value in interval scales, so the numbers cannot be interpreted as ratios. *Ratio scales* also have ordered, equal intervals, but unlike interval scales, they have an absolute, true zero point that represents none of whatever is being measured (e.g., weight, height). Therefore, numbers in ratio scales can be added, subtracted, multiplied, and divided.

II. Reliability of Measurement

Reliability refers to the extent to which the results of a study are consistent and precise, both of which are equated with the extent to which a test score is free from measurement error. For example, when the *standard error of measurement*, which estimates how repeated scores by the same participant on the same measure are consistently close to their "true score," is lower, the reliability coefficient is higher. There are several reliability estimates used to determine the reliability of an instrument. *Scorer reliability* or *interrater reliability* is the extent to which raters agree on their observations; the indicator of this reliability is *Cohen's kappa*. *Test-retest reliability* estimates the degree to which scores remain consistent over time. Test-retest estimates are gathered by administering the same test to the same group on two different occasions with a certain time interval (e.g., 4–6 weeks apart). The strength of the correlation between the two obtained scores is the test-retest reliability coefficient. *Split-half reliability,* or *alternate-form reliability*, is used to estimate the degree to which the content of two measures claimed to measure the same construct are correlated. High split-half reliability estimates suggest better reliability. *Coefficient alpha,* or *Cronbach's alpha,* is used to estimate inter item inconsistency, which results from fluctuations in items across an entire test. The Cronbach's alpha is higher when the number of items is increased and when the ratio of item score variance to total test score variance is decreased.

III. Validity of Measurement

Validity is "the degree to which evidence and theory support the interpretation of test scores for proposed uses of tests" (American Educational Research Association [AERA], American Psychological Association [APA], & National Council on Measurement in Education [NCME], 2014, p. 11). The sources of validity evidence include test content, response processes, internal test structure, and relations to other variables (AERA, APA, & NCME, 2014). *Face validity* is the extent to which the content of the measure reflects the construct it is intended to measure (Cozby & Bates, 2015). *Content validity* is the extent to which the content of the measure is representative of the larger universe of content reflective of the construct being measured. *Predictive validity* is the extent to which scores on a measure predict a criterion or outcome measured at a future time. *Concurrent validity* is the extent to which scores on a measure are related to a criterion measured at the same time. *Convergent validity* is the extent to which scores on a measure are related to other measures that claim to measure a similar construct (e.g., two different depression measures). *Discriminant validity* is the extent to which scores on a measure are not significantly correlated with, or inversely correlated with, measures to which they should not theoretically be linked (e.g., high depression and high self-esteem) (Cozby & Bates, 2015).

IV. Central Tendency

Measures of central tendency indicate where the majority of data falls in a dataset (Urbina, 2014). There are three measures of central tendency (Cozby & Bates, 2015): The *mean*, which is obtained by adding all the total scores in a distribution and dividing by the number of total scores. The *median* is the middlemost score, dividing the group in half, when all scores are lined up in order from lowest to highest. If there is no "middle" score due to an even number of scores, the median is the average of the two middlemost scores. The *mode* is the most frequent score. For example, if seven people scored 87, 91, 96, 99, 100, 100, and 111 on an IQ test, the mode would be 100, the median 99, and the mean 98. When the data distribution is skewed due to unusual or outlier scores (e.g., household income), the median or mode is a better indicator of central tendency.

V. Descriptive Statistics

Variability
Variability refers to the degree to which scores disperse or scatter within a particular distribution (Urbina, 2014). There are three variability indices (Cozby & Bates, 2015). The *range* is the distance between two extreme points or the difference between the highest and lowest score. The *variance* is the sum of the squared differences between each score and the mean of the data distribution, divided by the number of subjects. In other words, the variance is the average of the sum of the squared deviation values. The *standard deviation (SD)* is the square root of the variance, and is used to quantify the amount of variation or dispersion of a dataset, or the spread of the scores. The *SD* expresses the variance or spread of scores around the mean in units that are comparable to the mean. The *SD* is frequently used in research to describe the average deviation of scores from the mean. In the set of IQ scores from the previous example (i.e., 87, 91, 96, 99, 100, 100, and 111), the range is 24, the variance is 58.57, and the *SD* is 7.65.

Normal curve and standardized scores
The *normal curve* (a symmetrical bell curve) is a mathematically defined curve based on probability theory. The normal distribution is bilaterally symmetrical, meaning each half contains 50% of the area under the curve. The mean, median, and mode lie in the exact center of the distribution (Cozby & Bates, 2015). The normal curve is divided into *SDs* and associated percentile ranks: Approximately 68% of scores fall between one *SD* above and one *SD* below the mean, approximately 95% of scores fall between two *SDs* above and two *SDs* below the mean, and approximately 99% of scores fall between three *SDs* above and three *SDs* below the mean. Common standardized scores are *Z*-scores and *T*-scores (Cozby & Bates, 2015). A *Z-score* has a mean of zero and an *SD* of one. A *T-score* has a mean of 50 and an *SD* of 10.

VI. Basic Inferential Statistical Tests

Hypothesis testing

To test a hypothesis or research question, researchers test a null hypothesis and a research (alternative) hypothesis using inferential statistics. Inferential statistics go beyond descriptive analyses that describe the sample population, to allow the researcher to make inferences about the larger population based on the sample (Cozby & Bates, 2015). The *null hypothesis* assumes that the population means are equal. When the null hypothesis is true, the observed difference is due to random error and the independent variable has no effect on the dependent variable. The *research hypothesis* assumes that the population means are not equal. In other words, the observed difference is not due to random error and the independent variable has effects on the dependent variable. When the null hypothesis is rejected because there is a low probability that the results are due to random error, the result is considered significantly significant. When the null hypothesis is rejected when it is in fact true, *type I error* occurs. The probability of making a type I error is based on the statistical significance level—alpha level (α; e.g., .05). The alpha coefficient provides the researcher with the probability level to which the findings are in fact true. For example, an alpha of .05 suggests that there is only a 5% chance that the null hypothesis is true, and a 95% chance it is false. Similarly, if the alpha level is .01, there is a 1% chance the null hypothesis is true and a 99% chance that it is false. Thus, when the alpha is .05 or below, there is a small probability that the researchers are committing a type I error. Conversely, when the null hypothesis is accepted when it is false, a *type II error* (β) is committed. More specifically, when the null hypothesis is accepted and the research hypothesis rejected, when the researcher rejects the null when it is in fact true, a type II error occurs, suggesting the study did not have adequate power. The desired probability of correctly rejecting the null hypothesis is the power of the statistical test, which is the probability of making the correct decision if the research hypothesis is true and is statistically defined as $1 - \beta$. Researchers want to maximize power, desiring power to be .80 or greater and minimizing the type II error to .20 or less.

Sampling

Probability sampling occurs when the sample is gathered in a manner that does not give all individuals in the population an equal change of being selected (Cozby & Bates, 2015). This type of random sampling is designed to represent the population, resulting in higher external validity (generalizability). Probability sampling techniques include simple random sampling, stratified random sampling, and cluster sampling. *Nonprobability sampling* occurs when the sample is collected in a manner that does not allow all persons in the population an equal chance of being selected (Cozby & Bates, 2015). Therefore, nonprobability sampling is more biased due to the nonrandom nature of the collection method, and less generalizable to the intended population. Nonprobability sampling techniques include haphazard sampling, purposive sampling, and quota sampling. An important aspect of sampling is sample size; specifically, determining whether the sample size is big enough to obtain valid probability levels, power, and effect sizes. Small sample sizes are more likely to result in type I errors (rejecting the null, when it is true) and weak power. Larger sample sizes are less likely to result in type I errors and have stronger power, which protects against committing a type II error or concluding the null hypothesis is true, when in fact the research hypothesis is true. Simply put, type I errors could be characterized as "false positives" and type II errors as "false negatives." Sufficient a-priori sample size is determined before collecting the sample and is estimated by the type I error (e.g., $\leq$ .05), power (e.g., $\geq$ .80), and effect size (e.g., small, medium, or large effect sizes). These numbers allow the researcher to calculate the sample size needed to detect a statistical effect while not committing a type I or type II error.

Comparison

The *t* test is most commonly used to determine whether two groups are significantly different from each other (Cozby & Bates, 2015). The *F* test is used when there are more than two groups, commonly referred to as an analysis of variance (ANOVA). ANOVA determines between- and within-group variance or difference. The *F* test is the actual statistical test used in ANOVA when there are more than two independent variables or when there is a factorial design (when there are multiple independent variables in a single study). The *F* test is a ratio of systematic variance (between-group variance) and error variance (within-group variance).

Correlation analyses

The *Pearson product-moment correlation coefficient (r)* is used to find the strength of the linear relationship between two variables when both variables have interval or ratio scale properties (Cozby & Bates, 2015). The range of the correlation coefficient for a *negative linear relationship* is −1 to 0 and for a *positive linear relationship,* 0 to +1. When there is no linear relationship or there is a *curvilinear relationship*, the correlation coefficient is 0. Multiple regression analyses (MRAs) combine a number of predictors (e.g., age, GPA, socioeconomic status) to predict an outcome variable (e.g., years of college). The statistic used in MRAs is *R*-squared. The *R*-squared tells you how much of the variance in the outcome variable is accounted for by the predictor variable(s). For example, an *R*-squared of .23 for GPA and years in college suggests that 23% of the variance in years of college is accounted for by GPA, and thus 77% is accounted for by other variables. Structural equation modeling (SEM) is a multivariate statistical analysis used to analyze structural relationships among variables that have been theoretically linked. SEM is a combination of MRAs and factor analysis, and allows the researcher to make some causal inferences. For example, SEM may be used to examine a causal model of depression that includes variables linked in a specific theoretical order. For example, genetic vulnerability may influence response to environmental stress, which may influence loss of social support, which may influence isolation, which may influence depressive symptoms. SEM seeks to determine whether the proposed theoretical model provides a good fit to the data. Statistical tests determine the strength of the fit. A mediation analysis is often used when the researcher is interested in learning whether a predictor influences an outcome through another variable. In other words, does GPA influence years of college through social support (mediator)? Thus, a mediation analysis tests whether a third variable (s) influences the causal relationship between variable-x and variable-y when variable-x exerts its effect on variable-y (Hayes, 2013). Moderation analysis is used to determine whether there is an interaction between the predictor variable and another variable (moderator) that influences the outcome. For example, does GPA interact with social support to influence years of college (Hayes, 2013)?

Effect size

Effect size is the magnitude of the effect between variable-x and variable-y, or the strength of the association between variables (Cozby & Bates, 2015). For example, the correlation coefficients (r) of .10, .30, and .50 are considered conventional cutoff values for small, medium, and large effects, respectively. A correlation of .50 or greater is considered a large effect. Cohen's *d* is an effect size statistic for comparing two means. Cohen's *d* at 0.20, 0.50, and 0.80 are considered as conventional cutoff values for small, medium, and large effects, respectively.

For example, when Cohen's *d* is ≤ 0.20, the effect of one variable on another (predictor on outcome) or the strength of the relationship between two variables is considered to have a small effect. Notably, the effect size must be understood within the context of the literature and the construct; even small effects are significant for many psychosocial variables tested in our field.

Basic Quantitative and Qualitative Research Designs

Key Concepts

This section discusses experimental designs, quasi-experimental designs, single-case designs, developmental designs, and qualitative research designs.

I. Experimental Designs

Experimental design controls for the effects of confounding variables, which influence independent and dependent variables, compromising the internal validity of the study. Confounding variables are controlled by keeping them statistically constant and through the use of sample randomization controls for the effects of confounding variables, which influence independent and dependent variables, compromising the internal validity of the study (Cozby & Bates, 2015). There are several types of experimental designs, which all require randomization. The *posttest-only design* randomly assigns participants into two groups, introduces the independent variable, and uses a posttest-only dependent variable measure to determine whether the independent variable (treatment) differentially affects the two groups (e.g., means are significantly different). The *pretest–posttest design* randomly assigns participants into two groups, measures the dependent variable first, and then introduces the independent variable (treatment), followed by measuring the dependent variable after the treatment to determine change over time. *Solomon four-group design* is a combination of the posttest–only and pretest–posttest designs, wherein half the participants receive the posttest and the other half receive the pretest and posttest. *Independent groups design* involves two or more randomly assigned separate groups, each of which is composed of different participants. Each participant receives one test for each condition of the independent variable. In *repeated measures design*, each participant receives all conditions including treatment and control conditions. This type of design is often referred to as *within-subject design* and common in longitudinal studies. Repeated measures design needs fewer participants than independent groups design and is sensitive to finding statistically significant differences within a group. Because repeated designs require multiple measurements, order effects may occur, which are effects related to the order of the treatments versus the treatment itself. Scores may change because of practice or learning and fatigue, which negatively impact internal validity. A technique for controlling order effects is a *Latin square*, in which a limited set of orders is constructed so that each condition precedes and follows every other condition one time. A *matched pairs design* occurs when the participants in the sample are grouped into pairs based on similarity (e.g., age, sex, etc.) and within each pair, the participants are randomly assigned to different treatments. This approach controls for additional confounding variables such as age and sex. A *single-blind experimental design* refers to when participants do not know whether they are in a treatment or a control group, whereas a *double-blind experiment* occurs when both the researchers and the participants do not know whether they are in a treatment or control group. *Factorial designs* are used when there is more than one independent variable (factor). For example, a 2 × 2 factorial design includes two independent variables (or two factors), and each independent variable has two levels.

II. Quasi-Experimental Designs

Unlike experimental designs, quasi-experimental designs do not eliminate confounding variables through randomization (Cozby & Bates, 2015). Examples of quasi-experimental designs include one group posttest-only design, one-group pretest–posttest design, nonequivalent control group design, nonequivalent control group pretest–posttest test, interrupted time series design, and control series design. Quasi-experimental designs are subject to a number of confounding effects, including *history effects* (any confounding effect that happens between the first and second measurements that is not part of the manipulation), *maturation effects* (any change that occurs systematically over time that is not part of the manipulation), *testing effects* (the effect of simply taking the pretest changes the subjects' behavior), *instrument decay* (the basic characteristics of the instrument change over time), or *regression toward the mean* (when subjects' scores are extremely low or high on some variables, their scores will tend to change in the direction of the mean).

III. Single-Case Designs (small *N* design)

Single-case designs are used to determine whether an experimental manipulation has an effect on a single research participant (Cozby & Bates, 2015). The participant's behavior is measured at baseline, which is a control period before any manipulation is introduced. Later, a manipulation is introduced, and the participant's behavior is measured during this treatment period. Reversal of the manipulation is conducted to determine whether the independent variable was the cause of the effects. This is done by introducing a second baseline period after the treatment is removed; for example, A (baseline period) → B (treatment period) → A (base-line period) design (ABA design, a.k.a. a reversal design). Several variations of this design (i.e., ABAB or BAB) can be used, depending on research goals. Another variation is a *multiple baseline design*, where several baseline behaviors are measured at the same time and the treatment is introduced at different times for each behavior. The effectiveness of the treatment is demonstrated when measured behavior at a baseline period is changed after the treatment is applied.

IV. Developmental Research Designs

Developmental research designs can be used to study individual change as a function of age (Cozby & Bates, 2015). The *cross-sectional method* studies subjects of different ages at one point in time whereas the *longitudinal method* studies the same group of people at different points in time as they grow older.

V. Qualitative Research Designs

Qualitative research designs focus on collecting in-depth information on a relatively small number of participants or within a limited setting in order to describe their experience or behavior in their own words (Cozby & Bates, 2015). Qualitative research designs are based on several assumptions (Rumrill & Bellini, in press): Study hypotheses are not applicable, qualitative research is conducted to understand and describe a phenomenon versus explaining and generalizing, and triangulation (gathering data from multiple perspectives) and trustworthiness (e.g., credibility, transferability, dependability, and confirmability) are important to the validity of the research. Qualitative data is gathered from *structured interviews* (questions are determined in advance and all participants are asked identical questions), *semistructured interviews* (the interview is planned but may be modified while in progress), and *unstructured interviews* (questions are prompted by the flow of the conversation). *Focus groups* are a specific type of group interview used to gather qualitative data wherein members provide insight into a specific topic or issue. *Naturalistic observation* (i.e., field work, field observation) data collection occurs when the researcher observes participants in their natural setting and records their observations. Disadvantages associated with the naturalistic observation method include *observer effects* (the impact the observer has on participants), *observer expectations* (the observer's preconceived expectations that may not be true), and *observer bias* (observer's attitudes or beliefs affecting how events are observed or interpreted). Qualitative approaches include grounded theory, ethnographic research, phenomenological orientation, consensual qualitative research, and comprehensive process analysis. *Grounded theory* (Glaser & Strauss, 1967) is a qualitative research approach used to guide researchers in analyzing data and developing a theory from the data. *Ethnography* is the study of social interactions, behaviors, and perceptions that occur within groups, teams, organizations, and communities (e.g., the culture of the Trobriand Islands; Reeves, Kuper, & Hodges, 2008). *Phenomenology* studies people's subjective experiences and interpretations of everyday experience (Giorgi, 1985). *Consensual qualitative research* (CQR; Hill, 2012) incorporates elements from the phenomenological approach (Giorgi, 1985), grounded theory (Strauss & Corbin, 1998), and comprehensive process analysis (Elliott, 1989). The essential components of CQR include (a) open-ended questions in semistructured data collection techniques; (b) several judges throughout the data analysis process; (c) consensus to arrive at judgments about the meaning of the data; (d) at least one auditor to check the work; and (e) domains, core ideas, and cross-analyses in the data analysis (Hill, 2012).

Effectiveness of Rehabilitation Counseling Services

Key Concepts

Counseling/psychotherapy, working alliance, self-efficacy, motivational interviewing (MI), vocational rehabilitation services, and supported employment are empirically supported interventions used in the rehabilitation counseling context.

I. Program Evaluation

Program evaluation is routine, systematic, deliberate collection of information gathered to determine the factors that contribute to a success of a program and what actions need to be taken to address the findings of the evaluation (Durning & Hemmer, 2010). The logic model approach (Frechtling, 2007) suggests four components of program evaluation: (a) inputs (all relevant resources for defining the current status of a program); (b) activities (a set of "treatments," strategies, innovations, or changes planned for a program); (c) outputs (indication of each activity's "product"); and (d) outcomes (report of the short-term, medium-term, and longer-range changes). There are five phases of conducting a program evaluation: needs assessment (to study whether there are problems needed to be solved in program populations), assessment of program theory (to solve problems according to a theoretical assumption), process evaluation (to monitor the program), outcome evaluation (to assess the program's impact on outcomes), and efficiency assessment (to examine whether the program is worth its cost; Cozby, 2009).

II. Effectiveness of Vocational Rehabilitation

Meta-analytic studies show that clients benefit from counseling interventions and psychotherapy (Smith & Glass, 1977; Smith, Glass, & Miller, 1980; Wampold, 2001). Smith et al.'s (1980) meta-analysis of 475 controlled outcome studies concluded that clients receiving counseling were more than 80% better off than those not receiving counseling , with an effect size of 0.85. Likewise, Wampold concluded from several meta-analysis that the efficacy of counseling/psychotherapy falls within the range of 0.75 to 0.85. Furthermore, he suggested that the efficacy of counseling/psychotherapy is 0.80, a large effect size in the behavioral and social sciences. The working alliance is also an empirically supported counseling intervention (Chan, Shaw, McMahon, Koch, & Strauser, 1997). Wampold (2001) found that at least 70% of psychotherapeutic effects are due to common factors such as working alliance, empathic listening, and goal setting. In a study investigating working alliance and employment outcomes among rehabilitation clients, employed clients had a stronger working alliance than those who were unemployed ($d = 0.73$, large effect); the stronger the working alliance, the more positive the clients' perceptions of the future ($r = .51$, large effect; Lustig, Strauser, Rice, & Rucker, 2002). MI, another empirically supported treatment, has been broadly applied to rehabilitation practice, including assisting clients in managing medical issues, facilitating adjustment to disabling health conditions, improving psychosocial functioning, and returning to work (Wagner & McMahon, 2004). A meta-analysis of 72 studies investigating the efficacy of MI, 71% of which were alcohol-, smoking-, and drug-use interventions, found a large effect size, 0.77 (large effect), right after treatment, 0.30 (medium effect) after 3 to 6 months, and 0.11 (small effect) after 12 months of follow-up. However, the effect size of alcohol- and other drug-abuse treatment outcomes, 0.26, is relatively stable at all follow-up points. A meta-analysis analyzing 25 years of studies investigating MI and substance abuse, health-related behavior, engagement in treatment, and gambling variables found a small effect size, $g = 0.22$, yet MI was conducted in a significantly shorter time frame (over 100 fewer minutes) versus cognitive behavior therapies. Moreover, studies show that MI has a longer effect with positive changes lasting more than 2 years (Lundahl, Kunz, Brownell, Tollefson, & Burke, 2010).

Skills training has been empirically shown to reduce psychiatric symptoms, and increase social skill self-efficacy, coping skills, and job search and maintenance. A meta-analysis found that the average participants in the skills training programs exceeded 82% of the control nonparticipants on the outcomes, with a large effect size of .82 (Bolton & Akridge, 1995). A secondary analysis of the 2005 Rehabilitation Services Administration case services report (RSA-911) data found that job placement, on-the-job support, maintenance, and other services (e.g., medical care for acute conditions) improved the odds for obtaining competitive employment (Dutta, Gervey, Chan, Chou, & Ditchman, 2008).

Research Ethics

Key Concepts

The 1979 Belmont Report established three basic principles for ethical research on human subjects: beneficence, respect for persons (autonomy), and justice. Beneficence refers to doing no harm (Sims, 2010). The Commission on Rehabilitation Counselor Certification (CRCC) Code of Professional Ethics for Rehabilitation Counselors states that counselors are responsible for the welfare of participants throughout the research process and that counselors should take reasonable precautions to avoid causing psychological, physical, or social harm to participants (CRCC, 2016). Safeguards must be in place to address stress related to a research study (e.g., debriefing sessions). Risks must be evaluated as to whether the potential benefit of the research outweighs the risk to the individuals involved (Cozby & Bates, 2015). According to the CRCC Code of Professional Ethics for Rehabilitation Counselors, rehabilitation counselors must inform research subjects of experimental or relatively untried procedures. Rehabilitation counselors must disclose alternative procedures that would be advantageous for research subjects, describe any limitations on confidentiality, and provide participants with researcher contact information (CRCC, 2016).

Autonomy requires researchers to ensure study subjects are given the opportunity to make conscious and informed decisions regarding research participation. The informed consent process must state that clients are free to choose whether to participate in, and are free to withdraw from, a research study without adverse consequences (CRCC, 2016). Participants must also be informed in clear and easily understood language about the purposes of a study, its risks and benefits, and their right to refuse to participate in the study or to terminate their participation in the study (Cozby & Bates, 2015). The informed consent must be given freely and without coercion and the individual must be capable of providing consent. For example, individuals with cognitive impairments and minors are not presumed capable of providing informed consent (Cozby & Bates, 2015). According to the CRCC Code of Professional Ethics for Rehabilitation Counselors, participation in research by persons unable to provide informed consent may proceed if legally authorized informed consent on behalf of the individual is obtained. Finally, the CRCC Code states that informed consent also involves notifying the research subjects of the potential target audiences to whom the research information will be disseminated (CRCC, 2016). When the methodology of the research requires that information be withheld from participants, informed consent may be compromised. In general, it is considered ethically acceptable to withhold information if doing so would not affect a participant's decision to participate. For some types of studies, it may be impossible or unnecessary to obtain informed consent (e.g., observing behavior in a public setting).

Autonomy does not necessarily preclude the use of deception in behavioral research (Cozby & Bates, 2015). However, research involving deception should not be conducted unless alternative procedures are not feasible (CRCC, 2016). In addition, if deception might cause harm to the participants, the study is not conducted, regardless of the prospective value. When deception is used, the investigator explains the reasons using deception during the debriefing (CRCC, 2016). Debriefing also includes explaining the purpose of the study, what results the study yielded, and how the results may benefit others (Cozby & Bates, 2015).

Justice requires researchers to address fairness and equity when selecting research participants (Cozby & Bates, 2015; see also Table 8.1). The Belmont Report identifies racial minorities, those who have a low socioeconomic status, those who have chronic illness, and those living in institutions as disadvantaged populations that may unfairly be recruited to participate in research with potential risks (Harrison, 1993).

These ethical principles have been formalized through federal regulations issued and updated by the U.S. Department of Health and Human Services. These regulations require every institution receiving federal funding to have an institutional review board (IRB), an agency that reviews all research conducted by an institution to ensure that it complies with federal law regarding the protection of human research subjects (Cozby & Bates, 2015). When IRB approval is required, rehabilitation counselors provide accurate information about their research proposals and obtain approval prior to conducting their research. Research is conducted in accordance with the institution's approved research protocols (CRCC, 2016). When rehabilitation counselors conduct independent research and do not have access to an IRB, they are bound to the same ethical principles and laws pertaining to the review of the plan, design, conduct, and reporting of research. Independent researchers not familiar with IRB standards should seek appropriate consultation (CRCC, 2016).

TABLE 8.1   Summary of Key Concepts of Research and Program Evaluation

Key Concept	Interpretation
Positive linear relationship	As one variable value increases, the other increases too
Negative linear relationship	As one variable value increases, the other decreases
Curvilinear relationship	As one variable value increases, the other increases and decreases
Nominal scales	Mutually exclusive categories
Ordinal scales	Ordered categories
Interval scales	Each unit has equal interval
Ratio scales	Each unit has equal interval but includes an absolute zero point
Reliability	The estimate of the consistency or stability of a measure of behavior, such as test–retest reliability, split-half reliability, Cronbach's alpha, interrater reliability
Validity	The degree to which an instrument measures what it is supposed to measure, such as construct validity, face validity, criterion-oriented validity
Central tendency	Mode, median, mean
Variability	Range, variance, SD
Normal curve	68% of scores fall between one SD above and one SD below the mean; about 95% of scores fall between two SDs above and two SDs below the mean
Z-score	A mean of zero and an SD of one
T-score	A mean of 50 and an SD of 10
Type I error (α) (0.05, 0.01)	The probability when the null hypothesis is wrongly rejected
Type II error (β)	The probability when the null hypothesis is wrongly retained
t test, ANOVA, F test	Examine differences
Effect size	The magnitude of the effect between variable-x and variable-y, or the strength of association between variables
Program evaluation research	There are four components of conducting program evaluation, namely, inputs, activities, outputs, and outcomes.

(continued)

TABLE 8.1   Summary of Key Concepts of Research and Program Evaluation (*continued*)

Key Concept	Interpretation
Seven levels of evidence	From level 1 (a systematic review or meta-analysis of all relevant RCTs or evidence-based clinical practice guidelines based on systematic reviews of RCTs or three or more RCTs of good quality that have similar results), to level 7 (the opinion of authorities and/or reports of expert committees)
Research ethics	Beneficence (do not harm), respect for persons (autonomy; study subjects are provided the opportunity to make conscious and informed decisions), and justice (fairness and equity)

ANOVA, analysis of variance; RCTs, randomized controlled trials; *SD*, standard deviation.

Multiple-Choice Questions

1. In the hierarchy of evidence, which level contains evidence from a single descriptive or qualitative study?

   A. Level 6

   B. Level 7

   C. Level 8

   D. Level 10

2. Temperature is an example of which scale?

   A. Nominal

   B. Ordinal

   C. Interval

   D. Ratio

3. Reliability means that a measure is:

   A. Correct

   B. Consistent

   C. Proven

   D. Accepted

4. Predictive, concurrent, convergent, and discriminant validity are all types of what kind of validity?

   A. Construct

   B. Face

   C. Content

   D. Criterion oriented

5. Standard deviation is the average distance from the:

   A. Mode

   B. Median

    C. Variance

    D. Mean

6. What is the most common indicator of interrater reliability?

    A. Cohen's kappa coefficient

    B. Cronbach's alpha

    C. Pearson's product-moment correlation coefficient

    D. Hershenson's gamma

7. With the normal or bell-shaped curve, what percentage of scores fall within two *SD*s above and below the mean?

    A. 68

    B. 85

    C. 95

    D. 99

8. Which common standardized score has a mean of 50 and an *SD* of 10?

    A. Scaled score

    B. *T*-score

    C. Standard score

    D. Z-score

9. Not detecting a relationship between study variables in a sample when the variables are related in the broader population is known as:

    A. Type I error

    B. Level of significance

    C. Alpha level

    D. Type II error

10. Internal validity of a research study refers to _____.

    A. Generalizability

    B. The certainty of cause-and-effect conclusions

    C. Internal consistency of measurement instruments

    D. The inclusion in the study sample of adequate numbers of participants from racial and ethnic minority groups

Answer Key

1A, 2C, 3B, 4D, 5D, 6A, 7C, 8B, 9D, 10B

Advanced Multiple-Choice Questions

1. In which research design are participants randomly assigned to groups?

    A. Single-case experimental

    B. Independent groups

    C. Repeated measures

    D. Matched pairs

2. Qualitative research collects data through:

    A. Laboratory experiments

    B. Longitudinal studies

    C. Cross-sectional studies

    D. Interviews

3. In evidence-based practice, which level of evidence has evidence from randomized control trials?

    A. 2

    B. 3

    C. 4

    D. 5

4. Meta-analyses of studies of the effectiveness of counseling show what effect size?

    A. None

    B. Small

    C. Medium

    D. Large

5. What is the strength of correlation between interpersonal skills and job performance?

    A. None

    B. Small

    C. Small to moderate

    D. Moderate to strong

6. The process of seeking informed consent operationalizes the principle of:

    A. Justice

    B. Autonomy

    C. Beneficence

    D. Nonmaleficence

7. The principle that promotes respect for persons is:
   A. Justice
   B. Autonomy
   C. Beneficence
   D. Nonmaleficence

8. The principle that promotes fairness and equity is:
   A. Justice
   B. Autonomy
   C. Beneficence
   D. Nonmaleficence

9. Which scale has an absolute zero point?
   A. Nominal
   B. Ordinal
   C. Interval
   D. Ratio

10. In a set of scores, the highest score subtracted the lowest score provides the:
    A. Variance
    B. Standard deviation
    C. Mean
    D. Range

Answer Key and Explanation of Answers

1B: In independent groups design, participants are randomly assigned to the various conditions so that each participant is in only one group.

2D: Qualitative research deals with narrative descriptions and interpretations; data are generally collected through interviews, observations, and archival data.

3A: There are five levels of evidence. Level 2 evidence is defined as strong evidence from at least one properly designed randomized-controlled trial of appropriate size.

4D: Meta-analyses of studies of the effectiveness of counseling show effect sizes ranging from 0.75 to 0.85, all of which are in the large range.

5D: Meta-analyses of the correlation between interpersonal skills and job performance range between 0.39 and 0.93; that is, they are moderately to strongly correlated.

6B: The principle of autonomy requires that researchers ensure study subjects are provided the opportunity to make conscious and informed decisions about participating in research. Informed consent must be given freely and without coercion.

7B: The basic principle of ethical research that promotes respect for persons is autonomy, which is also the right to free choice.

8A: The basic principle of ethical research that promotes fairness and equity in the selection of individuals for research is justice.

9D: Ratio scales have ordered, equal intervals, as do interval scales, but they also have an absolute zero point that represents the absence of the variable being measured.

10D: The result of subtracting the lowest score from the highest score in a set of scores is the range of that set of scores. This is the simplest measure of variability.

References

Ackley, B. J., Swan, B. A., Ladwig, G., & Tucker, S. (2008). *Evidence-based nursing care guidelines: Medical-surgical interventions*. St. Louis, MO: Mosby Elsevier.

American Educational Research Association, American Psychological Association and National Council on Measurement in Education. (2014). *Standards for educational and psychological testing*. Washington, DC: American Educational Research Association.

Bolton, B., & Akridge, R. L. (1995). A meta-analysis of skills training programs for rehabilitation clients. *Rehabilitation Counseling Bulletin, 38*(3), 262–273.

Bossuyt, P. M., Reitsma, J. B., Bruns, D. E., Gatsonis, C. A., Glasziou, P. P., Irwig, L. M., … Standards for Reporting of Diagnostic Accuracy. (2003). Towards complete and accurate reporting of studies of diagnostic accuracy: The STARD initiative. *British Medical Journal, 326*(7379), 41–44.

Centre for Reviews and Dissemination. (2009). *Systematic reviews: CRD's guidance for undertaking reviews in health care*. Retrieved from http//www.york.ac.uk/inst/crd/pdf/Systematic_Reviews.pdf

Chan, A. W., Tetzlaff, J. M., Altman, D. G., Laupacis, A., Gøtzsche, P. C., Krleža-Jerić, K., … Moher, D. (2013). SPIRIT 2013 statement: Defining standard protocol items for clinical trials. *Annals of Internal Medicine, 158*(3), 200–207.

Chan, F., Shaw, L., McMahon, B. T., Koch, L., & Strauser, D. (1997). A model for enhancing consumer-counselor working relationships in rehabilitation. *Rehabilitation Counseling Bulletin, 41*(2), 122–137.

Colquhoun, H. L., Levac, D., O'Brien, K. K., Straus, S., Tricco, A. C., Perrier, L., … Moher, D. (2014). Scoping reviews: Time for clarity in definition, methods, and reporting. *Journal of Clinical Epidemiology, 67*(12), 1291–1294.

Commission on Rehabilitation Counselor Certification. (2016). *Code of professional ethics for rehabilitation counselors*. Schaumburg, IL: Author.

Cozby, P. C. (2009). *Methods in behavioral research* (10th ed.). Fullerton, CA: McGraw-Hill.

Cozby, P. C., & Bates, S. C. (2015). *Methods in behavioral research* (12th ed.). New York, NY: McGraw-Hill.

Dijkers, M. (2015). What is a scoping review? *KT Update, 4*(1). Retrieved from http//ktdrr.org/products/update/v4n1

Durning, S. J., & Hemmer, P. A. (2010). Program evaluation. In J. Ende (Ed.), *ACP teaching internal medicine*. Philadelphia, PA: American College of Physicians.

Dutta, A., Gervey, R., Chan, F., Chou, C., & Ditchman, N. (2008). Vocational rehabilitation services and employment outcomes for people with disabilities: A United States study. *Journal of Occupational Rehabilitation, 18*(4), 326–334.

Elliott, R. (1989). Comprehensive process analysis: Understanding the change process in significant therapy events. In M. J. Packer & R. B. Addison (Eds.), *Entering the circle: Hermeneutic investigations in psychology* (pp. 165–184). Albany, NY: SUNY Press.

Frechtling, J. (2007). *Logic modeling methods in program evaluation*. San Francisco, CA: Wiley.

Giorgi, A. (1985). Sketch of a psychological phenomenological method. In A. Girogi (Ed.), *Phenomenology and psychological research* (pp. 8–22). Pittsburgh, PA: Duquesne University Press.

Glaser, B. G., & Strauss, A. L. (1967). *The discovery of grounded theory: Strategies for qualitative research*. Chicago, IL: Aldine.

Harrison, L. (1993). Issues related to the protection of human research subjects. *Journal of Neuroscience Nursing, 25*(3), 187–193.

Hayes, A. F. (2013). *Introduction to mediation, moderation, and conditional process analysis: A regression-based approach*. New York, NY: Guilford Press.

Heppner, P. P., Wampold, B. E., Owen, J., Thompson, M. N., & Wang, K. T. (2016). *Research design in counseling* (4th ed.). Boston, MA: Cengage.

Hill, C. E. (2012). *Consensual qualitative research: A practical resource for investigating social science phenomena*. Washington, DC: American Psychological Association.

Kazdin, A. E. (2016). *Methodological issues and strategies in clinical research* (4th ed.). Washington, DC: American Psychological Association.

Lundahl, B. W., Kunz, C., Brownell, C., Tollefson, D., & Burke, B. L. (2010). A meta-analysis of motivational interviewing: Twenty-five years of empirical studies. *Research on Social Work Practice, 20*(2), 137–160.

Lustig, D. C., Strauser, D. R., Rice, N. D., & Rucker, T. F. (2002). The relationship between working alliance and rehabilitation outcomes. *Rehabilitation Counseling Bulletin, 46*(1), 24–32.

Moher, D., Liberati, A., Tetzlaff, J., Altman, D. G., & PRISMA Group. (2009). Preferred reporting items for systematic reviews and meta-analyses: The PRISMA statement. *Annals of Internal Medicine, 151*(4), 264–269.

Reeves, S., Kuper, A., & Hodges, B. D. (2008). Qualitative research methodologies: Ethnography. *British Medical Journal, 337*, a1020.

Rumrill, P., & Bellini, J. (in press). *Research in rehabilitation counseling* (3rd ed.). Springfield, IL: Charles C. Thomas.

Schulz, K. F., Altman, D. G., & Moher, D. (2010). CONSORT 2010 statement: Updated guidelines for reporting parallel group randomized trials. *Journal of Pharmacology & Pharmacotherapeutics, 1*(2), 100–107.

Sims, J. M. (2010). A brief review of the Belmont Report. *Dimensions of Critical Care Nursing, 29*(4), 173–174.

Smith, M. L., & Glass, G. V. (1977). Meta-analysis of psychotherapy outcome studies. *American Psychologist, 32*(9), 752–760.

Smith, M. L., Glass, G. V., & Miller, T. I. (1980). *The benefits of psychotherapy*. Baltimore, MD: Johns Hopkins University Press.

Strauss, A., & Corbin, J. (1998). *Basics of qualitative research: Grounded theory procedures and techniques* (2nd ed.). Thousand Oaks, CA: Sage.

Stroup, D. F., Berlin, J. A., Morton, S. C., Olkin, I., Williamson, G. D., Rennie, D., … Thacker, S. B. (2000). Meta-analysis of observational studies in epidemiology: A proposal for reporting. Meta-analysis Of Observational Studies in Epidemiology (MOOSE) group. *Journal of the American Medical Association, 283*(15), 2008–2012.

Urbina, S. (2014). *Essentials of psychological testing* (2nd ed.). Hoboken, NJ: Wiley.

von Elm, E., Altman, D. G., Egger, M., Pocock, S. J., Gøtzsche, P. C., & Vandenbroucke, J. P. (2014). The Strengthening the Reporting of Observational Studies in Epidemiology (STROBE) statement: Guidelines for reporting observational studies. *International Journal of Surgery, 12*(12), 1495–1499.

Wagner, C. C., & McMahon, B. T. (2004). Motivational interviewing and rehabilitation counseling practice. *Rehabilitation Counseling Bulletin, 47*(3), 152–161.

Wampold, B. E. (2001). *The great psychotherapy debate*. Mahwah, NJ: Erlbaum.

9

Biopsychosocial Aspects of Chronic Illness and Disability

CHUNGYI CHIU, JESSICA M. BROOKS, AND CONNIE SUNG

The World Health Organization (WHO, 1946) defined ideal health *as a state of complete physical, social and mental well-being, and not merely the absence of disease or infirmity and stated that health is a resource for everyday life, not the object of living, and is a positive concept emphasizing social and personal resources as well as physical capabilities. In 2001, the WHO proposed a new model—the International Classification of Functioning, Disability and Health (ICF)—to conceptualize health, function, and disability while accounting for personal and environmental factors. The ICF is composed of two parts: function and disability and contextual factors. Function and disability include body functions and structures, activities, and participation (WHO, 2013). Contextual factors include environmental factors and personal factors. Disability, therefore, is interpreted as the consequence of health conditions (e.g., spinal cord injuries [SCIs], multiple sclerosis [MS], depression), personal traits (e.g., self-efficacy, resilience, coping), and environmental characteristics (e.g., societal attitudes, social support, assistive technology [AT]). This chapter uses the ICF as a guiding framework to cover sections related to biopsychosocial aspects of common disability types and chronic illnesses, specifically in the areas of pathology, epidemiology, daily function, psychological aspects, vocational perspectives, and social-environmental accommodations.*

Learning Objectives

By the end of this unit you should be able to:

1. Understand the basic human body systems and diseases.
2. Understand medical terminology and diagnostic abbreviations.
3. Understand the existence, onset, severity, and progression of chronic illness and disability, associated functional limitations, and accommodations.
4. Understand accommodations, modifications, and AT.

Basic Overview of the Human Body Systems and Diseases

Key Concepts

The human body has 13 systems (Falvo, 2014). The *circulatory system* pumps and channels blood, which is relevant to cardiovascular disease. The *digestive system* digests and processes food, which is relevant to gastrointestinal hemorrhage and liver disease. The *endocannabinoid system* involves appetite, pain perception, mood, memory, and motor learning, which is relevant to mood disorders and movement disorders (e.g., Parkinson's disease, Huntington's disease). The *endocrine system* regulates bodily functions such as metabolism, growth, tissue function, reproduction, sleep, and mood, which is relevant to diabetes mellitus. The *integumentary system* protects the body, which is relevant to carcinoma. The *immune system* protects against disease, which is pertinent to allergies, lupus, rheumatoid arthritis, and AIDS. The *lymphatic system* circulates lymph, which is relevant to lymphadenopathy and lymphedema. The *musculoskeletal system* provides support, stability, and movement to the body, which is relevant to conditions such as osteoporosis, tendonitis, and carpal tunnel syndrome. The *nervous system* transmits signals between body parts, which is relevant to epilepsy, amyotrophic lateral sclerosis, and Alzheimer's disease. The *reproductive system* is available to humans for reasons related to procreation, which is relevant to diseases such as ovarian and prostate cancer. The *respiratory system* takes in oxygen and expels carbon dioxide, which is pertinent to asthma and chronic obstructive pulmonary disease (COPD). The *urinary system* produces, stores, and eliminates urine, which is relevant to urinary tract infection, interstitial cystitis, and kidney stones. The *vestibular system* controls balance and special orientation, which is relevant to vestibular and balance disorders.

Common Medical Terminology and Diagnostic Abbreviations

Commonly used medical abbreviations and terminology (described in the next section) improve efficiency and accuracy in reading medical records and communicating with rehabilitation counselors and other health professionals.

Key Concepts

The most common medical abbreviations are (Felton, 2002):

ABP: arterial blood pressure	Chol: cholesterol	Dx: diagnosis
AEA: above-elbow amputation	CNS: central nervous system	e: without, or "o," "s"
	c/o: complains of	FH: family history
AFO: ankle-foot orthosis	COPD: chronic obstructive	F/U: follow-up
amb: ambulating	pulmonary disease	Fx: fracture
A/O: alert and oriented	CRD: chronic respiratory	G.I.: gastrointestinal
aph: aphasia	disease	HBP: high blood pressure
c.: with	CVA: cerebrovascular	ICF: intracellular fluid
CAD: coronary artery disease	accident	IUC: intrauterine catheter
CHD: congenital/coronary	DD: discharge diagnosis	IV: intravenous
heart disease	DM: diabetes mellitus	LBP: lower back pain

L.E.: lower extremities
L.O.C.: loss/level of
   consciousness
MA: mental age
MH: marital history
n.: nerve
NG: nasogastric tube
OBS: organic brain syndrome
OD: right eye
O/E: on examination
OHD: organic heart disease
OPD: outpatient department
OS: left eye
PNI: peripheral nerve injury

PVD: peripheral vascular
   disease
quad.: quadriplegic
RDS: respiratory distress
   syndrome
RO,R/O: rule out
ROM: range of motion
Rx: therapy, prescription
STD: sexually transmitted
   disease
Sx: symptoms
TENS: transient electric nerve
   stimulation
THR: total hip replacement

TMJ: temporomandibular
   joint
Tx: treatment
UCD,
UCHD: usual childhood
   diseases
UGI: upper gastrointestinal
   series
XR: x-rays
u/o: under observation (for),
   urine output
URI: upper respiratory
   infection
UTI: urinary tract infection

Biopsychosocial Aspects of Physical, Sensory, Psychiatric, and Developmental Disabilities and Other Medical Conditions

Rehabilitation counselors and other health professionals serve persons with a broad spectrum of physical, psychiatric, cognitive, sensory, and developmental disabilities with a variety of functional limitations and needed accommodations.

Key Concepts

I. Physical Disability

Spinal cord injury

There are approximately 240,000 to 337,000 people with SCI in the United States (National Spinal Cord Injury Statistical Center [NSCISC], 2015). The average age at injury onset is 42 years. Vehicular accidents are the most common cause of traumatic injury affecting the spinal cord and account for 39.08% of SCI, followed by falls (29.54%), acts of violence (14.41%), and sports and recreational activities (8.39%). As many as 80% of new SCI cases are males (NSCISC, 2015). SCI labeled as "complete" results in no nerve, voluntary motor, and/or sensory function below the level of the injury. Incomplete SCI, in contrast, leaves the affected individual with residual motor and/or sensory function below the level of the injury. An injury below the first thoracic spinal nerve causes paraplegia, whereas an injury above the first thoracic spinal nerve results in quadriplegia (or sometimes called *tetraplegia*). People with injuries at cervical levels 1–4 (C1–C4) need respiratory assistance. For people with an injury at the C5 level, gross movement of the upper extremities is possible (e.g., bending the arm at elbow, holding a light object between the thumb and finger, independently operating an electric wheelchair). People with an injury at the C6 level can eat independently, write with hand splints, dress with the aid of special orthotic equipment, and use a manual wheelchair. People with an injury at the C7 to C8 levels can be almost completely independent with some environmental accommodations. People with an injury at the thoracic levels 1–3 (T1–T3) need support to maintain an upright position. People with an injury at the T7–T12 levels may be able to walk with long leg braces. People with an injury at the sacral level (S1–S4) may still have some impaired function in bowel and bladder. Potential complications associated with SCI include pressure sores (decubitus ulcers), spasticity, contractures, osteoporosis, chronic pain, cardiovascular complications (e.g., thrombophlebitis, pulmonary embolism, orthostatic hypotension), autonomic dysreflexia, pneumonia, urinary tract and bowel complications, diaphoresis (profuse sweating), and paresthesia (abnormal painful sensations below the level of injury).

SCI can cause drastic changes in daily life, including in the domains of employment and social relationships (Ottomanelli & Lind, 2009). The employment rate for people with SCI between 16 and 59 years of age at injury is 58.8%. On average, 8 years after injury, the employment rate for people with paraplegic SCI is 34.4%, with quadriplegic SCI at 24.3% (NSCISC, 2015). These life changes may cause altered self-concept, low self-esteem, and depression (Arango-Lasprilla, Ketchum, Starkweather, Nicholls, & Wilk, 2011). Persons with SCI need modifications in daily routine and in personal, social, and environmental contexts (e.g., transportation, building access, social support) (Falvo, 2014). Addressing issues related to sexual needs and changes is also important to psychosocial adjustment (Torriani, Britto, da Silva, de Oliveira, & Carvalho, 2014). Accommodations for activities of daily living (ADLs) may include a personal attendant to assist with basic needs for toileting, grooming, or eating. Accommodations for employment sites may include a height-adjustable desk or table, page turners and book holders, accessible parking, or arrangements for a service dog in the workplace (Carter Batiste & Loy, 2013).

Traumatic brain injury

Traumatic brain injury (TBI) occurs with unexpected physical damage to the brain that is caused by external or internal forces (Schwartz & Wild, 2014). The leading cause of TBI in young children and older adults is falls. In adolescents and young adults, motor vehicle accidents, especially those involving alcohol intoxication, are the leading cause, followed by violent assaults and suicide attempts (Schwartz, 2002). The major types of brain injuries are closed head injuries, blast injuries, open head injuries, and atraumatic brain injuries (Schwartz & Wild, 2014). With closed head injuries, brain contusions (bruises of the brain) are caused by the *coup*, or initial impact of the brain against the skull, which then causes the *contre coup* (when the side of the brain opposite the initial impact rebounds to hit the skull). The *Glasgow Coma Scale* (GCS) is a classification system used to determine the seriousness of brain injury by assessing the level of responsiveness of the patient, which yields a score from 3 (more severe injury) to 15 (least severe injury) (Falvo, 2014). Most often occurring during active duty military deployment, blast injuries are caused by explosions, which lead to injuries in multiple body systems such as the brain, lungs, and ears (Schwartz & Wild, 2014). An open head injury is caused by gunshots or stabbing incidents. Such an injury induces bleeding, localized brain damage, and even a state of coma. Finally, atraumatic brain injury occurs due to internal causes such as infection or stroke.

TBI impacts a wide range of daily functioning areas in the affected person's life, with any combination of physical, cognitive, and psychosocial manifestations (Falvo, 2014). Physical sequelae include balance problems, fatigue, pain, weakness on one side of the body (hemiparesis), uneven gait, movement coordination/gait problems (ataxia), motor planning problems (apraxia), decreased motor speed, seizure disorders, and sensory deficits. Cognitive sequelae include impairments in attention and concentration, memory, visual or auditory processing, verbal reasoning, critical thinking, language, and awareness. Psychosocial sequelae include personality changes, emotional lability, depression, flat affect, substance use/misuse, low frustration tolerance, impulsivity, disinhibition, and lack of initiative (Schwartz, 2002). A sustained brain injury requires immediate medical attention to stabilize the person and prevent further injury. Depending on the type and severity of injury, treatment plans may include imaging tests, physical therapy, speech therapy, occupational therapy, cognitive remediation, and AT for cognition (Schwartz & Wild, 2014). Possible work accommodations include written instructions, assignment of one task at a time, or additional time to perform assigned tasks (Job Accommodation Network [JAN], 2013a).

Stroke (cerebral vascular accident)

Strokes are the fifth leading cause of death in the United States, with about 800,000 people surviving and recovering from strokes (Mozzafarian et al., 2015). Strokes are caused by decreased blood flow and subsequent inadequate oxygen supply to part of the brain, leading to tissue damage, which causes neurological manifestations that can affect a number of body functions. As many as 34% of people hospitalized for strokes are younger than 65 years of age (Hall, Levant, & DeFrances, 2012). Atrial fibrillation is an independent risk factor for strokes, increasing risks by approximately fivefold. High blood pressure and high cholesterol are other important risk factors (Centers for Disease Control and Prevention [CDC], 2012). It is estimated that 87% of strokes are deemed to be ischemic; they occur when blood flow to the brain is blocked. A common cause of an ischemic stroke is a blood clot (thrombus) formed from inside an artery. A hemorrhagic stroke is due to the rupture of a blood vessel, causing intracranial hemorrhage. Individuals who experience strokes on the left side of the brain have manifestations that affect the right side of the body. The manifestations of right-sided brain damage include left-sided paralysis, spatial-perceptual deficits, quick impulsive behavior, and performance memory deficits. The manifestations of left-sided brain damage include right-sided paralysis, speech language deficits, slow and cautious behavior, language memory deficits, and problem-solving deficits. People with strokes may experience ataxia (inability to control the accuracy of muscle movement or limb position), apraxia (inability to carry out purposeful, coordinated voluntary motor skill movements), paresthesia (uncomfortable sensations such as tingling, burning, or pain), hemianopsia (inability to perceive half of the visual field), alexia (difficulty reading), agraphia (difficulty writing), agnosia (difficulty recognizing once-familiar images or objects), dysarthria (impaired coordination and accuracy of movement of the muscles, lips, tongue, or other parts of the speech mechanism), Broca's aphasia (nonfluent aphasia, articulation problems, word-finding difficulties [dysnomia]), Wernicke's aphasia (fluent aphasia, effortless speech but reduced information content), and global aphasia (inability to use and understand language). Complications associated with strokes include spasticity, contractures, poststroke seizures, central pain syndrome, shoulder pain, dysphasia (difficulty swallowing), problems with bowel and bladder control, emotional liability, and depression.

People with strokes may need to cope with extensive psychosocial issues such as loss of employment, unfulfilled social and leisure activities, emotional problems, disruption of self and identity, and diminished life satisfaction (Morris, 2011). The return-to-work rate following participation in vocational rehabilitation programs range from 12% to 49% (Baldwin & Brusco, 2011). Critical issues for return-to-work for stroke survivors include addressing depression and anxiety, coping with remaining ability and poststroke limitations, maintaining supportive relationships and good communication, and overcoming fatigue. Potential accommodations for persons experiencing motor limitations include mobility aids (canes, crutches, walkers, rolling walkers with seats, wheelchairs, and electric scooters), grooming/eating aids, and communication aids. For those experiencing cognitive impairments, certain accommodations may involve re-learning how to engage in conversation (e.g., reduce distractions in the work area, provide space enclosures), staying organized and meeting deadlines, handling memory deficits (e.g., tape meetings; use notebooks, calendars, or adhesive notes to record information for easy retrieval), handling problem-solving deficits (e.g., provide picture diagrams of problem-solving techniques), and maintaining stamina during the workday (e.g., use flexible scheduling, take longer or more frequent work breaks, adopt a self-paced workload) (Carter Batiste & Loy, 2013; JAN, n.d.).

Multiple sclerosis

MS is an inflammatory demyelinating disease of unknown origin. There are about 400,000 Americans diagnosed with MS, with disproportionately higher numbers of women and Whites. MS is caused by a disturbed regulation of the immune system. The symptoms depend on the severity of the immune reaction as well as the location and extent of the plaques. These plaques appear primarily in the brainstem, cerebellum, spinal cord, optic nerves, and white matter of the brain (National Institute of Neurological Disorders and Stroke [NINDS], 2015). MS is the most disabling neurological disease of young adults (NINDS, 2015). It is usually first diagnosed at the age of 20 to 40 years. Approximately 85% of affected people have relapsing-remitting MS, characterized by an unpredictable course of exacerbations and remissions. Approximately 15% of patients have primary progressive MS, characterized by a gradual physical decline with no noticeable remissions. Secondary progressive MS begins with a relapsing-remitting MS, followed by a later primary progressive MS. Progressive relapsing MS is characterized by a steady progress of disease with occasional exacerbations along the way. The first symptoms include vision problems, weak/stiff muscles (often with painful muscle spasms), tingling, numbness, difficulty walking, bladder control problems, and dizziness. The later symptoms include mental or physical fatigue, mood changes, declined cognitive function, and difficulty making decisions, planning, or prioritizing at work or in private life. Potential side effects of medications such as beta interferon drugs to slow down the relapsing symptoms include flu-like symptoms, such as fever, chills, muscle aches, and fatigue.

The unpredictable progress of MS and gradually worsening impairments can cause significant stress, interfering with attempts to adjust and live well with disability (Foley, 2016). It is therefore important to manage psychosocial factors in people with MS. For instance, state of mind and mood may impact a person's overall well-being and function, affect self-efficacy to cope with MS, impair cognitive function, and cause depression. Social support is also critical to maintaining and improving health-related quality of life in persons with MS (Costa, Sá, & Calheiros, 2012). Half of the people stop working within the first 5 years of being diagnosed, with only about 30% to 45% employed (Rumrill, 2015). For people with MS and cognitive impairments, potential job accommodations may include being given written job instructions when possible, reducing job stress, and allowing for periodic rest breaks to reorient. The accommodations for symptoms of fatigue/weakness may involve reducing or eliminating physical exertion and workplace stress, scheduling periodic rest breaks away from the workstation, and allowing for a flexible work schedule and flexible use of leave time. The accommodations for persons with issues related to heat sensitivity may include reducing worksite temperature, wearing a cooling vest or other cooling clothing, or using a fan/air-conditioner at the workstation. Last, for persons with MS experiencing mobility impairments, potential accommodations may include modifying the worksite to make it accessible, providing a parking space close to the worksite, and providing an accessible entrance (Carter Batiste, 2013).

Chronic pain

Throughout the world, nearly one out of three persons are impacted by chronic pain (Du et al., 2011). To diagnose pain as chronic instead of acute, pain must persist for 3 to 6 months or longer than the expected healing time (Institute of Medicine [IOM], 2011). The etiology of chronic pain can be influenced by numerous risk factors, including genetic predisposition (e.g., migraine), unknown cause (e.g., fibromyalgia), disability (e.g., MS), chronic disease (e.g., cancer), age (e.g., arthritis), postsurgical outcome (e.g., severed nerves), or injury (e.g., back pain) (IOM, 2011). The most common types of chronic pain include low back pain, arthritis, carpal tunnel syndrome, complex regional pain syndrome, fibromyalgia syndrome, and headaches (Du, Lindberg, & Bluestein, 2014). Low back pain has affected nearly 60% to 80% of all individuals in the United States at some point in their lives; however, in the majority of people with low back pain, symptoms resolve spontaneously within 1 month of onset (Gharibo & Khan, 2011). Conditions of arthritis such as osteoarthritis and rheumatic arthritis (RA) cause pain for individuals in single or multiple joints with a progressive disease course (Du et al., 2014). Carpal tunnel syndrome is a narrowing of the tunnels surrounding the median nerve in the wrist, which then compresses nerves and causes pain and paresthesia (a tingling, pricking sensation) in the hand (Falvo, 2014). Complex regional pain syndrome is a neuropathic pain syndrome that causes sensitivity to touch, tissue swelling, burning pain, excessive sweating, and changes in bone and skin (Du et al., 2014). Fibromyalgia syndrome is diagnosed primarily in women and is characterized by symptoms of persistent and widespread musculoskeletal pain as well as a decreased pain threshold and multiple tender points, fatigue, stiffness, sleep disturbances, emotional distress, and cognitive difficulties (Arnold et al., 2008; Wolfe et al., 2010). Individuals with headaches or migraines have severe pain from different origins, including chronic stress, diet, or secondary symptoms of other disorders (Du et al., 2014).

Treatment for chronic pain disorders should involve a multidisciplinary approach and begin as soon as possible following the time of injury (Gharibo & Khan, 2011). Effective pain-management programs provide medical intervention, physical therapy, occupational therapy, psychological treatment such as cognitive behavioral therapy, and vocational rehabilitation (McCarberg & Passik, 2005). Unfortunately, many clinicians use only medication as the primary treatment, and the major medication categories include anti-inflammatories, narcotic analgesics, nonnarcotic analgesics, muscle relaxants, and antidepressant; oral administration, injections, and implanted devices are used to deliver medications (Du et al., 2014). However, pharmacological treatment rarely eliminates chronic pain completely, and there are issues with long-term use of pain medication (Turk & McCarberg, 2005). For example, the permanent use of certain medications can increase risks for tolerance, tolerability, drug diversion, and adverse reactions, including neurotoxicity (Turk & McCarberg, 2005). Potential accommodations could focus on depression and anxiety (e.g., developing strategies to deal with work problems before they arise), fatigue and weakness (e.g., reducing or eliminating physical exertion and workplace stress), and muscle pain and stiffness (e.g., implementing an ergonomic workstation design) (Loy, 2015b).

II. Sensory Disability

Visual impairment

The Social Security Administration and other government agencies have adopted definitions by the WHO (2014b) to set standards to determine qualification for government services and benefits for vision impairment. *Functionally blind* is defined by individuals who are not able to perceive light. *Legal blindness* is based on a central visual acuity of 20/200 or less in the better eye with the best possible correction or a restriction in the visual field of 20° or less in the widest meridian of the better eye. *Visually impaired or partially sighted* refers to those with a best-corrected visual acuity of 20/70 to 20/180 in the better eye or a peripheral field of vision between 21° and 140°. *Fully sighted* describes people with a best-corrected visual acuity of 20/40 or better in the best eye (Takeshita, Langman, & Brod, 2009). Retinal hemorrhages occur secondary to diabetes, retinal tears and detachments, retinopathy, Stargardt's disease, retinitis pigmentosa, macular degeneration, and other retinal disorders. Persons with central retinal problems have blurred sight, poor color vision, reduced contrast perception, and sensitivity to light. Peripheral retinal problems cause difficulties with mobility, reduced night vision, and extreme sensitivity to light and glare. Retinal diseases, such as retinitis pigmentosa and complete retinal detachments, can result in total blindness. Abnormalities of the optic nerve, including glaucoma, optic nerve hypoplasia, optic nerve atrophy, and systemic illnesses (e.g., MS, brain tumors, increased intracranial pressure), are diagnostic of eye disease. Eye injuries and trauma to the head are also causes of optic nerve damage. Optic nerve disorders lead to varying degrees of blurred sight, color blindness, peripheral and central visual field defects, and total blindness (Takeshita et al., 2009). Glaucoma or retinitis pigmentosa creates an overall peripheral field defect, leaving only a small central field of vision intact. A cataract is a clouding that can occur in any and all parts of the lens and can result in decreased visual acuity, loss of contrast, and glare. Macular degeneration is one of the leading causes of visual impairments in older adults. Persons who lose vision later in life may find it more difficult to adapt and may experience grief and despair over the loss, become overly dependent on others, feel insecure in new situations, and avoid social interaction. People with visual impairment may have difficulty with social interaction because much of communication involves visual, nonverbal cues (Falvo, 2009). For persons with no vision, accommodations such as auditory versions of printed documents, documents formatted in Braille, and document readers such as optical character-recognition software may be useful. For persons with low vision, a closed-circuit television system that magnifies text, information in large print, magnifying devices, and frequent breaks to rest the eyes can be helpful accommodations. For persons with light sensitivity, lower-wattage overhead lights, full-spectrum lighting and/or filters, and flicker-free lighting can be useful accommodations (Loy, 2013).

Hearing impairment

As with many health conditions, hearing loss severity may range from a very mild loss to profound loss. However, not all definitions of hearing loss rely exclusively on numeric data, using functional self-reports or observations of hearing ability instead. As a result, both medical and cultural definitions related to hearing loss exist. Most *medical definitions* of hearing loss rely on the average of audiometric test results. In general, six levels of hearing loss are classified by sensitivity thresholds: normal hearing (0–25 dB), mild hearing loss (26–40 dB), mild-to-moderate hearing loss (41–55 dB), moderate hearing loss (56–70 dB), severe hearing loss (71–90 dB), and profound hearing loss (> 90 dB) (Saladin & Hansmann, 2009). People with hearing in the mild to moderate categories are considered "hard of hearing," whereas those with hearing loss in the severe and profound categories are considered "Deaf." *Cultural definitions* of Deafness, however, are grounded in personal choices about self-identification and language use. Thus, an individual may be identified as culturally Deaf, although he or she may only have a mild or moderate hearing loss from an audiological standpoint. The converse may also be true; a person may have an audiologically profound hearing loss but not identify with Deaf culture (Saladin & Hansmann, 2009). Deafness and hearing loss occur due to a wide variety of genetic, obstructive, neural, age-related, and environmental factors. There are four types of hearing loss: conductive (damage involving the outer or middle ear; e.g., Treacher Collins syndrome), sensorineural (damage involving the inner ear [cochlea] and/or auditory nerve), mixed (both conductive and sensorineural component), and central (damage along the auditory pathway or in the brain itself) (Eng & Lerner, 2011). *Presbycusis* describes progressive sensorineural hearing loss due to the aging process. *Ménière's disease* results from a cochlear lesion and is characterized by fluctuating sensorineural hearing and vestibular symptoms (e.g., vertigo, nausea, tinnitus, and fullness of the affected ear).

Medical interventions are used in conductive or mixed hearing loss, but most sensorineural hearing loss does not respond to medical or surgical intervention. American Sign Language may be the primary communication method used by persons who are severely hearing impaired; however, speech reading (lip reading) is ineffective as a stand-alone tool as up to two thirds of English speech sounds are not visible. Treatment and management of hearing loss is vital. The most common hearing-management method involves the use of assistive listening devices (ALDs) and telecommunication devices for the deaf (TDDs). ALDs include hearing aids and cochlear implants, whereas TDDs allow the individual with hearing impairment to send and receive typed messages to other TDD users via a telephone line (Eng & Lerner, 2011). In addition to daily life accommodations such as closed-caption decoders for television, flashing smoke detectors, and vibrator alarm beds, workplace accommodations may include the use of qualified interpreters, signaling devices, amplified telephones, flashing lights and alarms, enhanced lighting, vibrating pagers, and modified acoustics (JAN, 2013c).

III. Psychiatric Disability

Psychotic disorders

Psychotic disorders such as schizophrenia impact approximately 1% of a given population (American Psychiatric Association [APA], 2000). There is no known cause for schizophrenia, although it is likely due to interactions among genetic and environmental factors (Jarskog, Miyamoto, & Lieberman, 2007). According to the *Diagnostic and Statistical Manual of Mental Disorders* (5th ed.; *DSM-5*; APA, 2013), criteria for a diagnosis of schizophrenia include delusions, hallucinations, disorganized speech, grossly disorganized or catatonic behavior, and negative symptoms such as lack of emotional expression (affective flattening), poverty of speech (alogia), and lack of motivation (avolition). Delusions are erroneous beliefs involving a misinterpretation of perceptions or experiences. Hallucinations are perceptual distortions that can occur in any sensory modality such as gustatory (taste), visual, olfactory (smell), and touch (tactile), but auditory hallucinations are the most common. Disorganized symptoms of schizophrenia can appear in both the behavioral domain (e.g., unpredictable agitation, difficulties performing ADLs) and the language domain (e.g., loose associations, use of neologisms). Individuals with schizophrenia may experience impairments in verbal and nonverbal memory, working memory, attention, executive functioning, and processing speed.

Within the *DSM-5*, individuals with psychotic disorders are categorized along a gradient of severity for psychopathology from schizotypal personality traits (schizotypal personality disorder) to a brief psychotic episode (schizophreniform) to schizophrenia or to schizoaffective disorder (Peterson & Hong, 2014). If an individual experiences features of schizophrenia and a co-occurring affective disorder such as depression and/or mania, the individual is diagnosed with schizoaffective disorder (APA, 2013). Although there is no cure, individuals can recover and live well with a mental illness. For optimal management of psychotic disorders, both pharmacological and psychosocial interventions are recommended. Pharmacological treatment involves the use of antipsychotic medications that have significant side effects such as tardive dyskinesia, which causes involuntary stereotyped movements of the mouth and face. Other side effects include hypotension, tremors of the arms, rigidity in the extremities, listlessness (akinesia), internal listlessness (akathisia), dry mouth, blurred vision, sexual dysfunction, and weight gain (Kukla & Bond, 2011). Evidence-based programs of psychosocial treatment include assertive community treatment, individual placement and support, social skills training, and family systems–based psychotherapy (Drake, Bond, & Becker, 2012). Without family support and effective mental health services, individuals with disorders such as schizophrenia are faced with even lower rates of employment and with financial problems (Peterson & Hong, 2014). Possible work accommodations for individuals with psychotic disorders include allowing for a flexible scheduling, reducing work distractions, providing a mentor for guidance, and using task lists (Loy & Whetzel, 2015).

Personality disorders

Personality traits are considered longer term in nature than other mental health disorders, with personality disorders associated with persistent, inflexible ways of thinking of oneself and others that adversely affect functioning in social and work settings (APA, 2013). Personality disorders fall within 10 distinct types: paranoid, schizoid, schizotypal, antisocial, borderline, histrionic, narcissistic, avoidant, dependent, and obsessive-compulsive. Previously in the *Diagnostic and Statistical Manual of Mental Disorders* (4th ed., text rev.; *DSM-IV-TR*; APA, 2000), these types were organized into three clusters (Clusters A, B, and C) based on descriptive similarities. Cluster A included paranoid, schizoid, and schizotypal personality disorders, and individuals diagnosed with any of these would often appear to have odd or eccentric traits. Cluster B included antisocial, borderline, histrionic, and narcissistic personality disorders, and individuals diagnosed with any of these would often have dramatic, emotional, or erratic traits. Cluster C included avoidant, dependent, and obsessive-compulsive personality disorders, and individuals diagnosed with any of these would have anxious or fearful traits (APA, 2000). Certain personality disorders predispose an individual to an increased risk of developing another psychiatric disorder, complicating treatment (Peterson & Hong, 2014). Individuals with personality disorders often have no insight into their condition, which interferes with treatment options such as medication or psychosocial interventions such as dialectical behavioral therapy (Bohus et al., 2004). Possible work accommodations for individuals with personality disorders include developing clear expectations for responsibilities, permitting telephone calls to health care providers during work hours, or allowing the employee to work from home and/or have a flexible work schedule (JAN, 2015d).

Trauma- and stressor-related disorders

The category of trauma- and stressor-related disorders is new to the *DSM-5*, and it includes disorders that share in common the exposure to traumatic events and subsequent stressful reactions (Peterson & Hong, 2014). The three most common disorders in this category include adjustment disorder, acute stress disorder, and posttraumatic stress disorder (PTSD). Adjustment disorder is caused by a significant life-changing event, resulting in a state of distress and emotional disturbance such as depression or anxiety. Acute stress disorder is a severe reaction to a stressful event; the reaction lasts approximately 1 month, which is shorter in length than in PTSD (WHO, 2014a). PTSD develops in response to a traumatic event in which the individual witnessed, experienced, or was confronted with actual or threatened death or serious injury or a threat to the physical integrity of themselves or someone else (Peterson & Hong, 2014). Symptoms of PTSD may include feelings of detachment, lack of interest in social or daily activities, and reexperiencing of the event through nightmares. An individual with PTSD may avoid stimuli associated with the traumatic event and experience persistent symptoms of increased arousal, hypervigilance, insomnia, irritability, emotional outbursts, concentration difficulties, and exaggerated startle response (WHO, 2014a). Pharmacological treatment (e.g., antidepressants, antianxiety, blood pressure, and antipsychotic medications) and cognitive behavioral therapy have been proved to be useful in helping individuals with trauma- and stressor-related disorders to manage the body's reaction to stress and symptoms. Workplace accommodations may include reducing work-related stressors by allowing a flexible work environment or schedule (JAN, 2015e).

IV. Developmental Disability

Autism spectrum disorders

According to the *DSM-5*, autism spectrum disorders (ASD) are a group of neurodevelopmental disorders characterized by persistent deficits in social communication (e.g., initiating/sustaining conversations), impairments in social interactions (e.g., maintaining friendships), repetitive patterns of behaviors, restricted interests or activities, and the potential for sensory sensitivities (APA, 2013). When the *DSM-5* came into effect in May 2013, specific subcategories of ASD (e.g., Asperger's syndrome [AS] or Pervasive Developmental Disorders, Not Otherwise Specified) were eliminated and characteristics were included within the broader category of ASD. The prevalence of ASD has been steadily on the rise, with recent estimates suggesting that as many as 1 in 45 children have ASD in the United States (Zablotsky, Black, Maenner, & Schieve, 2015). This statistic represents a substantial increase from previous estimates of 1 of 68 in 2013 and 1 of 150 children in 2000 (CDC, 2014). ASD occur more often among boys, with a 4-to-1 ratio of boys to girls. Although the incidence of autism appears to be on the rise, it is unclear whether the growing number of diagnoses shows a real increase or improved detection. Possible reasons for increases in prevalence and incidence include (a) changes in diagnostic criteria; (b) variations in methods used in studies; (c) increased awareness among professionals, parents, and the general public; (d) the growth of specialist services; (e) probable causes and relation to age of onset; (f) association of autism conditions with other developmental or physical disorders; and (g) a possible true increase in numbers. Most cases of ASD are thought to be the result of a polygenic disorder (Gupta & State, 2007). In addition, likely environmental factors are interacting with genetic factors; however, the exact cause is unknown. Many people with ASD have comorbid psychiatric diagnoses, including anxiety disorder, depression, and attention deficit hyperactivity disorder (ADHD). Additional comorbid disorders include intellectual disability, sleep epilepsy, sleep problems, and gastrointestinal problems. In general, pharmacological treatment of persons with ASD has had limited success, with most drug treatments focusing on the reduction or alleviation of disruptive behaviors. It has been reported that approximately 70% of children who are older than age of 8 and who have been diagnosed with ASD receive some form of psychoactive medication in a given year.

The term *spectrum* refers to the wide range of symptoms, skills, and levels of impairment or disability that affect persons with ASD. Some persons are mildly impaired by their symptoms, whereas others are severely disabled. The trajectory of ASD is varied. Some persons lose skills over time and others reach a plateau in adolescence, while many persons may display patterns of continued development into adulthood (LeBlanc, Riley, & Goldsmith, 2008). Certain people with ASD have a higher capacity for functioning and may be labeled as "eccentric intellectuals" because they may tend to speak their mind and make insensitive remarks in social situations. These persons also tend to have long-standing difficulties in nonverbal expression, avoid mutual gaze, lack gestures, and have diminished facial expression. They may misunderstand the reactions of other people and lack empathy. There is also a lack of desire to share enjoyment, interests, and achievements with other people and a preference for solitary activities. In general, even when persons with ASD develop friendships, there is often more reported loneliness when compared with their counterparts without ASD. Although high-functioning individuals with ASD are more likely to report having friendships than those with less developed skills, their relationships often focus on common interests rather than social interactions. Besides difficulties with friendships, there is an overall reduction in participation in social and recreational activities and limited interest in planning for the future (LeBlanc et al., 2008).

For persons with ASD interested in pursuing employment options, potential accommodations may include emotional support (e.g., using coworkers as mentors), interactions with coworkers (e.g., providing training to coworkers), consideration of sensory sensitivity (e.g., sound/noise and light sensitivity), and visual support (e.g., visual schedule, pictures, images, other visual aids) (Whetzel, 2013a).

Intellectual disability

Intellectual disability (formerly known as *mental retardation*; an equivalent term for the *ICD-11* [WHO, 2017] diagnosis of Intellectual Developmental Disorders) is defined as significant limitations in both intellectual functioning and adaptive behavior (expressed in everyday social and practical skills) with onset during the developmental period (American Association on Intellectual and Developmental Disabilities, 2011; APA, 2013). It includes intellectual deficits and difficulty functioning in daily life in conceptual, social, and practical domains. The conceptual domain includes skills in language, reading, writing, math, reasoning, knowledge, and memory. The social domain refers to empathy, social judgment, interpersonal communication skills, the ability to make and retain friendships, and similar capacities. The practical domain centers on self-management in areas such as personal care, job responsibilities, money management, recreation, and organizing school and work tasks.

Intellectual disabilities have many different etiologies and may be seen as a final common pathway of various pathological processes that affect the central nervous system. Prior to the publication of *DSM-5* in 2013, diagnostic criteria for mental retardation required that a person score approximately two standard deviations below their expected IQ compared with same-age peers on standardized IQ tests (Full Scale Intellectual Quotient/IQ score ≤ 70). In the *DSM-5*, IQ scores have been deemphasized. There is no longer a "cut-off" score or threshold for establishing a diagnosis. Rather, scaled IQ scores are evaluated in the context of a person's entire "clinical picture." The rationale for this change was that scaled IQ scores represent approximations of conceptual functioning and may be insufficient in assessing reasoning in real-life situations and mastery of practical tasks within conceptual, social, and practical domains. As a result, although IQ scores are still relevant and important in assessing the level of intellectual disability, health professionals must consider the overall ability or impairment that impacts adaptive functioning (e.g., communication, social participation, independent living) across home, school, and recreation environments (APA, 2013). Intellectual disability is classified into four severity levels: mild, moderate, severe, and profound. The various levels of severity are defined on the basis of adaptive functioning (not IQ scores) because it is adaptive functioning that determines the level of supports as well as the type and amount of interventions required (Table 9.1).

Approximately 3% of the school-aged population are identified as having intellectual disability. Although up to 50% of cases of mental retardation have no known or recognizable etiology, there are many known causes of the condition. When physicians rule out specific syndromes and causes, they often cite other prenatal (before birth; e.g., Down's syndrome and phenylketonuria, chronic maternal illnesses, maternal use of alcohol, drugs, tobacco, maternal infections, and viruses), perinatal (during birth; e.g., extreme prematurity, cephalopelvic disproportion, asphyxia, hypoglycemia, infection, blood type diseases), and postnatal (after; e.g., malnutrition, acquired TBI, meningitis, encephalitis, chemical substances, seizure disorders, toxic-metabolic disorders, and environmental deprivation).

TABLE 9.1 Describing the Severity of Intellectual Disability

Severity	Conceptual Domain	Social Domain	Practical Domain
Mild	Preschoolers may show no obvious conceptual differences. School-aged children show difficulties in acquiring academic skills (e.g., reading, writing, arithmetic, telling time, using money). Abstract thinking and planning may be impaired; thinking tends to be concrete.	Communication, conversation, and language are more concrete or immature than the skills of peers. The child may have difficulty accurately understanding the social cues of others. There may be difficulties regulating emotion and behavior compared with peers.	The child may function in an age-expected manner with regard to personal care. In adolescence, assistance may be needed to perform more complex daily living tasks such as shopping, cooking, and managing money.
Moderate	Preschoolers' language and preacademic skills develop slowly. School-aged children show slow progress in academic skills. Academic skill development is usually at the elementary school level.	The child shows marked differences in social and communicative skills compared with peers. Spoken language is simplistic and concrete. Social judgment and decision making are limited. Friendships with peers are often affected by social or communicative deficits.	The child needs more time and practice learning self-care skills, such as eating, dressing, toileting, and hygiene, than peers. Household skills can be acquired by adolescence with ample practice.
Severe	The child generally has little understanding of written language or numbers. Caretakers must provide extensive support for problem solving throughout life.	There are limited spoken language skills with simplistic vocabulary and grammar. Speech may be single words/phrases. The child understands simple speech and gestures. Relationships are with family members and other familiar people.	The child needs ongoing support for all activities of daily living: eating, dressing, bathing, elimination. Caregivers must supervise at all times. Some youths show challenging behaviors, such as self-injury.
Profound	Conceptual skills generally involve the physical world rather than symbols (e.g., letters, numbers). Some visual spatial skills, such as matching and sorting, may be acquired with practice. Co-occurring physical problems may greatly limit functioning.	The child has limited understanding of symbolic communication. The child may understand some simple instructions and gestures. Communication is usually through nonverbal, nonsymbolic means. Relationships are usually with family members and other familiar people. Co-occurring physical problems may greatly limit functioning.	The child is dependent on others for all aspects of physical care, health, and safety, although participation may occur in some aspects of self-care. Some youths show challenging behaviors, such as self-injury. Co-occurring physical problems may greatly limit functioning.

For school-aged children or adults with intellectual disabilities who are interested in employment, accommodations in the workplace may involve assistance with reading (e.g., providing pictures), writing (e.g., use of a scribe), memory (e.g., prompting with verbal cues), calculations (e.g., using talking calculators), or organization (e.g., using color coding) (JAN, 2013d).

Epilepsy

Epilepsy is one of the most common chronic neurological disorders that involves recurrent and unprovoked seizures. Nerve cell activity in the brain becomes disrupted, causing seizures or periods of unusual behavior, sensations, and sometimes loss of consciousness. The word *epilepsy* is derived from the Greek word meaning "to be seized" and is a generic term that refers to a wide variety of seizure conditions. Nearly 10% of persons may have a single unprovoked seizure in the course of a lifetime. However, the incident of a single seizure does not mean that the person has epilepsy. At least two unprovoked seizures are generally required for an epilepsy diagnosis. There are 2.2 million people in the United States and more than 65 million people worldwide with a diagnosis of epilepsy. About 1 in 26 people in the United States develop a seizure disorder. Seizure symptoms can vary widely. The extent to which seizures affect brain functioning depends on both the duration of the seizure and its location within the brain. Some people with epilepsy simply stare blankly for a few seconds during a seizure, whereas others repeatedly twitch the arms or legs. Consequently, some seizures impair brain functioning slightly, whereas others result in a complete cessation of normal activities. Direct causes of epilepsy include TBI, birth trauma, anoxia (insufficient oxygen), brain tumors, infectious diseases in a pregnant woman, parasitic infections, vascular diseases affecting the brain's blood vessels, and substance abuse. Seizures are generally classified through a comprehensive review of clinical symptoms and supplemented by EEG and sometimes visual recording. There are two major types of seizures: generalized seizures that affect both cerebral hemispheres and partial (focal) seizures that affect a specific part of one cerebral hemisphere. The most common form of generalized seizure is the generalized tonic–clonic (grand mal) seizure, which occurs in only about 10% of the epilepsy population. This type of seizure involves two stages: the tonic stage, during which the body becomes rigid (tonic) for a period of seconds, and then the clonic stage, during which the individual begins to experience a series of rhythmic jerking (clonic) and convulsive movements (Fraser, Miller, & Johnson, 2011). This type of seizure usually lasts between 1 and 3 minutes, but when it lasts more than 10 minutes or when the individual has several seizures within 10 minutes and does not regain consciousness, it is known as *status epilepticus,* which is a medical emergency. The other commonly known type of generalized seizure is the absence (petit mal) seizure, which involves up to 5% of epilepsy cases. This type of seizure usually lasts only a few seconds and involves a brief disruption of consciousness (usually 10–20 seconds) and autonomic symptoms such as dilated pupils and mild rhythmic movements of the eyelids but sometimes may involve blank stares.

Partial seizures are divided into three categories: simple partial seizures with unimpaired consciousness, complex partial seizures with impaired consciousness, and partial seizures evolving into secondarily generalized seizures. Approximately 60% of those with epilepsy have seizures classified as partial. Simple partial seizures may involve motor, sensory, autonomic, or a combination of symptoms without impaired consciousness. They usually last less than 30 seconds and do not necessarily represent a significant problem with regard to job performance. Complex partial seizures are accompanied by impairment of consciousness and symptoms such as repetitive motor movements, fumbling with hands, lip smacking, and aimless wandering (Fraser et al., 2011). Many persons with complex partial seizures experience a brief aura or warning before an oncoming seizure, leading them to take precautionary safety measures.

Treatment for epilepsy usually involves the use of antiepileptic medications or sometimes surgery, which can control seizures for about 80% of people. The use of one medication (mono-therapy) is preferred, whenever possible, to control symptoms. One drug is often more effective and easier to manage, and one drug has less potential toxicity. Since persons with epilepsy are likely to have diverse patterns of cognitive impairment, a neuropsychological evaluation is essential when developing a rehabilitation plan. It is important to understand the degree to which the client is able to manage the seizure. It is also important to know whether there are patterns to seizure activity (e.g., during early mornings or sleep) and whether there are specific triggers/warning (e.g., flickering lights, aura). Recovery plans, medications, and co-occurring disabilities are also significant (Fraser et al., 2011). Accommodations may need to focus on work-place safety (e.g., keep aisles clear of clutter) or memory issues (e.g., provide written or pictorial instructions) (Whetzel, 2013b).

Cerebral palsy

Cerebral palsy (CP) is a group of neurological disorders that first appear in infancy or early childhood and permanently affect body movement, muscle coordination, and balance. CP is not a disease but the result of damage to the developing brain, which is nonprogressive and nonhereditary. Although the cause of CP is usually unknown, most often the problems occur during pregnancy. However, issues may also occur during childbirth or shortly after birth. Risk factors include preterm birth, twinship, certain infections during pregnancy such as toxoplasmosis or rubella, exposure to methylmercury during pregnancy, a difficult delivery, brain infection (e.g., bacterial meningitis, viral encephalitis), and head trauma during the first few years of life, among others. Common symptoms of include abnormal movements (twisting, jerking, or writhing) of limbs, abnormal muscle tones (too stiff/tight or too floppy), abnormal gait (crouched or "scissored"), exaggerated reflexes, tremors, unsteady gait, and loss of coordination. In addition to posture and motor abnormalities, persons may have secondary outcomes of brain damage, including epilepsy, intellectual disability, sensory and cognitive impairments (e.g., visual/hearing impairments), and orthopedic complications. Disorders of speech, such as dysarthria (slurred speech due to muscle tightness, weakness, or incoordination) and aphasia (impairment in the ability to communicate through speech or writing) are frequent impairments. However, not everyone experiences each of these impairments.

CP is generally classified in one of several ways: area of brain damage (neuroanatomical), type of movement disorder (spastic, dyskinetic, ataxic, and mixed), limb involvement (topographical), and function. Neuroanatomical classification describes the location of brain damage and is associated with the type of movement disorder (Falvo, 2009). Spasticity is a movement disorder that results from brain damage occurring in the cerebral cortex and pyramidal tracts. In spastic CP, limb muscles contract (tighten) abnormally, resulting in movement that is stiff and jerky. Over time, spastic muscles become shorter and exert differential pull around joints, gradually resulting in skeletal deformity as the limbs, pelvis, and spine become misaligned. Dyskinesia is a movement disorder that results from damage in the extrapyramidal tracts (i.e., basal ganglia). In dyskinetic CP, purposeful movement is distorted and muscles, especially in the arms, hands, and face, move randomly and involuntarily. Movement may range from writhing to jerking to tremor, depending on the type of dyskinesia. Muscle tone may be more normal when the person is asleep. Finally, ataxia is a movement disorder that results from damage in the cerebellum. In ataxic CP, individuals may have great difficulty stabilizing their gait and walk with feet wide apart while holding the arms out for balance. Rarely do these types of CP exist in "pure" forms. For example, a person may have both spasticity and dyskinesia, referred to as *mixed CP*. In addition to classification by neuroanatomy and type of movement disorder,

CP is classified by the location of limb involvement. *Monoplegia* refers to when only one limb is involved, which is uncommon in CP. *Paraplegia* refers to when only the legs are involved. *Hemiplegia* refers to when limbs on one side of the body are involved and an arm is usually more involved than the leg. *Triplegia* refers to when three limbs are involved, usually both legs and an arm. *Quadriplegia* refers to when all four limbs are involved. The trunk is often involved. *Diplegia* refers to greater involvement of the lower limbs than the upper limbs. *Double hemiplegia* refers to more involvement in the upper limbs than the lower limbs and one side of the body may be more involved than the other.

Potential accommodations for persons with CP may involve assistance with ADLs (e.g., accessibility in the restroom), fine motor aids (e.g., writing aids), gross motor aids (e.g., unobstructed hallways, incorporation of ramps, elevators, and other devices into physical structures), and work-related aids (flexible work schedules, cyber-commuting) (Whidden, 2013).

Attention deficit hyperactivity disorder

ADHD is one of the most common neurobehavioral disorders that affect 3% to 5% of American children and adults. It is a mental health condition exhibited by difficulty maintaining attention, as well as hyperactivity and impulsive behavior. It starts in early childhood, but in some cases, it is not diagnosed until later in life. It was once thought that ADHD was limited to childhood, but symptoms frequently persist into adulthood, with approximately 60% of those diagnosed in childhood still experiencing symptoms as an adult. The common characteristics of ADHD are impulsivity, inattention, and/or over-activity (APA, 2013). Persons with ADHD may find it difficult to focus/concentrate and prioritize, follow directions, remember information, organize tasks, and finish work on time. The inability to control impulses can range from impatience while waiting in line or driving in traffic to mood swings and outbursts of anger (APA, 2013). Although both inattention and hyperactivity symptoms may occur, many individuals predominantly display one symptom more than another. Therefore, the *DSM-5* identifies three subtypes that can be diagnosed. First, predominantly hyperactive-impulsive type involves fidgeting, talking excessively, interrupting others when talking, and impatience. Second, predominantly inattentive type involves distractibility, organization problems, failure to give close attention to details, difficulty processing information quickly and accurately, and difficulty following through with instructions. Third, combined type involves characteristics of both the hyperactive-impulsive and inattentive types (APA, 2013).

ADHD symptoms can lead to a number of problems, including unstable relationships, poor work or school performance, and low self-esteem. Although the exact cause of ADHD is not clear, many studies suggest that genetics play a large role. Like many other illnesses, ADHD probably results from a combination of factors. In addition to genetics, researchers are looking at possible environmental factors, such as brain injuries, nutrition, and the social environment (National Institute of Mental Health [NIMH], 2012). Although ADHD does not cause other psychological or developmental conditions, a number of other disorders often co-occur. These include mood disorders, anxiety disorders, personality disorders, and learning disabilities. As a result, the diagnosis of ADHD can be difficult, particularly in adults, because certain ADHD symptoms are similar to those caused by other conditions, such as anxiety or mood disorders. In addition, many adults with ADHD also have at least one other mental health condition, such as depression or anxiety. Treatment for ADHD includes stimulant drugs or other medications (e.g., Adderall, Ritalin), counseling/psychotherapy, education about ADHD, support/resources, and treatment for any mental health conditions that occur along with adult ADHD.

Accommodations for persons with ADHD often focus on concentration (e.g., reduce visual/auditory distractions by using headset or cubicle walls), organization and prioritization (e.g., use organizer and checklist, utilize coaching), time management (use timer, divide large assignments into several small tasks), multitasking (e.g., separate tasks that must be performed simultaneously and tasks that can be performed individually), control of impulsivity (e.g., provide structured breaks, work in private workspace to allow fidgeting), and memory recall (use flow-chart/adhesive notes/pictorial cues to lay out steps or as reminders) (JAN, 2015b).

Specific learning disorder

Specific learning disorders (SLD) are a group of conditions that affect a person's ability to acquire and/or use information through sources such as reading, writing, mathematical calculations, listening, speaking, and reasoning, but the individual does not have a diagnosis of a global intellectual disability (Falvo, 2009). Symptoms may include inaccurate or slow and effortful reading, poor written expression that lacks clarity, difficulties remembering number facts, or inaccurate mathematical reasoning. The person's difficulties must not be better explained by developmental, neurological, sensory (vision or hearing), or motor disorders and must significantly interfere with academic achievement, occupational performance, or ADLs. *ICD-10* (WHO, 2015) examples of SLD are dyslexia (impairment in the ability to interpret written language), dyscalculia (difficulty performing mathematical calculations), dysgraphia (inability to express oneself in writing), agnosia (inability to recognize and identify known objects through one or more senses), and dysphasia (impairments in language communication through speech) (Falvo, 2009). SLD is considered a high-incidence disorder that affects approximately 15% of the U.S. population, some of whom are never diagnosed. Learning disabilities are a heterogeneous set of disabilities that interfere with a person's ability to store, process, and produce information and are often hidden by the person's general level of functioning. Persons with SLD have difficulty recognizing crucial details and associating new information with what has previously been learned. This results in an inefficient memory system, making later retrieval of information difficult. Persons with SLD appear unorganized, especially in terms of their time-management skills. Because of the apparent disorganization, a person is often misperceived as lazy, unmotivated, or forgetful. SLD may occur with or be complicated by problems involving inadequate attention and inappropriate social skills (Givner & Brodwin, 2009).

Accommodations for persons with SLD may focus on difficulty reading text (e.g., reading back of written text), difficulty reading from a computer screen (e.g., screen-reading software), spelling (e.g., electronic dictionaries), cognitive processes of writing (e.g., creation of forms to prompt for information), physical process of writing (e.g., typewritten responses), mathematics (e.g., talking calculators), or speaking and communicating (e.g., written responses) (JAN, 2015c).

V. Other Medical Conditions and Chronic Illness

HIV infection

Approximately 1.2 million people in the United States live with HIV, and of these people, about 12.8% do not know that they are infected (CDC, 2015). Around 50,000 new HIV infections occur each year. HIV reduces the number of CD4 cells (T cells) in the body, making a person more likely to get other infections or infection-related cancers. These opportunistic infections or cancers take advantage of a very weak immune system and signal that the person has AIDS. People with AIDS have a damaged immune system, which causes an increasing number of severe illnesses. Treatment for HIV is often called *antiretroviral therapy* (ART). Persons who begin ART may develop immune reconstitution inflammatory syndrome (IRIS) (Meintjes et al., 2008). The IRIS syndrome is paradoxical worsening of an existing infection or disease process or appearance of a new infection/disease process soon after the initiation of therapy (Sharma & Soneja,

2011). The first stage of HIV is acute HIV infection; within 2 to 4 weeks after infection with HIV, people may experience a flu-like illness that may last for a few weeks. The second stage is clinical latency (HIV inactivity or dormancy), sometimes called *asymptomatic HIV infection* or *chronic HIV infection*. At this stage, HIV is still active but reproduces at very low levels. People may not have any symptoms or get sick during this time. The third stage is AIDS. Common symptoms of AIDS include chills, fever, sweats, swollen lymph glands, weakness, and weight loss. Without treatment, people with AIDS typically survive about 3 years (CDC, 2015). Only certain body fluids—blood, semen, preseminal fluid, rectal fluids, vaginal fluids, and breast milk—from a person who has HIV can transmit HIV. These fluids must come in contact with a mucous membrane or damaged tissue or be directly injected into the bloodstream (from a needle or syringe) for transmission to occur. HIV is spread mainly by having anal or vaginal sex with someone who has HIV or sharing needles or syringes, rinse water, or other equipment used to prepare drugs for injection with someone who has HIV. Although there is a problem of resistance of HIV to antiretroviral drugs, poor adherence is the major cause of therapeutic failure. Adhering to ART is a critical determinant of long-term outcome in HIV-infected individuals. Reasons for nonadherence could be behavioral, structural, and psychosocial barriers, including depression and other mental illnesses, neurocognitive impairment, low health literacy, low levels of social support, stressful life events, high levels of alcohol consumption and active substance use, homelessness, poverty, nondisclosure of HIV serostatus, denial, stigma, and inconsistent access to medications (Carr & Gramling, 2004; Halkitis, Shrem, Zade, & Wilton, 2005; Stirratt et al., 2006).

HIV has neurological, dermatological, pulmonary, cardiac, gastrointestinal, ophthalmological, kidney, and musculoskeletal complications and malignancies (e.g., non-Hodgkin's lymphoma, leukemia, colorectal cancer). Individuals with HIV are more likely to experience emotional distress such as major depression, dysthymia, generalized anxiety disorder (GAD), panic attacks, and substance abuse than the general population (RAND Corporation, 2007). Substance abuse and violence may lead to unsafe sex (RAND Corporation, 2007). The employment rate of persons with HIV is 45% (Rabkin, McElhiney, Ferrando, Van Gorp, & Lin, 2004). HIV-related stigma can result in a loss of job, unemployment, changes in job, or refusal of promotion, as well as a discriminatory attitude from coworkers (U.S. Department of Labor, 2012). Accommodations for fatigue/weakness may include reduction/elimination of lifting and walking, flexibility to sit or stand, and telecommute. Accommodations for chronic diarrhea may include a worksite or workstation near restroom, a flexible work schedule to allow for restroom breaks, and a flexible leave policy. Accommodations for vision impairment may include a larger monitor, screen-reading software, and improved lighting or task lighting. Accommodations for respiratory difficulties may include a clean work environment free from dust, smoke, odor and fumes; good ventilation; and avoidance of temperature extremes. Accommodations for skin infections may include avoidance of infectious agents and chemicals, avoidance of invasive procedures, and a flexible leave policy. Accommodations for weight loss may include an ergonomic chair with extra padding, alternate working positions to prevent sores from forming, and access to a refrigerator (to store food supplements or medications) (JAN, 2015a).

Diabetes mellitus

There are 29.1 million Americans living with diabetes, which equates to about 1 of every 11 people (CDC, 2016c). In 2011, 17.7 million adults with diagnosed diabetes reported taking medications (pills, insulin, or both), whereas 3.1 million (14.9%) did not report taking medication. Diabetes is a disease in which blood glucose levels are below or above normal. The symptoms are frequent urination, excessive thirst, unexplained weight loss, extreme hunger, sudden vision changes, tingling or numbness in the hands or feet, frequent fatigue, very dry skin, sores that are slow to heal, and a higher number of infections than usual. Type 1 diabetes, which was previously called *insulin-dependent diabetes mellitus* (IDDM) or *juvenile-onset diabetes,* may account for approximately 5% of all diagnosed cases of diabetes. Healthy eating, physical activity, and insulin injections are the basic therapies for type 1 diabetes. The amount of insulin taken must be balanced with food intake and daily activities. Type 2 diabetes, which was previously called *noninsulin-dependent diabetes mellitus* (NIDDM) or *adult-onset diabetes,* may account for 90% to 95% of all diagnosed cases of diabetes. Healthy eating, physical activity, and blood glucose testing are the basic therapies for type 2 diabetes. Gestational diabetes is a type of diabetes that occurs only in pregnant women. If not treated, it can cause problems for both mothers and babies. Gestational diabetes develops in 2% to 10% of all pregnancies but usually disappears when a pregnancy is over. Other specific types of diabetes resulting from specific genetic syndromes, surgery, drugs, malnutrition, infections, and other illnesses may account for 1% to 5% of all diagnosed cases. Diabetic complications include diabetic retinopathy (damaging the vessels in the retina), diabetic nephropathy (damaging the vessels in the kidney), and peripheral neuropathy (damaging the peripheral nerves, resulting in pain, tingling, or loss of sensation in the extremities).

Diabetes requires lifelong management to control blood glucose levels and complications by engaging in a healthy lifestyle and working with health care providers (CDC, 2016c). The national standards for diabetes self-management education (DSME) have been developed and have described diabetes self-management education as the ongoing process of facilitating the knowledge, skill, and ability necessary for prediabetes and diabetes self-care (Haas et al., 2014). This process incorporates the needs, goals, and life experiences of the person with diabetes or prediabetes into treatment and is guided by evidence-based standards. The overall objectives of DSME are to support informed decision making, self-care behaviors, problem solving, and active collaboration with the health care team and to improve clinical outcomes, health status, and quality of life (Haas et al., 2014). Seven essential self-care behaviors predict positive outcomes in people with diabetes: healthy eating, physical activity, monitoring of blood glucose, compliance with medications, good problem-solving skills, healthy coping skills, and risk-reduction behaviors (American Association of Diabetes Educators, 2010). Although diabetes usually does not impact the ability to work in a job, people with diabetes sometimes experience employment discrimination (American Diabetes Association, 2016). Accommodations for hypoglycemia/hyperglycemia may include allowing for storage of medications such as insulin and/or food, providing an area to test blood glucose levels, and providing appropriate containers for needles/syringe disposal. Accommodations for neuropathy may include modifying job tasks requiring fine finger dexterity, providing protective clothing and equipment, and eliminating or reducing the need to use sharp objects. The accommodations for kidney disease may include providing easy access to restroom facilities, allowing a flexible schedule or time off for treatment (dialysis), and allowing the individual to telecommute from a dialysis site (JAN, 2013b).

Rheumatic conditions

RA and systemic lupus erythematosus (SLE) are two of the major conditions of the 116 rheumatic conditions (Falvo, 2014). Rheumatic conditions affect the joints, connective tissues, and muscles and produce pain, fatigue, and loss of motion. RA is the most common form of autoimmune arthritis. More than 1.3 million Americans have this condition. RA often occurs in people at ages 40–60 years, and approximately 75% of those affected are women. RA has an unpredictable course of remissions and exacerbations. During an exacerbation, individuals develop synovitis, in which synovial tissue becomes red (erythema) and swollen (edema). Over time, repeated exacerbations cause joint destruction and irregularity, and ankylosis (stiffness and fixation of the joint), which impedes joint movement, develops. Although RA can affect any joint, the small joints (e.g., wrists, ankles, knees, elbows, fingers, and toes) are often symmetrically involved. Three main medications are used in combination for RA: nonsteroidal anti-inflammatory drugs (NSAIDs), disease-modifying antirheumatic drugs (DMARDs), and glucocorticoids. NSAIDs relieve pain, stiffness, and inflammation but do not slow the progression of RA. The side effects are somatic irritation and gastric bleeding. DMARDs slow the progression of RA. The side effects are bone marrow suppression and liver toxicity. Glucocorticoids rapidly suppress the inflammation, pain, and swelling as well as slow down the progression of RA. However, glucocorticoids cause serious side effects such as osteoporosis and hypertension. It is important for persons with RA to maintain physical activity. However, when RA flares, rest is helpful (American College of Rheumatology, 2016).

Persons with RA frequently suffer from anxiety, depression, and low self-esteem (Gettings, 2010). The unemployment rates of Americans with RA for the first 2 to 3 years after onset are 20% to 30% (Sokka, 2003). Accommodations for persons with RA may include use of a personal attendant and/or service animal at work, accessibility to and within the work facility, reduction of or eliminaton of physical exertion and workplace stress, periodic rest breaks away from the workstation, and ergonomic workstation design (Loy, 2015a).

SLE is the most common type of lupus (CDC, 2016d). About 1.5 million Americans have lupus, most of whom develop it between the ages of 15 and 44 years (Lupus Foundation of America [LFA], 2016). SLE is an autoimmune disease in which the immune system produces antibodies to cells in the body, leading to widespread inflammation and tissue damage (Duarte, Couto, Ines, & Liang, 2011). SLE can affect the joints, skin, brain, lungs, kidneys, and blood vessels. Persons experience remissions and flares of fatigue, pain or swelling in joints, skin rashes, and fevers. Most persons have a "butterfly rash" on the face and increased sensitivity to sunlight. Individuals with SLE have an increased frequency of other autoimmune problems, such as Sjögren's syndrome (i.e., dry eyes, dry mouth) and antiphospholipid syndrome (i.e., clotting problems, strokes, fetal loss) (Dall'Era, 2013). Two of three people with lupus completely or partially lose their income due to the inability to work full time (LFA, 2016). About 46% of persons with lupus are employed (Yazdany & Yelin, 2010). NSAIDs and low doses of corticosteroids are used to limit disease progression. Chronic pain, lifestyle changes, and emotional problems are common in those coping with lupus (LFA, 2016). Accommodations for people with lupus may include work from home, flexible work schedule, reduction or elimination of physical exertion and workplace stress, periodic rest breaks away from the workstation, minimization of outdoor activities between 10 a.m. and 4 p.m., and avoidance of reflective surfaces (e.g., sand, snow, concrete), and avoidance of infectious agents and chemicals (Dorinzi, 2014).

Chronic obstructive pulmonary disease

COPD refers to a group of diseases that cause airflow blockage and breathing-related problems, including emphysema, chronic bronchitis, refractory (nonreversible) asthma, and some forms of bronchiectasis (CDC, 2016b; COPD Foundation, 2016). Emphysema and chronic bronchitis often coexist and have similar pulmonary manifestations, including dyspnea (shortness of breath), especially on exertion; increased breathlessness; frequent coughing (with and without sputum); wheezing; and tightness in the chest (COPD Foundation, 2016). Smoking is the main risk factor for developing COPD (CDC, 2005). About 24 million Americans have COPD (COPD Foundation, 2016). COPD is most often diagnosed in people aged 65 to 74. Smoking cessation is an essential step for treating COPD. Pulmonary rehabilitation is an individualized treatment program that teaches COPD-management strategies to improve quality of life (CDC, 2016b). Plans may include breathing strategies, energy-conserving techniques, and nutritional counseling (CDC, 2016b).

Two breathing techniques, pursed-lips breathing and diaphragmatic (also called *belly* or *abdominal*) breathing, can help people with COPD. Bronchodilators relieve dyspnea by relaxing airways and are often delivered by an inhaler. The side effects of bronchodilators include trembling (particularly in the hands), nervous tension, dry mouth, constipation or diarrhea, nausea, vomiting, headaches, and a rapid heartbeat (National Health Service, 2014). Inhaled corticosteroid medications reduce airway inflammation and prevent exacerbations (Mayo Clinic, 2015). The side effects of these medications may include bruising, oral infections, and hoarseness (Mayo Clinic, 2015). There are four levels of the classification of airflow limitation in COPD (Global Initiative for Chronic Obstructive Lung Disease, 2017):

- GOLD 1-mild: FEV_1 (volume that has been exhaled at the end of the first second of forced expiration) $\geq$80% predicted, mild limitation of air and lack of awareness of abnormal lung function.

- GOLD 2-moderate: 50% $\leq FEV_1$ <80% predicted; limitation of airflow that causes coughing, coughing up of phlegm, and shortness of breath during exertion. Individuals usually seek medical treatment at this stage.

- GOLD 3-severe: 30% $\leq FEV_1$ <50% predicted, greater limitation of airflow. Individuals complain of worsening shortness of breath, fatigue, limitations to daily activities, and repeated exacerbations that all affect quality of life.

- GOLD 4-very severe: FEV_1 <30% predicted, limitation of airflow so severe that it also affects the heart and blood vessels. Daily administration of extra oxygen may be required. The symptoms are so severe that temporary worsening can be life-threatening.

Persons with COPD frequently experience a lower quality of live because they have difficulties or limitations in socializing and engaging in recreational activities, and these restrictions may also cause frustration and anger (Kim, Kunik, & Molinari, 2000; Zamzam, Azab, Wahsh, Ragab, & Allam, 2012). Compared with adults without COPD, persons with COPD are more likely to report being unable to work (24.3% vs. 5.3%), having an activity limitation caused by health problems (49.6% vs. 16.9%), having difficulty walking or climbing stairs (38.4% vs. 11.3%), or using special equipment to manage health problems (22.1% vs. 6.7%) (Wheaton, Cunningham, Ford, & Croft, 2015). Accommodations for people with COPD may include maintaining a clean and healthy work environment, providing air purification, and offering an accessible parking space with an unobstructed and easily traveled path into the workplace (JAN, 2013e).

Burn injury

Each year 1.1 million burn injuries require medical attention in the United States (CDC, 2016a). Approximately 50,000 of these injuries require hospitalization, and of this subgroup, approximately 20,000 are diagnosed with major burns involving at least 25% of the total body surface and approximately 4,500 die. The types of burn injuries include thermal burns (the most common type, caused by fire, hot liquids, or direct contact with a hot surface), chemical burns (caused by direct contact with strong acids, alkaline agents, and gases), radiation burns, electrical burns (caused by direct contact with electrical current or lighting), and inhalation injury (caused by inhalation of steam, toxic gases, or vapors). The severity of burn is determined by many factors, such as burn depth, the percentage of total body surface burned, and burn location (Falvo, 2014). First-degree burns (e.g., sunburn) are superficial burns involving the top layer of skin (the epidermis). The skin becomes red and painful to touch, and mild swelling is present. Second-degree (partial-thickness) burns involve the first two layers of skin—the epidermis and the dermis. The skin becomes reddened and very painful; there are blisters, glossy appearance from leaking fluid, and possible loss of some skin. Third-degree (full-thickness) burns penetrate the entire thickness of the skin and permanently destroy tissue. The burn destroys the dermis and epidermis and skin appendages (e.g., hair follicles, sebaceous glands, sweat glands). The skin, which is often painless, dry and leathery, charred, loses layers or has patches that appear white, brown or black. Fourth-degree burns damage the underlying subcutaneous fat, muscle, or bone.

The *rule of nines* is commonly used to calculate the amount of body surface injured (Falvo, 2014). General burn management includes wound management, nutritional support, splinting, pain management, and rehabilitation and wound remolding. After the acute phase of burn management, grafting procedures usually begin. The healing burn may be compressed with elastic dressings (e.g., pressure garments) to prevent or decrease the formation of hypertrophic (overgrowth) scarring (Falvo, 2014). At the critical stage of burn injuries, persons experience stressors of the intensive care environment, uncertainty about outcome, and a struggle for survival; cognitive changes such as extreme drowsiness, confusion, and disorientation are common during this phase, and even more severe cognitive changes such as delirium and brief psychotic reactions also occur (Dalal, Saha, & Agarwal, 2010). At the acute stage of recovery, persons may also experience depression, anxiety, sleep disturbance, pain, and grief (Dalal et al., 2010). At the long-term rehabilitation stage, individuals experience changing roles, return to work, body image distortion, sexual issues, anxiety, and depression. About 72% of previously employed individuals return to some form of work (Mason et al., 2012). Important factors for return-to-work include burn location, burn size, treatment variables, age, pain, psychosocial factors, job factors, and barriers. Accommodations may involve modifying the workstation to make it accessible, implementing an ergonomic workstation design, reducing the worksite temperature, and using a cool vest or other cooling clothing (Loy, 2015b). The accommodations for cold sensitivity may include increasing worksite temperature, using portable space heaters, and dressing in layers using thermal material or fleece. The accommodations for respiratory impairment may include prenotification of construction, painting, pesticide use, and heavy cleaning; use of nontoxic carpeting or an alternative floor covering such as tile or cotton throw rugs; use of nontoxic building materials and lawn products; and use of oxygen.

Cancer

Cancer is the second leading cause of death in the United States (Batra & Jajoo, 2011). Cancer is a general term used to describe a group of diseases characterized by the disorderly, uncontrollable growth and spread of abnormal cells (Orr & Orange, 2014). The exact cause of cancer has not been found, yet there are a variety of factors associated with cancer, including genetics (e.g., family history of breast, ovary, colon, lung cancers and malignant melanomas), diet (high fat intake, alcohol use), physical inactivity (e.g., limited exercise), and environmental factors (e.g., carcinogens, ultraviolet light). Some of the most common types of cancer are carcinoma (cancer of epithelial cells), sarcoma (cancer of the bone, muscle, or other connective tissue), lymphoma (cancer of the lymphatic system), leukemia (cancer of blood cells), and melanoma (cancer of pigment-producing cells such as skin) (Falvo, 2014).

Symptoms such as pressure, bleeding, a mass, unusual appearance, or interference with function may be early warning signs of certain forms of cancer (Orr & Orange, 2014). Formal diagnostic procedures involve physical examination, laboratory testing, imaging studies, interventional treatment, and biopsies. Once cancer is identified, staging is performed to determine the extent to which it has spread. The patient's functional capacity is also categorized, and the most commonly used scale is the Eastern Cooperative Oncology Group (ECOG) scale, ranging from zero (normal activity without physical limitation) to IV (the patient is in bed 100% of the time). There are several modalities, including surgery, chemotherapy, radiation, biologic therapy, and bone marrow transplantation, for treating or curing cancer (Falvo, 2014). Treatment side effects include hair loss, weight loss or gain, appetite loss or increase, fatigue, disfigurement from surgery, lack of concentration, nausea, vomiting, changes in skin tone, sleep disruption, and sexual dysfunction. Severe fatigue lasting for months is the most prominent side effect and can severely impact work performance (Orr & Orange, 2002). Potential accommodations for rehabilitation counselors working with individuals with cancer should focus on fatigue as well as ongoing psychological distress and adjustment reactions. For example, individuals with cancer may benefit from reducing physical exertion, scheduling rest breaks, and allowing time off for medical treatment (Loy, 2015c).

Assistive Technology and Universal Design

Key Concepts

Assistive technology (AT) is any item, piece of equipment, or product system, whether acquired commercially off the shelf, modified, or customized, that is used to increase, maintain, or improve the functional capabilities of people with disabilities (Individuals with Disabilities Education Act [IDEA], 1990). The device may be purchased commercially or modified to meet the individual's needs (IDEA, 1990). There are different categories of AT: (a) Aids for daily living are self-help aids for self-care that are used on a daily life basis, such as a fork with a built-up handle, bath lift/seat, button/shoe aids; (b) augmentative communication uses electronic and nonelectronic devices for expressive and receptive communication, such as a communication book/board, eye-controlled communicator; (c) computer applications enable people with disabilities to use a computer, including input and output devices (e.g., cursor-control accessories), alternate access aids (e.g., head sticks), modified keyboard, switches, and special software (e.g., computer access interfaces/instructions); (d) environmental control systems are electronic systems that enable people with mobility limitations to control various appliances, electronic aids, and security systems, such as a house with built-in automation and blinking locators; (e) home/worksite modifications are structural adaptations or fabrication in the home, worksite, or other area (ramps, lifts, bathroom, changes) for increasing accessibility, such as ramps, elevators, and stair lifts; (f) prosthetics and orthotics are a replacement, a substitution, or an augmentation of missing or malfunctioning body parts, such as a knee prosthesis or an ankle brace; (g) seating and positioning accommodations are made to a wheelchair or other seating system to increase stability, maintain posture, and reduce pressure on the skin surface, such as a cushion cover and trunk/pelvic supports; (h) aids for vision/hearing impaired are magnifiers, Braille, large-print materials, and a telecommunications device for the Deaf (Table 9.2); (i) wheelchairs/mobility aids include manual and electric wheelchairs, walkers, and mobility scooters; (j) vehicle modifications are for personal transportation, such as adaptive driving aids, hand controls, modified vans, and an acoustic cue system; and (k) recreational assistance methods and tools enable people with disabilities to enjoy recreational activities, such as three-wheel handcycles, homemade bowling ramps, and paintbrush holders. Although a rehabilitation counselor is in charge of introducing, evaluating, and selecting AT for a client, a client's involvement and support are important. It is critical to know a client's expectations for AT before its selection. It is also important to consider the extent to which the device fits a client's lifestyle, preferences, and values (Brodwin, Cardoso, & Star, 2004; Falvo, 2009). A rehabilitation counselor works with a client to make sure that a selected AT device is effective, reliable, easy, and comfortable to be used (Brodwin et al., 2004).

The Disability Act of 2005 defines universal design (UD) as (a) the design and composition of an environment so that it may be accessed, understood and used to the greatest possible extent, in the most independent and natural manner possible, in the widest possible range of situations, and without the need for adaptation, modification, assistive devices or specialized solutions, by any persons of any ages or sizes or having any particular physical, sensory, mental health, or intellectual abilities or disabilities; and (b) means, in relation to electronic systems, any electronics-based process of creating products, services or systems so that they may be used by any person. The seven principles of UD are equitable use, flexibility in use, simple and intuitive use, perceptible information, tolerance for error, low physical effort, and appropriate size and space for approach and use.

TABLE 9.2 Summary of Key Concepts of Diagnoses and Accommodations

Diagnosis	Key Information and Accommodation Needs
SCI	• Injuries at C1–C4 need respiratory assistance; injuries at C7–C8 can be mostly independent with some environmental accommodations. • Accommodations may include height-adjustable desk or table, page turners and book holders, and accessible parking.
TBI	• Physical damage to the brain includes closed head injuries, blast injuries, open head injuries, and atraumatic brain injuries. • Accommodations may include written instructions, assignments of one task at a time, and additional time to perform tasks.
Stroke	• Strokes are caused by decreased blood flow and subsequent inadequate oxygen supply to part of the brain, leading to tissue damage, including ischemic strokes and hemorrhagic stroke. • Accommodations may include mobility aids, rooming/eating aids, and communication aids.
MS	• MS is an inflammatory demyelinating disease of unknown origin. • Accommodations may include reducing physical exertion and workplace stress and scheduling periodic rest breaks away from the workstation.
Chronic pain	• Pain persists for 3–6 months or longer than the expected healing time. • Accommodations may include implementing ergonomic workstation design and reducing or eliminating physical exertion and workplace stress.
Visual impairment	• *Functionally blind* means that individuals are not able to perceive light. *Legal blindness* is based on a visual acuity of 20/200 or less or a central visual field restricted to 20° or less in the widest meridian of the better eye. • Accommodations may include auditory versions of printed documents and documents formatted in Braille.
Hearing impairment	• Six levels of hearing loss are classified by sensitivity thresholds (dB) (e.g., hearing at 41–55 dB indicating mild to moderate hearing loss). • Accommodations may include ALDs and TDDs.
Psychotic disorders	• Criteria for a diagnosis of schizophrenia include delusions, hallucinations, disorganized speech, grossly disorganized or catatonic behavior, and negative symptoms such as lack of emotional expression (affective flattening), poverty of speech (alogia), and lack of motivation (avolition). • Accommodations may include flexible scheduling and reducing work distractions.
Personality disorders	• Personality disorders are associated with persistent, inflexible ways of thinking of oneself and others that adversely affect functioning in social and work settings. • Accommodations may include developing clear expectations for responsibilities and permitting telephone calls to health care providers during work hours.

(continued)

TABLE 9.2   Summary of Key Concepts of Diagnoses and Accommodations (*continued*)

Diagnosis	Key Information and Accommodation Needs
Trauma- and stressor-related disorders	• Trauma- and stressor-related disorders share in common an exposure to traumatic events and the subsequent stressful reactions. • Accommodations may include reducing work-related stressors by allowing for a flexible work environment or schedule.
ASD	• ASD involves a group of neurodevelopmental disorders characterized by persistent deficits in social communication (e.g., initiating/sustaining conversations), impairments in social interactions (e.g., maintaining friendships), repetitive patterns of behaviors, restricted interests or activities, and the potential for sensory sensitivities. • Accommodations may include using coworkers as mentors and providing visual support.
Intellectual disability	• Intellectual disability involves significant limitations in both intellectual functioning and adaptive behavior (expressed in everyday social and practical skills) with onset during the developmental period. • Accommodations may include prompting memory with verbal cues and using color coding for assisting organization.
Epilepsy	• Epilepsy involves recurrent and unprovoked seizures. • Accommodations may include keeping aisles clear of clutter and providing written or pictorial instructions for assisting with memory problems.
CP	• CP refers to a group of neurological disorders that first appear in infancy or early childhood and permanently affect body movement, muscle coordination, and balance. • Accommodations may include accessibility in the restroom, unobstructed hallways, and incorporation of ramps, elevators, and other devices into physical structures.
ADHD	• People with ADHD exhibit difficulty maintaining attention, as well as hyperactivity and impulsive behavior. • Accommodations may include reducing visual/auditory distractions by using a headset or cubicle walls or using organizers and checklists.
SLD	• SLD refers to a group of conditions that affect a person's ability to acquire and/or use information through sources such as reading, writing, mathematical calculations, listening, speaking, or reasoning, but the person is not diagnosed with global intellectual disability. • Accommodations may include screen-reading software and electronic dictionaries.
HIV	• HIV reduces the number of CD4 cells (T cells) in the body, making the person more likely to get other infections or infection-related cancers. • Accommodations may include avoiding infectious agents and chemicals and avoiding invasive procedures.
Diabetes mellitus	• Diabetes is a disease in which blood glucose levels are below or above normal. • Accommodations may include modifying job tasks requiring fine finger dexterity and providing protective clothing and equipment.
RA	• Rheumatic conditions affect the joints, connective tissues, and muscle and produce pain, fatigue, and loss of motion. • Accommodations may include working from home and a flexible work schedule.
COPD	• COPD refers to a group of diseases that cause airflow blockage and breathing-related problems, including emphysema, chronic bronchitis, refractory (nonreversible) asthma, and some forms of bronchiectasis. • Accommodations may include maintaining a clean and healthy work environment and providing air purification.

(*continued*)

TABLE 9.2 Summary of Key Concepts of Diagnoses and Accommodations (*continued*)

Diagnosis	Key Information and Accommodation Needs
Burn injury	• The types of burn injuries include thermal burns, chemical burns, radiation burns, electrical burns, and inhalation injury. • Accommodations may include using nontoxic building materials and lawn products and allowing the use of oxygen.
Cancer	• Cancer is a general term used to describe a group of diseases characterized by the disorderly, uncontrollable growth and spread of abnormal cells. • Accommodations may include reducing physical exertion, scheduling rest breaks, and allowing time off for medical treatment.

ADHD, attention deficit hyperactivity disorder; ALDs, assistive listening devices; ASD, autism spectrum disorders; COPD, chronic obstructive pulmonary disease; CP, cerebral palsy; MS, multiple sclerosis; RA, rheumatic arthritis; SCI, spinal cord injury; SLD, specific learning disorders; TBI, traumatic brain injury; TDDs, telecommunication devices for the deaf.

Multiple-Choice Questions

1. An environment or a device conceived to be accessed in the most independent and natural manner and without the need for assistive devices by people with disabilities is:

   A. Total access

   B. Assistive technology

   C. Universal design

   D. Specialized accommodation

2. Diabetes mellitus is related to which body system:

   A. Circulatory system

   B. Endocannabinoid system

   C. Immune system

   D. Endocrine system

3. Alzheimer's disease is related to which body system:

   A. Nervous system

   B. Musculoskeletal system

   C. Vestibular system

   D. Immune system

4. Rank the causes of spinal cord injury from highest to lowest in incidence?

   A. Acts of violence, vehicular accidents, falls

   B. Vehicular accidents, acts of violence, falls

   C. Vehicular accidents, falls, acts of violence

   D. Falls, vehicular accidents, acts of violence

5. The leading cause of traumatic brain injury in young children and older adults is:
   A. Falls
   B. Vehicular accidents
   C. Sports and recreational activities
   D. Viruses

6. Ischemic stroke is due to:
   A. Hemorrhage into the brain tissue
   B. Aneurysm
   C. Intracerebral hemorrhage
   D. Occlusion of a blood vessel

7. What is the most common type of multiple sclerosis?
   A. Relapsing-remitting
   B. Primary-progressive
   C. Secondary progressive
   D. Progressive-relapsing

8. The first stage of HIV is:
   A. A flu-like illness that may last for a few weeks
   B. HIV dormancy
   C. Asymptomatic HIV infection or chronic HIV infection
   D. Chronic HIV infection

9. Which of the following is not a symptom of diabetes:
   A. Excessive thirst
   B. Frequent urination
   C. Loss appetite
   D. Extreme hunger

10. There are four levels of airflow limitation in chronic obstructive pulmonary disease. Which of the following is referring to level 2?
    A. Mild limitation of air flow, but persons may not be aware of abnormal lung function
    B. Coughing, coughing up phlegm, and shortness of breath during exertion
    C. Greater limitation of airflow
    D. Worsening shortness of breath, fatigue, limitations to daily activities, and repeated exacerbations

11. A condition of chronic pain that predominantly causes pain in single or multiple joints with a progressive disease course is:
    A. Rheumatic arthritis
    B. Fibromyalgia syndrome

    C. Carpal tunnel syndrome

    D. Complex regional pain syndrome

12. Treatment for chronic pain should include which pain management approach?

    A. Pharmacological

    B. Physical therapy

    C. Educational

    D. Multidisciplinary

13. A common side effect of cancer treatment that often affects work performance is:

    A. Hair loss

    B. Nausea

    C. Weight loss

    D. Fatigue

14. The most prevalent group of psychiatric disorders are:

    A. Mood disorders

    B. Psychotic disorders

    C. Substance use disorders

    D. Anxiety disorders

15. Which of the following is *NOT* an evidence-based program of psychosocial treatment for individuals with psychotic disorders?

    A. Assertive community treatment

    B. Dialectical behavioral therapy

    C. Social skills training

    D. Individual placement and support model

16. Traumatic brain injury can lead to which of the following symptoms:

    A. Impulsivity

    B. Depression

    C. Substance use/misuse

    D. All of the above

17. What is the prevalence rate for chronic pain across the world?

    A. 10%

    B. 20%

    C. 33.3%

    D. 65%

18. What is the etiology for cancer?

    A. Genetics

    B. Environmental factors

    C. Physical inactivity and diet

    D. All of the above

19. Which of the following is *NOT* an anxiety disorder?

    A. Panic disorder

    B. Bipolar disorder

    C. Generalized anxiety disorder

    D. Agoraphobia

20. Which of the following is NOT a trauma- and stressor-related disorder?

    A. Traumatic brain injury

    B. Adjustment disorder

    C. Acute stress disorder

    D. Posttraumatic stress disorder

21. The prevalence of autism spectrum disorder has been steadily increasing throughout the years. What is the most current estimated prevalence now?

    A. 1 of 150 children

    B. 1 of 88 children

    C. 1 of 68 children

    D. 1 of 45 children

22. Many individuals with autism spectrum disorder have comorbid psychiatric diagnoses. Which of the following is *NOT* an example of a comorbid disorder?

    A. Anxiety disorder

    B. Depression

    C. Asperger's syndrome

    D. Gastrointestinal problems

    E. Attention deficit hyperactivity disorder

23. There are four severity levels of intellectual disability. Which of the following is not one of them?

    A. Mild

    B. Moderate

    C. Pervasive

    D. Severe

    E. Profound

24. For individuals with epilepsy, several accommodations can be provided in a workplace. These accommodations include:

    A. Focus on workplace safety

    B. Memory cues

    C. Onsite automated external defibrillator

    D. A and B

    E. All of the above

25. Which of the following criteria can be used to define intellectual disability?

    A. Intellectual functioning that is significantly below average

    B. Impairments in adaptive behavior

    C. Early onset during the developmental period

    D. All of the above

26. Early manifestation of symptoms such as rigid muscle tones, twisting movements of limbs, and abnormal gaits can be diagnosed as which of the following?

    A. Infantile autism

    B. Cerebral palsy

    C. Intellectual disabilities

    D. Down syndrome

    E. Traumatic brain injury

27. Clinical features of cerebral palsy include:

    A. Exaggerated reflexes

    B. Tremors

    C. Unsteady gait

    D. Abnormal muscle movement

    E. All of the above

28. Attention deficit hyperactivity disorder is a _____ disorder.

    A. Congenitally based

    B. Academically related

    C. Chemically induced

    D. Neurobehavioral

29. A child with dyslexia but with no other difficulties would be classified as having:

    A. Autism spectrum disorder

    B. A learning disability

    C. A specific learning disorder

    D. Attention deficit hyperactivity disorder

30. Which of the following is the criteria for legal blindness?

    A. Best-corrected visual acuity of 20/70 to 20/180 in the better eye

    B. Peripheral field of vision between 21° and 140°

    C. Visual acuity of 20/200 or less

    D. Inability to perceive light

    E. None of the above

Answer Key

1C, 2D, 3A, 4C, 5A, 6D, 7A, 8A, 9C, 10B, 11A, 12D, 13D, 14C, 15B, 16D, 17C, 18D, 19B, 20A, 21D, 22C, 23C, 24D, 25D, 26B, 27E, 28D, 29C, 30C

Advanced Multiple-Choice Questions

1. Design relevant to buildings, products, and environments can be made accessible to people with diverse abilities and disabilities. This type of design uses which principle of universal design:

    A. Simple and intuitive use

    B. Equitable use

    C. Flexible use

    D. Low physical effort

2. If a design discourages unconscious action in tasks that require vigilance, it uses which principle of universal design:

    A. Simple and intuitive use

    B. Equitable use

    C. Tolerance for error

    D. Size and space for approach and use

3. Parkinson's and Huntington's diseases are related to which body system?

    A. Musculoskeletal system

    B. Endocannabinoid system

    C. Vestibular system

    D. Integumentary system

4. At which spinal level does a person with complete spinal cord injury maintain some gross movement of the upper extremities (e.g., bending the arm at elbow, holding a light object between the thumb and finger, independently operating an electric wheelchair)?

    A. C3

    B. C5

C. T1

D. T7

5. At which spinal level does a person with complete spinal cord injury be almost independent with some environmental accommodations?

A. C5

B. C7

C. T7

D. S1

6. What does it mean if a person's Glasgow Coma Scale score was in the range of 4–8?

A. Moderate head injury

B. Severe head injury

C. Coma

D. Deep coma or brain death

7. Manifestations of right-sided brain damage include which of the following?

A. Speech language deficit and spatial-perceptual deficits

B. Spatial-perceptual deficits and quick impulsive behavior

C. Quick impulsive behavior and language memory deficits

D. Speech language deficits and language memory deficits

8. An inability to carry out purposeful, coordinated voluntary motor skills movements is:

A. Apraxia

B. Ataxia

C. Aphasia

D. Paresthesia

9. Wernicke's aphasia includes which of the following symptoms?

A. Fluent aphasia, word-finding difficulties

B. Nonfluent aphasia, word-finding difficulties

C. Fluent aphasia, effortless speech but reduced information content

D. Nonfluent aphasia, effortless speech but reduced information content

10. The later symptoms of MS include which of the following symptoms?

A. Weak/stiff muscles (often with painful muscle spasms), difficulty walking

B. Mental or physical fatigue, difficulty walking

C. Mental or physical fatigue, reduced cognitive function

D. Reduced cognitive function, difficulty walking

11. _____ is a chronic pain syndrome diagnosed primarily in women.
    A. Carpal tunnel syndrome
    B. Complex regional pain syndrome
    C. Fibromyalgia syndrome
    D. All of the above

12. Which of the following is *NOT* a medication used for pain management?
    A. Anti-inflammatory
    B. Narcotic analgesic
    C. Antidepressant
    D. Antipsychotic

13. Which of the following is considered a rare form of cancer?
    A. Chordoma
    B. Sarcoma
    C. Melanoma
    D. Carcinoma

14. Which symptom is *NOT* part of the diagnostic criteria for anxiety disorders?
    A. Nervousness
    B. Sweating
    C. Sadness
    D. Worrying

15. Which model of therapy is particularly effective for persons with personality disorders?
    A. Dialectical behavior therapy
    B. Psychoanalysis
    C. Cognitive behavioral therapy
    D. Motivational interviewing

16. What model of therapy is particularly effective for persons with anxiety disorders?
    A. Dialectical behavior therapy
    B. Psychoanalysis
    C. Cognitive behavioral therapy
    D. Motivational interviewing

17. Which of the following is *NOT* a commonly used and misused substance?
    A. Cannabis
    B. Alcohol

C. Sedatives

D. Cough syrup

18. Which symptom is *NOT* part of the diagnostic criteria for mood disorders?

    A. Irritable mood

    B. Increased or decreased appetite

    C. Substance misuse

    D. Suicidal thoughts

19. Through which means can an open head injury to the brain be caused?

    A. Gunshot

    B. Stabbing

    C. Car accident

    D. All of the above

20. Which symptom is *NOT* part of the diagnostic criteria for posttraumatic stress disorder?

    A. Emotional outbursts

    B. Concentration difficulties

    C. Mania

    D. Hypervigilance

21. Autism varies widely in severity and symptoms. Which of these behaviors is *NOT* one of the characteristics of autism spectrum disorders?

    A. Difficulties in maintaining social conversations

    B. Impairment in maintaining friendships

    C. Repetitive patterns of behaviors

    D. Exceptional math skills

    E. Lack of empathy

22. One of the characteristics of a person with autism spectrum disorder is having difficulty interacting with others. Which of the following statements is an example of this?

    A. The person avoids maintaining eye contact with other people

    B. The person seems unaware of other's feelings toward him or her

    C. The person often misunderstands the reactions of other people

    D. The person prefers solitary activities instead of sharing with other people

    E. All of the above

23. Which of the following skills is *NOT* listed as one of the adaptive behaviors that people use to function in their everyday lives?

    A. The conceptual skills

    B. The social skills

C. The accommodating skills

D. The practical skills

24. *Intellectual disability* is the current term used in the *DSM-5*, which replaces the old diagnostic label:

    A. *Autism*

    B. *Mental retardation*

    C. *Learning disability*

    D. *Microcephaly*

25. This type of seizure, also called *petit mal*, is an episode of brief disruption of consciousness and mild rhythmic movements of the eyelids.

    A. Myoclonic seizure

    B. Absence seizure

    C. Infantile seizure

    D. Tonic–clonic seizure

26. Common symptoms of cerebral palsy include all of the following *EXCEPT*:

    A. Abnormal gait

    B. Abnormal muscle tone

    C. Below-average IQ

    D. Loss of coordination

27. Which of the following is *NOT* one of the three manifestations of attention deficit hyperactivity disorder?

    A. Hyperactivity

    B. Inability to maintain social interactions

    C. Inattention and distractibility

    D. Impulsivity

28. Symptoms of specific learning disorder may include impairment in the ability to use acquired information. Which of the following is not an example of a symptom of specific learning disorders?

    A. Dysphoria

    B. Dyslexia

    C. Dyscalculia

    D. Dysgraphia

    E. Agnosia

29. For individuals with visual impairments, several possible accommodations can be provided in a workplace. Which is an accommodation for light sensitivity?

    A. Braille documents

    B. Large-print documents

    C. Auditory versions of forms

    D. Lower-wattage overhead lights

    E. Magnification of text with a closed-circuit television system

30. The most common hearing-management method for persons with hearing impairment is:

    A. Hearing aids

    B. Cochlear implants

    C. Telecommunication devices for the deaf

    D. All of the above

    E. None of the above

Answer Key and Explanation of Answers

1B: Universal design uses the principle of equitable use to provide the same means of use for all users.

2C: Universal design's principle of tolerance for error means the design minimizes hazards and the adverse consequences of accidental or unintended actions.

3B: The endocannabinoid system involves appetite, pain perception, mood, memory, and motor learning, which is relevant to mood disorder and movement disorders (e.g., Parkinson's disease and Huntington's disease).

4B: A person with an injury at the C5 level can have some gross movement of the upper extremities (e.g., bending the arm at elbow, holding a light object between the thumb and finger, independently operating an electric wheelchair).

5B: A person with an injury at the C7 to C8 levels can be almost independent, with some environmental accommodations.

6C: The Glasgow Coma Scale is a classification system used to determine the seriousness of brain injury by assessing the level of responsiveness of the patient. It yields a score from 3 (more severe injury) to 15 (least severe injury). The score range of 4 to 8 indicates a comatose status.

7B: Manifestations of right-sided brain damage include left-sided paralysis, spatial-perceptual deficits, quick impulsive behavior, and performance memory deficits. Manifestations of left-sided brain damage include right-sided paralysis, speech language deficits, slow and cautious behavior, language memory deficits, and problem-solving deficits.

8A: Apraxia is an inability to carry out purposeful and coordinated voluntary motor skills and movements.

9C: Broca's aphasia presents with nonfluent aphasia, articulation problems, and word-finding difficulties (dysnomia); Wernicke's aphasia presents with fluent aphasia and effortless speech but reduced information content; and global aphasia presents with an inability to use and understand language.

10C: The first symptoms of multiple sclerosis include vision problems, weak/stiff muscles (often with painful muscle spasms), tingling, numbness, difficulty walking, bladder-control problems, and dizziness. Later symptoms include mental or physical fatigue, mood changes, reduced cognitive function, and difficulty making decisions, planning, or prioritizing at work or in private life.

11C: Fibromyalgia affects approximately 2% to 8% of the population and more women than men by a ratio of 9:1. Women tend to have more pain-related clinical conditions due to a variety of possible risk factors such as cultural factors or female hormones. However, the gender gap is most significant for the case of fibromyalgia.

12D: Anti-inflammatory, narcotic analgesic, and antidepressant medications are used as pharmacological approaches to pain management. People with chronic pain may receive a prescription or recommendation to take any one of these medications for dealing with persistent issues related to pain. Antipsychotic medications are *not* endorsed for chronic pain. They are a class of psychiatric medications and are used primarily to manage psychosis.

13A: Chordoma is a rare form of cancer. It is less common than sarcoma, melanoma, and carcinoma. In the United States, chordoma affects roughly 300 people per year. Approximately 14,000 people are diagnosed with sarcoma each year. Melanoma is found in about 76,380 people in the United States every year. Finally, carcinoma is the most common form of cancer and may affect the breast, lung, prostate, colon, and other epithelia tissues, with more than 1,685,210 new cases diagnosed on an annual basis in the United States.

14C: Common symptoms for anxiety disorders include nervousness, sweating, and worrying. Anxiety disorders are prevalent mental health disorders that primarily involve excessive anxiety and worry. Symptoms such as sadness or depressed mood can occur with anxiety, but they are *not* a part of the diagnostic criteria for anxiety disorders.

15A: Personality disorders involve a persistent pattern of long-term issues with maladaptive emotions, thoughts, and behaviors, such as mood, self-image, or social functioning. It is often recommended that persons diagnosed with personality disorders seek treatment from a multidisciplinary team, including primary care providers, psychiatrists, and psychologists. For psychological services, the model of therapy that has been deemed evidence based is called *dialectical behavior therapy*. It is a comprehensive form of cognitive behavioral treatment, and it is especially useful for people with borderline personality disorder.

16C: Cognitive behavioral therapy is a short-term, goal-oriented, and directive form of treatment for anxiety and other mental health problems. It often involves hands-on and problem-solving approaches to psychological issues. It has been shown to be particularly useful for anxiety relief. Cognitive behavioral therapists provide psychoeducation to persons with anxiety and offer suggestions for self-management tools and homework assignments. Over time and with practice, persons are able to gradually reduce anxiety in various contexts.

17D: Cannabis, alcohol, and sedatives are commonly used and misused substances in the general population. In 2013, 4.2 million Americans met diagnostic criteria for cannabis use disorder. Alcohol has the highest rate of abuse among all drug classes. In 2013, 17.3 million Americans had problems related to alcohol use. Sedative misuse is less common, with 0.2% of persons 12 or older with reported use. National surveys on the abuse of cough syrup have estimated rates to be as high as 3% to 4%, but it seems to be a problem documented predominantly among teenage groups.

18C: Clinical criteria for mood disorders involve symptoms such as irritable mood, increased or decreased appetite, change in sleep, fatigue, guilt, reduced concentration, and decreased interest or pleasure in daily activities. In severe cases, people with depression may report suicidal thoughts or plans. Persons with mental illness are often screened for substance use and are frequently labeled with the "dual diagnoses" of substance misuse and mental health disorders. Substance misuse symptoms may even mimic mental health problems but are *not* a part of the diagnostic criteria for depression.

19D: Open head brain injury can be caused by any penetration in which the outer brain layer or the skull is breached. Gunshot, stabbing incidents, and car accidents are common reasons for such trauma inflicted on and entering the brain.

20C: A medical diagnosis for posttraumatic stress disorder (PTSD) may include symptoms such as nightmares, flashbacks, distressing recollections of the event, avoidance of triggers, and heightened reactivity to stimuli. Persons with PTSD are frequently diagnosed with co-occurring mental health disorders such as bipolar disorders, which lead to even more severe PTSD symptoms or problems such as substance misuse. Although PTSD symptoms may present with significant mood and other psychological issues, manic symptoms are *not* a part of the diagnostic criteria.

21D: Difficulty in maintaining social conservations, impairment in maintaining friendships, repeated patterns of behavior, and lack of empathy are characteristics of autism spectrum disorder. Lack of math skills is not.

22E: According to *DSM-5*, autism spectrum disorder is characterized by persistent deficits in social communication (e.g., initiating/sustaining conversations), impairment in social interactions (e.g., maintaining friendships), repetitive patterns of behaviors, restricted interests or activities, and the potential for sensory sensitivities.

23C: Adaptive behaviors include conceptual, social, and practical domains. Conceptual skills are skills in domains such as language, reading, writing, and math. Social domains include interpersonal communication skills and the ability to make and maintain friendships. The practical domain includes self-management skills, such as personal care and money management, while the accommodating domain includes skills to adapt or adjust to changes and be flexible.

24B: *Mental retardation* was replaced by *intellectual disability* in *DSM-5*.

25B: Absence seizure is one common type of generated seizure, which is also called a *petit mal seizure*. This type of seizure usually lasts only a few seconds and involves a brief disruption of consciousness (usually 10–20 seconds) and autonomic symptoms such as dilated pupils and mild rhythmic movements of the eyelids, but sometimes the episode may involve blank stares.

26C: Common symptoms include abnormal movements (twisting, jerking, writhing) of limbs, abnormal muscle tones (too stiff/tight or too floppy), abnormal gaits (crouched or "scissored"), exaggerated reflexes, tremors, unsteady gait, and loss of coordination. Below-average IQ is not one of the common symptoms of cerebral palsy.

27B: Attention deficit hyperactivity disorder is a condition exhibited by difficulty maintaining attention, as well as hyperactivity and impulsive behavior. Being unable to maintain appropriate social interactions is one of the characteristics of individuals with autism spectrum disorder.

28A: Dysphoria is a profound state of unease or dissatisfaction. It is unrelated to autism spectrum disorders.

29D: Braille documents are an accommodation for persons with no vision; large-print documents, auditory versions of forms, and text magnification using a closed-caption television system are accommodations for persons with low vision. Lower-wattage overhead lights are an accommmodation for persons who are sensitive to light.

30D: The most common hearing-management method involves the use of assistive listening devices (ALDs) and telecommunication devices for the deaf (TDDs). ALDs include hearing aids and cochlear implants, whereas TDDs allow the person with a hearing impairment to send and receive typed messages to other TDD users via a telephone line.

References

American Association of Diabetes Educators. (2010). AADE7 self-care behaviors. Retrieved from https://www.diabeteseducator.org/patient-resources/aade7-self-care-behaviors

American Association on Intellectual and Developmental Disabilities. (2011). Frequently asked questions on intellectual disability. Retrieved from https://aaidd.org/intellectual-disability/definition/faqs-on-intellectual-disability

American College of Rheumatology. (2016). Rheumatoid arthritis. Retrieved from http://www.rheumatology .org/I-Am-A/Patient-Caregiver/Diseases-Conditions/Rheumatoid-Arthritis

American Diabetes Association. (2016). Employment discrimination. Retrieved from http://www .diabetes.org/living-with-diabetes/know-your-rights/discrimination/employment-discrimination/?referrer=https://www.google.com

American Psychiatric Association. (2000). *Diagnostic and statistical manual of mental disorders* (4th ed., text rev.). Washington, DC: Author.

American Psychiatric Association. (2013). *Diagnostic and statistical manual of mental disorders* (5th ed.). Arlington, VA: American Psychiatric Publishing.

Arango-Lasprilla, J. C., Ketchum, J. M., Starkweather, A., Nicholls, E., & Wilk, A. R. (2011). Factors predicting depression among persons with spinal cord injury 1 to 5 years post injury. *NeuroRehabilitation, 29*(1), 9–21.

Arnold, L. M., Crofford, L. J., Mease, P. J., Burgess, S. M., Palmer, S. C., Abetz, L., & Martin, S. A. (2008). Patient perspectives on the impact of fibromyalgia. *Patient Education and Counseling, 73,* 114–120.

Baldwin, C., & Brusco, N. K. (2011). The effect of vocational rehabilitation on return-to-work rates post stroke: A systematic review. *Topics in Stroke Rehabilitation, 18*(5), 562–572.

Batra, R., & Jajoo, P. (2011). The role of rehabilitation in cancer patients. In S. R. Flanagan, H. Zarestsky, & A. Moroz (Eds.), *Medical aspects of disability* (4th ed., pp. 103–117). New York, NY: Springer Publishing.

Bohus, M., Haaf, B., Simms, T., Limberger, M. F., Schmahl, C., Unckel, C., … Linehan, M. M. (2004). Effectiveness of inpatient dialectical behavioral therapy for borderline personality disorder: A controlled trial. *Behaviour Research and Therapy, 42*(5), 487–499.

Brodwin, M. G., Cardoso, E., & Star, T. (2004). Computer assistive technology for people who have disabilities: Computer adaptations and modifications. *Journal of Rehabilitation, 70*(3), 28–33.

Carr, R. L., & Gramling, L. F. (2004). Stigma: A health barrier for women with HIV/AIDS. *Journal of the Association of Nurses in AIDS Care, 15*(5), 30–39.

Carter Batiste, L. (2013). Accommodation and Compliance Series: Employees with multiple sclerosis. Retrieved from https://askjan.org/media/MS.html

Carter Batiste, L., & Loy, B. (2013). Accommodation and Compliance Series: Employees who use wheelchairs. Retrieved from https://askjan.org/media/Wheelchair.html

Centers for Disease Control and Prevention. (2005). Annual smoking-attributable mortality, years of potential life lost, and productivity losses—United States, 1997–2001. *Morbidity and Mortality Weekly Report, 54*(250), 625–628.

Centers for Disease Control and Prevention. (2012). Vital signs: Awareness and treatment of uncontrolled hypertension among adults—United States, 2003–2010. *Morbidity and Mortality Weekly Report, 61*(35), 703–709.

Centers for Disease Control and Prevention. (2014). *Community report from the Autism and Developmental Disabilities Monitoring (ADDM) network: A snapshot of autism spectrum disorder among 8-year-old children in multiple communities across the United States in 2010.* (No. SS2). Washington, DC: Author.

Centers for Disease Control and Prevention. (2015). HIV fact sheets. Retrieved from http://www.cdc.gov/hiv/library/factsheets/index.html

Centers for Disease Control and Prevention. (2016a). Burns. Retrieved from http://www .cdc.gov/masstrauma/factsheets/public/burns.pdf

Centers for Disease Control and Prevention. (2016b). Chronic obstructive pulmonary disease. Retrieved from https://www.cdc.gov/copd/index.html

Centers for Disease Control and Prevention. (2016c). Diabetes. Retrieved from http://www .cdc.gov/diabetes/home

Centers for Disease Control and Prevention. (2016d). Lupus. Retrieved from http://www.cdc.gov/lupus

COPD Foundation. (2016). What is COPD? Retrieved from http://www.copdfoundation.org/What-is-COPD/Understanding-COPD/What-is-COPD.aspx

Costa, D. C., Sá, M. J., & Calheiros, J. M. (2012). The effect of social support on the quality of life of patients with multiple sclerosis. *Arquivos de Neuro-Psiquiatria, 70*(2), 108–113.

Dalal, P. K., Saha, R., & Agarwal, M. (2010). Psychiatric aspects of burn. *Indian Journal of Plastic Surgery, 43*(Suppl.), S136–S142.

Dall'Era, M. (2013). Systemic lupus erythematosus. In J. B. Imboden, D. B. Hellman, & J. H. Stone (Eds.), *Current rheumatology diagnosis and treatment* (3rd ed.). New York, NY: McGraw-Hill.

Dorinzi, L. (2014). Accommodation and Compliance Series: Employees with lupus. Retrieved from https://askjan.org/media/Lupus.html

Drake, R. E., Bond, G. R., & Becker, D. R. (2012). *Individual placement and support: An evidence-based approach to supported employment.* Oxford, UK: Oxford University Press.

Du, A. T., Lindberg, J., & Bluestein, B. W. (2014). Chronic pain management. In M. G. Brodwin, F. W. Siu, J. Howard, E. R. Brodwin, & A. T. Du (Eds.), *Medical, psychosocial, and vocational aspects of disability* (4th ed., pp. 131–142). Athens, GA: Elliott & Fitzpatrick.

Du, S., Yuan, C., Xiao, X., Chu, J., Qui, Y., & Qian, H. (2011). Self-management programs for chronic musculoskeletal pain conditions: A systematic review and meta-analysis. *Patient Education and Counseling, 85*, 299–310.

Duarte, C., Couto, M., Ines, L., & Liang, M. H. (2011). Epidemiology of systemic lupus erythematosus. In R. G. Lahita, J. Buyon, & T. Koike (Eds.), *Systemic lupus erythematosus* (5th ed., pp. 673–696). London, UK: Elsevier.

Eng, N., & Lerner, P. K. (2011). Speech, language, hearing, and swallowing disorders. In S. R. Flanagan, H. Zarestsky, & A. Moroz (Eds.), *Medical aspects of disability* (4th ed., pp. 195–222). New York, NY: Springer Publishing.

Falvo, D. (2009). *Medical and psychosocial aspects of chronic illness and disability* (4th ed.). New York, NY: Jones & Bartlett.

Falvo, D. (2014). *Medical and psychosocial aspects of chronic illness and disability* (5th ed.). Burlington, MA: Jones & Bartlett Learning.

Felton, J. S. (2002). Medical terminology. In M. G. Brodwin, F. Tellez, & A. Browin (Eds.), *Medical, psychosocial and vocational aspects of disability* (pp. 15–26). Athens, GA: Elliott & Fitzpatrick.

Foley, F. (2016). *Taming stress in MS.* Retrieved from http://www.nationalmssociety.org/NationalMSSociety/media/MSNationalFiles/Brochures/Brochure-Taming-Stress.pdf

Fraser, R. T., Miller, J. W., & Johnson, E. K. (2011). Epilepsy. In S. R. Flanagan, H. Zarestsky, & A. Moroz (Eds.), *Medical aspects of disability* (4th ed., pp. 65–87). New York, NY: Springer Publishing.

Gettings, L. (2010). Psychological well-being in rheumatoid arthritis: A review of the literature. *Musculoskeletal Care, 8*(2), 99–106.

Gharibo, C. G., & Khan, M. F. (2011). Chronic pain syndromes. In S. R. Flanagan, H. Zarestsky, & A. Moroz (Eds.), *Medical aspects of disability* (4th ed., pp. 147–158). New York, NY: Springer Publishing.

Givner, C. C., & Brodwin, M. G. (2009). Learning disabilities. In M. G. Brodwin, F. W. Siu, J. Howard, & E. R. Brodwin (Eds.), *Medical, psychosocial, and vocational aspects of disability* (3rd ed., pp. 355–365). Athens, GA: Elliott & Fitzpatrick.

Global Initiative for Chronic Obstructive Lung Disease. (2017). *Pocket guide to COPD diagnosis, management, and prevention: A guide for health care professionals.* Retrieved from http://goldcopd.org/wp-content/uploads/2016/12/wms-GOLD-2017-Pocket-Guide.pdf

Gupta, A. R., & State, M. W. (2007). Recent advances in the genetics of autism. *Biological Psychiatry, 61*, 429–437.

Haas, L., Maryniuk, M., Beck, J., Cox, C. E., Duker, P., Edwards, L., … Youssef, G. (2014). National standards for diabetes self-management education and support. Retrieved from http://care.diabetesjournals .org/content/37/Supplement_1/S144.full

Halkitis, P. N., Shrem, M. T., Zade, D. D., & Wilton, L. (2005). The physical, emotional and interpersonal impact of HAART: Exploring the realities of HIV seropositive individuals on combination therapy. *Journal of Health Psychology*, *10*(3), 345–358.

Hall, M. J., Levant, S., & DeFrances, C. J. (2012). *Hospitalization for stroke in U.S. hospitals, 1989–2009*. NCHS data brief, No. 95. Hyattsville, MD: National Center for Health Statistics.

Individuals With Disabilities Education Act of 1990 (IDEA). (1990, October 30). PL 101–476, Title 20, U.S.C. 1400 et seq. U.S. Statutes at Large, 104, 1103–1151.

Institute of Medicine. (2011). *Relieving pain in America: A blueprint for transforming prevention, care, education and research*. Washington, DC: National Academies Press.

Jarskog, L. F., Miyamoto, S., & Lieberman, J. A. (2007). Schizophrenia: New pathological insights and therapies. *Annual Review of Medicine*, *58*, 49–61.

Job Accommodation Network. (n.d.). Accommodation ideas for stroke. Retrieved from https://askjan .org/media/stro.htm

Job Accommodation Network. (2013a). Accommodation and Compliance Series: Employees with brain injuries. Retrieved from https://askjan.org/media/BrainInjury.html

Job Accomodation Network. (2013b). Accommodation and Compliance Series: Employees with diabetes. Retrieved from https://askjan.org/media/Diabetes.html

Job Accommodation Network. (2013c). Accommodation and Compliance Series: Employees with hearing loss. Retrieved from https://askjan.org/media/Hearing.html

Job Accommodation Network. (2013d). Accommodation and Compliance Series: Employees with intellectual or cognitive disabilities. Retrieved from https://askjan.org/media/intcog.html

Job Accommodation Network. (2013e). Accommodation and Compliance Series: Employees with respiratory impairments. Retrieved from https://askjan.org/media/respiratory.html

Job Accommodation Network. (2015a). Accommodation and Compliance Series: Accommodation ideas for HIV/AIDS. Retrieved from https://askjan.org/media/HIV.html

Job Accomodation Network. (2015b). Accommodation and Compliance Series: Employees with attention deficit hyperactivity disorder. Retrieved from https://askjan.org/media/adhd.html

Job Accomodation Network. (2015c). Accommodation and Compliance Series: Employees with learning disabilities. Retrieved from https://askjan.org/media/LD.html

Job Accommodation Network. (2015d). Accommodation and Compliance Series: Employees with personality disorders. Retrieved from https://askjan.org/media/personality.html

Job Accommodation Network. (2015e). Accommodation and Compliance Series: Employees with post traumatic stress disorder (PTSD). Retrieved from https://askjan.org/media/ptsd.html

Kim, H., Kunik, M., & Molinari, V. (2000). Functional impairment in COPD patients: The impact of anxiety and depression. *Psychosomatics*, *41*, 465–471.

Kukla, M., & Bond, G. R. (2011). Psychiatric disabilities. In S. R. Flanagan, H. Zarestsky, & A. Moroz (Eds.), *Medical aspects of disability* (4th ed., pp. 441–466). New York, NY: Springer Publishing.

LeBlanc, L. A., Riley, A. R., & Goldsmith, T. R. (2008). Autism spectrum disorders: A lifespan perspective. In J. L. Matson (Ed.), *Autism spectrum disorders: Evidence based assessment and intervention across the lifespan* (pp. 65–81). San Diego, CA: Elsevier.

Loy, B. (2013). Accommodation and Compliance Series: Employees with vision impairments. Retrieved from https://askjan.org/media/Sight.html

Loy, B. (2015a). Accommodation and Compliance Series: Employees with arthritis. Retrieved from https:// askjan.org/media/Arthritis.html

Loy, B. (2015b). Accommodation and Compliance Series: Employees with chronic pain. Retrieved from https://askjan.org/media/ChronicPain.html

Loy, B. (2015c). Accommodation and Compliance Series: Employees with cancer. Retrieved from https://askjan.org/media/Cancer.htm

Loy, B., & Whetzel, M. (2015). Accommodation and Compliance Series: Employees with mental health impairments. Retrieved from https://askjan.org/media/Psychiatric.html

Lupus Foundation of America. (2016). Statistics on lupus. Retrieved from http://www.lupus.org/about/statistics-on-lupus

Mason, S. T., Esselman, P., Fraser, R., Schomer, K., Truitt, A., & Johnson, K. (2012). Return to work after burn injury: A systematic review. *Journal of Burn Care and Research, 33*(1), 101–109.

Mayo Clinic. (2015). Chronic obstructive pulmonary disease. Retrieved from http://www.mayoclinic.org/diseases-conditions/copd/basics/treatment/con-20032017

McCarberg, B. H., & Passik, S. D. (Eds.). (2005). *Expert guide to pain management.* Philadelphia, PA: ACP Press.

Meintjes, G., Lawn, S. D., Scano, F., Maartens, G., French, M. A., Worodria, W., … International Network for the Study of HIV-associated IRIS. (2008). Tuberculosis-associated immune reconstitution inflammatory syndrome: Case definitions for use in resource-limited settings. *Lancet Infectious Diseases, 8*(8), 516–523.

Morris, R. (2011). The psychology of stroke in young adults: The roles of service provision and return to work. *Stroke Research and Treatment, 2011.* doi:10.4061/2011/534812

Mozzafarian, D., Benjamin, E. J., Go, A. S., Arnrr, D. K., Blaha, M. J., Cushman, M., … American Heart Association Statistics Committee and Stroke Statistics Subcommittee. (2015). Heart disease and stroke statistics—2015 update: A report from the American Heart Association. *Circulation, 131*, e29–e322.

National Health Service. (2014). Side effects of bronchodilator medicines. Retrieved from http://www.nhs.uk/conditions/bronchodilator-drugs/pages/side-effects.aspx

National Institute of Mental Health. (2012). Attention deficit hyperactivity disorder (ADHD). Retrieved from https://www.nimh.nih.gov/health/publications/attention-deficit-hyperactivity-disorder-adhd-the-basics/qf-16-3572_153275.pdf

National Institute of Neurological Disorders and Stroke. (2015). Multiple sclerosis: Hope through research. Retrieved from https://www.ninds.nih.gov/Disorders/All-Disorders/Multiple-Sclerosis-Information-Page

National Spinal Cord Injury Statistical Center. (2015). *Facts and figures at a glance.* Birmingham: University of Alabama at Birmingham.

Orr, L. E., II, & Orange, L. M. (2002). Cancer. In M. G. Brodwin, F. Tellez, & S. K. Brodwin (Eds.), *Medical, psychosocial, and vocational aspects of disability* (2nd ed., pp. 171–184). Athens, GA: Elliott & Fitzpatrick.

Orr, L. E., II, & Orange, L. M. (2014). Cancer. In M. G. Brodwin, F. W. Siu, J. Howard, E. R. Brodwin, & A. T. Du (Eds.), *Medical, psychosocial, and vocational aspects of disability* (4th ed., pp. 37–50). Athens, GA: Elliott & Fitzpatrick.

Ottomanelli, L., & Lind, L. (2009). Review of critical factors related to employment after spinal cord injury: Implications for research and vocational services. *Journal of Spinal Cord Medicine, 32*(5), 503–531.

Peterson, D. B., & Hong, G. K. (2014). Psychiatric diagnoses. In M. G. Brodwin, F. W. Siu, J. Howard, E. R. Brodwin, & A. T. Du (Eds.), *Medical, psychosocial, and vocational aspects of disability* (4th ed., pp. 269–284). Athens, GA: Elliott & Fitzpatrick.

Rabkin, J., McElhiney, M., Ferrando, S. J., Van Gorp, W., & Lin, S. H. (2004). Predictors of employment of men with HIV/AIDS: A longitudinal study. *Psychosomatic Medicine, 66*, 72–78.

RAND Corporation. (2007). *Mental health and substance abuse issues among people with HIV.* Santa Monica, CA: Author.

Rumrill, P. (2015). *Q & A on employment of people with physical disabilities: Employment and multiple sclerosis—August 2014*. Retrieved from http://vcurrtc.org/resources/content.cfm/1127

Saladin, S. P., & Hansmann, S. (2009). Hearing loss, deafness, and related vestibular disorders. In M. G. Brodwin, F. W. Siu, J. Howard, & E. R. Brodwin (Eds.), *Medical, psychosocial, and vocational aspects of disability* (3rd ed., pp. 171–184). Athens, GA: Elliott & Fitzpatrick.

Schwartz, S. H. (2002). Traumatic brain injury. In M. G. Brodwin, F. Tellez, & S. K. Brodwin (Eds.), *Medical, psychosocial, and vocational aspects of disability* (2nd ed., pp. 363–373). Athens, GA: Elliott & Fitzpatrick.

Schwartz, S. H., & Wild, M. A. (2014). Traumatic brain injury. In M.G. Brodwin, F. W. Siu, J. Howard, E. R. Brodwin, & A. T. Du (Eds.), *Medical, psychosocial, and vocational aspects of disability* (4th ed., pp. 155–168). Athens, GA: Elliott & Fitzpatrick.

Sharma, S. K., & Soneja, M. (2011). HIV & immune reconstitution inflammatory syndrome (IRIS). *Indian Journal of Medical Research*, 134(6), 866–877.

Sokka, T. (2003). Work disability in early rheumatoid arthritis. *Clinical and Experimental Rheumatology*, 21 (Suppl. 31), S71–S74.

Stirratt, M. J., Remien, R. H., Smith, A., Copeland, O. Q., Dolezal, C., Krieger, D., & SMART Couples Study Team. (2006). The role of HIV serostatus disclosure in antiretroviral medication adherence. *AIDS and Behavior*, 10(5), 483–493.

Takeshita, B., Langman, R., & Brod, R. (2009). Visual disabilities. In M. G. Brodwin, F. W. Siu, J. Howard, & E. R. Brodwin (Eds.), *Medical, psychosocial, and vocational aspects of disability* (3rd ed., pp. 171–184). Athens, GA: Elliott & Fitzpatrick.

Torriani, S. B., Britto, F. C., da Silva, G. A., de Oliveira, D. C., & Carvalho, Z. M. (2014). Sexuality of people with spinal cord injury: Knowledge, difficulties and adaptation. *Journal of Biomedical Science and Engineering*, 7, 380–386.

Turk, D. C., & McCarberg, B. (2005). Non-pharmacological treatments for chronic pain: A disease management context. *Disease Management & Health Outcomes*, 13, 19–30.

U.S. Department of Labor. (2012). *HIV and employment*. Retrieved from http://www.dol.gov/odep/pdf/20120728hivaidsreports.pdf

Wheaton, A. G., Cunningham, T. J., Ford, E. S., & Croft, J. B. (2015). Employment and activity limitations among adults with chronic obstructive pulmonary disease—United States, 2013. Retrieved from http://www.cdc.gov/mmwr/preview/mmwrhtml/mm6411a1.htm

Whetzel, M. (2013a). Accommodation and Compliance Series: Employees with autism spectrum disorder. Retrieved from https://askjan.org/media/ASD.html

Whetzel, M. (2013b). Accommodation and Compliance Series: Employees with epilepsy. Retrieved from https://askjan.org/media/epilepsy.html

Whidden, E. (2013). Accommodation and Compliance Series: Employees with cerebral palsy (CP). Retrieved from https://askjan.org/media/CP.html

Wolfe, F., Clauw, D. J., Fitzcharles, M. A., Goldenberg, D. L., Katz, R. S., Mease, P., … Yunus, M. B. (2010). The American College of Rheumatology preliminary diagnostic criteria for fibromyalgia and measurement of symptom severity. *Arthritis Care & Research*, 62(5), 600–610.

World Health Organization. (1946). Constitution of WHO: Principles. Retrieved from http://www.who.int/about/mission/en

World Health Organization. (2001). *The International Classification of Functioning, Disability and Health (ICF)*. Geneva, Switzerland: Author. Retrieved from http://www.who.int/classifications/icf/en

World Health Organization. (2013). *How to use the ICF: A practical manual for using the International Classification of Functioning, Disability and Health (ICF). Exposure draft for comment*. Geneva, Switzerland: Author.

World Health Organization. (2014a). *International classification of disease* (10th revision). Clinical Modification (ICD-10-CM). Geneva, Switzerland: Author.

World Health Organization. (2014b). Visual impairment and blindness. Retrieved from http://www.who .int/mediacentre/factsheets/fs282/en

World Health Organization. (2015). International classification of diseases, tenth revision (ICD-10). Retrieved from http://apps.who.int/classifications/icd10/browse/2015/en

World Health Organization. (2017). International classification of diseases, eleventh revision (ICD-11). Retrieved from http://apps.who.int/classifications/icd11/browse/l-m/en#

Yazdany, J., & Yelin, E. (2010). Health-related quality of life and employment among persons with systemic lupus erythematosus. *Rheumatic Disease Clinics of North America, 36*(1), 15–32.

Zablotsky, B., Black, L. I., Maenner, M. J., & Schieve, L. A. (2015). *Estimated prevalence of autism and other developmental disabilities following questionnaire changes in the 2014 National Health Interview Survey.* (National Health Statistics Reports; No. 87). Hyattsville, MD: National Center for Health Statistics.

Zamzam, M. A., Azab, N. Y., Wahsh, R., Ragab, A. Z., & Allam, E. M. (2012). Quality of life in COPD patients. *Egyptian Journal of Chest Diseases and Tuberculosis, 61*(4), 281–289.

10

Rehabilitation Services, Case Management, and Related Services

Malachy Bishop, Veronica I. Umeasiegbu, and Christina Espinosa Bard

This chapter reviews rehabilitation counseling legislation, case management, and a variety of services that rehabilitation counselors provide or arrange in the public sector (i.e., the state-federal vocational rehabilitation (VR) system and other public VR agencies), the private nonprofit sector, and the private for-profit sector. Topics covered include

- *VR*
- *Case and caseload management*
- *Independent living (IL)*
- *School-to-work transition services*
- *Disability management (DM)*
- *Forensic rehabilitation, vocational expert practices, and life care planning*
- *Substance abuse (SA) treatment and rehabilitation*
- *Wellness and illness-prevention concepts*
- *Community resources and community-based rehabilitation programs (CRPs)*
- *Insurance programs and Social Security*
- *Assistive technology (AT) and rehabilitation counseling*

Vocational Rehabilitation

Overview

This section reviews the history and status of the public VR program in America and identifies important elements and outcomes of key VR legislation.

Learning Objectives

By the end of this unit you should be able to:

1. Describe the history, status, and purpose of the state-federal VR program.
2. Identify key VR legislation, legislative mandates, and outcomes.

Key Concepts

The state-federal VR program is a federally funded program authorized under the Rehabilitation Act of 1973 and subsequent amendments, with the most recent amendment in 2014. The state-federal VR program funds state VR agencies to provide employment-related services for persons with disabilities to enable preparation for and engagement in gainful employment. This program is founded on the principle that individuals with disabilities, including those with the most significant disabilities, can achieve competitive integrated employment when provided the necessary skills and supports. The Rehabilitation Services Administration (RSA) within the U.S. Department of Education is the federal agency that oversees the program. The state-federal VR program operates in each state, Washington, DC, and several U.S. territories, and many states operate separate VR programs for individuals who are blind (Fabian & MacDonald-Wilson, 2012). The state-federal VR program provides employment-related services for individuals with disabilities, giving priority to those individuals who have the most significant disabilities.

The state-federal VR program is an eligibility, rather than an entitlement program. To be eligible for VR services, an applicant must have a physical or mental impairment that constitutes or results in a substantial impediment to employment, and it must be determined that the applicant requires VR services to prepare for, secure, retain, advance in, or regain employment consistent with the individual's strengths, resources, priorities, concerns, abilities, capabilities, interests, and informed choice. In addition, in the state-federal VR program, there is a *presumption of eligibility* based on eligibility for Social Security benefits, which means that any applicant who has been determined eligible for Social Security benefits under title II or title XVI of the Social Security Act is presumed to be eligible for VR services. There is also a *presumption of benefit*, which means that any applicant who meets these eligibility requirements is presumed to be able to benefit in terms of an employment outcome.

Once eligibility has been determined, a written plan for employment, called an Individualized Plan for Employment (IPE), is developed and approved by the individual or a representative and the VR counselor. The IPE must be designed to achieve a specific employment outcome that is selected by the individual and is consistent with the individual's unique strengths, resources, priorities, concerns, abilities, capabilities, interests, and informed choice. Although generally developed in collaboration with the state VR counselor, an eligible individual or the individual's representative may develop all or part of the IPE independently. The IPE is developed and implemented to give eligible individuals the opportunity to exercise informed choice in selecting the employment outcome, employment setting, and VR services that will be needed to achieve the employment outcome. The VR counselor and the client review the IPE at least annually to evaluate progress toward the employment outcome. Services that may be provided under the plan include (a) medical, psychological, vocational, and other diagnostic assessments and evaluation services; (b) counseling and guidance; (c) physical and mental restoration therapy or treatments; (d) occupational and vocational training and education; (e) interpreter services, reader, and orientation and mobility training and services; (f) job search and placement and job-retention services; (g) supported employment services; (h) personal assistance services; (i) rehabilitation technology services, including vehicular modification, telecommunications, and sensory and other technological aids and devices; (j) postemployment services; and (k) transition services for students and youth with disabilities to facilitate postsecondary transition.

I. Historical Foundation of Vocational Rehabilitation in America

Before establishment of public VR in the Unites States, rehabilitation services were provided by private religious, philanthropic, and charitable organizations. A combination of factors during the end of the 19th century and the first two decades of the 20th century created the conditions for the establishment of the state-federal VR: (a) the Industrial Revolution, which led to a national shift from an agrarian, or farm based, economy to an industry-based economy and a relocation of the population base to the cities; (b) a federal policy shift characterized by economic, social, and political reform and an increased government role in creating opportunities for individuals to compete; (c) compulsory public education, in large part as a means of teaching vocational skills and creating productive workers in cities that had large populations seeking to become employed and needing to be appropriately educated for employment; and (d) the federal income tax, which resulted in moneys that could, in part, be used in the federal sponsorship of VR programs for soldiers, veterans, and civilians. The income tax also enabled tax write-offs for rehabilitation ventures and established the economic argument for VR (i.e., an investment of funds in VR will, by enabling persons with disabilities to become employed tax payers, result in a several-fold increase in federal income over time).

The public VR of Americans with disabilities emerged from federal legislation, including the Soldier's Rehabilitation Act of 1918 and the Smith-Fess Act in 1920. These acts and the subsequent federal VR-related legislation prior to the Rehabilitation Act of 1973 are presented in Table 10.1.

TABLE 10.1   Key Vocational Rehabilitation–Related Legislation 1935–1973

Legislation and Year	Key Mandates/Outcomes
The Smith Hughes Act of 1917 (also known as the Vocational Education Act)	Made federal monies available on a matching basis to states that developed a vocational education program. The act created the Federal Board of Vocational Education, which would become the first administrative agency for the vocational rehabilitation program.
Soldier's Rehabilitation Act 1918	First U.S. program for vocational rehabilitation of people with disabilities. The Federal Board of Vocational Education had responsibility for developing vocational rehabilitation programs and training for military veterans with physical disabilities for whom employment was seen as a feasible result of services.
The Smith-Fess Act of 1920	This act provided federal money at a 50-50 match with states that provided vocational guidance, vocational education, placement, and occupational adjustment to civilians with physical disabilities (defined as a physical defect or infirmary). Because of the 50-50 match, there was a strong incentive for states to develop such programs, and 18 months after the act was passed, 34 states had developed vocational rehabilitation programs. The law was temporary and had to be extended every few years until 1935 when the Social Security Act of 1935 made the state-federal vocational rehabilitation program a permanent program that could be discontinued only through congressional action.

(continued)

TABLE 10.1 Key Vocational Rehabilitation-Related Legislation 1935–1973 (*continued*)

Legislation and Year	Key Mandates/Outcomes
Barden-LaFollette Act of 1943	Expanded services to persons with mental retardation and mental illness and expanded physical restoration services that could be provided. Established federal support for agencies that served people who were blind.
Rehabilitation Act Amendments of 1954	Increased the federal share of the state-federal match to 66%; expanded services and funding to persons with mental retardation and chronic mental illness; established research and demonstration grants aimed at the discovery of new knowledge in vocational rehabilitation; provided grants to colleges and universities to develop preservice training programs for rehabilitation counselors.
Social Security Amendments of 1956	Authorized Social Security disability allowances for persons permanently disabled, aged 50 or over, who were deemed incapable of returning to competitive employment.

A. Rehabilitation Act of 1973

The Rehabilitation Act of 1973 was significant because of its several mandates and outcomes. Among these, the act (a) mandated that states serve individuals with the most severe disabilities before serving persons with less severe disabilities; (b) promoted and ensured client involvement in rehabilitation plan development through the joint (counselor and client) development of an Individualized Written Rehabilitation Program (IWRP), which identified vocational objective, subobjectives, and related services, as well as the criteria for evaluating client progress; (c) implemented pilot Client Assistance Programs (CAPs), which became required for every state in 1984, through which clients could receive assistance with application and advocacy services; (d) established demonstration projects in IL rehabilitation services; (e) mandated program evaluation, so that states became accountable for collecting information on the target population being served, the timeliness and adequacy of VR services, the suitability of placements and retention of clients in employment, and client satisfaction with services; (f) increased funding for rehabilitation and disability research, establishing the National Institute of Handicapped Research, which later became the National Institute on Disability and Rehabilitation Research (NIDRR); and (g) advanced the civil rights of people with disabilities through Title V. Title V included sections covering:

- Section 501 mandated nondiscrimination and affirmative action in federal hiring.

- Section 502 established the Architectural and Transportation Barriers Compliance Board to oversee compliance to the Architectural Barriers Act of 1968.

- Section 503 prohibited discrimination in employment on the basis of disability, required affirmative action plans among recipients of federal contracts and their subcontractors of amounts in excess of $10,000, and required a written affirmative action plan of employers/contractors receiving over $50,000 or with 50 or more employees.

- Section 504 prohibited disability-based exclusion of otherwise qualified persons with disabilities from any federal program or activity or any program or activity receiving federal funding (including school districts, colleges and universities, hospitals, day-care programs, public welfare agencies, or nursing homes).

B. Rehabilitation Act Amendments of 1992

Important mandates and outcomes of the Rehabilitation Act Amendments of 1992 included (a) increased client involvement at the individual level by ensuring increased client choice and participation in the development, implementation, and evaluation of the IWRP; (b) increased client involvement at the agency level by requiring the establishment of Rehabilitation Advisory Councils to guide state VR policies and procedures, as well as mandates that the majority of members be persons with disabilities; and (c) increased access to VR services by incorporating the presumption of benefit (presumption that the applicant with a disability applying for services can become employed and will therefore benefit from services), the use of existing data, and requirements that eligibility decisions be made within 60 days of application. The Amendments also mandated the preparation of more people ation of from minority backgrounds as professional rehabilitation counselors and increased the federal share of the state-federal funding match to 78.7%.

C. Workforce Investment Act of 1998, Including the Rehabilitation Act Amendments of 1998

The Workforce Investment Act (WIA) of 1998 linked state-federal VR program to the state's workforce-development system. WIA consolidated several employment and training programs into a unified statewide workforce-investment system. The link did not affect the integrity of the state-federal VR program as an individual and separate entity. The purposes of the act were to streamline services by integrating multiple employment and training programs in one agency, where customers could easily access the employment information and services they require through a "One-Stop" system. Every state has at least one One-Stop center in each major population area. VR is a mandated partner and must provide services to some extent via the One-Stop system. The degree of participation varies by state.

Key elements of the 1998 Rehabilitation Act Amendments

The Rehabilitation Act Amendments of 1998 streamlined VR administrative procedures by establishing eligibility for people already receiving Supplemental Security Income (SSI) or Social Security Disability Insurance (SSDI) benefits. The IPE replaced the IWRP to emphasize the employment focus of the VR program. Consumers were given an expanded role in the development of their IPEs and the opportunity to either develop their own plans or to develop a plan with the assistance of the rehabilitation counselor. The amendments stressed the need to expand outreach to minorities and recognized that people from minority background experience higher rates of disability. The amendments also improved due-process provisions by requiring state VR agencies to establish policies and procedures relating to the mediation of disputes and provide hearings before impartial hearing officers. Increased opportunities for obtaining employment were provided through an emphasis on telecommuting, self-employment, and small business operation as legitimate employment outcomes.

D. Workforce Innovation and Opportunity Act of 2014

The Workforce Innovation and Opportunity Act (WIOA), signed by President Obama in 2014, included the most recent amendments to the Rehabilitation Act of 1973, and provided for many important changes. WIOA represented an effort to develop a 21st-century public workforce-development system by building closer alignment between business leaders, state and local workforce-development boards, labor unions, community colleges, nonprofit organizations, youth-serving organizations, and state and local officials in order to enhance job-driven training and skills development. WIOA amended key provisions of the Rehabilitation Act of 1973. Specifically, WIOA:

- Increased federal commitment to postsecondary transition services to students and youth with disabilities by amending the VR program to expand not only the population of students with disabilities who may receive VR transition-related services, but also the breadth of services that the VR agencies provide to youth or students with disabilities

- Defined *students with disabilities* as meaning students enrolled in educational programs, including postsecondary education programs, homeschooling programs, and other nontraditional secondary educational programs (provided students satisfy age requirements) and defined *youth with a disability* as an individual with a disability who is aged 14 to 24

- Strengthened coordination between VR and local education agencies in transition services provided under the Individuals with Disabilities Education Act (IDEA) and preemployment transition services (PETS) to students with disabilities under the VR program

- Required that states reserve at least 15% of their federal allotment to provide and arrange for the provision of PETS to students with disabilities

- Emphasized integrated, community employment by closing access to most long-term sheltered workshops by 2016

- Promoted access for people with disabilities to the American job center system

- Required state VR agencies to emphasize competitive, integrated employment opportunities for people with disabilities (The WIOA definition of *competitive integrated employment* is summarized as work performed on a full- or part-time basis [including self-employment] for which an individual is compensated at a rate not less than minimum wage or higher and not less than the rate paid by the employer for the same or similar work performed by employees without disabilities, in a location where the employee is fully integrated with workers without disabilities, and that presents opportunities for advancement that are similar to those for employees without disabilities who have similar positions.)

- Transferred the state IL services program and centers for independent living (CIL) program from the RSA in the U.S. Department of Education to the Administration for Community Living (ACL) in the U.S. Department of Health and Human Services

- Transferred the NIDRR to the ACL (NIDRR is now called the National Institute on Disability, Independent Living, and Rehabilitation Research [NIDILRR].)

Case and Caseload Management

Overview

This section defines *case management* and *caseload management*, two critical elements of the rehabilitation counseling job function, and discuss certification as a case manager.

Learning Objectives

By the end of this unit you should be able to:

1. Define and distinguish between case management and caseload management.
2. Describe the case management knowledge domains underlying rehabilitation counseling case management practice.

Key Concepts

Case management is the process of coordinating and integrating case services and, in rehabilitation counseling. It involves functions and processes such as intake interviewing; assessment and evaluation; planning, evaluating, coordinating, and evaluating the rehabilitation plan and related services; and recording and reporting of case information. Each of these functions is associated with a specified set of knowledge, skills, and abilities (Leahy & Phillips, 2011; Roessler & Rubin, 2006). For example, intake interviewing requires counseling and time-management skills applied to the process of learning about consumers and their rehabilitation goals and objectives through a comprehensive interview and providing information about the agency, its policies, data necessary for informed consent and professional ethics, expectations, services, and limits of services. In the assessment function, relevant information for status and planning is obtained. In the planning function, information obtained in the intake interview and assessment, as well as other information about the consumer, is used to develop a plan for service provision and goal achievement. In the services coordination function, the case manager establishes contacts with other professionals for services, including referrals for evaluations and assessments. The case manager arranges for and monitors the services and assessments with, for example, psychologists and psychiatrists, vocational evaluators, and medical and health-related professionals. The recording and reporting function entails maintaining records and files, reporting on progress, and preparing summary reports (Roessler & Rubin, 2006).

Case management has consistently been identified, along with personal and vocational counseling and client advocacy, as among the most important activities of rehabilitation counselors (Leahy, Chan, & Saunders, 2003; Leahy, Chan, Sung, & Kim, 2013; Rubin, Roessler, & Rumrill, 2016). Knowledge domains underlying rehabilitation counseling case management practice generally include the following: (a) **medical treatment and services** (e.g., pharmaceutical and pharmacological management, assessment of clinical information for use in developing treatment plans, and establishment of treatment goals that meet the client's health care and safety needs), (b) **community resources and services** (e.g., coordination of community-based funding resources, eligibility for community-based care, crisis intervention), (c) **professional judgment and problem solving** (e.g., legal and ethical issues related to confidentiality, planning and goal-development techniques, and application of problem-solving techniques), (d) **cost containment** (e.g., understanding of cost analysis and methods for determining cost-effectiveness), and (e) **psychosocial aspects of disability** (e.g., theories of personality, understanding of the interaction of psychological and social factors as they pertain to wellness and independence; Leahy, Chan, Shaw, & Lui, 1997).

Caseload management refers to a system based on the systematic synthesis of client information from diverse sources to enhance counselor decision making and ensure the effective and efficient delivery of appropriate services for accomplishing successful consumer outcomes within agency and ethical guidelines (Wheaton & Berven, 1994). Caseload management is to the management of the total caseload, as opposed to a single client. It is a systematic process of using both counseling and managerial skills to ensure efficient and effective decision making and coordination of services. Caseload-management approaches and styles vary by agency, so it is generally learned on an organizational level, and counselors adopt the style of caseload management that is practiced within their agency while following state and federal guidelines and ethical principles of the overseeing professional organizations. It is imperative for caseload management that all activities, professional referrals, collaborative efforts, timing, and planning be specifically documented during the caseload procedure.

Independent Living

Overview

This section defines and describes the history of the IL movement, reviews the legislative basis for IL, and describes the roles of statewide independent living councils (SILC) and centers for independent living (CIL).

Learning Objectives

By the end of this unit you should be able to:

1. Define *independent living* and describe the history of the IL movement.
2. Describe the legislative basis for IL services.
3. Define and describe SILC and CILs.

Key Concepts

I. Definition and History of IL

IL can be defined as being in control of one's life, choosing one's own goals and activities, and ultimately deciding one's own support system, including the strategies, people, and animal supports necessary to accomplish any given objective in the entire environment in which the support system is needed (Litvak & Enders, 2001). The major precepts of the IL philosophy are that (a) it is not disability that prevents people with disabilities from living independently but rather external barriers such as stigmatizing attitudes, interpretations of disabilities, and architectural, legal, and educational barriers; (b) people with disabilities have the right to self-determination and to learn from their experiences; (c) people with disabilities can be experts in their own self-care; (d) people with disabilities must set the agenda for research and political actions in disability policy; and (e) IL services are managed and administered mostly by consumers (Braddock & Parish, 2001; Fabian & MacDonald-Wilson, 2012; Pratt, Gill, Barrett, & Roberts, 2007). The first IL center in the United States was established in the early 1970s in Berkeley, California; it served as a model for the development of other such centers across the country.

II. Legislative Basis

The Rehabilitation Act of 1973 called for an investigation of the feasibility of providing services to individuals with the most severe disabilities, who due to the severity of their disability and other factors, were not expected to be rehabilitated for employment but for whom rehabilitation services may improve the ability to live independently or function within their family and community. In the Rehabilitation Act Amendments of 1978, funds were authorized for the provision of IL services, and this funding has been maintained in subsequent amendments. Title VII of the Rehabilitation Act Amendments of 1998 mandated services and administrative systems through which IL services are provided, including SILCs and CILs. Under WIOA, oversight for IL services and independent living centers (ILCs) was transferred to the IL Administration in the ACL, U.S. Department of Health and Human Services.

Authorized under the Rehabilitation Act and amended by WIOA, the CIL Program provides grants to consumer-controlled, community-based, cross-disability, nonresidential, private nonprofit agencies to provide IL services to individuals with significant disabilities. CILs funded by the CIL Program are required to provide, at a minimum, five IL core services, including (a) information and referral; (b) IL skills training; (c) peer counseling; (d) individual and systems advocacy; and (e) new under WIOA, services that facilitate transition from nursing homes and other institutions to home and community-based residences with the necessary supports and services, provide assistance to those at risk of entering institutions, and facilitate transition of youth to postsecondary life.

Under WIOA, to be eligible for IL and CIL funding, states must establish and maintain a SILC. SILCs are composed of a majority of people with disabilities and include other IL stakeholders. SILC members are generally appointed by the state's governor. Each state is also required to prepare a state plan for independent living (SPIL). This plan establishes the principles and policy framework for the state's IL programs and is developed by the SILC with the agency that acts on behalf of the state for IL programs. The SPIL is required to be jointly developed by the chairperson of the SILC, and the directors of the CILs in the state, after receiving public input from individuals with disabilities and other stakeholders. Key concepts associated with IL are presented in Table 10.2.

TABLE 10.2 Key Concepts Associated With Independent Living

Key Concept	Summary
IL	A consumer-driven movement to achieve control over one's life, choosing one's own goals, activities, and support system, including the strategies, people, and animal supports necessary to accomplish objectives.
IL philosophy	Barriers and stigma, not the disability, prevent community inclusion of people with disabilities; people have the right to self-determination; people with disabilities are experts in their own self-care.
SILC	A consumer-controlled council authorized by WIOA to establish state IL plans.
CIL	CIL are cross-disability, nonresidential, community-based nonprofit programs that provide, at a minimum, the following cores services: (a) information and referral; (b) IL skills training; (c) peer counseling; (d) individual and systems advocacy; and (e) services that facilitate transition from nursing homes and other institutions to home and community-based residences with the necessary supports and services, provide assistance to those at risk of entering institutions, and facilitate transition of youth to postsecondary life.

CIL, centers for independent living; IL, independent living; SILC, statewide independent living council; WIOA, Workforce Innovation and Opportunity Act of 2014.

School-to-Work Transition Services

Learning Objectives

By the end of this unit you should be able to:

1. Understand the history of school-to-work transition services in the United States.
2. Outline the roles and functions of DM specialists.

Key Concepts

In 1975 the Education for All Handicapped Children Act (PL 94-142) called national attention to the public education of children and youth with disabilities. This legislation mandated (a) free and appropriate education for all students with disabilities through age 21 or graduation; (b) required states to identify, locate, and evaluate all children in the state who required special education and related services; (c) required that education be provided for students in the least restrictive environment (LRE), and to the maximum extent possible, with students without disabilities; and (d) mandated nondiscrimination in testing and evaluation services for children with disabilities.

In the mid to late 1980s, professional and political attention turned to postsecondary outcomes for students with disabilities as increasingly research suggested that special education students were more likely to drop out of school; significantly less likely to be employed after finishing school and, if employed, earned lower wages; more likely to live at home with their parent; and less likely to participate in further education, community integration, or IL. As a result of increased attention to and awareness of these problems, there was an increased legislative response.

I. Individuals with Disabilities Education Act

The IDEA of 1990 (subsequently reauthorized several times, most recently in 2004) increased the focus on postschool transition and firmly placed transition planning in the individualized education plan (IEP). The IEP is a written plan that specifies the special education goals and services that the school must provide to meet the unique educational needs of a student with a disability. (Students with disabilities who do not have an IEP but have a disability and require reasonable accommodation while attending school may have a plan under section 504 of the Rehabilitation Act of 1973, referred to as a 504 plan.)

In the 2004 reauthorization of IDEA, *transition* is defined as a coordinated set of activities for a child with a disability that is designed to be within a **results**-oriented process, that is **focused on improving the academic and functional achievement of the child with a disability to facilitate the** movement from school to postschool activities, including postsecondary education, vocational education, integrated employment (including supported employment), continuing and adult education, adult services, IL, and community participation. IDEA states that transition is based on the individual child's needs, taking into account the child's strengths, preferences and interests, and includes instruction, related services, community experiences, the development of employment and other postschool adult living objectives, and if appropriate, acquisition of daily living skills and functional vocational evaluation. (Individuals with Disabilities Education Act, 2004)

For each student, beginning at age 16 (or younger, if determined appropriate by the IEP team), the IEP includes a statement of the needed transition services for students, including, when appropriate, a statement of the interagency responsibilities or linkages before the student leaves the school setting. IDEA identifies rehabilitation counselors as related service providers.

II. Rehabilitation Act Amendments of 1998

The Rehabilitation Act Amendments of 1998 described the state rehabilitation agency's role in transition. Each state is required to develop a plan containing policies and procedures for coordination with education officials responsible for the provision the public education of students with disabilities. The plan is designed to facilitate the transition of students receiving services in school to receiving VR services. It includes information on a formal interagency agreement between the state educational agency and the state rehabilitation agency that provides for (a) consultation and technical assistance to help educational agencies in planning for transition from school to postschool activities, including VR services; (b) transition planning by state agency and educational agency personnel that facilitates the development and completion of the IEP; (c) roles and responsibilities, including financial responsibilities, of each agency; and (d) procedures for outreach to and identification of students with disabilities who need transition service (Rehabilitation Act Amendments of 1998).

III. Rehabilitation Act Amendments of 2014

The 2014 WIOA amendments to the Rehabilitation Act represent a significant increase in the role of VR in postsecondary transition, and several significant changes were made with respect to VR requirements related to transition services. The increased attention to transition services is reflected in the new requirement that at least 15% of each state's federal VR funding be used for preemployment transition services (PETS), which include the following required transition services: job exploration counseling, work-based learning experiences, counseling on postsecondary opportunities, workplace readiness training, and instruction in self-advocacy. VR is authorized, but not required, to provide nine additional services if funding is available.

The definition of *transition services* in the Rehabilitation Act reflects some differences and expansions compared with the language in IDEA. Specifically, in WIOA transition services refers to a coordinated set of activities for a student or youth with a disability that (a) are designed within an outcome-oriented process promoting movement from school to postschool activities, including postsecondary education, vocational training, competitive integrated employment, supported employment, continuing and adult education, adult services, IL, and community participation; (b) are based on the individual student's or youth's needs, taking into account the student's or youth's preferences and interests; (c) include instruction, community experiences, development of employment and other postschool adult living objectives, and, if appropriate, acquisition of daily living skills and functional vocational evaluation; (d) promote or facilitate the achievement of the employment outcome identified in the student's or youth's IPE; and (e) include outreach to and engagement of the parent or, as appropriate, the representative of such a student or youth with a disability. In WIOA, a *student with a disability* is defined as a student aged 16–21 who is eligible for and receiving IDEA services or is an individual with a disability for purposes of section 504, and a *youth with a disability* is defined as between the ages of 14–24. PETS must be provided only to "students with a disability."

Under WIOA, local VR offices have expanded responsibilities with respect to the transition process, including attending IEP meetings for students with disabilities when invited; working with local workforce-development boards, One-Stop centers, and employers to develop employment opportunities for students with disabilities; working with schools to coordinate and ensure that PETS are provided; and attending person-centered planning meetings, when invited.

In addition, several requirements concerning transition must now be included in the unified or combined state plan. The unified state plan is a required four-year plan that outlines the state's workforce-development strategy for the six core WIOA workforce-development programs (adult, dislocated worker, youth, employment services provided under the Wagner-Peyser Act, adult basic education, and VR). Under WIOA the VR services portion must describe plans, policies, and procedures for coordination between VR offices and education officials responsible for the public education of students with disabilities. This coordination is designed to facilitate the transition of students with disabilities from the receipt of educational services to the receipt of VR services. These plans must provide for the development and approval of an IPE as early as possible in the transition-planning process and no later than the time a student with a disability is determined to be eligible for VR services leaves the school setting. The plan must include information on a formal interagency agreement between VR and the state educational agency that provides for the following: (a) consultation and technical assistance to assist educational agencies in planning for the postsecondary transition of students with disabilities, including PETS and other VR services; (b) transition planning by VR and school personnel that facilitates the development and implementation of the IEPs of students with disabilities; (c) identifying the roles and responsibilities (including financial responsibilities) of each agency; and (d) procedures for outreach and identification of students with disabilities who need transition services, as early in the transition planning process as possible, which at minimum must provide a description of the purpose of the VR program, information on eligibility requirements and application procedures, and the scope of services that may be provided. Key concepts associated with school-to-work transition services are presented in Table 10.3.

TABLE 10.3   Key Concepts Associated With School-to-Work Transition

Education for All Handicapped Children Act (PL 94-142) of 1975	Concerning the public education of children and youth with disabilities, mandated (1) free and appropriate education for all students with disabilities through age 21 or graduation; (2) required states to identify, locate, and evaluate children who required special education and related services; (3) required that education be provided in the LRE; and (4) mandated nondiscrimination in testing and evaluation services for children with disabilities.
IDEA	Amendment and subsequent reauthorization of the Education for All Handicapped Children Act. Ensures that children with disabilities have available a free appropriate public education that includes special education and related services to meet their needs and prepare them for employment and independent living. Increased the focus on postschool transition and mandated transition planning in the IEP.
IEP	Written plan that specifies the special education goals and services to meet the unique educational needs of a student with a disability, including beginning at 16 (or younger), a statement of needed transition services and interagency responsibilities or linkages before the student leaves school.

IDEA, Individuals with Disabilities Education Act; IEP, individualized education plan; LRE, least restrictive environment.

Disability Management

Learning Objectives

By the end of this unit you should be able to:

1. Understand the need for DM.
2. Outline the roles and functions of DM specialists.

Key Concepts

DM is an increasingly important component of professional rehabilitation counseling. In a recent survey of private sector rehabilitation counselors, almost 17% reported holding certification in DM (Beveridge, Karpen, Chan, & Penrod, 2016). DM has been described as a workplace program using prevention, early intervention, and return-to-work strategies to reduce the impact of work injury and disability and accommodate employees who experience work-related functional limitations (Ethridge, Rodgers, & Fabian, 2007).

DM involves prevention and remediation strategies to prevent disability from occurring in the workplace and early intervention following the onset of disability. DM may involve the use of both proactive and reactive techniques. Proactive techniques, such as wellness programs, safety awareness, and illness/injury prevention, are used to reduce occupational disabilities. Reactive techniques include employee assistance programs, transitional work programs, outplacement, and work hardening (Dunn, 2001).

Job functions and knowledge and skill requirements involved in DM include case management, psychosocial interventions, vocational aspects of disability, managed care and managed disability, and human resources and business (Chan et al., 2000). Other important skills and knowledge include comprehensive individual case analysis and disability case management, performance of worksite/job analysis, vocational counseling, development of individualized return-to-work and work-retention plans, coordinating services and collaboration with other services providers and employers to provide needed services for clients, development of prevention and workplace intervention plans, ergonomic evaluation, health and wellness program development, and the development of worksite modifications and job accommodations (Certification of Disability Management Specialists Commission [CDMSC], 2009; Rosenthal, Hursh, Lui, Zimmermann, & Pruett, 2005). It is also important that disability managers be skilled in organizational change strategies, negotiation, systems analysis, mediation, labor relations, rehabilitation engineering, and human resource management (Olsheski, Rosenthal, & Hamilton, 2002), understanding of insurance regulations, workers' compensation laws, and legislative aspects of work and disability. They should also be aware of relevant legislation, including the Americans with Disabilities Act (Ethridge et al., 2007). Key concepts associated with DM are presented in Table 10.4.

TABLE 10.4 Key Concepts Associated With Disability Management

Key Concept	Summary
DM	A workplace prevention and remediation strategy involving the development and implementation of integrated services that promote the recovery and return to work of an injured worker, prevent injury or exacerbation of injury or disability, and control costs associated with the injury.

(continued)

TABLE 10.4   Key Concepts Associated With Disability Management (*continued*)

Key Concept	Summary
CDMSC	An independent body that protects the public by monitoring the competency of DM specialists.
Work interruption case management	A knowledge domain of DM that includes comprehensive individual case analysis/disability case management, and so forth.
Disability-prevention and workplace-intervention plan	A knowledge domain of DM that involves risk mitigation, ergonomic evaluation and recommendations, health and wellness initiation, development of worksite modifications, and job accommodations.

CDMSC, Certification of Disability Management Specialists Commission; DM, disability management.

Forensic Rehabilitation, Vocational Expert Practices, and Life Care Planning

Learning Objectives

By the end of this unit you should be able to:

1. Define forensic rehabilitation and vocational expert services.
2. Describe key concepts in workers' compensation.
3. Understand the purpose of the emerging professional area of life care planning.

Key Concepts

Black's Law Dictionary (Black, 1990) defines *forensic rehabilitation* as the use or practice of principles of rehabilitation within the legal environment. Shaw and Betters (2004) posited that *forensic rehabilitation* refers to a variety of rehabilitation counseling services that are provided in legal or quasi-legal settings or that pertain to legal proceedings. Involvement in the court system or in the courtroom is relatively a new concept to the rehabilitation counseling profession. The Code of Professional Ethics for Rehabilitation Counselors (Commission on Rehabilitation Counselor Certification, 2010) stipulates the essential involvement of rehabilitation counselors in the legal system in positions such as expert witnesses. Individuals preparing for the certified rehabilitation counselor (CRC®) examination are encouraged to consult the Code of Professional Ethics for Rehabilitation Counselors for detailed consideration of forensic rehabilitation.

According to the International Association of Rehabilitation Professionals (IARP, 2016), forensic rehabilitation counselors can practice in three major content areas: analysis of the vocational capabilities, medical care/life care plans, and economic components.

A forensic rehabilitation professional can work as a forensic expert who testifies in court or a consultant (who does not testify in court). The services provided by forensic rehabilitation counselors may include testifying as a vocational expert in workers' compensation or Social Security Administration (SSA) hearings, civil court proceedings, personal injury litigation, life care planning, marriage dissolution or family court hearings, employment discrimination, or medical malpractice cases (Brodwin, 2008; Shaw & Betters, 2004). Required qualifications for serving as a vocational expert witness include completion of a graduate degree in rehabilitation counseling or the behavioral sciences, several years of experience in rehabilitation counseling practice, and knowledge of and experience in the medical aspects of disabilities, functional limitations, rehabilitation and vocational potential, transferable skills analysis, marketability, employability (Brodwin, 2008; IARP, 2016), and understanding of various court procedures and rules (IARP, 2016).

I. Workers' Compensation

The workers' compensation program is regarded as the oldest social insurance for injured workers in the United States. It is focused on the following programs: medical care, disability payments, and VR services for injured workers. Two primary goals of workers' compensation are the provision of medical care and wage replacement for workers who sustain justifiable injury during active duty and the protection of employers through the development of a "no fault" system that removes the need for legal action by employees against employers (Beveridge & McDaniel, 2014).

Workers' compensation is an insurance-based program designed to provide monetary compensation for workers who are injured on the job. Historically, before workers' compensation laws, an injured worker was forced to sue an employer to obtain payment for medical services and to recover wages. However, the existence of three defenses made success in such lawsuits doubtful. These included (a) the assumption of risk, which held that injury was a normal and accepted danger associated with employment; (b) the fellow servant doctrine, which prevented recovery if the injury was caused by a fellow worker's negligence; and (c) contributory negligence, which prevented recovery if the worker's own negligence contributed to the accident or injury. Workers' compensation essentially guarantees compensation benefits for workers who forego most of their rights to sue their employer in the event of injury. It is described as a "no-fault" system. Benefits are paid regardless of who is at fault for the injury, as long as the injury or disease happened at work or was caused by work. Persons injured on the job receive money to replace lost wages at a fixed amount, medical expenses, and usually VR.

In the Unites States, workers' compensation is an employer-funded program achieved either through the purchase of commercial insurance or by the setup of a self-insurance account. Most states have exclusion criteria for small companies and for domestic and agricultural workers (Guyton, 1999). Claims by injured workers are generally handled by state-based compensation boards, and statutes regulating eligibility, compliance, and the administrations of benefits and services are legislated at the state level. Certain basic standards for the provision of workers' compensation are set by the federal government. Federal employees, workers on interstate railroads, seamen, persons loading and unloading vessels, and some construction workers working around navigable waters are covered by federal laws. Federal workers' compensation programs include the Federal Employees' Compensation Act (FECA), Longshore & Harbor Workers' Compensation Act, and the Railroad Retirement & Railroad Unemployment Insurance Acts.

A. Workers' Compensation Laws

Germany is said to have started the first form of industrial accident–related insurance in 1884 (Marini, 2012; Sengupta & Reno, 2007). In 1908, with the enactment of the Federal Employers' Liability Act the United States began a similar industrial accident-related insurance program. Workers' compensation programs rapidly spread in the Unites States, and by 1920, 42 of the then-48 states adopted such programs (Marini, 2012).

Workers' compensation programs use a unique calculation system to determine work-related losses. Wage-loss benefits are calculated using an impairment rating, a wage-loss system, or loss-of-earning capacity. The impairment rating system has five categories: temporary total disability (TTD), temporary partial disability (TPD), permanent partial disability, permanent total disability, and survivor (death) benefits. With TTD, wages are usually paid to claimants while they are off work from a workers' compensation claim. If the injured worker can return to the former employment in some modified capacity, but at reduced function or earnings compared with the preinjury status, then the worker is classified into the TPD status. The worker receives income maintenance at a percentage of the difference between preinjury and postinjury earnings. TPD usually covers the medical bills and a wage differential if the claimant is able to work, but not in the same capacity, while recovering from a work-related injury. Permanent total disability means that the worker is unable to work in any capacity. Permanent partial disability means the worker is able to work, but has a permanent, residual deficit. TTD is the worker's status after an industrial injury or illness and a brief qualifying period of generally days or weeks. TTD usually involves the period of time a worker receives reimbursed medical services directed toward maximum medical improvement (MMI) or medical stability. During this period, the worker receives wage-loss benefits based on preinjury earnings while regarded by the attending physician as unable to work. Wage-loss benefits are often *two-thirds* of the injured worker's average weekly wage at the time of injury.

Scheduled and unscheduled injuries

In cases of permanent total or partial disability, at the point of MMI, the attending physician determines the degree of loss, disability, or impairment, if any, through guidelines established by the American Medical Association's (1990) *Guides to the Evaluation of Permanent Impairment*. The "impairment rating" is determined by medical guidelines, as well as by individual state statues that classify the injury as either "scheduled" or "unscheduled." "Scheduled" injuries involve the extremities, eyes (vision), or ears (hearing). Schedules of impairment list the disability and the corresponding compensable payment for the loss. Industrial injuries not found in the statutorily defined schedule generally become "unscheduled" injuries (e.g., spinal cord injury, double amputation). The benefits for unscheduled injuries are calculated differently. At the date of MMI and release to return to work by the attending physician, the injured worker is entitled to compensation based on the difference between preinjury and postinjury earnings. The benefit is paid over the life of the worker and periodic adjustments can be made if the earnings capacity of the individual worker changes.

Earning capacity

At the time that permanent partial or total disability is determined, the state workers' compensation regulatory body receives a petition from the insurer with evidence of the degree of loss and offering a specific compensation settlement or award, at which point litigation becomes germane. The worker has the right to protest the award and then may hire an attorney. This is an area where VR interventions may be effective. The vocational expert may play a vital role in the hearing process by presenting evidence on behalf of either the plaintiff (injured worker) or the defendant (insurer, employer).

B. Purpose of Rehabilitation Services in Workers' Compensation

VR has been an important benefit in workers' compensation since the 1970s. The primary goal of VR services is the early return to work and minimized loss of earnings capacity by the injured worker to help mitigate insurer and employer losses. Early physical and psychosocial interventions are necessary to promote return to work and reduce complications such as social withdraw, loss of self-esteem, and addition to alcohol or prescription medications (Marini, 2012).

C. Knowledge and Skill Domains Related to Workers' Compensation

The major rehabilitation knowledge domains were identified by Matkin (1985) as including human disabilities, case management, job placement, vocational assessment, rehabilitation disability legislation, rehabilitation resources, and forensic issues. More recently, Leahy, Chan, Taylor, Wood, and Downey (1998) identified seven empirically derived knowledge factors as important for effective private rehabilitation practice. These knowledge factors include vocational assessment and planning, case management and reporting, expert witness testimony, employment- and disability-related legislation and regulations, community resources, psychosocial and functional aspects of disability, and job analysis and modification.

D. Return-to-Work Hierarchy in Workers' Compensation

A return-to-work hierarchy is described in workers' compensation VR that describes the preferred order of service goals and seeks to capitalize on existing capacities and relationships with the injured worker's employer. These are:

- Return to work in the same job, with the same employer
- Return to work in the same but modified job with the same employer
- Return to work in a different job (capitalizing on transferable skills), with the same employer
- Return to work in the same job, with a different employer
- Return to work in the same but modified job, with a different employer
- Return to work in a different job (capitalizing on transferable skills) with a different employer
- Return to work in a different job with retraining with the same or a different employer
- Return to work in self-employment

II. Life care planning services

Although life care planning as a specialty is relatively new, this field has grown fast in the last 30 years. Life care planning is regarded an interdisciplinary specialty area involving both health care and legal practitioners (Beveridge & McDaniel, 2014). As an interdisciplinary specialty, life care planning has medically been used to assess and document an individual's functioning and medical needs. Vocationally, life care planning serves to inform the social, education, and vocational history and needs of the person. Legally, life care plans can be used to plan for litigation and compensation from insurance companies (Beveridge & McDaniel, 2014).

Life care planning services are forms of medical and catastrophic case management involving the design of a plan of comprehensive and long-term rehabilitation and related services for an individual who has experienced a catastrophic injury or has significant chronic health care needs (Brodwin, 2008; McCollom, 2002). Life care plans are designed to identify and communicate the details of care that will be necessary from the point of evaluation through the projected end of the individual's life. Among the areas that may be addressed in a life care plan are projected needs for evaluations and therapies, diagnostic testing, educational assessments, vocational and educational planning, equipment needs and aids for independent functioning, medication and medical supply needs, care setting considerations and the need for architectural renovation, transportation, health maintenance and services, and leisure and recreational services (Brodwin, 2008).

Professionals that may be involved in the development of the life care plan include physicians and medical specialists, physical and occupational therapists, rehabilitation professionals, rehabilitation counselors, lawyers, and economists, as well as the individual and family and friends. The health care specialty of life care planning attracts a variety of professionals, including rehabilitation counselors, rehabilitation nurses, rehabilitation psychologists, psychiatrists, case managers, and others. A long-term approach is usually the mainstay in life care planning to ensure that the needs of the individual receiving the care will be met and to bridge any gap between acute care and long-term medical care and rehabilitation services (Beveridge & McDaniel, 2014).

Substance Abuse Treatment and Rehabilitation

Learning Objectives

By the end of this unit you should be able to:

1. Define the key terms used in SA counseling and rehabilitation.
2. Discuss the relationships between SA and disability.
3. Describe major models of SA and counseling theories related to SA treatment and rehabilitation.

Key Concepts

I. SA and Substance Dependence

SA and *substance dependence* (4th ed., text rev.; *DSM-IV-TR*; American Psychiatric Association [APA], 2000) have been replaced with a new single term, *substance use disorder* (5th ed.; *DSM-5*;

APA, 2013). The *DSM-5* defines *substance use disorder* as a group of cognitive, behavioral, and physiological symptoms that show that an individual persistently uses the substance regardless of significant substance-related problems (APA, 2013). Substance use disorder is characterized as an underlying circuit change in the brain that persists even after detoxification. This change in the brain may contribute to repeated relapses that occur when the individual is exposed to a substance.

According to the *DSM-5*, the diagnosis for *substance use disorder* "is based on a pathological pattern of behaviors related to use of the substance" (APA, 2013, p. 483) grouped as the following criteria: (a) impaired control (criteria 1–4), (b) social impairment (criteria 5–7), (c) risky use (criteria 8–9), and (d) pharmacological criteria (criteria 10–11). According to the Substance Abuse and Mental Health Services Administration (SAMHSA, 2016) SA and substance dependence in the United States are major public health concerns. Statistics show that "approximately 1 in 12 (21.5 million) people had a substance use disorder in the past year; almost one quarter engaged in binge drinking in the past month; and over 10 percent used illicit drugs in the past month" (SAMHSA, 2016, p. 2). A national study in 2013 reported similar results, indicating that an estimated 21.6 million individuals 12 years and older have SA or substance dependence (SAMHSA, 2014).

II. SA, Disability, and Rehabilitation

The prevalence of SA disorder is almost twice as high among adults with disabilities compared with the general population, and more than 20% of persons eligible for VR services experience SA or dependence (Krahn, Deck, Gabriel, & Farrell, 2007). In certain circumstances, the presence of SA may increase the risk for acquiring a secondary disability. For instance, driving under the influence may result in motor vehicle accident and traumatic brain injury; risky behavior may lead to HIV infection (Falvo, 2014). People with disabilities in addition to SA disorders have the lowest successful closure rates in VR agencies (Hollar, McAweeney, & Moore, 2008). The presence of a disability significantly increases the risk for SA, alcohol and illicit drug use, and prescription abuse (Brucker, 2007). Among people with disabilities, young adults are more likely to use illicit drugs and older adults are more likely to abuse prescription medication. SA disorders are the most frequently occurring comorbid disability in persons with a mental health diagnosis (Bachman, Drainoni, & Tobias, 2004). Access to, and completion of SA treatment for persons with disabilities may be affected by physical, attitudinal, or communication barriers and failure of physicians to identify and refer such individuals for treatment (West, Graham, & Cifu, 2009; West et al., 2009).

III. Models of SA and Addiction

The moral model
The moral model explains the etiology of substance addiction based on beliefs about right and wrong or acceptable and unacceptable behavior. SA is seen as a personal choice, and individuals as capable of making alternate choices. This model is still prevalent in public policies and attitudes (Capuzzi & Stauffer, 2012).

The disease model

Addiction is seen in terms of a medical orientation resulting from genetic predisposition or pathological metabolism from an acquired disease caused by repeated exposure. SA is seen as a primary disease with progressive and irreversible stages and as chronic and incurable, thus the term *recovering*, rather than *recovered*, is used by adherents of this perspective, and abstinence, rather than cure, is seen as the goal of treatment (Capuzzi & Stauffer, 2012; Janikowski, Cardoso, & Lee, 2005).

Genetic, biological, and neurobiological models

Biological and genetic models of SA suggest that the individual's biological and genetic constitution can predispose the individual to substance dependency. Research on addiction suggests that SA and alcohol dependency is associated with genetic factors; however, it is difficult to distinguish between the genetic factors and the social and environmental factors, which also are likely to contribute to the development of addiction or dependence. The neurobiological model suggests that the actions of neurotransmitters (chemical messengers) cause chemical changes in the limbic system of the brain that may lead to addiction.

Psychological models

Several psychological models of SA and addiction exist. The ***cognitive behavioral models*** state that people perceive or derive certain satisfactions and reinforcement from substance use. Addiction results from an inability to regulate or control the reward system. The ***learning models*** suggest that substance use is a result of faulty learning, and that use is reinforcing and leads to repeating the behavior, which may lead to addiction. They also suggest that social or environmental conditions may be associated with or trigger the behavior. The aversive effects and tension associated with withdrawal may motivate continued SA. The ***psychodynamic models*** view SA as a symptom of other basic psychopathology and problems with regulation of affect link SA to inadequate parenting, ego deficiencies, attachment disorders, masturbation, homosexuality and other issues. The ***personality theory models*** assume that certain personality traits (e.g., dependency, immaturity, inability to express anger) lead to addiction.

IV. Treatment and Rehabilitation

A wide range of treatment and rehabilitation models and approaches are used, based on different models and theories of addiction, historical and emerging treatment theories and approaches, and the substance or addiction involved. These include residential models, including in-patient treatment programs (frequently based on the Alcoholics Anonymous [AA] 12-step orientation), therapeutic communities (based on a social learning approach to prevention and skill development), intensive outpatient treatment programs, halfway houses, self-help groups (e.g., AA, Narcotics Anonymous, Rational Recovery), family programs (e.g., Al-Anon, Alateen), and pharmacological therapies, which may be combined with the other treatment options. (Janikowski et al., 2005).

SA is known to present significant barriers to employment. VR may be helpful in bridging the vocational barriers and improving treatment outcomes. According to Atherton and Toriello (2012, p. 291), "vocational services are not only important but should be a priority in treatment programs, a stated goal in the treatment plan, and targeted to consumers' individualized needs."

Wellness and Illiness-Prevention Concepts

Learning Objectives

By the end of this unit you should be able to:

1. Define and distinguish between health and wellness.
2. Define and describe self-management, adherence, and major models of health promotion and health behavior.

Key Concepts

For many people, the impact of disability on health and wellness is minimal, but for others, disability or chronic illness (CI) can limit participation in health-related activities and affect access to correlates of wellness, including social support, basic financial needs, optimism, and self-determination. Having a disability does not necessarily mean that one experiences poor health, but disability increases the risk for further CI and disability. Rehabilitation counselors are increasingly recognizing that promoting the health and wellness of consumers with disabilities is both a critical role and a function of their work, one that may increase the consumers' ability to achieve rehabilitation goals. Research on the impact of health on employment outcomes suggests that (a) poorer health is associated with being unemployed, (b) being unemployed significantly increases the odds for poor general physical and mental health (Jamoon, Horner-Johnson, Suzuki, Andresen, & Campbell, 2008; Jiang & Hesser, 2006; Scanlan & Beltran, 2007), and (c) health problems are a significant impediment to employment among unemployed working-age persons with disabilities (Harrington, Fogg, & McMahon, 2010).

I. Health and Wellness

Health is increasingly defined as a multidimensional concept. For example, the World Health Organization (WHO) International Classification of Functioning, Disability and Health (ICF; WHO, 2001) incorporates a multidimensional view of health, including both environmental and personal factors, as well as body, individual, and societal perspectives. The multidimensional and interrelated ICF approach to health incorporates (1) environmental factors external to the individual that may include the built environment and structural access, the physical environment, and the social environment, including social support, societal attitudes, and cultural, legal, and political systems; and (2) personal factors, including characteristics such as gender, race/ethnicity, socioeconomic status, as well as education and individual personal features and characteristics; (3) body structure and function, or the physiological and psychological functioning of body parts and systems; (4) activities, or tasks in which the individual engages in; and (5) participation, or the involvement and ability of the individual to participate in activities (WHO, 2001).

Wellness is a concept related to, but also distinct from, health. Common to most definitions of wellness are that (1) wellness is a process, or a way of living, rather than an end state; and (2) wellness involves striving for or achieving and maintaining the optimal level of well-being and health of which one is capable. Health and wellness can be seen as existing on separate but parallel continuums, such that an individual could achieve or exist at different ends of each simultaneously. Thus having a disability or CI does not preclude being well or engaging in a wellness lifestyle (Sperry, Lewis, Carlson, & Englar-Carlson, 2005).

Rehabilitation counseling requires an understanding of the concepts and effective methods of practice in illness prevention and health promotion, including self-management, adherence, health assessment, and health promotion. It also requires helping clients make informed personal decisions about health and wellness.

II. Self-Management

Self-management is defined as learning and practicing the skills necessary to carry on an active and emotionally satisfying life in the face of a chronic condition (Lorig, 1993). It includes concepts such as managing one's condition, including medication and treatment management, communicating with physicians, and exercising and dieting; maintaining, changing, and creating new, meaningful behaviors and roles; engaging effectively in work and leisure activities; maintaining social relationships; coping emotionally with the feelings associated with living with illness; and realizing and developing a new sense of future (Corbin and Strauss, 1988). Self-management programs have been found to result in decreased pain, disability, anxiety, and health care use and increased psychological functioning, role functioning, adherence, and use of cognitive coping techniques. Lorig and Holman (2003) suggested that the following should be included in counseling to promote self-management: teaching and helping clients to develop problem-solving skills, helping consumers to become informed and aware of their illness or disability and its treatment, helping consumers find and use health information and resources, form effective relationships with health care providers, and take actions that promote their health and manage their condition.

III. Models of Health Promotion and Health Behavior

Many models of health and wellness promotion have been suggested. Generally, these are based on models of health behavior and health behavior change. Among the more frequently discussed and researched of these models in rehabilitation counseling are the following.

Health Beliefs Model
The basic tenets of the health beliefs model are that behavior depends on two variables: the value placed by an individual on a particular goal and the individual's estimate of the likelihood that a given action will result in achievement of that goal (Becker, Drachman, & Kirscht, 1974). The correlate in health behavior is that engaging in recommended health behavior depends on the value placed on avoiding illness (maintain/achieve health) and the belief that a health behavior will prevent illness (achieve/maintain health). Elements that moderate this relationship include perceived susceptibility (e.g., risk of threat of illness or poor health), perceived severity or seriousness of the risk, perceived benefits of engaging in the behavior, perceived barriers to taking action, and cues to action (availability of stimuli that trigger the decision-making process). More recently, self-efficacy has also been incorporated into this model.

Theory of Reasoned Action

According to this theory, the intention to perform a behavior is the primary determinant of behavior (Ajzen & Fishbein, 1980; Fishbein & Ajzen, 1975). This intention is influenced by attitudes toward the behavior, including (1) individuals' beliefs that the action will lead to a certain outcome, (2) the value attached by individuals to the outcome, and (3) subjective norms (the extent to which people believe that others think that they should engage in the behavior, weighed by their desire to comply with their wishes).

Theory of Planned Behavior

Like the theory of reasoned action, this theory posits that health behavior is driven by behavioral intentions. It is further delineated that behavioral intentions are a function of (1) the individual's attitude toward the behavior (i.e., the individual's positive or negative feelings about performing the behavior), (2) the subjective norms surrounding the performance of the behavior (i.e., the extent to which people who are important to the individual are perceived as thinking the behavior should be performed), and (3) behavioral control (i.e., the individual's perception of the ease with which the behavior can be performed) (Ajzen, 1991).

Social Cognitive Theory

This model suggests that behavior change and maintenance are a function of expectations about whether the behavior will achieve certain outcomes and efficacy beliefs (expectations about one's ability to execute the behavior) (Bandura, 1989).

Transtheoretical Model

This model can be seen as a model of health decision making and describes the stages of change, which are represented as categories along a continuum of readiness to change a behavior (precontemplation, contemplation, preparation, action, and maintenance). Transitions between the stages are modified by factors such as self-efficacy (confidence in the ability to change) and psychological, environmental, cultural, socioeconomic, and other variables or behaviors specific to the context of change (Prochaska & DiClemente, 1983).

Health Action Process Approach

Schwarzer's (1992) health action process approach (HAPA) model of health promotion has received increased attention from health researchers, and the model appears to be valid for people across many cultures. The HAPA model integrates health self-efficacy, the theory of planned behavior, and the transtheoretical model to predict engagement in health behavior. The HAPA model indicates that the adoption, initiation, and maintenance of health behaviors can be seen as a process involving motivation and volition phases. Action self-efficacy, outcome expectancies, and risk assessment contribute to the formation of intention in the motivation phase. In the volition phase, action planning, coping planning, maintenance self-efficacy, and recovery self-efficacy are used to bridge the gap between intention and action. Perceived situational barriers and support also influence engagement and maintenance of health behavior. Key concepts in wellness and illness-prevention concepts are presented in Table 10.5.

TABLE 10.5 Key Concepts in Wellness and Illness Prevention

Key Concept	Summary
Health	A multidimensional concept referring to physical, social, and emotional well-being and influenced by environmental, social, and personal factors.
Wellness	A lifestyle and process of striving for and maintaining the optimal level of well-being and health of which one is capable.
Self-management	Learning and practicing the skills necessary to have an active and emotionally satisfying life with a chronic condition, including caring for oneself; managing of one's condition; maintaining, changing, and creating new meaningful behaviors and roles; and coping.
Adherence to treatment	The degree to which health care recipients follow, or adhere to, treatment recommendations.

Community Resources and Community-Based Rehabilitation Programs

Learning Objectives

By the end of this unit you should be able to:

1. Understand the importance of community resources for people with disabilities.
2. Identify existing community resources and how to provide access to them for people with disabilities.
3. Understand the need for collaborations with community service providers.

Key Concepts

To effectively refer, transfer, or coordinate rehabilitation counseling services, the rehabilitation counselor needs to know about the different services provided by agencies, facilities and organizations is needed (Crimando & Riggar, 2005). Community resources may be unique to a community and counselors must become aware of organizations and services that deal with inclusive education, inpatient and outpatient rehabilitation programs, medical resources and facilities, IL services, AT services, accessible public transportation, and advocacy organizations in the community (Patterson, DeLaGarza, & Schaller, 2005).

Community resources that rehabilitation counselors should be aware of include:

- **Health and diagnostic services** include medical services, home-based rehabilitation, mental and behavioral health care, and dental care. Disparities in the delivery of health care services across a wide variety of medical conditions have been documented among the U.S. population of persons with disabilities. One of the reasons to pay attention to issues of health and diagnostic services is the current health disparity that exists in the nation, especially within the population of persons with disabilities. "Although there are disparities in access to health care in the general population, these disparities are more pronounced with the population of people with disabilities when compared to the general population" (Umeasiegbu, 2013, p. 11).

It is necessary to assist individuals with disabilities in gaining access to health and diagnostic services during the rehabilitation process and at all times to maximize and promote health and prevent secondary health conditions.

- **Rehabilitation and vocational services** include VR and supported employment, AT services, forensic rehabilitation, and educational and human services. Rehabilitation and vocational services are indispensable tools for community participation for individuals with disabilities. Effective vocational and rehabilitation services reduce and or remove a variety of barriers and increase the quality of life of persons with disabilities.

- **Career and technical education** includes adult education, special education, CIL, and public/specialized transportation.

- **Community living resources** include public housing assistance, supported housing for persons with disabilities, state or local housing and rental assistance programs, accessible recreation and leisure resources, and informational resources.

- **Legal and advocacy services** include availability of pro bono legal services, services and networks from the Americans with Disabilities Act, and advocacy groups and resources. Persons with disabilities experience discrimination, negative attitudes from society, and sometimes, abuse. Persons with disabilities, like minority groups, can be regarded as vulnerable, so advocacy and legal actions are needed to maintain their human rights. Counselors can advocate on behalf of rehabilitation clients and provide information on legal resources that clients can use when they need such services.

- **Social services.** Social services are the same as those offered to low-income citizens and older adults, including SSDI and SSI, Medicaid, children and family services, family planning, and financial assistance.

I. Community-Based Rehabilitation Programs

CRPs are community-based nonprofit organizations that provide a range of employment and rehabilitation services. These programs directly provide or facilitate the provision of VR services to individuals with disabilities. Employment-related CRP services frequently include testing or assessment; job development, training, placement, and retention services; supported employment services; and job coaching. Frequently, these services are provided through contracts with the state VR agencies. Other sources of income include public and private agency sources.

Insurance Programs and Social Security

Learning Objectives

By the end of this unit you should be able to:

1. Define and describe the SSA disability benefits: SSDI and SSI, including eligibility criteria.
2. Define and distinguish between Medicare and Medicaid.
3. Describe work incentives associated with SSI and SSDI.

Key Concepts

The SSA provides disability benefits through the SSDI program and the SSI program. The SSA defines *disability* as the inability to engage in any substantial gainful activity (SGA) by reason of any medically determinable physical or mental impairment that can be expected to result in death or has lasted or can be expected to last for a continuous period of not less than 12 months.

I. Social Security Disability Insurance

Established in 1954, SSDI provides eligible people with disabilities with monthly income benefits and Medicare insurance. SSDI is an eligibility program; a person must have worked and paid Social Security taxes, be permanently disabled, and earn less than SGA. Eligibility is based on contributions the worker (or in some cases the spouse or parents) made to Federal Insurance Contributions Act (FICA) while employed.

II. Supplementary Security Income

SSI provides monthly benefits and Medicaid to adults and children with disabilities who have limited income and resources, people with low income who are age 65 or older, and people who are blind. The amount of benefit received is based on the individual's other sources of income and living situation. The federal government determines the base SSI benefit rate annually.

III. Medicaid and Medicare

Medicaid is a federal-state matching program available to certain low-income and eligible individuals and families. It is state-administered, and each state sets its own guidelines regarding eligibility and services. Medicaid provides payments not to the individual but directly to the health care provider. Depending on the state's rules, the individual may also be asked to pay a copayment for some services. Medicaid covers hospital and doctor visits, medication, and in some states, personal assistant services.

Medicare is a federal health insurance program, established in 1965, for people age 65 or older and others who meet certain criteria, including people under age 65 who have a disability (received SSDI benefits for at least 24 months) and people who receive Social Security disability benefits because they have amyotrophic lateral sclerosis or permanent kidney failure. Medicare is financed by payroll taxes and monthly premiums deducted from Social Security checks.

Medicare coverage includes hospital insurance (Part A) and supplementary medical insurance (Part B). People who receive Parts A and B through the government are covered under "original Medicare." Medicare Part C refers to Medicare advantage plans, which are plans offered through private companies approved by Medicare. These plans combine the benefits of Parts A, B, and sometimes Part D (prescription drug coverage) in a single plan through a private insurer. These plans may also provide additional benefits coverage. Part D refers to a voluntary outpatient prescription drug benefit, established in 2006, that is delivered through private plans, either through Part C or as a separate plan. Within established limits, Medicare Part A helps cover inpatient hospital services, skilled nursing facility services, home health care, hospice care, and inpatient psychiatric care. In addition, with various limits, Part B provides for physicians services (including office visits and annual wellness visits), durable medical equipment, outpatient hospital services, outpatient mental health services, and laboratory and diagnostic tests.

IV. Work Incentives and Terms Associated With Social Security Benefits

Through work incentives established in recent decades, and most recently through the Ticket to Work and Work Incentives Improvement Act (1999), SSI/SSDI recipients are eligible for several employment incentives to promote work and reduce dependence on SSA benefits.

Trial work period

A trial work period allows SSDI recipients to engage in a work trial for at least 9 (not necessarily consecutive) months. During this period, the person continues to receive full Social Security benefits regardless of earnings. Medical coverage through Medicare is also continued for at least 93 months beyond the 9-month trial work period, beginning the month after the last month of the trial. After this period, some people may purchase continued Medicare coverage. If the person is considered able to work (trial work met the earning criteria for SGA), cash benefits automatically continue for a 3-month grace period.

Extended period of eligibility

SSDI recipients who complete a trial work period can, for a 36-month period, still receive benefits for any month in which earnings are below SGA (Rubin et al., 2016).

Plan to achieve self-support

A plan to achieve self-support (PASS) allows SSI recipients to set aside income or resources so that the income/resource will not be considered when calculating initial and continuing eligibility for SSI payments. This helps the person establish and maintain SSI eligibility and increase SSI payment amounts.

Impairment-related work expenses

In determining SGA, the cost of certain impairment-related items and services that are related to work are deducted from the individual's earnings. To qualify as impairment-related work expenses (IRWEs) the item or service must be necessary for the individual to work, be related to the individual's disability, be paid for by the individual, and be paid for in a month during which the individual worked. Examples of IRWEs that may be deductible include attendant care services that help the person prepare for work (e.g., activities of daily living [ADLs]) or get to and from work and costs associated with modifications to a vehicle that is needed to drive to work or be driven to work.

Ticket to work

Rehabilitation researchers (Fraser, McMahon, & Danczyk-Hawley, 2004; Marini & Reid, 2001) have demonstrated that only a very small percentage of SSDI beneficiaries resume substantial gainful employment once they begin receiving benefits. The cost savings associated with even a small percentage of recipients returning to work could be substantial. For example, according to the U.S. General Accounting Office, the SSA would save several billion dollars if only 1% of those receiving SSI or SSDI benefits returned to work (Strauser, 2013). To overcome the real and perceived barriers faced by the recipients capable of returning to work, in addition to the work incentives improvements previously addressed, the Ticket to Work Program was developed. The Ticket to Work Program is a voluntary program in which SSI and SSDI recipients may choose to engage in employment or other support services that enable self-support through a qualified vendor or provider of their choosing. These vendors, referred to as *Employment Networks*, may consist of both public and private providers, including the federal-state rehabilitation VR program or private rehabilitation companies or counselors (Rubin et al., 2016). The services are paid for directly to providers through the Ticket to Work Program.

AT and Rehabilitation Counseling

Learning Objectives

By the end of this unit you should be able to:

1. Define *AT* and related terms.
2. Describe categories of AT.
3. Describe the process and important components of AT assessment.

Key Concepts

AT is technology used by individuals with disabilities to perform functions that might otherwise be difficult or impossible. *AT* is defined as technological tools used to access education, employment, recreation or communication so that the individual can live as independently as possible. AT can include mobility devices, computer hardware or software, and devices that help people with disabilities access computers or other information technologies. (National Center on Accessible Information Technology in Education [NCAITE], 2011).

Rehabilitation engineering is defined in the 1998 Rehabilitation Act as the systematic application of engineering sciences to design, develop, adapt, test, evaluate, apply, and distribute technological solutions to problems confronted by individuals with disabilities in functional areas, such as mobility, communications, hearing, vision, and cognition, and in activities associated with employment, IL, education, and integration into the community. *Rehabilitation technology* refers to the systematic application of technologies, engineering methodologies, or scientific principles to meet the needs of, and address the barriers confronted by, individuals with disabilities in areas that include education, rehabilitation, employment, transportation, IL, and recreation. Thus, the term *rehabilitation technology* includes rehabilitation engineering, AT devices, and AT services. The availability of rehabilitation technology assessment and AT devices is mandated in the Rehabilitation Act as a primary benefit to be considered in IPEs.

According to the Assistive Technology Act of 2004, PL 108-364, AT is any item, piece of equipment or product system, whether acquired commercially off the shelf, modified, or customized, that is used to increase, maintain, or improve the functional capabilities of children with disabilities. This act required states to provide a variety of ATs to children and adults with disabilities, as well as their parents and guardians.

I. Categories of AT

AT can be applied and used in a wide variety of applications, including aids for daily living, augmentive communication, computer applications, environmental-control systems, home and worksite modifications, health promotion, prosthetics and orthotics, seating and positioning, mobility aids, aids for vision and hearing impairment, and vehicle modifications (Rubin et al., 2016). Assistive technology for cognition (ATC) uses a wide range of tools, including computer technologies, to compensate for cognitive impairment. ATC supports the completion of functional activities in natural settings, which increases independence for individuals with processing deficits (Sohlberg, 2011).

AT may involve low-tech solutions (such as screen magnifiers), as well as medium- and hi-tech devices. It can be equipment to help people work, study, participate in recreation opportunities, or navigate the community. It can be used across environments, resulting in an increase of independence at home, school, and work and in the community.

II. AT Assessment and Rehabilitation Counseling

AT can reduce the impact of limitations related to disability, and improve quality of life. The responsibility of rehabilitation counselors in providing AT services varies among states. Some states might be required to identify, need, purchase, and coordinate services, as well as provide information to consumers. Other states have specialists or counselors designated to provide AT to clients (Noll, Owens, Smith, & Schwanke, 2006). It is critical that a careful assessment be conducted. Specifically, the following should be considered: the consumer's goals and the role of AT; the consumer's abilities and disabilities as related to job performance and functions and AT use; the environment in which AT will be used; completion of a job/task analysis; barriers to job/task performance; research and identification of the most effective available options for meeting the goals identified; the likelihood of continued use of AT by the consumer and potential revisions/modifications; consumer training; and follow-up to explore whether the equipment meets the needs of the consumer or intervention/modification is required. The individual user should always be included in the design and device-selection process. Finally, it is important to consider funding sources for initial and continued AT products and services, which may include AT loans, private funding, VR, schools, Medicare or Medicaid, the Veterans Administration, and regional lending libraries or AT centers.

Multiple-Choice Questions

1. Which of the following is an accurate statement about the state-federal vocational rehabilitation (VR) program?

   A. The program funds state agencies to provide VR services for persons with disabilities, prioritizing services to those with the least significant disabilities.

   B. To be eligible for VR services, an applicant must have an impairment that is, or results, in a substantial impediment to employment.

   C. The program is an entitlement, rather than an eligibility, program.

   D. The *presumption of benefit* means that any applicant with a disability will be able to receive Social Security disability benefits.

2. Rehabilitation professionals who are engaged in testifying as a vocational expert in workers' compensation or Social Security Administration hearings, vocational capabilities analyses, and life care planning are most likely:

   A. State-federal program VR counselors

   B. Forensic rehabilitation counselors

   C. Substance abuse and addiction specialists

   D. Rehabilitation engineers

3. Which of the following statements is accurate?

   A. More than 1 of 5 persons who are eligible for VR services experience substance abuse or dependence.

   B. Among those with a diagnosed substance abuse disorder, there is a decreased risk for acquiring a secondary disability.

   C. Among people with disabilities, young adults are more likely to abuse prescription medication than older adults.

   D. The prevalence of substance abuse disorders is higher in the general population than it is among adults with disabilities.

4. Centers for independent living are community-based private nonprofit agencies mandated to provide, at a minimum, five core services. Which of the following is a new core service mandated under the Workforce Innovation and Opportunity Act?

   A. Independent living skills training

   B. Information and referral services

   C. Services to help with the transition from nursing homes and other institutions to home or community-based residences

   D. Peer counseling

5. Which of the following is not true of postsecondary transition services under WIOA?

   A. Transition services are designed to promote movement to postschool activities, such as postsecondary education, vocational training, competitive integrated employment, supported employment, independent living, or community participation.

   B. Transition services are based on the parent's or legal guardian's preferences for the transition-age youth.

   C. Transition services may include instruction, community experiences, the development of employment, and other postschool adult living objectives.

   D. Transition services should include outreach to and engagement of parents or a representative of the student or youth with a disability.

6. The Rehabilitation Act of 1973 was seen as important because it:

   A. Created a mandate that individuals with the most significant disabilities receive services before those with less severe disabilities

   B. Mandated client involvement in rehabilitation planning so that clients were partners in the development of their Individualized Written Rehabilitation Program

    C. Was critical in establishing VR client assistance programs and independent living services

    D. Created a federal program that removed from the states the responsibility for collecting information about individuals with disabilities and their satisfaction with VR services

7. Which of the following statements is *NOT* accurate?

    A. Having a disability does not necessarily mean that one experiences poor health.

    B. A disability increases the risk for further chronic illness and disability.

    C. Poorer health is associated with being unemployed.

    D. Being employed significantly increases the odds for physical and mental health problems.

8. Which of the following is a program in which prevention, early intervention, and return-to-work strategies are used to reduce the impact of injury and disability in employment?

    A. Independent living

    B. Supported employment

    C. Disability management

    D. Self-management

9. The preferred order of return to work for an injured worker, in order to capitalize on capacities and relationships with the worker's employer, is:

    A. Retraining, modified job, self-employment, transferable skills training

    B. Return to work in self-employment, return to work in a different job, return to work in the same job with a different employer, return to work in the same job with a different employer

    C. Return to work in the same job with the same employer, return to work in a different job with the same or a different employer, return to work in the same job with a different employer, self-employment

    D. Return to work in the same job with the same employer, return to work in the same but modified job with the same employer, return to work in a different job with the same employer, return to work in the same job with a different employer

10. A counselor who views a client's substance addiction as resulting from genetic predisposition or pathological metabolism or from an acquired disease resulting from repeated exposure is most likely operating within which model of addiction?

    A. Moral model

    B. Disease model

    C. Psychological model

    D. Psychodynamic model

Answer Key

1B, 2B, 3A, 4C, 5B, 6D, 7D, 8C, 9D, 10B

Advanced Multiple-Choice Questions

1. Legally, the people who may have responsibility for the development of a life care plan include all but which one of the following:

    A. Physicians and medical specialists

    B. Rehabilitation counselors

    C. Family and friends of the individual

    D. The individual

    E. All of the above

2. The Workforce Innovation and Opportunity Act made a number of changes to the Rehabilitation Act of 1973. Among these was a significantly increased emphasis on:

    A. Health-related services to aging Americans with chronic illnesses

    B. Preemployment services to children with disabilities

    C. Postsecondary transition services to students and youth with disabilities

    D. Transportation and employment services for persons living in rural and remote areas

3. In the state-federal vocational rehabilitation (VR) program, because of the *presumption of eligibility:*

    A. Any applicant who has been determined eligible for Social Security Disability Insurance is presumed to be eligible for VR services.

    B. Any applicant who meets the eligibility requirements is presumed to be eligible for VR services.

    C. Any eligible applicant may develop all or part of the Individualized Plan for Employment independently.

    D. Eligibility for any other federal disability program makes one ineligible for the state-federal VR program.

4. In the state-federal VR program, the Individualized Plan for Employment:

    A. Is written by the rehabilitation counselor, who has the knowledge, training, and awareness of local resources to complete the plan

    B. Is generally not reviewed or changed without Rehabilitation Services Administration authority

    C. Identifies a wide range of employment-related services to be provided

    D. Is authorized by the Individuals with Disabilities Education Act and represents a continuation of the individualized education plan initiated when the client was a student

5. Social Security disability benefits include Social Security Disability Insurance (SSDI). Which of the following is *NOT* true of SSDI?

    A. SSDI provides eligible people with disabilities with monthly income benefits and Medicare insurance.

    B. SSDI is an eligibility program for people who have worked and paid Social Security taxes, are permanently disabled, and earn less than substantial gainful activity.

    C. A large percentage of SSDI beneficiaries resume substantial gainful employment after they begin receiving benefits.

    D. SSDI beneficiaries are eligible for the Ticket to Work Program.

6. In the calculation of substantial gainful activity, an individual with a disability may be eligible to deduct the cost of certain disability-related items or services if they are necessary for the individual to work and are paid for by the individual. These deductions are referred to as:

    A. Medicaid-reimbursable items and services (MRSI)

    B. A personal assistant service or system

    C. Plans for achieving self-support

    D. Impairment-related work expenses

7. The stages of readiness for health behavior change, including precontemplation, contemplation, preparation, action, and maintenance, are most associated with which of the following models of health and wellness promotion?

    A. Transtheoretical model

    B. Health beliefs model

    C. Theory of reasoned action

    D. Health action process approach model

8. The provision of assistive technology to consumers who either do not subsequently use the device or use it for a short period of time and then abandon it is a significant problem that could be reduced through:

    A. Increased fees for AT services

    B. Policies that reduce the cost of AT devices and services

    C. Careful assessment

    D. Consumer-based insurance systems

9. *Self-management* is best defined as an approach to health promotion in which:

    A. Clients are encouraged to manage their health services through private insurance.

    B. Clients or health care recipients are encouraged to follow or comply with beneficial treatment recommendations.

    C. Clients are encouraged to develop the skills necessary to take responsibility for managing their self-care and health care and to cope with role changes.

    D. Clients are encouraged to develop the skills for managing pain, anxiety, and depression through cognitive coping techniques.

10. The economic argument for VR is best described as the idea that

    A. VR will be a more effective program economically if services are provided to individuals with the most significant disabilities before serving persons with less severe disabilities.

    B. VR will be a more economical program if services are provided to individuals with the less severe disabilities before serving persons with more significant disabilities.

C. Investment in VR enables persons with disabilities to become employed tax payers.

D. A society will generally benefit economically from providing "a square deal" to all its citizens.

Answer Key and Explanation of Answers

1E: A variety of professionals and persons may be involved in the development of the life care plan, including physicians and medical specialists, physical and occupational therapists, rehabilitation professionals, rehabilitation counselors, lawyers, and economists, as well as family and friends of the individual and the individual.

2C: The Workforce Innovation and Opportunity Act (WIOA) of 2014 amended a number of key provisions of the Rehabilitation Act of 1973, but among the most significant was the increased federal commitment to postsecondary transition services to students and youth with disabilities. It expanded the population of students with disabilities who may receive vocational rehabilitation transition–related services and increased the range of services that vocational rehabilitation agencies may provide to youth or students with disabilities. In addition, WIOA required that states reserve at least 15% of their federal funding to provide and arrange for preemployment transition services to students with disabilities.

3A: In the state-federal vocational rehabilitation (VR) program, *presumption of eligibility* refers to the fact that any applicant who has been determined eligible for Social Security benefits under Title II or Title XVI of the Social Security Act (including Social Security Disability Insurance) is presumed to be eligible for VR services. There is also a *presumption of benefit*, which refers to the fact that any applicant who meets the eligibility requirements for VR services can benefit in terms of an employment outcome.

4C: The Individualized Plan for Employment (IPE) identifies services that may be provided under the plan, which may include a wide range of employment-related services, including medical, psychological, vocational, and other diagnostic assessments and evaluations; counseling and guidance; occupational and vocational training and education; interpreter services, reader, and orientation and mobility training and services; job search and placement and job-retention services; supported employment services; and personal assistance services, among others. The IPE is a written employment plan authorized in the Rehabilitation Act of 1973, unrelated to the IPE authorized under IDEA. Although generally developed in collaboration with the state vocational rehabilitation counselor, an eligible individual or the individual's representative may develop all or part of the IPE independently. The plan must be consistent with the individual's unique strengths, resources, priorities, concerns, abilities, capabilities, interests, and informed choice. The vocational rehabilitation counselor and the client review the IEP at least annually to evaluate progress toward the employment outcome and make changes as required.

5C: A very small percentage of people who are receiving Social Security Disability Insurance (SSDI) (or Supplemental Security Income) return to employment after they begin to receive benefits. This is the issue that the Ticket to Work Program was developed to address. SSDI provides eligible people with disabilities with monthly income benefits and Medicare insurance. To be eligible for SSDI, one must be a person who has worked and paid Social Security taxes, be permanently disabled, and earn less than substantial gainful activity.

6D: When substantial gainful activity is determined, the cost of certain impairment-related work items and services are deducted from the individual's earnings. Impairment-related work expenses may include a number of services and items, such as attendant care services or the costs associated with vehicle modifications.

7A: The transtheoretical model is a model of health decision making that describes the stages of change, categories along a continuum of readiness to change a behavior, including precontemplation, contemplation, preparation, action, and maintenance.

8C: In working with a consumer to provide effective assistive technology, it is critical that a careful assessment be conducted and include the consumer's goals and abilities, the environment in which assistive technology will be used, the most effective available options to meet the goals identified, and the likelihood of continued use of the assistive technology by the consumer.

9C: Self-management involves learning and practicing skills to carry on an active and emotionally satisfying life in the face of a chronic condition through self-care, management of one's condition, medication, treatment, effective communication with health care providers, exercise and diet, social relationships, and coping.

10C: The economic argument concerns the cost and benefit of vocational rehabilitation (VR). The question of effectiveness and accountability is critical to the public tax-payer–funded VR program. The idea behind the argument is that the investment of funds in VR will, by enabling persons with disabilities to become employed tax payers and contribute to the tax base, result in a several-fold increase in federal income over the working years of the individual who receives VR services. Researchers have consistently shown that, overall, VR services provide a positive return on investment.

References

Ajzen, I. (1991). The theory of planned behavior. *Organizational Behavior and Human Decision Processes*, *50*(2), 179–211.

Ajzen, I., & Fishbein, M. (1980). *Understanding attitudes and predicting social behavior*. Englewood Cliffs, NJ: Prentice Hall.

American Medical Association. (1990). *Guides to the evaluation of permanent impairment*. Chicago, IL: Author.

American Psychiatric Association. (2000). *Diagnostic and statistical manual of mental disorders* (4th ed. Text Rev.). Washington, DC: Author.

American Psychiatric Association. (2013). *Diagnostic and statistical manual of mental disorders* (5th ed.). Arlington, VA: American Psychiatric Publishing.

Atherton, W. L., & Toriello, P. J. (2012). Re-conceptualizing the treatment of substance use disorders: The impact on employment. In P. L. Toriello, M. L. Bishop, & P. D. Rumrill (Eds.), *New directions in rehabilitation counseling: Creative responses to professional, clinical, and educational challenges* (pp. 289–312). Linn Creek, MO: Aspen Professional Services.

Bachman, S. S., Drainoni, M., & Tobias, C. (2004). Medicaid managed care, substance abuse treatment, and people with disabilities: Review of the literature. *Health and Social Work*, *29*, 189–196.

Bandura, A. (1989). Social cognitive theory. In R. Vasta (Ed.), *Annals of child development: Six theories of child development* (Vol. 6, pp. 1–60). Greenwich, CT: JAI Press.

Becker, M. H., Drachman, R. H., & Kirscht, J. P. (1974). A field experiment to evaluate various outcomes of continuity of physician care. *American Journal of Public Health*, *64*, 1062–1070.

Beveridge, S., Karpen, S., Chan, C., & Penrod, J. (2016). Application of the KVI-R to assess current training needs of private rehabilitation counselors. *Rehabilitation Counseling Bulletin*, *59*(4), 213–223.

Beveridge, S., & McDaniel, R. S. (2014). Private practice in vocational rehabilitation. In D. R. Strauser (Ed.), *Career development, employment, and disability in rehabilitation: From theory to practice* (pp. 361–388). New York, NY: Springer Publishing

Black, H. C. (1990). *Black's law dictionary: Definitions of the terms and phrases of American and English jurisprudence, ancient and modern* (6th ed.). St. Paul, MN: West.

Braddock, D. L., & Parish, S. L. (2001). An institutional history of disability. In G. L. Albrecht, K. D. Seelman, & M. Bury (Eds.), *Handbook of disability studies* (pp. 11–68). Thousand Oaks, CA: Sage.

Brodwin, M. (2008). Rehabilitation in the private-for-profit sector: Opportunities and challenges. In S. E. Rubin & R. T. Roessler (Eds.), *Foundations of the vocational rehabilitation process* (6th ed., pp. 501–524). Austin, TX: Pro-Ed.

Brucker, D. (2007). Estimating the prevalence of substance use, abuse, and dependence among Social Security disability benefit recipients. *Journal of Disability Policy Studies, 18*, 148–159.

Capuzzi, D., & Stauffer, M. D. (2012). History and etiological models of addiction. In D. Capuzzi & M. D. Stauffer (Eds.), *Foundations of addictions counseling* (2nd ed., pp. 1–15). Boston, MA: Pearson.

Certification of Disability Management Specialists Commission. (2009). *CDMSC guide for candidate certification.* Schaumburg, IL: Author.

Chan, F., Leahy, M. J., Downey, W., Lamb, G., Chapin, M., & Peterson, D. (2000). A work behavior analysis of certified case managers. *Care Management, 6*(4), 50–62.

Commission on Rehabilitation Counselor Certification. (2010). *Code of professional ethics for rehabilitation counselors.* Schaumburg, IL: Author.

Corbin, J., & Strauss, A. (1988). *Unending work and care: Managing chronic illness.* San Francisco, CA: Jossey-Bass.

Crimando, W., & Riggar, T. F. (2005) *Community resources.* Long Grove, IL: Waveland Press.

Dunn, P. L. (2001). Trends and issues in proprietary rehabilitation. In P. D. Rumrill, Jr., J. L. Bellini, & L. C. Koch (Eds.), *Emerging issues in rehabilitation counseling: Perspectives on the new millennium* (pp. 173–191). Springfield, IL: Charles C Thomas.

Ethridge, G., Rodgers, R. A., & Fabian, E. S. (2007). Emerging roles, functions, specialty areas, and employment settings for contemporary rehabilitation practice. *Journal of Applied Rehabilitation Counseling, 38*(4), 27–33, 49–50.

Fabian, E. S., & MacDonald-Wilson, K. L. (2012). Professional practice in rehabilitation service delivery systems and related system resources. In R. M. Parker & J. B. Patterson (Eds.), *Rehabilitation counseling basics and beyond* (5th ed., pp. 55–87). Austin, TX: Pro-Ed.

Falvo, D. R. (2014). *Medical and psychosocial aspects of chronic illness and disability* (5th ed.). Burlington, MA: Jones & Bartlett Learning.

Fishbein, M., & Ajzen, I. (1975). *Belief, attitude, intention, and behavior: An introduction to theory and research.* Reading, MA: Addison-Wesley.

Fraser, R., McMahon, B., & Danczyk-Hawley, C. (2004). Progression of disability benefits: A perspective on multiple sclerosis. *Journal of Vocational Rehabilitation, 19*(3), 173–179.

Guyton, G. P. (1999). A brief history of workers' compensation. *Iowa Orthopedic Journal, 19*, 106–110.

Harrington, N. P., Fogg, P. E., & McMahon, B. T. (2010). The impact of the Great Recession upon the unemployment of Americans with disabilities. *Journal of Vocational Rehabilitation, 33*, 193–202.

Hollar, D., McAweeney, M., & Moore, D. (2008). The relationship between substance use disorders and unsuccessful case closures in vocational rehabilitation agencies. *Journal of Applied Rehabilitation Counseling, 39*, 48–52.

Individuals with Disabilities Education Act (IDEA) of 2004, Pub. L. No. 108-446. [34 CFR 300.43 (a)] [20 U.S.C. 1401 (34)].

International Association of Rehabilitation Professionals. (2016). Overview of forensic services in rehab. Retrieved from https://connect.rehabpro.org/forensic/news/forfocus/forinrehab

Jamoon, E., Horner-Johnson, W., Suzuki, R., Andresen, E., Campbell, V., & RRTC Expert Panel on Health Status Measurement. (2008). Age at disability onset and self-reported health status. *BMC Public Health*, *8*, 10.

Janikowski, T., Cardoso, E., & Lee, G. K. (2005). Substance abuse counseling in case management. In F. Chan, M. Leahy, & J. Saunders (Eds.), *Case management for rehabilitation health professionals* (pp. 247–274). Osage Beach, MO: Aspen Professional Services.

Jiang, Y., & Hesser, J. (2006). Associations between health-related quality of life and demographics and health risks: Results from Rhode Island's 2002 behavioral risk factor survey. *Health and Quality of Life Outcomes*, *4*, 14–24.

Krahn, G., Deck, D., Gabriel, R., & Farrell, N. (2007). A population-based study on substance abuse treatment for adults with disabilities: Access, utilization, and treatment outcomes. *American Journal of Drug and Alcohol Abuse*, *33*, 791–798.

Leahy, M., Chan, F., & Saunders, J. (2003). Job functions and knowledge requirements of certified rehabilitation counselors in the 21st century. *Rehabilitation Counseling Bulletin*, *46*, 66–81.

Leahy, M., Chan, F., Shaw, L., & Lui, J. (1997). Preparation of rehabilitation counselors for case management practice in health care settings. *Journal of Rehabilitation*, *63*(3), 53–59.

Leahy, M., Chan, F., Taylor, D., Wood, C., & Downey, W. (1998). Evolving knowledge and skill factors for practice in private sector rehabilitation. *The NARPPS Journal*, *6*(1), 34–43.

Leahy, M. J., Chan, F., Sung, C., & Kim, M. (2013). Empirically derived test specifications for the certified rehabilitation counselor examination. *Rehabilitation Counseling Bulletin*, *56*(4), 199–214.

Leahy, M. J., & Phillips, B. (2011). Certification: Practitioner certification in the delivery of vocational rehabilitation services to individuals with disabilities in the United States. In J. H. Stone & M. Blouin (Eds.), *International encyclopedia of rehabilitation*. Retrieved from http://cirrie.buffalo.edu/encyclopedia/en/article/42

Litvak, S., & Enders, A. (2001). Support systems: The interface between individuals and environments. In G. L. Albrecht, K. D. Seelman, & M. Bury (Eds.), *Handbook of disability studies* (pp. 711–733). Thousand Oaks, CA: Sage.

Lorig, K. (1993). Self-management of chronic illness: A model for the future (self care and older adults). *Generations*, *17*(3), 11–14.

Lorig, K. R., & Holman, H. R. (2003). Self-management education: History, definitions, outcomes, and mechanisms. *Annals of Behavioral Medicine*, *26*(1), 1–7.

Marini, I. (2012). The psychosocial world of the injured worker. In I. Marini, N. M. Glover-Graf, M. Millington (Eds.), *Psychosocial aspects of disability: Insider perspectives and strategies for counselors* (pp. 235–259). New York, NY: Springer Publishing.

Marini, I., & Reid, C. (2001). A survey of rehabilitation professionals or alternate provider contractors with Social Security: Problems and solutions. *Journal of Rehabilitation*, *67*(2), 36–41.

Matkin, R. E. (1985). *Insurance rehabilitation: Service applications in disability compensation systems*. Austin, TX: Pro-Ed.

McCollom, P. (2002). Guiding the way: The evolution of life care plans. *Continuing Care*, *21*(6), 26–28.

National Center on Accessible Information Technology in Education (NCAITE). (2011). *What is accessible electronic and information technology?* Retrieved from http://www.washington.edu/accessit/articles?110

Noll, A., Owens, L., Smith, R. O., & Schwanke, T. (2006). Survey of state vocational rehabilitation counselor roles and competencies in assistive technology. *Work*, *27*, 413–419.

Olsheski, J. A., Rosenthal, D. A., & Hamilton, M. (2002). Disability management and psychosocial rehabilitation: Considerations for integration. *Work*, *19*, 63–70.

Patterson, J. B., DeLaGarza, D., & Schaller, J. (2005). Rehabilitation counseling practice: Considerations and interventions. In R. M. Parker, E. M. Szymanski, & J. B. Patterson (Eds.), *Rehabilitation counseling: Basic and beyond* (4th ed., pp. 155–186). Austin, TX: Pro-Ed.

Pratt, C. W., Gill, K. J., Barrett, N. M., & Roberts, M. M. (2007). *Psychiatric Rehabilitation* (2nd ed.). San Diego, CA: Elsevier Academic Press.

Prochaska, J. O., & DiClemente, C. C. (1983). Stages and processes of self-change of smoking: Toward an integrative model of change. *Journal of Consulting and Clinical Psychology, 51*, 390–395.

Rehabilitation Act Amendments of 1998, 29 U.S.C. § 701 et seq.

Roessler, R., & Rubin, S. E. (2006). *Case management and rehabilitation counseling: Procedures and techniques* (4th ed.). Austin, TX: Pro-Ed.

Rosenthal, D. A., Hursh, N. C., Lui, J., Zimmermann, W., & Pruett, S. R. (2005). Workplace disability management: Case management implications. In F. Chan, M. J. Leahy, & J. L. Saunders (Eds.), *Case management for rehabilitation health professionals* (2nd ed., Vol. 1, pp. 330–365). Linn Creek, MO: Aspen Professional Services.

Rubin, S. E., Roessler, R. T., & Rumrill, P. D. (2016). *Foundations of the vocational rehabilitation process* (7th ed.). Austin, TX: Pro-Ed.

Scanlan, J. N., & Beltran, R. O. (2007). Work in unemployment: Occupied or preoccupied? A review. *Work, 28*, 325–334.

Schwarzer, R. (1992). Self-efficacy in the adoption and maintenance of health behaviors: Theoretical approaches and a new model. In R. Schwarzer (Ed.), *Self-efficacy: Thought control of action* (pp. 217–243). Washington, DC: Hemisphere.

Sengupta, I., & Reno, V. (2007). Recent trends in workers compensation. *Social Security Bulletin, National Academy of Social Insurance, 67*(1), 17–26.

Shaw, L. R., & Betters, C. J. (2004). Private sector rehabilitation. In T. F. Riggar & D. R. Maki (Eds.), *Handbook of rehabilitation counseling* (pp. 236–252). New York, NY: Springer Series.

Sohlberg, M. M. (2011). Assistive technology for cognition. *American Speech-Language-Hearing Association Leader, 16*, 14–17.

Sperry, L., Lewis, J., Carlson, J. D., & Englar-Carlson, M. (2005). *Health promotion and health counseling: Effective counseling and psychotherapeutic strategies* (2nd ed.). Boston, MA: Allyn & Bacon.

Strauser, D. (2013). *Career development, employment, and disability in rehabilitation.* New York, NY: Springer Publishing.

Substance Abuse and Mental Health Services Administration. (2014). *Results from the 2013 National Survey on Drug Use and Health: Summary of national findings*, NSDUH Series H-48, HHS Publication No. (SMA) 14-4863. Rockville, MD: Author.

Substance Abuse and Mental Health Services Administration. (2016). Substance use and suicide: A nexus requiring a public health approach. Retrieved from http://store.samhsa.gov/shin/content//SMA16 -4935/SMA16-4935.pdf

Umeasiegbu, V. I. (2013). Determinants of health care access after spinal cord injury. *Journal of Applied Rehabilitation Counseling, 44*(2), 11–17.

West, S. L., Graham, C. W., & Cifu, D. X. (2009). Rates of alcohol/other drug treatment denials to persons with physical disabilities: Accessibility concerns. *Alcoholism Treatment Quarterly, 27*, 305–316.

West, S. L., Luck, R. S., Capps, C. F., Cifu, D. X., Graham, C. W., & Hurley, J. E. (2009). Alcohol/other drug problems screening and intervention by rehabilitation physicians. *Alcoholism Treatment Quarterly, 27*, 280–293.

Wheaton, J. E., & Berven, N. L. (1994). Education, experience, and caseload management practices of counselors in a state vocational rehabilitation agency. *Rehabilitation Counseling Bulletin, 38*(1), 44–58.

World Health Organization. (2001). *International classification of functioning, disability and health.* Geneva, Switzerland: Author.

Index